T0387882

USING VIDEO TO DEVELOP TEACHING

Since video has gone digital, new opportunities for raising the quality of teaching and learning have come within reach. This book provides the first integrated account of how digital video can be used to develop teaching.

Framed within a research-based vision on what is quality in teaching and learning, the book gives an overview of the development from analog to digital video and describes a variety of applications in teacher competence development. A systematic review of the latest research shows how using video helps teachers improve instruction. The author's own research and development work clarifies how viewing guides support teachers in setting and achieving targets for improvement. An indepth case study of peer coaching with video spanning seven years uncovers how the participating teachers succeeded in making sustainable changes in their instruction. This book shows not only how using video can help teachers move towards more dialogic forms of teaching and learning, but also how such change benefits pupils' learning and behaviour.

Using video to develop teaching takes the everyday needs of teachers as its point of departure. It explains the activities, processes and organisational conditions needed for raising the quality of instruction through video use. The evidence base involved serves as a basis for practical application. The book concludes with concise recommendations and resources for producing video and using it for professional learning and instruction.

This book offers readers a wealth of knowledge, practices and resources concerning a powerful medium, which will benefit them in their work.

Niels Brouwer is a leading teacher educator and researcher whose work focusses on the effectiveness of teacher education and professional development. His work received international awards and reaches audiences worldwide.

"Digital video has in the last decades become the single most helpful tool for advancing teaching and teacher education. This comprehensive and multi-faceted book covers the power and effectiveness of this seminal medium in an impressive way."

Kurt Reusser, *Professor emeritus, Universität Zürich, Switzerland*

"The Visual Teacher Learning model developed by Niels Brouwer places at the core of teachers' work how they bring learners to engage with the content of learning, which entails the cognitive, emotional and social domains. The principles of learning that the author expects teachers to enact in their inter-actions with pupils are also the principles to be modelled by teacher educators when using the VTL model, thus successfully bridging theory and practice. In the numerous examples of the uses and benefits of this approach to enhance teachers' work with learners, the author and his collaborators recognise and address the demands faced by teachers, whether novice, beginning or experi-enced. This book will make a significant contribution to developing teacher educators' competencies for using Visual Teacher Learning in their work."

Carmen Montecinos, *Professor of Psychology, Pontificia Universidad Católica de Valparaíso, Chile*

USING VIDEO TO DEVELOP TEACHING

Niels Brouwer

Routledge
Taylor & Francis Group

LONDON AND NEW YORK

Cover image: © Getty Images

First published 2022
by Routledge
2 Park Square, Milton Park, Abingdon, Oxon OX14 4RN

and by Routledge
605 Third Avenue, New York, NY 10158

Routledge is an imprint of the Taylor & Francis Group, an informa business

© 2022 Niels Brouwer

British Library Cataloguing-in-Publication Data
A catalogue record for this book is available from the British Library

Library of Congress Cataloging-in-Publication Data
Names: Brouwer, Niels, author.
Title: Using video to develop teaching / Niels Brouwer.
Description: First Edition. | New York : Routledge, 2022. | Includes bibliographical references and index. | Identifiers: LCCN 2021048651 | ISBN 9780367353797 (Hardback) | ISBN 9780367353803 (Paperback) | ISBN 9780429331091 (eBook)
Subjects: LCSH: Digital video. | Interactive videos. | Educational technology.
Classification: LCC LB1028.75 .B76 2022 | DDC 371.33--dc23/eng/20220110
LC record available at https://lccn.loc.gov/2021048651

ISBN: 978-0-367-35379-7 (hbk)
ISBN: 978-0-367-35380-3 (pbk)
ISBN: 978-0-429-33109-1 (ebk)

DOI: 10.4324/9780429331091

Typeset in Bembo
by SPi Technologies India Pvt Ltd (Straive)

Graphics by Lennart Brouwer

CONTENTS

FIGURES

TABLES

BOXES

PREFACE

Learning and education are as necessary as daily bread. Teachers, in large majority, form a loyal workforce which makes vast contributions to the life chances of generations. At the same time, many governments seem to take education for granted, without wondering what teachers need to do their work well. Teaching is known as a profession in which workload and turnover are high, salary is mediocre and social status uncertain. Still, thousands of people choose teaching as a living and find satisfaction in it.

Teaching can be demanding and its outcomes hard to determine. There is always a need to examine it critically and develop it further. In my work as a teacher, teacher educator and researcher, I have sought ways to develop teaching by grounding it in theory and research. During the last twenty years, I have become convinced that digital video has great potential for raising the quality of teaching and learning. In this book, I present what I have learned.

I was told that teachers are my heroes. They are indeed! I find teaching a noble profession, noble as music. I hope that the practices and knowledge described in this book will benefit teachers and teacher educators around the world, from the global North to the global South, from embattled inner-city schools to outlying rural districts and everywhere in between.

ACKNOWLEDGEMENTS

The research and development work underlying this book has greatly benefitted from the cooperation of many people. Not all can be named here, but I want to thank especially the following people for their generous support – substantive, material or both.

In the Netherlands, I extend my gratitude to teachers, pupils and management of the Urban Gymnasium Nijmegen. In particular, I thank those teachers who gave follow-up interviews about their participation in peer coaching with video for sharing personal experiences from their working lives. I also thank management, staff and students of Iselinge College of Primary Teacher Education in Doetinchem for providing the resources and effort needed for the research and development projects I proposed to them. Equally, I thank the management teams of the Eindhoven School of Education and the Kennisnet Foundation and project leaders from the Open University of the Netherlands for the resources and cooperation they contributed.

As representatives for all the Dutch teachers and teacher educators with whom I had the fortune to cooperate in and through the above institutions I thank Ellen van den Berg, Perry den Brok, Wim Drenth, Maarten Franken, Walter Geerts, Wim Jochems, Fred Korthagen, Karel Kreijns, Marc van Laeken, Gert Muller, Erik Roelofs, Roel Scheepens and Eddy Stortelder. Equally, I thank my co-authors Ida Oosterheert and Eric Besselink (Chapter 4), Fokelien Robijns (Chapter 5) and Harmen Schaap (Chapter 6).

International cooperation has been a tremendous source of inspiration for the writing of this book. It was a privilege and a joy to organise and participate in symposia about video use for teacher development at the conferences of the American Educational Research Association (AERA) and the European Association for Research on Learning and Instruction (Earli). I warmly thank the following colleagues for their professional companionship and hospitality, which I experienced during these meetings and during expert seminars and working visits.

In the US: François Tochon (Departments of Curriculum and Instruction and French & Italian, University of Wisconsin-Madison); Karen Givvin and Jim Stigler (Psychology Department, University of California at Los Angeles); Rossella Santagata and Beth van Es (School of Education, University of California at Irvine), who hosted me during a sabbatical stay; Kevin Miller (College of Literature, Science, and the Arts, University of Michigan at Ann Arbor); Nanette Seago (WestEd, San Francisco); and Brian Yusko (College of Education, Cleveland State University).

In Germany: Alexander Gröschner (Lehrstuhl für Schulpädagogik und Unterrichtsforschung, Friedrich-Schiller-Universität Jena) and Marc Kleinknecht (Institut für Bildungswissenschaft, Leuphana Universität Lüneburg).

In Switzerland: Kathrin Krammer (Pädagogische Hochschule Luzern); Kurt Reusser (Institut für Erziehungswissenschaft, Universität Zürich); Valérie Lussi Borer and Simon Flandin (Faculté de Psychologie et des Sciences de l'Éducation, Université de Genève); and Florinda Sauli and Alberto Cattaneo (Swiss Federal Institute for Vocational Education and Training, Lugano).

In France: Cyrille Gaudin (Unité Mixte de Recherche Éducation, Formation, Travail, Savoirs, Université de Limoges).

In Chile: Carmen Montecinos, who invited me to teach a masterclass for the staff of the Escuela de Pedagogía of the Pontificia Universidad Católica de Valparaíso and José Miguel Garrido Miranda, who organised and helped me prepare it.

I thank Lennart Brouwer for his creative work on the graphics. At Routledge, I thank Bruce Roberts for his swift and enthusiastic acceptance of my proposal for this book and Ann-Kathrin Klein and Molly Selby for their constructive and friendly editorial assistance. At Straive, I thank Saritha Srinivasan for her careful work on the production of the book.

Finally, I thank from the bottom of my heart my partner Ursula, my daughter Sara, her husband Bruce and my sons Lennart and Yannick for their understanding and support throughout my absorption in this book.

Niels Brouwer

1

INTRODUCTION

Niels Brouwer

Teachers worldwide fulfil vital functions for human society. Through their work, teachers help – or hinder – generations of learners, who in turn populate countries, drive economies and shape cultures. Teachers' work determines to a large extent how learners are qualified to lead productive lives, how they are allocated to economic positions and how they become integrated into society (Fend, 1974). The extent to which countries' citizens can unfold their potential depends a great deal on the quality of teachers' work (OECD, 2005). For these reasons, teacher education and professional development (PD) have a multiplier function for society, a function that is usually little acknowledged (Sarason, 1996; Stones, 1994). All the same, it is of crucial, I would even say of historical importance to equip teachers fully for their demanding work.

How teachers do their work is the most important single influence on learners' achievement, whether in upcoming or in established economies (Hanushek, 2005; Hattie, 2009). Raising the quality of teaching and learning, then, deserves careful attention and sustained investment. Video as a medium has contributed to teacher education and professional development for at least half a century, but since it has gone digital, powerful new opportunities for developing teaching have come within reach. I therefore aim, in this book, to provide an integrated account of the special opportunities which digital video (DV) offers for teacher competence development.

Aims of this book

Video was introduced to teacher education already in the 1960s. Then as now, its attraction to teachers and teacher educators is that a picture tells more than a thousand words, as the saying goes. Rather than reading or listening to abstract information, viewing video may directly address teachers' practical concerns. This would help solve an old problem in teacher education and PD.

DOI: 10.4324/9780429331091-1

Teacher learning is firmly rooted in practical concerns rather than in theoretical concepts, as scholars have noted time and again, among others Schön (1983), Guskey (1986) and Korthagen, Kessels, Koster, Lagerwerf and Wubbels (2001). Still, much of teacher education and PD remains "front-loaded" (Eraut, 1994, p. 10) and orchestrated from a "theory first" perspective (Wideen, Mayer-Smith, & Moon, 1998, p. 152–156, 160–162, 166–170). Small wonder then that prospective and experienced teachers alike often experience the programmes offered to them as removed from their practical needs and concerns. Explaining practice through theory is apparently difficult and applying theory to improve practice even more so. In the teaching profession, two-way traffic or transfer between practice and theory does not function very well. This is what I call the "transfer problem" of teaching.

Video has a number of properties which make it a promising medium for connecting practical concerns with theoretical insights. Visualising teaching and learning has the potential to foster transfer between practice and theory.

What explains the attraction of video is that it can make human interactions accessible and understandable in all their complexity and subtlety. Because of their realism, video images can display to teachers what happens in the classic "instructional triangle", i.e. during the dynamic interaction between their own actions, the content of learning and their learners' actions and reactions. Also, because of their concreteness, video images invite teachers to make their analysis of teaching and learning specific to the school subject at hand. Furthermore, video enables teachers to engage in repeated analysis of their classroom interaction and to do so from different perspectives, without the immediate need to draw consequences for action. This opens up possibilities for considering alternative courses of action. Last but not least, moving images invoke an "as if" experience, which approaches the reality of practice, but is not identical with immediate, live experience. This virtual or "vicarious" experience, as Laurillard (1993, p. 114) calls it, can engage the viewer not just cognitively, but also emotionally, whether in the sense of acceptance or rejection.

Since the turn of the millennium, the digitisation of video has revitalised its use. The medium has become much more affordable and versatile. This is why, during the last twenty years, video has again captured the imagination of teacher educators and a host of research and development (R&D) work has been undertaken. A risk here is that technological advances develop faster than the pedagogies they enable. This may cause undue enthusiasm about video as a panacea for all sorts of challenges. The central question to keep asking is what are the goals and effects of using video in professional education (Brophy, 2004, p. ix–x). In the case of teachers, the central issue to attend to remains how video use can help them understand and improve what they do to foster learning.

The core of teachers' work is how they bring learners to engage with the content of learning. Teaching and learning are deeply intertwined. Accordingly, teachers' own professional learning should be understood in relation to pupils' learning. Using video can help raise the quality of teaching, when it encourages teachers to understand how they influence learning. This is why I have introduced the concept of "Visual Teacher Learning" (VTL) (Brouwer, 2011). I define VTL as: all forms of competence development in which teachers use video representations of their interaction with learners and content in order to improve their instructional behaviour.

An essential element in this definition is that it does not take teacher perception and thought as its end point, as most research since 2000 into video use for teacher learning has done. I focus in addition on whether and how teachers put into practice what they discover by examining their work in the classroom through video. My interest is what VTL can contribute to raising the effectiveness of teachers' teaching and pupils' learning. VTL, then, is considered here as a means to a broader social goal.

The specific objectives of this book are:

A. to provide an up-to-date account of the special opportunities offered by digital video for raising the quality of teaching and learning through teacher competence development and
B. to draw lessons for practice from the relevant theory and research.

The book is addressed to teachers and teacher educators active in R&D. These professionals include mentor teachers and school leaders in primary, secondary and vocational education as well as supervisors and coordinators of student teaching, providers of PD and researchers working in colleges and universities.

In all these contexts, raising the quality of instruction requires bridging the well-known gap between practice and theory. Taking up this challenge is possible in collaboration between schools and teacher education institutions. The insights, evidence and resources contained in this book are intended to support this collaboration. Based on reviews of the relevant research and on my own studies of practical interventions, it explains the activities, processes, outcomes and conditions involved in VTL. Due attention is paid to implementation, which is why the book concludes with lessons drawn in the form of resources for practitioners.

Making research into teaching and learning useful for practice requires in my view that it should not only describe what teachers learn. It should also explain how they learn. Otherwise, one cannot underpin recommendations for action. In my own research, I therefore consistently follow a mixed-methods approach (Brouwer, 2010). My approach to teaching and learning is inspired by cultural-historical activity theory (CHAT) (Daniels, Cole, & Wertsch, 2007; Engeström, Miettinen, & Punamäki, 1999; Kozulin, Gindis, Ageyev, & Miller, 2003; Vygotsky, 1977; Yasnitsky, Van der Veer, & Ferrari, 2014). In this theory, it is assumed that the practice of education is at the same time determined by and itself shapes the social and historical context in which teachers work with pupils. This assumption entails that I try to relate individual teacher learning (on the micro-level) to issues of organisation and culture in (the cooperation between) schools and teacher education institutions (on the meso-level) and to education as a social system (on the macro-level).

Before embarking on the subject of VTL, it is necessary to clarify in this introduction a number of foundational issues. First of all, when we speak of "raising the quality of teaching and learning" and of "improving teaching", it should be clear how quality in education is defined. This issue is addressed in the following section. Secondly, as Brophy (2004) has noted, it is decisive for the value of video use how it is embedded in the context in which teachers' professional learning takes place. This context differs depending on their career phase. Teachers who complete a career in education, develop their professional competence in the contexts of preservice teacher education (PTE), induction for beginning teachers, alternative certification programmes (ACPs) for career changers and/or PD for experienced teachers. Together, I denote these institutional forms of teacher learning as "teacher development". Whichever pathways individual teachers pursue through these contexts, they should ideally be designed and provided as a continuum of opportunities for learning (Feiman-Nemser, Schwille, Carver, & Yusko, 1999). I therefore explicate in this chapter quality standards for programmes for these four contexts. Against this background, the introduction concludes with an overview of the remaining chapters of the book.

Quality learning and quality teaching

If one wants to know how teacher development can contribute to raising the quality of teaching and learning, this requires a clear vision of what "quality" means. In the following, I therefore discuss three related questions: What are valuable goals for education in modern societies? What are effective forms of teaching to achieve these goals? What kinds of instruction should teachers be able to enact?

These questions can never be answered definitively or exhaustively. They require permanent debate. Also, they can be examined on different grounds: firstly, on the basis of religious, moral, philosophical and/or political values; secondly, on the basis of practical experience and craft knowledge; thirdly, on the basis of theory and research evidence. Each of these three perspectives has a role to play, but they have different strengths and weaknesses. Building only on religion, philosophy or politics risks ending in dogma. Building only on practical experience risks ending in misguided activism. Building only on theory and research risks ending in arbitrary scientism.

The relation between teaching and learning

What I try to do here is stake out what kinds of teaching behaviour are needed in order to foster desirable outcomes of learning.

Desirable aims of education

What are desirable aims of education can be delineated in terms of the three general functions of education distinguished by the German sociologist Helmut Fend, to whom I referred earlier (Fend, 1974). Contributing to the qualification function would mean nowadays that teaching helps equip pupils to function productively in industrialised and digitised 21st-centry economies. Contributing to the allocation function entails carrying out a curriculum oriented towards the differentiated demands of working life. Contributing to the integration function means educating

pupils towards being conscious citizens willing and able to participate in demo-
cratic societies. Making these broad goals concrete means, in my view, that teaching
should aim at learning with active understanding instead of passive reproduction.

Let me explain this with an example from my own teaching. In teaching the
Dutch language to English-speaking foreigners I built on the idea of the "germ
cell" advocated by the Russian psychologist Vassily Davydov (1977). This means
that the content of learning should be sequenced by introducing the most powerful abstraction right in the beginning and then differentiating it progressively from
there. According to this idea, I began the first lesson of each course by presenting to
my students two or more simple sentences consisting of a subject, a predicate and an
object, such as: "Ik koop brood" (I buy bread), "Mijn zus schrijft een brief" (My sis-
ter writes a letter) and "De kat vangt een muis" (The cat catches a mouse). I would
then ask the students to compare these sentences and formulate what they have in
common. During the resulting conversation, I used their answers and comments to
produce the abstract scheme "subject–predicate–object" on the blackboard and to
explain how it is used to create complete sentences. I then had the students practise
this by themselves, using the activity format of "think–pair–share" (Lyman, 1981).
This activity would of course bring complications into play, such as different kinds
of objects (direct, indirect and prepositional), the addition of adjuncts (of time, place
and mode), predicates consisting of two or more verb forms etcetera. I included
these differentiations in subsequent cycles of instruction, practice and feedback.
Together, these cycles constituted the curriculum underlying the course. Over the
years, I have finetuned these cycles and their sequence in order to accommodate the
specific learning processes that I observed in my students.

The intent behind this system of structured learning activities was to encourage
students to build up a generalisable mental apparatus that they would be able to use
by themselves in order to express their own meanings and messages in speaking and
writing. To promote this ability, I concluded each lesson with conversation exercises, in which dyads of students role-played scenes from daily life such as shopping,
buying tickets, asking for information, searching for housing etcetera. Just as the
grammar exercises, these conversation exercises began in a strongly structured form,
consisting of question–answer sequences fully written out, followed by incomplete
sentences that students then adapted and supplemented to fit their own intentions.
I chose to have this activity carried out in dyads in order to avoid plenary situations
in which students might feel embarrassed about making mistakes.

In sum, grammar functioned here not as an incomprehensible, tedious subject,
but as a tool to be used in daily life. The Dutch word for grammar, fittingly, is *spraakkunst*, which literally means "the art of speaking" (Brouwer & Kerssies, 1983).

The cyclical nature of learning

What is effective in the approach illustrated above is that teacher and learners move
repeatedly through cycles of instruction, practice and feedback. During each cycle,
the initial phase of instruction is subdivided in presentation and explanation of new

content, specification of the learning activities that learners need to carry out and dialogue between teacher and learners. This cyclical structure is present in teaching approaches which have been shown to promote achievement in group learning, notably direct instruction (Brophy & Good, 1986; Rosenshine, 2010) and mastery learning (Bloom, 1968; Guskey, 2005). What is essential to bring about effective learning is that teaching activates learners' cognition (Mayer, 2008; Reusser, 2019) and that this cognitive activation takes place in an environment where making mistakes is not discouraged, but used as an opportunity for learning with and from each other (Stanford, 1977).

As noted earlier, the core of teachers' work is how they bring learners to engage with the content of learning. This is what teachers' work in the "instructional triangle" is about (see Figure 1.1).

In the instructional triangle, the content component should be understood broadly. This component represents all possible objects of learning, i.e. not only knowledge, but also cognitive and motor skills as well as the attitudes involved in their deployment in social contexts. The sides of the triangle symbolise different processes.

The basis of the instructional triangle, stretching between learners and content, symbolises that learners must acquire the knowledge, master the skills and develop the attitudes set by society as the goals of learning. Without the need for this challenge, education would not exist. In other words, the basis of the triangle represents the *raison d'être* of education. The side stretching between teacher and content symbolises the teacher's task of presenting and explaining the content of learning. Without mastering this content, no teacher can do her or his work. The side stretching between teacher and learners symbolises the need to create and uphold suitable learning environments, in which teachers succeed in encouraging prosocial behaviour and effort in learners.

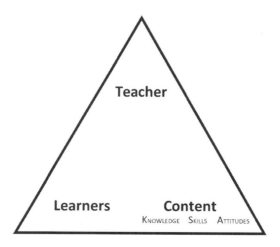

FIGURE 1.1 The instructional triangle

These processes are never separate. They always take place simultaneously and continually interact. The focus of teachers' and learners' attention is forever in motion throughout the triangle.

Consequences for the nature of teaching

The teacher's task within the instructional triangle is to lead, guide and encourage learners to move from their zones of actual development into their zones of proximal development. These epoch-making concepts introduced in the early twentieth century by the Russian psychologist Lev Semyonovich Vygotsky denote the difference between what a child can accomplish independently and what she or he can accomplish with the help of another person who has progressed further in the issue at hand, usually an adult – parent or teacher – or another child. By helping learners bridge the gap between the two zones of development, teachers make social interaction productive for transforming existing knowledge, skills and attitudes into new capabilities (Kozulin et al., 2003; Vygotsky, 1977).

The foregoing argument and the teaching approaches referenced have one thing in common: what teachers should be able to do is determined from the perspective of what learning requires of teaching. This latter question appears simple enough, but surprisingly, educational science has not systematically addressed it. A valiant attempt to do this was undertaken by the psychologist Carel van Parreren, who has done much to introduce CHAT in the Netherlands. In his work, Van Parreren distinguished six types of school learning and twelve principles of teaching to promote them.

Van Parreren's six types of learning are generic categories referring primarily to elementary education, but they are also valid for preschool learning and secondary, vocational and tertiary education. The first type of learning that schools should foster in pupils is the ability to analyse problem situations, so that they develop the insight and the thinking habits they need to understand not only current learning tasks, but also different and new problems. This includes distinguishing relevant aspects and becoming aware of underlying relationships such as commonalities and differences or cause and effect. Acquiring the habit to analyse tasks and using concepts and methods to complete them will raise pupils' chances of solving new types of problems successfully. Secondly, a necessary condition for learning is acquiring knowledge of facts. These facts become really meaningful when pupils are encouraged to place them in relation to each other. Thirdly, memorising and reproducing cultural symbol systems, such as the alphabet and the decimal system, are necessary conditions for further learning. The same is true, fourthly, for automating cognitive and motor skills. This enables pupils to free their attention for dealing with other topics. Learning to learn or developing successful learning strategies is the fifth type of learning that schools should foster. Finally, spontaneous or unintentional learning, such as takes place especially during play, lays the foundation for later, purposeful learning (Van Parreren, 1990).

All these forms of learning, according to Van Parreren, have their own value and none should override or exclude others. By promoting them, the school must contribute to pupils' ability to recognise patterns and regularities in phenomena, to think abstractly and to make justified generalisations. To achieve this, teachers can and should follow certain principles in their instructional behaviour. Van Parreren (1988) expects that by doing so, teachers will exert a formative influence on pupils.

These principles of formative teaching are summarised in Box 1.1. They are not meant to be exhaustive, Van Parreren cautions, nor can they be applied or combined in each and every lesson. However, in teaching practice, they do deserve more attention than they often receive. The first nine principles address cognitive learning, while the last three are about motivation.

BOX 1.1   PRINCIPLES OF FORMATIVE TEACHING BY VAN PARREREN (1988)

I. Motivating the learning task

Clarify at the beginning of the lesson why it is useful to do the learning task.

Linking content and examples to pupils' experiences is sensible, but should not be the only option. During the middle part of the lesson, concepts, abstractions and symbolic representations should be presented as such. These, too, can rouse pupils' interest.

II. Dialogic teaching

Use dialogue to find out and tune in to how pupils understand the lesson content.

The teacher should combine functioning on two levels: following the main course of the lesson content, while keeping track of pupils' thinking about it. Upholding dialogue with pupils makes it possible to ask questions, give additional explanations and adapt lesson planning where necessary.

III. Diagnostic teaching

Find out how pupils carry out their learning activities and which strategies they use.

During teaching, teachers should determine how pupils understand and misunderstand lesson content. Teachers should use diagnostic instruments as a basis for providing specific feedback and remediating activities to pupils.

IV. Sequencing learning tasks

Design a series of learning tasks which will lead the pupil towards the learning goal.

Teachers should design series of learning tasks which show to pupils the steps they need to take to achieve learning goals. These steps should be chosen not on the basis of the desired end product, but of the learning activities leading to it. The steps should be neither too large nor too small and each task should orient pupils towards the next task.

V. Acting on different levels

Organise learning activities on different levels.

Building concepts is facilitated when pupils perform material, perceptual, verbal and mental acts, in that order. Teachers should shape and vary this stepwise procedure – developed by Gal'perin (Haenen, 2001) on the basis of Vygotsky's theory of internalisation – depending on the specific learning goal and the starting points of the pupils involved.

VI. Pace and channels of instruction

Instruct for learning activities in a concise form, at a quiet pace and using two or more channels.

For learning to be effective, it is essential that instructions for learning activities are crystal clear. Teachers should therefore make instructions available and retrievable through both visual and verbal channels.

VII. Behaviour-oriented instruction and correction

Orient instructions and corrections to pupils' behaviour, not to the desired end product.

To make pupils understand how they can be successful at a learning task, teachers should observe and analyse their behaviour during learning. On this basis, it becomes possible to provide the specific feedback needed.

VIII. Reflection

Encourage pupils to analyse mistakes as well as successes during learning.

To achieve learning outcomes that are generalisable and versatile, it is essential that pupils understand which learning activities do or do not lead to success. Teachers should foster such understanding by helping pupils analyse mistakes and successes and by helping them discover rules for arriving at correct solutions. This is possible by promoting dialogue about the how of learning and recapitulating how learning tasks were carried out.

IX. Varied practice

Provide opportunities for practise in varied instead of repetitive forms.

To promote understanding and the ability to apply rules in different problem situations, teachers should present exercises in varied instead of repetitive forms. This avoids developing blind routine and reliance on tricks. It will also motivate pupils.

X. Fostering initiative and creativity

Reward pupils' initiative and creativity foremost in how they learn.

The foregoing principles advocate well-structured forms of teaching and learning. Within these bounds, it is productive to allow pupils to practise initiative and creativity while developing learning strategies. In developing their knowledge, however, teachers should prevent misconceptions.

XI. Supporting pupil motivation

Help pupils plan, monitor and adjust their learning activity.

Teachers should contribute to upholding pupils' motivation. They can do so by supporting self-regulation, i.e. helping them plan, monitor and adjust their learning activity and generally by paying attention to how they go about their learning.

XII. Pedagogical climate

State clear goals, challenge pupils to progress and justify rules.

Pupils learn best, when teachers make their zones of proximal development accessible. They should do so by stating clear goals and challenging them with learning tasks whose relevance they can understand. Similarly, rules for behaviour should be clearly stated and justified.

Characteristic for the principles of teaching in Box 1.1 is what they imply about the role of the teacher. These implications become apparent in a typical piece of advice that Van Parreren gives to teachers. When instructing learners how to carry out learning tasks, assignments or exercises, he says, you should take care that the learner knows the answers to the following four questions (Van Parreren, 1988, p. 60):

- What should I do exactly?
- Why should I do it?
- How should I do it?
- Why should I do it in this way?

This advice sends two important messages to teachers. Firstly, there is an inextricable relation between human activity, cognition and emotion. In their interaction with learners, teachers should therefore attend not only to matters of knowledge, but also to how they can encourage learners' motivation to acquire that knowledge.

Secondly, all instructional behaviour is to be motivated by how it is adjusted to the activity of learning. Teachers should therefore base their instructional behaviour on an understanding of what goes on in the learner.

The search for effective teaching behaviours

The above two messages have, in turn, consequences for how we should determine what are effective teaching behaviours. The search for such behaviours began with process-product research in the 1970s and similarly paid attention to the relation between cognition and motivation in teaching and learning (Brophy, 1986; Brophy & Good, 1986; Dunkin & Biddle, 1974). Later research, building on this tradition, has produced evidence that the interaction between teachers and pupils can be characterised in terms of three interrelated domains: Emotional Supports, Classroom Organisation and Instructional Supports. Factor analyses of observational data from more than 4,000 US schools suggested that the effectiveness of teaching depends on how teachers, within the conditions of classroom organisation, enact instruction and encourage pupils' motivation (Hamre et al., 2013). The concrete teaching behaviours involved were specified in the Classroom Assessment Scoring System (CLASS) (Pianta, La Paro, & Hamre, 2008). Constructive interaction between teacher and pupils requires, in sum, adequate physical conditions, an orderly learning environment including uninterrupted time for learning activity and a social climate providing emotional safety. Such conditions can be created when class sizes remain within a range of 20–30 pupils (Finn, Pannozzo, & Achilles, 2003).

The advice given by Van Parreren on the basis of CHAT and the outcomes of process-product research point in the same direction. This convergence can inform how we should define quality learning and quality teaching.

Quality learning encompasses not only memorisation and reproduction of knowledge, but also higher levels of learning. In terms of Bloom's taxonomy of educational objectives, reproducing factual knowledge remains important, but only as a condition for understanding concepts, applying knowledge, analysing problems, making sound judgements and working with knowledge creatively (see the updated version of Bloom's taxonomy of educational objectives in Anderson & Krathwohl, 2014). The latter are forms of higher-order learning, characterised by the ability to use abstract symbol systems and to transfer learning to new domains (Haskell, 2001).

Quality teaching aims for active learning leading to understanding and higher-order learning, as opposed to teacher-centred instruction eliciting pupil passivity, reproduction and memorisation. The greatest challenge currently facing teacher development is to promote the shift from teacher-dominated and reproduction-oriented learning towards active, higher-order learning, in which pupils develop an understanding of foundational, transferable concepts. Such higher-order learning is increasingly being demanded by technological developments in industrialised, as well as industrialising economies. Teachers should be able to promote this kind of learning. To describe the professional competence that they need to do so, I would like to speak – as do Tharp and Gallimore (1988, p. 248–266) – of "higher-order teaching".

Higher-order teaching

Just as the issue what are desirable outcomes of learning, what constitutes higher-order teaching cannot be determined definitively or exhaustively. There are, however, three forms of teaching which I see as decisive goals for teacher development if schooling is to contribute to higher-order learning. These forms are responsive or dialogic teaching, giving feedback on mounting levels and contingent teaching. Below, I elaborate on each of these.

Dialogic teaching

Traditionally, much of school learning has been dominated by a type of discourse that makes pupils passive and reproduces rote learning. This problem was pointed out time and again by linguists and social scientists. Hoetker and Ahlbrand Jr. (1969, p. 163) have characterised the type of instruction involved as "persistence of the recitation", meaning the time-worn "rapid-fire, question-answer pattern of instruction" which elicits from pupils no more than the memorisation and reproduction of facts. This pattern was later termed Initiation-Response-Follow-up (IRF) by Sinclair and Coulthard (1975) and Initiation-Response-Evaluation (IRE) by Mehan (1979) (see the overview in Mercer & Dawes, 2014).

Already before the work of these authors, Bellack, Kliebard, Hyman and Smith Jr. (1966) demonstrated the existence of this pattern in their pioneering study *The Language of the Classroom*. These researchers characterised classroom discourse in terms of four types of speech acts or conversational "moves": Structuring, Soliciting, Responding and Reacting. Structuring is the type of move that teachers use to direct the course of a lesson, as when they start a lesson, introduce a new topic, explain content, instruct for activities or make transitions to a new lesson phase. Soliciting occurs when a teacher or pupil takes the initiative to ask a question or elicit a response from another person, as when a teacher checks pupils' homework. Responding is the necessary complement to soliciting, as when a pupil answers a teacher's question. Reacting is a voluntary type of move, which follows any of the other moves. For example, a pupil may react – without having to do so – to a teacher's explanation or another pupil's remark.

Theoretically, both teachers and pupils can use all types of moves, but Bellack and his colleagues found that teachers usually do most of the talking. Most of the structuring and soliciting moves are performed by teachers, while responses and reactions from pupils are more infrequent and relatively short. Even when teachers do elicit such responses and reactions, they often do not follow up on them, because of time pressure, habit, stress or other reasons. Still, engaging pupils in discussing the lesson content or "academic talk and dialogue", as researchers now call it (Resnick, Asterhan, & Clarke, 2015), is exactly what is needed to foster higher-order learning. To activate learners cognitively, teachers need to reduce their own amount of talk and increase pupils' contribution to content-focussed dialogue.

Overcoming teacher-centred routines in the interaction with learners is not an easy thing to do for teachers, but recent R&D work shows that it is possible, also in the existing setting of classroom teaching and learning. Collaborative learning is a suitable setting within which teachers can promote dialogue. In combination with the rise of e-learning, this setting opens up new possibilities for teaching and learning. Since the Information Age was ushered in, teachers are no longer the sole or main providers of subject matter. Electronic learning environments can be of great help in presenting lesson content, enabling teachers to orchestrate blended learning and shift their energies to guiding and supporting pupils while they engage with subject matter.

To activate learners in such settings, questioning is one of the most important skills, perhaps even the prime skill that teachers need. This skill can be trained. What is especially demanding, however, is to respond adequately to pupils' responses and reactions, after having elicited them. This requires the teacher, in the moment, not only to diagnose what a pupil thinks, but also which follow-up response is best suited to help a pupil move her or his thinking forward, all the while monitoring what the rest of the class is doing. Jacobs and Empson (2016, p. 185) call what is needed here "responsive teaching", i.e.

> a type of teaching in which teachers' instructional decisions about what to pursue and how to pursue it are continually adjusted during instruction in response to children's content-specific thinking, instead of being determined in advance.

In a study of one expert mathematics teacher's classroom interaction, these researchers have explored what kinds of conversational moves she used during responsive teaching. These moves often had the form of questions and served, besides diagnosing pupils' current thinking, to encourage them to consider alternative solution strategies and to pose related problems that might help them progress into their zones of proximal development. In the resulting dialogue, the teacher maintained a "caring and respectful stance" (Jacobs & Empson, 2016, p. 189, 196).

In another study, Webb, Franke, Turrou and Ing (2015) have shown that during mathematics teaching, moves such as asking probing questions and encouraging peer discussion and explanation among pupils can help raise achievement. Chi and Menekse (2015) studied how during collaborative learning in small groups, teachers' conversational moves influenced pupils' achievement. They found that effects on learning were due not so much to the collaborative learning setting per se as to the nature of teachers' discourse. The more their discourse activated pupil thinking, the more learning was promoted. Gillies (2015), finally, showed how two-day PD workshops helped teachers increase their use of questioning and communication

TABLE 1.1 Feedback on mounting levels

Correctness	Is my answer right or wrong?
Localisation	Where is my error?
Identification	What is right or wrong?
	What is essential?
Error analysis	Why is my answer right or wrong?
Alternatives	What can I do differently?
	What should I do better?

strategies during pupils' cooperative group discussions in order to challenge and move forward their thinking about subject matter.

These examples show that teachers' questioning and responding during dialogue with pupils have a key role to play in fostering higher-order learning. A crucial function of these instructional behaviours is to give pupils feedback on their thinking.

Giving feedback

Feedback is one of the most powerful factors influencing learning, as Hattie (2009) has noted. It has been conceptualised in many different ways, but seldom from the perspective of learners themselves. Teachers often limit their feedback to telling pupils whether an answer or solution is right or wrong. This is what Shute (2008, p. 160) calls "simple feedback". However, pupils would and should benefit far more, when they also receive more "elaborated feedback", which provides them with more information about how they can arrive at an understanding of the issues at hand. In lectures and workshops, I have used the questions in Table 1.1 to support teachers in giving pupils feedback on mounting levels. These levels are similar to the types of elaborated feedback distinguished by Shute, but they are presented in a different form, i.e. as questions that learners need an answer to in order to be able to bring their learning forward. This form was inspired by the questions formulated by Van Parreren for instructing learning tasks (see the previous section).

Giving learners information that allows them to bring their own learning forward requires that teachers place themselves in their learners' shoes and adjust their instruction to learners' current levels of understanding. Such fine-tuning is more easily said than done.

Contingent teaching

To describe what teachers need to do to fine-tune their dialogue with pupils, Janneke van de Pol (2012) has developed the "model of contingent teaching" in pioneering dissertation research at the University of Amsterdam. Proceeding from a Vygotskyan perspective, Van de Pol developed the idea that in order to help learners bring their learning forward, teachers need to determine appropriate levels of challenge. To help learners move from their zones of current into their zones of proximal development, instructional action should be based on neither an underestimation nor an overestimation of their current understanding. Only then can teachers provide effective scaffolding, i.e. "temporary support provided for the completion of a task that learners otherwise might not be able to complete" (Van de Pol, 2012, p. 29).

The "model of contingent teaching" specifies four steps taking place consecutively during teacher–pupil interaction (Van de Pol, 2012, p. 85):

> (1) applying diagnostic strategies (discovering a student's actual understanding); (2) checking one's diagnosis with the student (summarising what the student said and asking whether this is correct to create common understanding or intersubjectivity); (3) applying intervention strategies (the actual support, adapted to the information gathered in steps 1 and 2); and (4) checking a student's understanding (verifying whether the student learned something).

After each step, the teacher needs to receive, perceive and interpret a response from the learner. Otherwise, she or he will not be able to determine how to take the next step. To promote contingent teaching, Van de Pol developed, conducted and evaluated a video-based PD programme for teachers in two cycles of design-based research. Groups of prevocational social studies teachers participated in this programme, while they taught collaborative learning projects. The evaluation findings showed that participating teachers developed more contingent teaching behaviours than non-participating teachers (Van de Pol, 2012, p. 123–157, also in Van de Pol, Volman, & Beishuizen, 2012; Van de Pol, 2012, p. 157–197, also in Van de Pol, Volman, Oort, & Beishuizen, 2014). In a third cycle, the impact of contingent teaching on pupils was studied. The pupils of teachers participating in the PD programme appeared to appreciate their teachers' contingent support, but their on-task behaviour decreased, possibly because their teachers lacked sufficient opportunities for timely interaction with all pupil groups (Van de Pol, 2012, p. 197–233, also in Van de Pol, Volman, Oort, & Beishuizen, 2015). This outcome shows that class size can be a serious contextual constraint on contingent teaching. Nonetheless, Van de Pol's work points an important way forward for developing higher-order teaching.

The instructional skills needed to promote higher-order learning place high demands on teachers. Still, as the research described above suggests, teachers can learn to master them. We will see in Chapter 3 that to develop skills for higher-order teaching, video use can be especially helpful.

Quality standards for teacher learning

The formal acquisition and development of teaching competence take place in the four contexts of PTE, induction, ACPs and PD. If video use for teacher learning is to be effective, I assume that in each of these contexts, specific conditions must be fulfilled. The more these conditions are fulfilled, the better opportunities will exist for video use to contribute to teachers' professional competence and raising the quality of teaching and learning. In this section, I describe these conditions in the form of quality standards for each context. The quality standards I put forward here are based on the literature about teacher learning and on my own work in Dutch teacher education.

These standards recognise two fundamental characteristics of the teaching profession. The first is that competent teaching requires using many different skills simultaneously. Classrooms are highly interactive places where a multitude of events, partly unpredictable, unfold (Doyle, 1986, p. 394–395). This is why teaching competence can only be acquired through a lot of varied practice. Developing it further requires teachers – regardless of their amount of experience – to engage in active learning.

The second fundamental characteristic is that the work of teaching is cyclical in nature. It involves going through repeated cycles of preparing, conducting and reflecting on lessons. Many cyclical models to guide teachers' work – among others Korthagen's ALACT model, referring to the five phases of Action, Looking back on the action, Awareness of essential aspects, Creating alternative methods of action and Trial (Korthagen et al., 2001); Santagata's Lesson Analysis Framework (Santagata & Guarino, 2011); and the Problem-solving Cycle developed by Borko, Jacobs, Eiteljorg, and Pittman (2008) – testify to this fundamental characteristic of teaching. The sequence of a preactive, an interactive and a postactive phase is inherent in teachers' work (Stones, 1994, p. 29).

At the same time, the quality standards I put forward differ between contexts, because student teachers, beginning teachers, ACP candidates and experienced teachers have different backgrounds and different amounts of teaching experience. Preservice teachers have by definition no experience. ACP candidates do have work experience, but not in teaching. For these two groups, who lack teaching experience, I also use the term "*prospective teachers*". Beginning teachers have experience only from student teaching, which in many countries is of limited duration. Experienced teachers, finally, differ in the number of years they have taught as well as the opportunities they have received for engaging in PD.

Preservice teacher education

The transfer problem noted above (see the section *Aims of this book*) is a persistent challenge in teacher development. Worldwide, teacher educators are grappling with the question how to achieve a productive relationship between knowledge construction and competence development. Traditionally, theoretical knowledge is taught to prospective teachers in methods courses, which they are then expected to apply during student teaching. This is a deductive, "theory-to-practice" approach. The problem with this approach is that the demands of teaching are usually too complex for student teachers to succeed in applying the theories presented to them. The idea of presenting theories about teaching and then expecting prospective teachers to "do it yourself" stems from the old days when teacher education programmes were not yet fully institutionalised and well-meaning professors provided evening lectures for anyone who wanted to enter teaching.

The opposite inductive "practice-to-theory" approach of letting competence development depend wholly on practical experience runs the risk of unreflected reproduction of traditional, teacher-centred instructional practices whose effectiveness is unclear. Instead, the key challenge is how to unite theory and practice. Deductive and inductive teacher learning ought to complement each other (Korthagen et al., 2001).

Which conditions should teacher education programmes fulfil, if they are to encourage their participants to develop themselves as competent and thoughtful teachers? For an answer to this question, empirical evidence is needed about relationships between programme features on the one hand and learning outcomes in graduates on the other. So far, such a knowledge base is incomplete (Cochran-Smith & Zeichner, 2005; Sleeter, 2014; Zeichner & Schulte, 2001). Before describing the quality standards I propose for PTE, I give an overview of research that has produced some important evidence.

The influence of occupational socialisation on teacher learning

The transfer problem in teacher education can be traced to the phenomenon of occupational socialisation and its influence on teacher learning.

The first research relating programme features to outcomes in graduates was carried out in the 1970s by Hanns-Dietrich Dann and colleagues from the University of Konstanz in Germany. What this research sought to address was the problem of "reality shock" or "practice shock", meaning the phenomenon that beginning teachers are overwhelmed by the complex demands of their first student-teaching placement or job. In the US, Corcoran (1981) has named this same problem "transition shock". It should not be underestimated what consequences this has for young teachers' development in the profession. The main symptoms of practice shock found in beginning teachers are work stress, changes in behaviour and attitudes, negative feelings about the self and dropout from the profession (Müller-Fohrbrodt, Cloetta, & Dann, 1978, p. 32). Similar findings have been reported from many other countries (see the review by Veenman, 1984).

The research by Dann and colleagues has shown that during practice shock, prospective teachers go through "discrepancy experiences". This means that the reality of teaching differs so radically from their expectations that they feel bewildered and have to struggle for control. In the process, they tend to discard any ideas or ideals about innovative teaching that PTE programmes may have tried to inculcate and quickly resort to the type of transmissive teaching behaviour that encourages passivity and resistance in pupils. The concomitant attitude change follows a U-shaped pattern, which has become known as the "Konstanz bath tub" (Dann, Cloetta, Müller-Fohrbrodt, & Helmreich, 1978; Dann, Müller-Fohrbrodt, & Cloetta, 1981). Similar findings were reported from Hamburg by Hinsch (1979).

The mechanism underlying attitude change in beginning teachers is that "counterattitudinal action", i.e. behaviour inconsistent with a person's existing beliefs, forces the individual to rethink and adjust those beliefs (Kelman, 1974). This mechanism can explain what Lortie (1975) called the "apprenticeship of observation", meaning that the experience of practice shock causes prospective teachers to resort to the kinds of teaching they have experienced themselves during years of being pupils in schools. The phenomena described above are forms of occupational socialisation which cause traditional teaching practices to be reproduced (Lacey, 1977).

The German studies referenced above have yielded indications that PTE programmes in which student teachers' practical experiences are closely linked to theoretical reflection can strengthen in-service teaching competence in graduates. My own dissertation research built on these studies. This was a longitudinal study conducted in the Netherlands among 357 students, 128 cooperating teachers and 31 university supervisors from 24 graduate university teacher education programmes. Quantitative survey data as well as in-depth qualitative data were collected over a period of 4½ years. The development of teaching competence was followed from candidates' enrolment until their third year as in-service teachers (Brouwer, 1989, 2010; Brouwer & Korthagen, 2005).

The findings showed that beginning teachers' work is characterised by setbacks, especially during their first in-service year. During this period, what innovative teaching practices they may have practised during PTE programmes are often forced underground. In a number of cases, however, this is a temporary or latency effect (Brouwer & Korthagen, 2005, p. 212). The resurgence of innovative teaching behaviours, notably the ability to activate learners, was stronger in graduates from programmes which had systematically encouraged them to move back and forth between action and reflection in collaborative settings. Findings pointing in the same direction have also become available in the US (Boyd, Grossman, Lankford, Loeb, & Wyckoff, 2009; Darling-Hammond, 2000, p. 167–168). The evidence accumulated in these studies suggests that programmes which carefully integrate practice and theory *can* have a noticeable influence on how teachers do their work.

The impact of PTE programmes probably depends to an important extent on how programme features are combined within one coherent learning environment. This means that, in order to raise the effectiveness of teacher education, a number of conditions should be fulfilled simultaneously. The five quality standards I present in Box 1.2 are meant to serve this purpose.

Longitudinal programming

The first quality standard for PTE entails that for learning to teach, goals are set and activities are planned whose complexity gradually increases, in combination with creating opportunities for mutual support and reflection on individual experiences and concerns. Such a gradual build-up of practical experience coupled with collaborative analysis and reflection helps graduates increase and sustain innovative teaching competence during the first years in the profession.

BOX 1.2 QUALITY STANDARDS FOR PRESERVICE TEACHER EDUCATION

I. Longitudinal programming

Goals and activities for learning to teach are programmed in consecutive cycles which gradually increase in complexity.

II. Networking with schools

Teacher education institutions and schools maintain stable collaboration for a continuous number of years, so that student teachers' learning needs and concerns can be served.

III. Professional development of teacher educators

Teacher educators and mentor teachers have completed professional development in the areas of curriculum development, mentoring and action research.

IV. Electronic learning environments

An ICT infrastructure specifically geared to teacher learning is available and student teachers, mentor teachers and teacher educators know how to use it for supporting each others' and their own learning.

V. Balancing formative and summative assessment

In formative and summative assessments underlying intake, progress and cer-tification decisions, instruments and procedures are used which support candi-dates in directing their learning trajectories.

This standard is best operationalised in a curriculum in which student-teaching and college-based periods alternate in ways that enable student teachers to move through repeated cycles of planning lessons, conducting them in realistic classroom settings and then reflecting on them. Over time, a gradual increase in the com-plexity of student-teaching activities creates opportunities to acquire the manifold teaching skills needed for competent teaching.

During the 1990s, my colleagues and I have embodied this principle of increas-ing complexity in a four-year curriculum structured in consecutive one-year stages revolving around the following student-teaching periods: the Orientation stage, in which the student teacher explores whether teaching is a realistic perspective for him or her; the Basic stage, in which the acquisition of basic instructional skills

TABLE 1.2 Intermediate goals for teacher learning

TASK DOMAIN	Orientation stage	Basic stage	Elaboration stage	Transition stage
1 ORGANISATION Solving problems in the organization of (educational) activities	• agree on and perform duties as an *assistant teacher* in and *outside* the classroom	*prepare a whole lesson* including making materials and media ready for use	• collect *materials* and *advice* among colleagues and • use them in preparing and giving lessons	• function as a *team member* and • show *initiative* *cooperate* with colleagues • of the same and • other subjects contribute towards *curriculum development*
2 CONTENT Transmitting knowledge and stimulating insight in specific subject matter areas	assist with teaching in *group settings*, e.g.: • tutor pupils in small groups • help with homework • support second-language acquisition • teach *part of a lesson*	use *direct instruction*: • *present and explain* subject matter • give *instructions* and *assignments* • help pupils *practice* • give *feedback* on assignments	• *relate to pupils'* existing knowledge • *explain* in correct language and without undue simplifications • ask and answer *questions*	arrange *learning environments* in accordance with curricular objectives support pupils in *self-directed learning*, notably the acquisition of domain-specific • understanding and • skills
3 SEQUENCING Planning and carrying out (educational) activities in a premeditated sequence	*support the teaching-learning process* by e.g.: • registering pupil attendance • helping pupils with seatwork • tidying the classroom	• make a *time plan* for a lesson and • *maintain* it in carrying out the lesson	purposefully • determine and • vary the *pace* of lessons give adequate *feedback* at suitable moments • design and • carry out *series of lessons*	make lessons *flow*, especially during • start, • transitions and • ending *alternate* • teacher *control*, • shared control and • pupil control of learning activity

4 MEDIA Selecting, producing and presenting learning materials	collect and present learning *materials*, using among others • blackboard and whiteboard, transparencies, slides, video and digital media *assist* with: • exhibitions • school paper • library and media workshop • ICT lessons	give a whole lesson using existing *materials* *use ICT* for • retrieval, documentation, administration, planning and presentation in own lessons	present subject matter using • succinct *figures* and *tables* • telling *examples*	make use of • current *news* and • pupils' *interests* utilise the *affordances of ICT* for • interactivity and • feedback in pupil learning
5 METHODS Selecting and using work forms	support *groups of pupils* in making assignments *assist* with • laboratory lessons • sports events • excursions	alternate • whole-class *teacher-centered* delivery and • *supporting* pupils individually and in dyads	conduct whole-class *question-answer* sessions use assignments and group work to encourage *pupil activity and cooperative learning*	moderate *whole-class discussions* monitor and support *pupil traineeships* use forms of • homogeneous and • heterogeneous *differentiation*
6 EVALUATION Evaluating learning and development processes in pupils	*help pupils individually* with • understanding subject matter • assignments and home work *assist* in • *administering* and • *rating tests*	*check* by direct individual questioning *whether pupils understand* an explanation	*evaluate regularly and validly pupils'* • starting points for learning, • progress and • achievements	• *signal* and • when necessary (help) *remediate* • cognitive, • affective and • regulative *learning problems*

(*Continued*)

TABLE 1.2 (Continued). Intermediate goals for teacher learning

TASK DOMAIN	Orientation stage	Basic stage	Elaboration stage	Transition stage
7 **INTERACTION** Interacting with pupils in ways which stimulate (experiences of) active involvement	*Assist* with • canteen supervision • activities outside school • projects • festivities	while teaching *perceive* when pupils want to say or ask something	"maintaining discipline" for beginners: • clarify, • agree on and • maintain *rules for behaviour*	"maintaining discipline" advanced: with *respect* for pupils • create and • maintain a conducive *working climate*
8 **REFLECTION** Critically investigating and if necessary modifying one's way of teaching	*open* oneself to others' • experiences and • comments	*utilise experiences* with earlier lessons in • planning and • carrying out subsequent lessons	put forward pedagogical *arguments* for • content and • form of own teaching	• *investigate* and • *improve* own work as a teacher by engaging in • collegial support groups, • action research and • professional development work

and self-confidence in classroom performance are central concerns; the Elaboration stage, in which the student teacher consolidates and elaborates these skills and develops an awareness of pupils' learning and his or her own influence on it; and the Transition stage, in which the student teacher functions as a team member and develops a professional identity. Table 1.2 shows the goals we set for each stage.

The goals for each stage were further operationalised in the form of observation protocols or "viewing guides", which student teachers, mentors and supervisors used for lesson planning and feedback (Brouwer et al., 2002). A PTE curriculum based on longitudinal programming such as this offers many opportunities for video use. In Chapters 4 and 5, we will see how video feedback in combination with structured viewing guides can benefit teacher learning. This approach can of course be used with other observation systems such as the CLASS (Pianta & Hamre, 2009) or those developed by Danielson (2007) and Stronge (2002).

Networking with schools

Student teachers' learning needs and concerns can be addressed through forms of clinical supervision in small-group settings in which student teachers, cooperating teachers and college or university supervisors cooperate. To achieve this, a stable and workable division of labour between teacher education institutions and schools is needed, i.e. the school contributes a local environment in which prospective teachers gather authentic practical experiences and receive mentoring enabling them to acquire teaching competence, while the teacher education programme provides them with training opportunities and resources eliciting them to interpret their experiences on more generalised levels.

Stable working relationships allow for the placement of student teachers in schools which commit themselves to creating opportunities for professional learning. This is possible only when collaboration lasts for a continuous number of years. In addition, teacher educators and school mentors should maintain regular contact in order to develop a shared understanding of programme content, to monitor individual students' progress and to coordinate the support given them.

Professional development of teacher educators

The multiplier function of teacher education for society makes it of great importance that programmes are implemented and developed on the basis of up-to-date knowledge. This is why all staff involved in promoting teacher learning need and deserve opportunities to develop themselves in their work – just as pupils and teachers (Tharp & Gallimore, 1988).

It is not generally acknowledged that educating teachers is a specific expertise. However, teacher educators perform quite a variety of roles. For them, it is especially important to be able to make explicit and model effective teaching behaviour, to bring theory to bear on the dilemmas facing teachers, to support their learning in informed and empathetic ways, to make valid assessments of teacher competence and to work on programme development and research. Since the rise of school-based teacher education, the same increasingly applies to school mentors. In practice, however, it is rather the exception than the rule that personnel responsible for educating teachers is capable of performing all of these roles (Koster, Dengerink, Korthagen, & Lunenberg, 2008; Lunenberg, Dengerink, & Korthagen, 2013).

If teacher educators and school mentors are to link practice and theory, three areas of expertise appear to be of crucial importance. Firstly, they should contribute to the systematic improvement of school curricula and programmes for teacher education and PD. Secondly, they should be trained in mentoring skills. Supporting teachers' professional learning requires more than giving practical, local advice and moral support. It is also about facilitating and eliciting personal, reflective learning (Crasborn & Hennissen, 2010). Thirdly, teacher educators and school mentors should be able to perform action research (e.g. Mills, 2013). When teacher educators and mentor teachers are qualified in these three areas, this will favour the creation of learning environments for student teachers which combine challenge and support.

Electronic learning environments

In the digital age, knowledge acquisition and communication no longer occur in personal contact only. They increasingly take place anytime anywhere through computer-supported collaborative learning (CSCL). Digitisation is bringing about profound changes in schooling (Roschelle, Pea, Hoadley, Gordin, & Means, 2000). This is a cultural shift with considerable implications for the work of both teachers and teacher educators. Searching, selecting and structuring content are becoming more important tasks than transmitting it. In addition to being leaders of interaction in groups, teachers and teacher educators must work as "e-moderators" in electronic learning environments (Salmon, 2011), where they act more as a "guide on the side" than as a "sage on the stage" (King, 1993) to support learners in processing information and transforming it into personally meaningful knowledge.

Modern teacher education programmes may be expected to maintain secure online environments for CSCL which fulfil standards for the use of information technology (Fulton, 2000). We should bear in mind, however, that implementing CSCL places high demands on learners' capacity for self-direction and thus also on how learning environments are structured (Smith, 2003). Combining learning in personal contact with online learning – "blended learning" – therefore appears to hold the most promise (Ko & Rossen, 2010; Littlejohn & Pegler, 2007).

CSCL environments in teacher education should preferably be accessible for all groups involved, i.e. student teachers, mentor teachers and teacher educators. These environments should provide information about the curriculum content in the school types served as well as the teacher education programme itself. These resources should be made accessible in understandable and navigable ways and be accompanied by activity formats for learning from them. In such environments, video representations of teaching can be shared and discussed to serve the goal of teacher learning. Chapters 2, 7 and 9 in particular show which possibilities and requirements are involved in achieving this goal.

Balancing formative and summative assessment

Summative as well as formative assessment is necessary in all stages of PTE. To control the quality of teaching, teacher education programmes are legally responsible for taking valid intake, progress and certification decisions. These are typically part of high-stakes performance assessment (Andrews & Barnes, 1990; Shinkfield & Stufflebeam, 1995). At the same time, teacher candidates have a moral right to receive not only information about selection decisions and the criteria and procedures involved, but also feedback and advice about their personal achievements and perspectives.

Summative and formative assessment have different functions, i.e. appraisal and selection versus diagnosis and feedback. A drawback of summative assessments is that they tend to take the form of "one-shot" procedures capitalising on self-reports and other kinds of indirect data such as contained in portfolios. Accordingly, they risk producing a meagre or even biased representation of a teacher's competence and development. The formative approach tends to be more context-bound and longitudinal and to use more qualitative instruments, as is the case in repeated direct observations. It seeks to maintain an evidence-based dialogue with candidates about their progress through mounting levels of competence.

Summative and formative assessment should not be seen as categorically different or separate. Rather, they represent the opposite ends of one continuum. The challenge is to balance both functions, but this can be hard to achieve (Shepard, 2000). Candidates should receive timely and acceptable motivations for decisions, not only in the case of positive decisions, but especially in the case of negative ones. Whoever is rejected at any time has a right to receive advice about remediation or redirection of his or her efforts.

Figure 1.2 shows which functions summative and formative assessments have to serve during the main stages of professional learning through which teacher candidates proceed.

Before being admitted to a programme, an intake procedure should generate some assessment of candidates' suitability and chances of success. Then, during further orientation, they need advice about the question whether and how they should continue learning to teach. While they progress through competence development, they are well served when mid-term as well as end-of-term assessments enable them

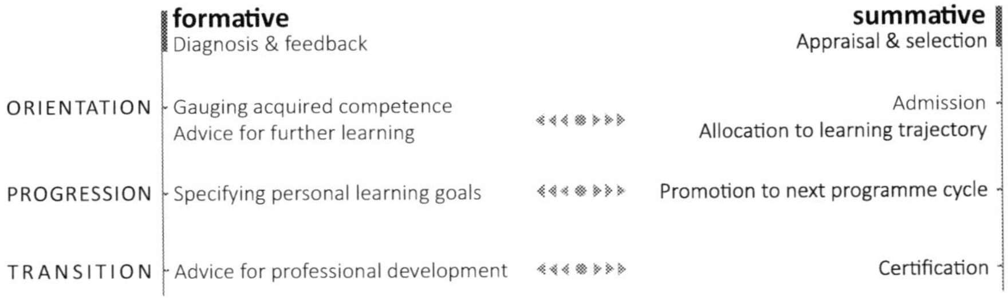

	formative Diagnosis & feedback		**summative** Appraisal & selection
ORIENTATION	Gauging acquired competence Advice for further learning	◀◀◀ ✹ ▶▶▶	Admission Allocation to learning trajectory
PROGRESSION	Specifying personal learning goals	◀◀◀ ✹ ▶▶▶	Promotion to next programme cycle
TRANSITION	Advice for professional development	◀◀◀ ✹ ▶▶▶	Certification

FIGURE 1.2 Functions of assessment in teacher development

to reformulate their learning goals. Finally, before and while making the transition to in-service teaching, they will benefit from a specification of their current competence and suggestions for professional development.

From a validity point of view, assessments should be based on criteria and indicators specifying effective teacher behaviours. For this purpose, categorisations of goals such as presented in Table 1.2 can be used. While such goals specify certain standards about teaching quality and teacher competence, they also leave space for individual teachers to focus on developing specific professional skills, depending on their current progress and learning needs.

Procedurally, assessments should ideally be based on repeated direct observations of practice as well as competence ratings by different stakeholders, particularly school mentors, teacher educators and school leaders acquainted with a teacher's learning. Schools and teacher education institutions share an obligation to provide explicit norms and practicable procedures for assessment.

Induction of beginning teachers

The phenomenon of practice shock discussed in the previous section generally extends from the start of student teaching until at least the second year of beginning teaching. The first year of teaching with a full workload and full responsibilities is a pivotal phase in teachers' competence development (Feiman-Nemser et al., 1999, p. 6). The problems that beginning teachers experience are well known and well researched, but still, during enculturation into the profession, they receive too little support. This is a persistent and worldwide problem (Veenman, 1984), but in comparison to other professions, teaching cuts a particularly bad figure. It frequently exposes novices to a "sink or swim" experience which has a particularly deleterious impact, not only on teachers personally, but also on the quality of the workforce. The lack of adequate induction causes costly rates of teacher attrition and turnover (Ingersoll & Strong, 2011, p. 202; Kearney, 2014, p. 4; Tynjälä & Heikkinen, 2011, p. 12–13). In many countries, the teaching profession is plagued by a "revolving door effect", meaning that adverse working conditions lead teachers to switch schools or leave the profession altogether (Ingersoll, 2001).

Since Lortie (1975) drew attention to the problem of teachers' occupational socialisation, increasing efforts to introduce programmes for teacher induction have been made in many countries. The most common forms of induction are the provision of information, orientation and workshops, workload reduction, lesson observation and feedback, mentoring and collaboration with colleagues. However, the implementation of these measures is variable (Tynjälä & Heikkinen, 2011, p. 23–25) and far from systematic (Kearney, 2014). Also, evidence-based knowledge has become available about what features make induction effective. From their critical review of induction research, Ingersoll and Strong (2011, p. 201) conclude that "support and assistance for beginning teachers have a positive impact on three sets of outcomes: teacher commitment and retention, teacher classroom instructional practices, and student achievement." There are also indications that the higher the duration and intensity of induction, the more effects can be expected, but it remains unclear what are optimal levels of induction. In disadvantaged contexts, indications are that induction can alleviate, but not offset, the impact of the challenges facing teachers (Ingersoll & Strong, 2011, p. 228).

Relatively effective forms of induction appear to be those focussing on daily teaching practice, i.e. orientation, mentoring, lesson observation and feedback and collegial collaboration. For example, Smith and Ingersoll (2004) studied the relationship between induction and turnover in a nationally representative sample of 3,235 beginning teachers in the US, who experienced different "induction packages". 3% received no induction. 56% experienced "basic induction", i.e. mentoring from a colleague and "supportive communication" with a teacher in a leadership function. 26% experienced "basic induction + collaboration", i.e. mentoring and supportive communication, complemented with "common planning time or regularly scheduled collaboration with other teachers in their subject area; and … a seminar for beginning teachers". Less than 1% received all the above forms of support plus "participating in an external network of teachers, having a reduced number of preparations, and being assigned a teacher's aide". The statistically significant outcome of this study was that the more elaborate the induction package was, the lower was the likelihood that beginning teachers switched schools or left the profession altogether (Smith & Ingersoll, 2004, p. 704–706).

The findings and conclusions from the review by Ingersoll and Strong (2011) were confirmed by a randomised controlled trial by Helms-Lorenz, Van de Grift and Maulana (2016), who followed 338 beginning teachers in Dutch secondary schools from their first into their third year of teaching, using their pupils' perceptions as outcome measures. Also this study showed that the more elaborate induction was, the lower teachers' turnover rates were. Interestingly, beginning teachers switching schools or leaving the profession lacked, according to their pupils, especially instructional skills in providing goal clarity, explaining, classroom management and fostering engagement and motivation. "The strongest effect was shown for teachers being observed and coached" (Helms-Lorenz, Van de Grift, & Maulana, 2016, p. 11–15).

Given that induction has been shown to be effective in reducing turnover and fostering teaching skills, it is possible to derive standards for a systemic implementation of support for beginning teachers (cf. Tynjälä & Heikkinen, 2011). Based on a review of available research, Kearney (2014, p. 7, 13) has listed requirements for effective induction which may serve as such standards. These requirements are situated on the three levels of school organisation, teacher teams and individual teacher learning.

On the level of school organisation, beginning teachers will benefit from a reduced teaching load and/or release time as well as from professional support and/ or networking.

On the level of teacher teams, they will benefit from participating in collaborative PD which provides opportunities for professional communication and dialogue.

On the level of individual learning, beginning teachers need support in the form of mentoring, based on regular and structured observation of their teaching.

Alternative certification programmes

Teacher shortages have led governments in many countries to introduce ACPs with the aim of attracting career changers from other professions to teaching (Brouwer, 2007; Dangel & Guyton, 2005; Grossman & Loeb, 2008). These programmes come in many forms and shapes, but they share two basic features. Firstly, they are usually dual programmes, i.e. they are designed as a form of workplace learning. Secondly, they are abridged or accelerated, i.e. their duration is shorter than that of regular preservice programmes. The assumption behind this feature is that because of their earlier work experience, career changers can learn to teach faster than student teachers in regular preservice programmes. However, as a review of ACP research shows (Tigchelaar, Brouwer, & Korthagen, 2008), there is little evidence supporting this idea. On the contrary, large-scale survey data about attrition patterns in US teachers have shown that the longer teachers' preparation lasted, the lower were their dropout rates from the profession (Shen & Bierlein Palmer, 2005). ACP participants risk entering teaching in ways that are too abrupt, and this can cause dropout (Donaldson & Graham, 2001; Kasworm, 2001). This risk may aggravate the revolving-door effect already at work in the teaching profession. Such phenomena also surfaced in the early German research into "practice shock" (see the previous sections).

For these reasons, I consider the quality standards for PTE presented above equally applicable to ACPs. However, the fact that ACPs are often dual and accelerated programmes requires specific consideration. Heeding the first quality standard of longitudinal programming is particularly important in ACPs in order to ensure a gradual buildup of activities for teacher learning. What should at least be guaranteed to counter the risk of reproducing practice shock is the provision of a preliminary period in ACPs, during which candidates do not yet teach, but orient and prepare themselves for workplace learning (McCabe, 2004).

The second quality standard requires ACP providers and schools to pay special attention to creating suitable environments for workplace learning, for instance by ensuring maximum hours for work and minimum hours for mentoring. Just as for beginning teachers, support for career changers in the form of induction – specifically mentoring and collegial collaboration – can reduce turnover between schools and promote retention in teaching. Following the third standard, such support should be provided by qualified mentor teachers and teacher educators.

The fourth standard calling for the use of electronic learning environments is especially relevant for career changers because of their specific need for a flexible organisation of their learning. As adult learners they often combine family and work responsibilities. This makes it all the more important that well-functioning electronic learning environments are available to them.

Finally, the fifth standard of balancing formative and summative assessment is especially important for ACP participants, because from a socioeconomic perspective, a career change to teaching is a high-stakes enterprise. In their situation, a great deal depends on receiving careful and timely feedback and advice during their learning trajectories.

Professional development

Compared to student teachers and career changers, experienced teachers generally have a greater mastery of professional competence and a more crystallised understanding of what is necessary and desirable to carry out and develop their work. Quality standards for experienced teachers' professional learning must therefore also differ. During the last decades, educational research has pursued the question what PD efforts contribute to in-service teachers' work and how. This has led to a degree of consensus about what constitutes effective PD. Reviews have allowed identifying a "canon" of critical features of effective PD. Using the reviews by Kennedy (1998), Desimone (2009), Timperley, Wilson, Barrar and Fung (2007), Cordingley, Bell, Thomason and Firth (2005) and Van Veen, Zwart and Meirink (2012) as a basis, I have summarised this canon in Box 1.3. It lists seven quality standards describing PD features ranging from the level of individual teacher learning through characteristics of teamwork and school organisation to policy issues on a larger scale. In the following discussion of each standard, I pay particular attention to the mechanisms that may explain how experienced teachers' learning takes place.

A shared finding in most research on PD effectiveness is that "one-shot" PD offerings, in which teachers are exposed passively to single lectures or demonstrations by experts specialised in specific aspects of education, usually do not have any influence on how teachers do their daily work. Just as in PTE, this traditional deductive approach is ineffective. As Guskey (1986, 2002) has shown, teachers do not change their instruction as a consequence of theoretical ideas, but in response to how learners react when they try out new ways of teaching. Teachers judge the value of their work foremost by how, in their perception, it influences the learning processes and outcomes in the learners entrusted to their responsibility (Fishman, Marx, Best, & Tal, 2003, p. 643–646). It is teachers' experiences during teaching which influence in the first place whether and how they will change their practices. This explains why changes in teachers' beliefs generally follow rather than precede changes in their actions (cf. Clarke & Hollingsworth, 2002, p. 958–962).

What is involved in how teachers change their instruction has been clarified by the research underlying the canon of features of effective PD. Depending on the scope and resources available, this research has used varying criteria to determine what counts as effective. The most rigorous studies have employed observations and measurement to assess what influence PD contents and activities have on changes in teachers' behaviour and eventually on pupils' learning. Other studies have relied on changes in practice, knowledge and beliefs as reported by teachers themselves.

Coherence with current practice

If teachers are to learn through PD, it should be embedded in their daily work (Wilson & Berne, 1991). This means that it should take account of their current practice and how their knowledge and beliefs relate to that practice. For the teachers participating in PD, it should be recognisable how its contents and

BOX 1.3 FEATURES OF EFFECTIVE PROFESSIONAL DEVELOPMENT

I. Coherence with current practice

PD contents and activities are recognisably related to teachers' current practice and how their knowledge and beliefs relate to that practice.

II. Focus on subject-matter content and pedagogy

Attention is paid to the following issues: which specific subject matter is taught, on which grounds it is selected, how it is structured and how learners are encouraged to engage with it actively.

III. Active learning

Teachers engage in activities aiming to sustain or increase effective teaching practices. This includes evaluating and redesigning teaching plans.

IV. Collegial collaboration

Teachers collaborate voluntarily in groups of colleagues providing them with opportunities to address the concerns and challenges they face in their daily work. This includes giving and receiving feedback on the basis of equality and trust.

V. Duration

PD activities comprise enough time and extend over periods long enough for teachers to develop new perspectives on their work and to adapt their teaching accordingly.

VI. Support and sustainability

School management provides working time and creates opportunities for teachers to examine and alter their practice. This includes access to evidence-based expertise. After PD efforts end formally, follow-up support promotes sustainability.

VII. Examination of existing theories and policies about learning

Teachers are encouraged to examine critically existing theories about pupils' learning in relation to educational policies.

activities address their interests, concerns and needs. If any other learning activities were or are undertaken in the school, it should also be clear how they relate to the PD involved.

Focus on subject-matter content and pedagogy

As noted earlier, teachers' work is inherently situated in the instructional triangle. Teachers participating in PD will therefore always want to address its consequences for one or more of the following issues: which specific subject matter is taught, on which grounds it is selected, how it is structured and how learners are encouraged to engage with it actively (Kennedy, 1998). The more opportunities are available to do so, the more effective PD can be.

What is especially conducive to teacher learning is when PD encourages teachers to examine pupil learning as a function of their own instructional actions, in other words when the relationship between teaching and learning is analysed with the intent to discover alternative ways in which teaching can foster learning (Timperley et al., 2007, p. 183–192).

Active learning

The fact that classroom teaching requires teachers to deploy a host of skills simultaneously makes it imperative that effective PD should include ample opportunities for practising (Garet, Porter, Desimone, Birman, & Yoon, 2001). This applies in particular to the interactive and the preactive phases of teachers' work. Teachers can only develop interactive skills such as explaining, questioning and giving feedback by exercising them actively. For example, during PD, role-play is useful for this purpose, not only in the role of teacher, but also in the role of pupil. In the latter case, teachers can experience vicariously what impact different teaching actions have on pupils. Similarly, when teachers consult pupils about how they experience their teaching, this can generate valuable insights to guide their professional learning.

The cyclical nature of teachers' work entails that PD can become more effective, when it includes opportunities for them to evaluate and redesign teaching plans. Changing instruction requires reorganising how one thinks about and plans to shape and manage pupils' learning, followed by trial and evaluation (Fenstermacher & Richardson, 1993; Yinger, 1979). This is an iterative process, during which teachers engage in repeated fine-tuning of their plans and actions, resulting in incremental change. The outcome consists not only of changes in instruction, but also of changes in teachers' understanding of how they influence learning (Silver, Kogut, & Huynh, 2019).

PD should not be *for* teachers, but *by* teachers. If it is to be effective, it is not enough when they talk about their work in general terms (Little, 1990). When during PD, teachers focus on examining concretely the interplay between teaching and learning, this raises the chances of their enhancing pupil learning eventually (Ermeling, 2010; Vescio, Ross, & Adams, 2008).

Collegial collaboration

The one feature surfacing in virtually all research into effective PD is teacher collaboration with colleagues. But what is it that makes collaboration so valuable for teacher learning?

Joyce and Showers (2002) point out that teachers' PD is effective when a professional learning community (PLC) enables them to participate in R&D work aiming at improving the outcomes of student learning. Assessing pupils' learning processes and outcomes together is a key characteristic of this work, which contributes to having a shared purpose. Also Timperley et al. (2007, p. xxxii–xxxiv and 201–205) have identified this as a feature of effective PD.

The reviews by Cordingley et al. (2005, 2015) point out specific aspects of collaboration explaining when teachers feel supported by it. Teachers value collaboration when it provides opportunities for exchanging practical experiences in an atmosphere of trust. This happens especially when they observe each other's lessons, give and receive feedback on them and, on this basis, engage in professional dialogue. In addition, benefits experienced through peer support are strengthened when teachers identify personal learning needs as starting points and foci for their PD activities, in other words when they have ownership over their PD.

A point of discussion is whether teachers' participation in PD should be voluntary or not. The review by Timperley et al. (2007, p. 194) is clear about this:

> Volunteering was not associated with successful outcomes any more frequently than compulsion. What was important was that teachers engaged in the learning process at some point. Engagement depended more on the purpose behind the initiative and the content and form of the professional development than whether teachers volunteered or not.

Duration

When it comes to the time teachers spend on PD, it is important to distinguish between three different factors: the total number of hours involved, the time span within which PD activities take place and the opportunities present to engage in cycles of preactive, interactive and postactive activities. Combinations between these factors can influence the nature and intensity of teachers' PD experience considerably.

It is not clear from research how long PD efforts should last minimally before they become effective. Besides determining the numbers of hours spent, it is probably more illuminating to consider over which periods teachers' activities should extend and which kinds of activities teachers should undertake how regularly in order to achieve the goals set. Most reviewers do agree that for significant out-comes to result from PD, it should extend over sustained periods (Garet et al., 2001; Desimone, 2009). Cordingley et al. (2015, p. 4) suggest that at least two academic terms are necessary to allow for embedding new practices in the school organisation.

Support and sustainability

To make PD efforts possible, structural measures in the school organisation are clearly necessary. Teachers need some form of release time for carrying out PD activities, such as visiting each other's classes, discussing R&D work and studying resources. Ermeling (2010) advocates in addition protecting time slots for doing PD work.

Making resources for PD available is in fact a minimum option. Timperley et al. (2007, p. 192–196) conclude that PD becomes more effective, when school man-agement also engages itself in the substance of teachers' work and cultivates a cul-ture of professional learning. This includes contributing to formulating a vision and deriving concrete goals from it; establishing priorities; staying focussed; and distributing leadership. Similarly, Joyce and Showers (2002) emphasise that school development should be a collective enterprise.

A specific issue is whether specific expertise from outside the school should be employed in PD. Most reviews are in favour of doing so. This may indeed counter the risk that teachers limit their perspectives to their own experience and forego benefitting from the available knowledge base about teaching and learning (Little, 1990). What is essential, however, is not where this expertise comes from, but that teachers get access to it and that different parties involved – teachers, subject spe-cialists, researchers – pool their resources (Joyce & Showers, 2002; Timperley et al., 2007, p. 201–205).

A familiar problem in school development is that once resources and facilities for PD projects are withdrawn, the related practices and outcomes fade away. It appears difficult to prevent this from happening, even when a school promotes a culture of professional learning. The sustainability of PD outcomes has been little studied. However, research by Carpenter (2012) suggests that teachers' social networks play an important part in it. The extent to which teachers succeed in upholding improvements in their work appears to depend on the level of expertise they build up, the strength of their ties with colleagues – i.e. the frequency and intensity of their contacts – and the depth of their interactions with colleagues. "High-depth" interaction was defined as dialogue about not only preparing and conducting lessons, but specifically about what, how and why pupils learned as a function of teaching.

Examination of existing theories and policies

One feature that has found its way into the canon of effective PD is "consistency with school, district and state policy". This feature stems from quantitative studies of large-scale PD initiatives in mathematics and science in the US, but its causal status is unclear. It does differ from the first feature of coherence with teachers' current practice and learning activities.

Policy mandates have an uneasy relationship with teachers' existing theories about their pupils' learning. While such mandates do not necessarily result in improved outcomes of schooling, teachers' existing theories do influence pupils' learning. This is why it is important for PD providers to acknowledge those theories and to encourage teachers to examine them critically (Timperley et al., 2007, p. 196–201). The same applies in my opinion to educational policies. Teachers can and should develop their professionalism also by examining what those policies entail for their work in the classroom. PD initiatives should offer them the opportunities to do so.

Overview of chapters

Given the aims of this book, I have addressed in the preceding sections which kinds of outcomes of schooling are valuable to aim for and what kinds of instruction teachers should be able to enact to achieve such outcomes. I then explicated which conditions the four contexts of teacher learning – PTE, induction, ACPs and PD – should fulfil to create the best opportunities for teachers to acquire and develop professional competence. Within this framework, the following chapters address how video use can contribute to raising the quality of teaching and learning.

Chapter 2 provides an overview of the field. It opens with background information about the development from analog to digital video in teacher development. Then, a variety of applications is described which represents the possibilities DV offers for teacher learning. Building on these examples, the terminology used in this book is defined and the main paradigms underlying VTL research are outlined. On this basis, conclusions are drawn about the outcomes, processes and conditions involved in VTL and the VTL model is introduced, which addresses how VTL can support teaching and learning.

Chapter 3 is an up-to-date systematic review of empirical research carried out since 2000, focussing on the effects of VTL on teachers' instructional behaviour. The available scientific knowledge is synthesised with special attention to changes in teachers' instructional action, their impact on pupil learning, their development and their sustainability. The main conclusion is that VTL is a strategy especially suitable for raising the quality of instruction by developing teachers' competence in fostering higher-order learning.

In Chapters 4, 5 and 6, I report my own research, which strategically addresses how VTL can influence teaching and learning.

The study in Chapter 4 shows that using structured viewing guides for examining subject-specific lessons, in this case in reading and writing, has consistently positive effects on the quality of teachers' instruction. The study in Chapter 5 then shows how the use of different kinds of viewing guides influences the ways in which preservice teachers attend to and reason about instruction.

In Chapter 6, an in-depth case study is reported exploring the impact of reciprocal peer coaching with video on 45 experienced secondary teachers' work. The aim of this study was to find out if and what this form of VTL can contribute to the quality of instruction and what activities, processes and organisational conditions are needed for implementing it in the context of daily schooling. The teachers were followed over seven years. The findings show that they strengthened and expanded their teaching repertoires, both during and after peer coaching. The main conclusion from this study is that reciprocal peer coaching with video has the potential to alter the interplay between teaching and learning by eliciting and driving changes in teachers' classroom behaviour. This type of collegial collaboration can bring about sustainable increases in the quality of instruction and encourage teachers to shift their instruction towards more dialogic forms of teaching and learning. What makes this study ground-breaking is that it demonstrates not only *that* VTL can foster sustainable changes in instruction, but also *how*.

While in Chapters 2 through 6, the emphasis is on describing and explaining VTL on the basis of research, it shifts in Chapters 7 through 9 to recommendations for practice.

Chapter 7 addresses an issue which has so far been little studied, i.e. which features of video clips of teaching and learning – whether published on video platforms or produced by teachers themselves – help teachers judge and decide if and how they want to adopt or adapt the instructional behaviour shown. In this chapter, guidelines for video production are presented in the form of a checklist. This list specifies clip features promoting VTL under four headings. Video producers should consider firstly what they portray as good teaching. Secondly, there are decisions to take during planning, capture and editing. The third issue to take into account is how to frame video clips by means of context information and perspectives for analysis. Finally, privacy issues and data protection are addressed.

Drawing on insights from research, Chapter 8 illustrates how teachers can encourage active and differentiated learning by developing and using video as a medium for instruction. As an example, applications of hypervideo (HV) in vocational education are described. Another example from secondary education, involving a module about Electricity, illustrates how teachers can use video to consult pupils about their learning experiences and thus come to understand their learning better as a basis for developing teaching. These examples show how instructional video and VTL can converge to strengthen the cooperation between teachers and learners.

In the final Chapter 9, lessons drawn from the preceding chapters are summarised in the form of resources for practitioners. Publicly accessible video platforms are listed. Organisational conditions favouring peer coaching with video are specified, minimum requirements for guarding privacy are formulated and features to include in structured viewing guides are listed. Then follows a do-it-yourself guide for teachers who want to engage in peer coaching with video. For the purpose of video production, clip features promoting VTL are summarised. Guidelines are presented for making collaborative lesson analysis constructive as well as for selecting, producing and using instructional video clips. The chapter concludes with a series of steps to take during pupil consultation.

To conclude this introduction, I want to make clear what this book is *not* about. It does not address uses of video purely as a method of educational research, such as in eye-tracking studies. I also exclude video use for purposes of teacher assessment, evaluation or appraisal. This application is in my view burdened with unresolved issues of validity and trust. Finally, I do not review video software and hardware. Technical details are left aside, unless they are especially relevant to using video to develop teaching.

2

IMAGING TEACHER LEARNING

From analog to digital

Niels Brouwer

Since the turn of the millennium, an impressive array of DV applications has been developed for promoting teachers' professional learning. As these applications have proliferated, we need to know how effective are the uses that are being made of them and especially why they are effective. If teachers are to benefit from using DV, the medium should be implemented in evidence-based ways. This is why I have undertaken a literature review of the empirical research that has become available about teacher learning with DV. The aim of this review is to help build a knowledge base for promoting effective uses of VTL.

In this chapter, I first formulate the questions guiding this review and explain why these questions are formulated as they are, followed by an account of the review method. Then, against the background of three analog precursors, the specific properties of DV as a medium for teacher learning are identified, followed by a description of a series of DV applications which represent the variety of ways in which DV is used to develop teaching competence. On this basis, I delineate different functions that DV can serve for teachers' professional learning, and I introduce concepts and terminology for communicating about VTL. Also, the main paradigms underlying the research reviewed are characterised. Finally, I present my conclusions. These underpin the Visual Teacher Learning model.

Review questions

This review is guided by three questions:

I. *What* do teachers learn when using digital video?
II. *How* do teachers learn when using digital video?
III. *In what kinds of learning environments* do teachers learn when using digital video?

DOI: 10.4324/9780429331091-2

These review questions address different aspects: I. the outcomes, II. the processes and III. the conditions involved in VTL. In other words, the review aims not only at identifying outcomes of teacher learning, but also at understanding the ways and the circumstances in which these outcomes are produced. This is because knowledge about all these aspects is necessary in order to determine which features should be incorporated in the design of effective VTL. One cannot explain learning without reconstructing the events taking place in the causal chain leading to its outcomes (Brouwer, 2010).

Teachers' instructional action forms a crucial element in this causal chain. In addressing the first review question, I therefore pay particular attention to how VTL influences teachers' professional behaviour and their thinking about it. The second review question is directed especially at what happens while teachers view, review, analyse and interpret DV records of teaching. These processes take place in different learning environments. How these environments are created and organised is addressed in review question III.

Method

Since 2000, research into VTL has become a booming field. In fact, the sheer mass of research being undertaken makes it impossible to exhaust the available evidence. I therefore do not claim to do so. What I want to show in this chapter is, rather, what kinds of teacher learning are made possible by different types of DV applications. For this purpose, I have selected a number of applications whose design rests on an explicit rationale and about which empirical evidence is available. The sources for this review were collected and analysed as follows.

Source selection

The DV applications presented in this chapter were selected on the basis of four criteria: relevance and methodological quality of the available research, period and geographical origin.

Relevance

First of all, to be included, the evidence available about a DV application should be relevant to one or more of the review questions. When this was the case, studies were included irrespective of the theoretical paradigms within which they were situated or the kinds of research design that were used. I choose, rather, to benefit from a diversity of perspectives. This does have consequences for the kinds of findings the studies produce and the conclusions they allow. I discuss these consequences in connection with the conclusions.

Methodological quality

Secondly, studies about DV applications should conform to basic methodological standards. Most studies reviewed here were published or presented after some form of peer review, i.e. as articles in recognised scientific journals, chapters in scholarly books or dissertations. Papers accepted at conferences organised by associations for educational research were also eligible, notably the American Educational Research Association (AERA) and the European Association for Research on Learning and Instruction (Earli) as well as smaller expert meetings. However, about a few DV applications, only exploratory data or policy studies were available. Whether peer-reviewed or not, I only present findings from studies in which (1) sufficient information is provided about response rates and representativeness, (2) the validity of operationalisations is evident or well argued and (3) it is clear how data were analysed. These criteria delimit what I consider to be dependable findings.

Period

Thirdly, all studies used were published after 2000, as by far the most VTL research began to appear from that year onwards.

Geographical origin

Finally, I have sought to present DV applications from as many different countries as possible. As most relevant studies are published in English or German, a bias towards English- or German-speaking countries can easily occur. However, R&D work in the area of VTL also takes place in French- and Spanish-speaking countries and in non-Western countries generally.

Procedure

The search for sources was conducted through search systems provided by university libraries in the Netherlands, Germany and the United States as well as Google Scholar. The search terms used were straightforward, i.e. "teach*" OR "video". Other terms, notably "visual*" were tried, but these yielded no additional sources. In this way, sources were also found relating to uses of video as an instructional medium. These, however, were excluded as not relevant to the review questions. In addition, both during and after this search, I identified sources relevant for this review through contacts and correspondence with VTL researchers. This collaboration often took place in connection with symposia during AERA and Earli conferences, several of which were organised by myself.

The sources selected for review were analysed as follows. First, I retrieved information about the genesis of the DV application, the audience(s) it intends to serve, the substantive topic(s) covered and the school subject(s) involved. Then, I described its design and the rationale behind it and summarised the available research evidence. Finally, I drew conclusions as a basis for answering the review questions.

Analog video use

In the 1960s and 1970s, important analog precursors of DV use for teacher learning were developed: Microteaching, Self-confrontation and Self-modelling. The significance of these approaches lies in how they pointed the way towards making teacher education more realistic and more relevant to everyday teaching practice. They did so by creating opportunities for developing professional skills.

This section opens with a description of these approaches. On this basis, important commonalities between them are identified.

Microteaching

Video has been used as a medium for teacher learning since it was developed by Dwight Allen, Kevin Ryan and colleagues in the Microteaching Clinic at Stanford University (Allen & Ryan, 1969; Cooper & Allen, 1970). In this approach, student teachers acquire skills needed for effective classroom instruction such as explaining, questioning and using "wait time", i.e. giving pupils more time to think about the lesson content and contribute to classroom discourse. Stanford staff were unsatisfied with the gap existing between the content and activities programmed during the university-based periods in the preservice teacher education (PTE) curriculum and students' experiences during their practice periods in schools. For most students, usually white girls from middle-class backgrounds, their first acquaintance with the practice of teaching worked out as a shock.

Microteaching (MT) was intended as a more realistic preparation. It consists of a rapid "teach-reteach cycle", in which a student teacher studies an introduction to and a video demonstration of a specific teaching skill, prepares and teaches a lesson in which she or he practices this skill, and receives immediate feedback from a facilitator with the help of a "student response form" specifying aspects of how the skill involved can best be used. These forms were based on a range of study materials about effective teaching behaviour. As soon as possible after this succession of activities, the student teacher reteaches the same lesson, after which changes and improvements are discussed anew. This teach–reteach cycle was originally conducted in laboratory settings with real pupils, who came to visit the university especially for this purpose. Later, simulation versions were developed, in which peer students played the roles of pupils (for an overview of the development of MT, see McKnight, 1980).

An important assumption behind MT, denoted as the "component skills approach", is that when students practice distinct teaching skills one at a time in a setting in which the complexity of real classrooms is reduced, this will allow them to develop a command of that skill. Developing mastery in this way should lay the basis for professional judgement and decision-making. As Allen and Ryan (1969, p. 23–24) wrote,

> When the teacher has control over several teaching skills and knows what the effects of each are, the next step is to apply these skills to achieve his instructional aims. For this teacher the teaching act involves decisions about when and where to apply his skills. For the individual so trained, teaching is not a series of happenstances, but a series of professional decisions.

In order to support the use of MT, study materials about a range of teaching skills, accompanied by examples on videotape, were developed. To serve also in-service teachers and schools, this effort was systematised by Walter Borg and colleagues from the Far West Laboratory for Educational Research and Development. Just as the creators of MT at Stanford University, they proceeded from the assumption that just telling teachers what are effective teaching behaviours and then leaving it to them to "go and do it" is not effective. In traditional PTE and PD programmes, they argued,

> Most of the information ... is ... presented to the teacher in the form of abstractions. The teacher must apply these abstractions to concrete educa-tional situations, and this leap from abstract information to concrete appli-cations is a difficult one for most teachers to make. As a result, teachers ... are often extremely critical of this aspect of their training because they can generally recognize that the information they need is not being given in a form that they can use.
>
> (Borg, 1968, p. 1)

This gap was closed by the development of Minicourses. A Minicourse is "a self-contained package of training materials" intended for independent use by teachers in their own school situation with feedback being provided not by trained supervisors, but by informed peers (Borg, 1968, p. 2). It consists of an introduction film, a fifteen-minute instructional film illustrating the teaching skill to be trained with narrator comments focussing attention on major points and printed materials including a handbook, self-evaluation forms, a follow-up programme and instructions for train-ees and the school course coordinator. Teachers used these materials to engage in repeated MT cycles over extended periods. Examples of Minicourses are: 1. and 3. *Effective Questioning* in elementary and secondary classrooms, respectively; 2. *Thought and Language* to develop skills in encouraging language acquisition; 8. *Organizing the Kindergarten for Independent Learning and Small Group Instruction*; and 14. *Improving Teacher and Pupil Skills in Discussing Controversial Issues* (Borg, 1968, p. 4–5).

Each Minicourse was produced and revised on the basis of an R&D cycle includ-ing repeated field tests among teacher samples of increasing sizes. Evaluations rested on the comparison of classroom observation measures before and after Minicourse implementation. The research designs also included retention measures months after Minicourses were completed. The findings showed statistically significant improve-ments in teaching behaviour in a clear majority of cases.

Over the years, MT has gained considerable popularity both within and outside the US. Still, its effectiveness has met with academic scepticism, for example in an encyclopaedia contribution by MacLeod (1995). Nevertheless, a review of 225 empirical studies of MT some 30 years after its introduction has produced clear evidence of its effectiveness. Klinzing (2002) reviewed two questions: I. Do MT programmes raise the probability that target behaviours are acquired quickly and effectively? and II. Can what is learned in MT training be transferred to teaching practice after graduation? In this review, only studies were included about training programmes which provided trainees with conceptual knowledge about teaching skills as well as opportunities to practice these skills and receive feedback. The studies reviewed were both about the classical MT version, in which real pupils are engaged in a laboratory setting and about the simulation version, in which student teachers' peers play the roles of pupils. In these studies, MT outcomes were determined by means of direct observation systems consisting of low-inference categories or by means of ratings. Evidence about transfer to graduates' teaching practice was obtained through interviews.

Out of 39 studies about the laboratory version of MT, 34 showed statistically significant outcomes. Out of 74 studies about the role-play version, 59 showed statistically significant outcomes. Also the studies about the transferability to real-life teaching yielded predominantly positive findings. Out of 56 studies about the laboratory version, 43 showed positive outcomes. The same was true for fourteen out of seventeen studies about the role-play version. All these studies took place in PTE. In addition, Klinzing found 39 studies about MT in PD settings. 37 of these showed positive outcomes.

The overall conclusion is clear: teaching competencies were shown to improve under the influence of MT in the short as well as the long run, both in PTE and in PD.

Self-confrontation

Slightly later in time than MT, Frances Fuller and colleagues at the Research and Development Center for Teacher Education of the University of Texas at Austin incorporated video use in the "self-confrontation approach" (Fuller & Manning, 1973). Just as with MT, the central idea in this approach is that student teachers should learn to confront the discrepancy between initial images and expectations of being a teacher and the reality of functioning in classrooms. Viewing and analysing video representations of their teaching and receiving feedback on them were the learning activities employed to encourage student teachers to focus on points for improvement and seek alternative courses of action.

Fuller emphasises that becoming a teacher is uniquely different for every student teacher. In her conceptualisation, this process is to a large extent determined by personal concerns. Still, Fuller hypothesised that these concerns follow a common pattern, i.e. by and large, student teachers progress through three phases. In the Preteaching Phase, first non-concern, then concern with classroom management is paramount. Then, during the Early Teaching Phase, student teachers wonder about the questions "Where do I stand?" and "How adequate am I?" Finally, in the Phase of Late Concerns, concern with pupils and with how their learning takes place arises (Fuller, 1969, p. 218–221; Fuller & Bown, 1975, p. 36–39).

Due to earlier experiences with learning and personal characteristics, each individual student takes her or his own particular course through these phases. These individual differences are the reason why teacher education programmes should follow a "personalised" approach (Fuller, 1974). This means that programme design and implementation should ensure the following. Firstly, personal concerns should form the basis for target setting, monitoring and directing progress while learning to teach. Secondly, practice activities should be sequenced gradually in order to ensure that each student finds realistic opportunities to master the teaching behaviours targeted (Fuller, 1974, p. 114–116; Fuller & Bown, 1975, p. 44–45).

Thirdly, it is of crucial importance that video feedback should fulfil a number of conditions. In a review of theory and research about self-confrontation by means of video – in teaching as well as other professions – Fuller and Manning (1973) have specified these conditions as follows. Effective video feedback should be given as soon as possible after teaching practice and come from different sources, such as university supervisors, mentor teachers and pupils. Feedback should further be focussed, i.e. related to personal learning goals and provide feasible alternatives for action. Also, it should preferably address the impact of a student teacher's behaviour on pupils. It will be most powerful, when it specifies discrepancies between a student teacher's self-image and her or his actual behaviour, as is often the case when feedback comes from pupils (Fuller & Manning, 1973, p. 491).

Fulfilling these conditions obviously requires expertise from supervisors and mentors. While providing feedback, they should take care to distinguish observations from evaluations, to communicate with the trainee in a non-threatening manner and show empathy and authenticity (Fuller & Manning, 1973, p. 499).

Self-modelling

"Self-modelling" is a video application developed by Peter Dowrick to assist children, adolescents and adults with disabilities (Dowrick, 1991). It is used to help people with forms of autism, but has spread to other domains such as social skills (Kehle & Gonzales, 1991) and sports training (Franks & Maile, 1991). The idea behind self-modelling is that an individual takes a video representation of her or his own best performance in a particular skill as the springboard for developing it further. The video medium is often used where verbal approaches are ineffective, either because the clearest way of presenting a skill is visual or because the individual's language development is weak or both.

There are two forms of self-modelling: positive self-review and feedforward. For positive self-review, videos are used in which only positive examples of a person's performance are shown. Lapses or other instances of less-than-best performance are omitted. In the case of feedforward, more deliberate measures are taken to bring the person to display the desired behaviour while being recorded, for instance leaving a care worker or therapist modelling the behaviour out of the image. Evaluations of the effect of successive viewing of self-modelling videos have demonstrated success in diverse therapeutic settings, with frequency and maintenance of target behaviours and generalisation to other settings as the criteria. Other trials have resulted in lack of maintenance and/or generalisation (Krantz, MacDuff, Wadstrom, & McClannahan, 1991).

Self-modelling appears to be used by teachers only to assist pupils or clients, not for their own PD. The latter does, however, seem to be feasible and to carry some promise. Colleagues of mine have reported about using it to promote teacher learning (Leisink & Kienstra, 2002, p. 105).

The work by Dowrick and colleagues has yielded a useful distinction between three types of video: model, trigger and action videos. This distinction is quite suitable to characterise video use for teacher learning. "Model videos" demonstrate exemplary teacher behaviour, often in combination with study materials in which the behaviours presented are explained, justified and/or discussed. "Trigger videos" show complex situations or dilemmas in which teachers can choose to act or react in different ways. These situations are deliberately left unresolved, so that viewers are confronted with cognitive friction or conflict and thus encouraged to engage in rethinking and discussing preexisting ideas. "Action videos" show teachers at work, not primarily with the goal of advocating certain teaching behaviours, but to support teachers in recognising, distinguishing and examining different behaviours as a basis for expanding and diversifying their own repertoires of instructional behaviour (Dowrick, 1991, p. 92–127; Fortkamp, 2002, p. 11–13).

Microteaching, self-confrontation and self-modelling compared

At first sight, MT, self-confrontation and self-modelling may appear to proceed from quite different assumptions. MT is sometimes seen as a "hard", behaviouristic, technocratic or instrumental approach and self-confrontation as a "soft", humanistic, personalistic approach, while self-modelling seems limited to therapeutic applications. However, these three approaches actually share commonalities concerning issues that are of undiminished relevance today.

Firstly, what is common to all three approaches is that learning proceeds from experience. The concept of training underlying both MT and self-confrontation departs from the tradition of deductive programming, which overvalues knowledge acquisition and undervalues competence development (see the section *Quality standards for teacher learning* in Chapter 1). Instead, they emphasise the need to offer teachers opportunities to practise the many skills needed for teaching and to reflect on their experiences in doing so.

In the second place, all three approaches involve cycles of learning activities. MT and self-confrontation emphasise the need to sequence teachers' professional learning gradually and to practice concrete instructional skills during repeated cycles of preparation, enactment and evaluation. The idea behind this is that teachers should have the opportunity not only to acquire, but also to integrate new teaching skills in routine behaviour and the judicious use of it. In the self-modelling approach, different terminology is used – performance, feedback and behaviour modification – but the cyclical character of learning is clearly present. Interestingly, the study of visual models and the principle of a rapid "teach–reteach cycle" in MT are akin to the self-modelling approach.

Last but not least, the learning outcomes and experiences engendered by all three approaches confirm the central importance of providing learners with feedback.

The generally accepted definition of feedback is information about a person's functioning. If feedback about behaviour is to be effective, it should be frequent, fast and focussed, or in shorthand: FFF. Self-modelling adds an important element here. It stresses the importance of positive feedback. In contrast to negative feedback, positive feedback has two advantages. It exploits the power of good examples as it encourages emulation as well as motivating towards performing better.

Digital video use

As a basis for answering the three review questions formulated above, I begin this section by pointing out what exactly distinguishes digital from analog video use. I then describe a series of nineteen DV applications which represent the diverse ways in which DV is nowadays used with the aim of developing teaching. These descriptions are grouped primarily on the basis of comparable purposes that they aim to serve. The first group concerns applications which serve mainly to support an understanding of what teaching means and how one can prepare for practising it. In the second group, DV is used predominantly to support reflection in groups of teachers. In the third group, it is used for training specific teaching skills. The fourth group is about online video platforms aiming to support teachers in their work. In the fifth group, applications are described where video is the central element in computer-supported collaborative learning (CSCL). The last group is about online video use for supporting teachers on an individual basis.

The sequence in which the applications are described roughly follows the preactive, interactive and postactive phases of teaching. However, they are also sequenced chronologically, so applications developed earlier are presented earlier.

For each application, as far as possible, the following elements are described:

- *genesis:* where and how the application was developed
- *audience(s):* which group(s) of teachers it intends to serve
- *topic(s):* which topic(s) it mainly covers
- *school subject(s):* which school subject(s) it is about
- *design and use:* what is the rationale underlying the application and which learning activities are involved
- *research findings:* which empirical evidence is available about the
  - I.   outcomes,
  - II.   processes and/or
  - III. conditions

of VTL as addressed in the review questions.

The presentation of each group of applications concludes with a summary of the main findings. The applications to which these findings refer are mentioned in the text or between brackets.

The special affordances of digital video

The development and use of the MT, Self-confrontation and Self-modelling approaches show that already in the analog era, the advantages of using video for developing teaching were well known. As stated at the outset of this book (see the section *Aims of this book* in Chapter 1), the realism of moving images makes video a particularly suitable medium to help teachers attend to the interplay between teaching and learning taking place in the instructional triangle. Because of its concreteness, video entails domain specificity of observations. It also enables repeated analysis from different perspectives without the need for immediate action. Finally, it invokes vicarious experience and emotional engagement in the viewer. What these properties of video can do for teachers is to let them experience the full complexity of teaching and learning without having to act on this experience immediately, thus enabling them to examine what is actually happening and consider alternative courses of action. Now, if these advantages were already known, what explains the renewed interest in using video since its digitisation?

DV as a medium distinguishes itself from analog video not only by its increased affordability, but especially by the host of versatile ways in which it can be used. Not only training institutions, but also individual professionals nowadays have access to hardware and software which enable them (1) to view, review and edit video footage in any order they wish, (2) to embed video material in hypermedia and (3) to communicate about it anytime anywhere. These are new "affordances", which distinguish DV from analog video and consequently, have caused radical changes in tool use. The term "affordances" was introduced by James Gibson (1979) in his book *The ecological approach to visual perception*. This approach characterises the relationship between perceiving organisms and their environment as a configuration within which properties of the environment afford the organisms particular ways of perceiving it. As applied in information technology (IT), the term "affordance" has come to refer to the specific ways in which IT tools shape humans' perceptual relations to the world. In the case of DV, the following affordances can be distinguished.

Firstly, unlike analog video, DV can be traversed without delay at the user's will. In more technical terms: video records of teaching and learning can now be edited and studied in non-linear sequences. Smart phones have replaced cumbersome tape cameras and instead of winding and rewinding, we now swipe forwards and backwards along a time line, having the events practically at our fingertips. Navigation has also been greatly facilitated since exact moments in a video can be accessed from specific places in a text and from specific items in a hyperlinked index. Non-linear control features such as these have revolutionised playback and sped up opportunities for feedback.

Secondly, being one type of digital medium, DV can be used alongside other types, notably still images, sound, text and graphics. When these media are available through separate software applications, they are called "multimedia". When they are purposefully connected within one application, they are called "hypermedia" (Chan, 2003, p. 7). An early example of hypermedia are the video ethnographies developed by Harris and colleagues, i.e. digital video cases representing teaching and learning situations that teachers can peruse and study from different angles which they can choose themselves (Chan & Harris, 2005; Harris, Pinnegar, & Teemant, 2005).

So far, hypermedia for professional uses by teachers are available only through dedicated applications such as these. Hypermedia functionalities were, for a while, available to the general computer user through PowerPoint Producer, a piece of beta software that unfortunately never made it into Microsoft's standard Office suite.

A feature included in hypermedia applications that can particularly enhance collaboration among teachers is video annotation. The significant innovation introduced by video annotation is the possibility to place a tag on the timeline of a video precisely where significant events in a lesson occur. This tagging option enables teachers to identify such events precisely and give each other feedback on them. For example, the application VideoPaper (http://vpb.concord.org/) enables teachers to share with colleagues video fragments from their lessons hyperlinked to other resources such as still images, lesson plans, instructional materials and reflective writing. As the creators of VideoPaper write,

> The intellectual work the VideoPaper assignment demands arises from the fact that video, text, and slides must be connected in order for the narrative to emerge. This interconnectedness pushes the author to closely examine the relationship between the images and their text, to think carefully about exactly how to generate meaning from their media. The exactness of the medium demands that one make precise choices in editing and concentrate on discrete themes in the video.
>
> (Beardsley, Cogan-Drew, & Olivero, 2007, p. 489)

Video annotation tools have become a part of the landscape of teacher development that is undoubtedly here to stay. Among the earliest were Video Analysis Support Tool (VAST; cf. Van Es & Sherin, 2002) and V-share (Henning, Massler, Ploetzner, & Huppertz, 2007; Huppertz, Massler, & Ploetzner, 2005; Huppertz, Ploetzner, & Massler, 2007; Ploetzner, Massler, & Huppertz, 2005), now available as a plug-in for Moodle (www.v-share.de). Rich and Hannafin (2009a) have reviewed six video annotation tools: VAST, Video Interactions for Teaching And Learning (VITAL), VAT 2.0, Video traces, VideoPaper, MediaNotes and StudioCode. They conclude that these tools have the potential to support reflection on teaching and linking practice and theory in more realistic ways than were available in the past. Still, more empirical evidence is needed about how video annotation tools can be used effectively (cf. Evi-Colombo, Cattaneo, & Bétrancourt, 2020).

Thirdly, when video as a part of hypermedia goes online, as it does through video platforms and in electronic learning environments, professional communication is greatly facilitated. For teachers, this means that they can access visual records of each other's teaching and related resources independently from time and place and exchange interpretations and ideas.

Integration of the above three affordances in one interface has led to the creation of "interactive video" or "hypervideo" (HV), the most advanced form of DV so far. Alberto Cattaneo and colleagues describe the affordances of HV as "control features, hyperlinks and exchange options" (Cattaneo, Van der Meij, Aprea, Sauli, & Zahn, 2018, p. 2–6). Not only can HV be navigated with maximum flexibility, but it also allows immediate access to additional resources, quizzing and communication with colleagues. An overview of these new possibilities is given in a review by Sauli, Cattaneo and Van der Meij (2018) (see Figure 2.1).

The three technological developments described above are profoundly changing the practice of teacher education and PD. Already in 1993, Merseth and Lacey foresaw that case-based learning, once digitised, would further turn "the delivery system of teacher education on its head" as it enables representing "the complexity of teaching … accurately, yet manageably" (Merseth, 1996; Merseth & Lacey, 1993, p. 289). In 2003, Wang and Hartley explored in a perceptive literature review how

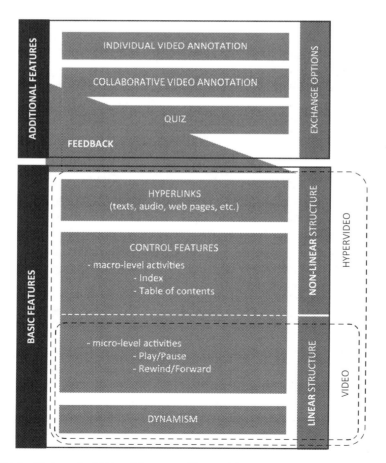

FIGURE 2.1   Basic and additional features of hypervideo

DV technology might contribute to teacher education reform. They expected that this technology could expose teachers to a wide variety of classroom situations and help them interpret how children learn, examine exemplary subject-specific teaching practices and reflect in realistic ways on their own and colleagues' teaching. The changes in tool use caused by DV indeed have this potential. As the special affordances of DV expand those already present in analog video, they enhance the impact of video use on teacher learning.

Preparing for teaching

The DV applications in the group I present first share the purpose of clarifying what it means to be a teacher. This includes orienting aspiring teachers towards the profession and making concrete what planning for instruction entails.

Docucases

Docucases is a collection of video documentaries about teaching developed by Traci Bliss of Idaho State University at Locatello, US, and researched in collaboration with Anne Reynolds (Bliss & Reynolds, 2004). Bliss wanted to solve a familiar problem in preservice teacher education: while it is necessary to clarify to students what is quality teaching, doing so in the form of abstract concepts and generic standards will cause it to remain a dead letter to them. It was therefore decided to produce a number of video documentaries, in which four domains of quality teaching – planning, instruction, classroom environment and professional responsibilities as defined by the Interstate New Teacher Assessment and Support Consortium (INTASC, 1992) – should be brought to life. For this purpose, eight expert teachers, certified on the basis of the National Board of Professional Teaching Standards (NBPTS), were filmed during teaching. Their lessons should serve as cases exemplifying the INTASC standards.

In order to ensure that viewers would be able to experience concretely what quality teaching means the production team sought to fulfil three principles for creating professional video: authenticity, aesthetics and accessibility. Their aim was to enable viewers to interpret and understand the lessons shown on an analytical as well as an intuitive level.

The principle of authenticity entailed giving the video a focus. In Docucases, this focus is how teachers can engage pupils in higher-level thinking. To show what this aspect of quality teaching looks like in real life, two cameras were used, one following the teacher, one following the pupils. Also, to achieve a maximum of realism, no retakes were made of any lesson event. The raw footage captured in this way was then edited to a condensed 22–25 minute record representing the essential events and transitions during the lesson. Their chronology was preserved. Great care was taken to validate this editing process, as each video case underwent critical review by a jury consisting of NBPTS-certified teachers, high-performing student teachers and/or members of other professions. These juries assessed to what degree the sequence and content of the recorded lesson was clear and understandable and how well the video illuminated the teaching standards to be represented. The juries' comments led to repeated revisions.

The principles of aesthetics and accessibility were pursued as follows. The use of two cameras made it possible to recreate close-up the interaction between teachers and pupils. Narration in the form of voiceovers was used to introduce each video and to clarify links between lesson components. Interviews with teachers illuminated what they intended in their lessons. Annotations and graphical pop-ups were included to highlight moments when teachers' actions exemplified specific standards.

Within the PTE curriculum, students first completed reading assignments about the relevant teaching domains and standards. Against this background, they viewed the Docucases in subgroups, each of which focussed on a different domain or standard, and then discussed them in the whole class.

An evaluation was conducted among 34 prospective middle or high school teachers aged 21–25 and 74% female. This study addressed whether teaching standards became more accessible through the Docucases process and how it influenced students' comprehension of the standards about quality teaching. The students provided scores on a retention test about the information they received about teaching standards, wrote reflections about the videos they viewed and completed evaluation forms about the subgroup sessions.

Descriptive statistics of the quantitative data and content analyses of the qualitative data yielded the following findings. 91% of the students preferred viewing a video to reading a written case. The main reasons given for this assessment were that the video enabled them to gain a richer and more realistic understanding of the lessons viewed, notably of how teachers, through their communicative behaviour, engaged pupils in learning. Comparison of the retention scores before and after the Docucases experience indicated that the number of students correctly identifying key aspects of teaching standards increased. Finally, the students felt that exchanging ideas with fellow students during the class discussion following video viewing helped them deepen their understanding of the lessons viewed.

In conclusion, the evaluation of Docucases suggests that video documentaries aiming at a realistic representation of teaching and learning can help preservice teachers develop a deeper understanding of how teachers foster learning than written information alone.

Didiclass

Didiclass is a collection of video cases developed by Walter Geerts and Matthias Mitzschke of the Noordelijke Hogeschool Leeuwarden (NHL) Stenden University of Applied Sciences and Marc van Laeken of the Open University in the Netherlands (available both online and offline through www.didiclass.nl and www.coutinho.nl/didiclass). This collection shows the real-life dilemmas of classroom management that student teachers in primary and secondary education confront. Showing teachers' dilemmas in their full complexity is at the heart of the rationale behind Didiclass.

The video cases are in Dutch and usually include an introduction by the student teacher recorded, who presents her or his problem statement; lesson fragments; and interviews with the student teacher, mentor teachers and/or pupils. Didiclass cases are mostly viewed and discussed by student teachers during course meetings in PTE programmes, but they can also be studied individually offline and online.

A fine example of a Didiclass case – the only one in English and available at https://www.coutinho.nl/didiclass/studiemateriaal/casusbank/videocases/deel-a/a126.html – is the case of Derek, a secondary teacher of English from the US, who struggles with what he perceives as the classroom culture in the Netherlands. In lesson fragments, one can see how he tries to handle counterproductive pupil behaviour. In the interview with Derek, he describes his approach to teaching as friendly, but also strict. Two pupils, on the other hand, describe in an interview in which respects they feel that Derek fails their expectations of a good teacher. The contrast between teacher and pupil perceptions is stark and remains unresolved.

In another video case, Olga, a secondary teacher of German, is shown during attempts at achieving an orderly beginning of a lesson. She states her own problem and lesson fragments show how she gradually moves into a productive type of interaction with pupils in a whole-group setting. In a third video case from a kindergarten classroom, the teacher removes Ali, a sweet little boy, from the classroom. After a while, he is called back and reluctantly rejoins the ongoing learning activities. The viewer can also witness an individual exchange between the teacher and Ali, in which she explains why she sent him off and does her best to restore an understanding between Ali and herself. These video cases, too, are open-ended in their own way.

The disarming honesty of the teachers and pupils portrayed in Didiclass makes for a convincing demonstration of the challenges of teaching. What the makers of Didiclass aim for is developing situated knowledge in teachers, i.e. using their personal experiences as starting points for arriving at well argued professional judgements and decisions. Important assumptions behind Didiclass are that teaching and learning are never 100% controllable, life is always stronger than dogma and there is no one truth. Rather, teachers have diverging personal perceptions of practice, which reality forces them to reconsider again and again. These assumptions are nicely symbolised by the surrealist paintings of René Magritte which adorn the covers of several supporting materials published for teachers and teacher educators. The title of one of these, *What would you do?* (Geerts, Van Laeken, & Mitzschke, 2009), points to the need for teachers to view and review each other's work and give each other advice. Central to this effort is making available diverse perspectives and encouraging teachers to compare and inquire into them.

So far, two small-scale empirical studies have been conducted into the effectiveness of working with Didiclass (Geerts, 2018). In the first study, seventeen second-year student teachers in English, 76% female and aged 22 years on average, participating in a two-month course about classroom management were divided in an experimental group of nine students using Didiclass and a control group of eight students, who used written or verbalised cases. Interview responses and written advice from the students were examined through content analysis to find out if both groups differed in their interpretation of the cases studied. In the second study, the advice about a Didiclass video case written by two fourth-year students out of a group of 33 students – 75% female and aged 26 years – was examined to find out to what extent they identified possible alternatives for teaching action and formulated general principles for teaching. In both studies, some indications were found that studying the Didiclass video cases did promote student teachers' understanding of teaching. However, the samples analysed in these studies were too small to establish any systematic patterns.

Web-based cognitive apprenticeship model for instructional planning

Experienced teachers know how important instructional planning is for successful teaching. Traditional deductive PTE programmes, however, often allow student teachers insufficient opportunities for practising and understanding the significance of instructional planning. This is the problem that Tzu-Chien Liu and colleagues sought to solve in a PTE programme for primary education in Jung-li City, Taoyuan, Taiwan.

The existing design in this programme for training instructional planning consisted of three phases. In the Preparing phase (two weeks), student teachers read assigned textbook chapters about instructional planning, visited and observed in groups of twelve an expert teacher's lesson in school and discussed it there with her or him. In the Designing-Implementing Phase (four weeks), they designed an instructional plan themselves and consulted with expert teachers through visits or email in order to modify it. They then taught this lesson in the expert teacher's school and received feedback on it from the expert teacher and fellow students. In the Reflecting Phase (one week), they wrote a report about their lesson planning and teaching experience and received comments on this from the expert teacher.

This design had two main drawbacks that Liu and colleagues wanted to remove. Firstly, its exclusive reliance on verbal information hindered students in imagining how instructional plans may work out in actual practice. Secondly, opportunities for reflective interaction with the expert teachers were limited to one school visit and asynchronous communication by email, whereas inexperienced students are often in need of just-in-time assistance. To improve on the existing design, Liu and colleagues chose to develop a "web-based cognitive apprenticeship model". This also consisted of three phases, but the students' learning activities took place in a web-based learning environment, which included multimedia materials encouraging visualisation and facilitated not only asynchronous, but also synchronous communication. The latter made more intensive and timely communication with the expert teachers possible.

The first phase of the web-based training design is Modelling–Observing. During this phase, the students studied online an expert teacher's instructional plan and viewed a video case in which the expert teacher either explained how and why the instructional plan was designed or could be seen teaching a lesson based on it. In the second phase, Scaffolding–Practicing, the students prepared their own instructional plans in an online conferencing environment called the Instructional Planning Assisting SyStem (IPASS). Here, expert teachers followed and commented on their work just in time to help them modify their plans, if necessary referring them back to the multimedia materials. The student teachers then taught a lesson based on their plans in the expert teachers' schools and received feedback on it from the expert teacher and fellow students. In the third phase, Guiding–Generalising, the student teachers recorded their reflections about their planning and teaching experience. The expert teachers then reacted in the electronic conferencing environment so as to support the students in deriving more general principles for instructional planning from their experience.

The changes in the training design described above were inspired by constructivist theories of learning, notably the Cognitive Apprenticeship Model proposed by Collins, Brown and Newman (1989). Their impact on student teachers' learning was studied as follows. Two groups of twelve students each were randomly assigned to a control and an experimental group. The control group followed the existing training design for instructional planning, the experimental group the web-based design.

Before and after training, the quality of the instructional plans produced by the students in both groups was rated anonymously by one expert teacher using five-point Likert scales consisting of 28 items with reliabilities ranging between .84 and .95. These scales measured six aspects: activity; goals and objectives; method and procedure; material resources; assessment; and the reasonability and effectiveness of the overall plan. In addition, attitudes towards instructional planning were measured before and after training in both groups on four-point self-report scales, which also consisted of 28 items. The reliabilities of these scales ranged between .94 and .97. These scales measured three aspects: identification with the importance and the functions of instructional planning and willingness to design and implement instructional plans in the future. In the experimental group, also qualitative data were collected, consisting of all texts generated during online conferencing and of students' responses during semi-structured interviews.

A 2x2 mixed analysis of variance (ANOVA) yielded the following results. The control and experimental groups began training on a similar baseline of instructional planning performance. During training, both groups progressed, but the experimental group outperformed the control group by one scale point. This difference was statistically significant ($p < .05$). In their attitudes towards instructional planning, both groups began training on a moderately positive baseline. After training, the control group remained on this level, but the experimental group showed more positive attitudes. These were .76 scale points higher. This difference was statistically significant ($p < .05$).

From these quantitative findings Liu concludes that "the web-based cognitive apprenticeship model has the potential to more effectively enhance preservice teachers' performance and attitudes towards instructional planning than the traditional course" (Liu, 2005, p. 144). The qualitative findings lead him to the following interpretations of this outcome. Firstly, "the web-based multimedia provided clear and effective cognitive modelling as a response to the needs of the pre-service teachers." Secondly, "the integrated application of web-based multimedia and Internet conferences benefited the pre-service teachers' learning." Thirdly, "the web-based course seemed to offer the pre-service teachers more sophisticated and timely support than that from the traditional course." Finally, "the last phase of the web-based course, 'Guiding-Generalizing', helped to elaborate and extend the conceptual model of the pre-service teachers." Liu attributes the positive change in their attitudes towards instructional planning to the use of multimedia cases and web-based conferencing with expert teachers (Liu, 2005, p. 144–146). These features of the learning environment have probably allowed and encouraged the students in the experimental group to deepen their understanding of instructional planning and of its significance for orchestrating pupils' learning.

Video for Interactive Lesson preparation by Mentor and Student

What happens between student teachers and their mentors when they use video while collaborating on lesson planning has been researched in depth in a series of design-based studies carried out by Maaike Vervoort in a primary teacher education programme in Hengelo, the Netherlands. In this programme, rich media cases, i.e. multimedia cases – meaning video cases linked to text, images and/or audio – had already been used to encourage student teachers to interpret video records of teaching and learning in terms of relevant theory. However, research had shown that this approach, even if it included structured assignments, did not lead student teachers to apply in their own teaching practice innovative ideas that they had observed in the video cases (Blijleven, 2005; Oonk, 2009). It was therefore decided to develop Video for Interactive Lesson preparation by Mentor and Student (VILMS), an intervention in which mentor teachers in the schools would support their student teachers in designing lesson plans. For this purpose, a rich-media package called Multimedia Interactive Learning Environment (MILE) Nederlands, which aims at innovative literacy teaching, served as a basis.

Second-year students and their mentors viewed the videos in this package together and then had a dialogue about how the students might include innovative practices they had seen in the videos in a lesson plan of their own, which they would then carry out. This procedure was tried out and revised in three rounds, in the first by six mentors and their second-year students, in the second by 30 students and twenty mentors, in the third by 45 students and 23 mentors. Almost all students and mentors were female. Analyses of surveys and video portfolios showed that the intervention had the intended effect. The student teachers applied innovative ideas derived from MILE Nederlands in their teaching and argued their instructional approach on the basis of the dialogues they had with their mentors. In these dialogues, the mentors made their practical knowledge about literacy teaching explicit to the students. Influential in this process was how mentors connected their general knowledge about goals and instructional practices for literacy learning with their local knowledge about pupils' learning (Vervoort, 2013, p. 139–141).

The above design iterations pointed towards the crucial role of the dialogues between mentors and student teachers. Vervoort therefore focussed a fourth and final study on the issue how such dialogues influenced student teachers' teaching. Five pairs of student teachers and mentors, all female, were studied in depth during their collaboration. Data collection took place in three steps. Each student first described her lesson idea in a five-minutes conversation with the researcher. Then each pair viewed and discussed, during a dialogue lasting 27 minutes on average, a video case and the related assignment for designing a lesson plan. Finally, in a conversation with the researcher lasting ten minutes on average, the student teacher described her final lesson plan to the researcher. All dialogues and the ensuing conversations with the researcher were recorded on video. Analysis of the transcripts revealed that during the dialogues, the student teachers' lesson plans were modified in different ways. Most frequent were additions to and refinements in the lesson plans. Also, certain elements were omitted, as these seemed too difficult for pupils. In a single case, a lesson plan was completely revised.

An interesting experience during the above series of design-based studies was that mentor teachers expressed uncertainty about their role in the dialogue with their mentee. They did not want to prescribe ideas to them, but found it difficult to take a different role. When the programme staff explained that they were expected to discuss with students the merits of different ideas for lesson planning, they were happy to do so. The videos viewed were rich enough to elicit such discussions and this, together with the role instructions to the mentors, tended to change the mentor–student relationship from a vertical exchange between expert and novice into a horizontal one between professionals – the one aspiring and the other experienced – engaging in the same practice.

The studies by Vervoort indicate that it was not the video or the multimedia material in itself that influenced lesson planning and implementation, but rather the way in which the learning environment and the learning activities invited the student teachers and mentors to use them for engaging in professional dialogue.

Child-Friendly School

Can video be used to develop teaching in non-Western contexts? This important question was at stake in a project for training preservice and in-service primary teachers in Battambang, Cambodia. In 2007, the Cambodian Ministry of Education, Youth and Sports initiated its programme Child-Friendly School (CFS). As a part of this programme, a digital video disc (DVD) with good-practice videos and an accompanying booklet were developed in collaboration with the Dutch non-governmental organisation (NGO) Voluntary Services Overseas (VSO), the Open Institute, an NGO aiming at ICT innovations, and United Nations Children's Emergency Fund (UNICEF) Cambodia in order to support teachers in developing the competencies needed to implement student-centred teaching methods (SCM). Two trials with these materials were facilitated and researched by Leandra Lok (2019).

As a VSO volunteer, Lok supported three Cambodian teacher educators in teaching a two-month course to primary student teachers, in which they studied nine videos showing SCM. These videos focussed specifically on cooperative learning, teachers' questioning practices, their use of teaching resources such as cards and pictures as well as games and other activating learning activities. Guidelines for viewing in the booklet accompanying the DVD were used to conduct whole-class discussions about these practices. In addition, Lok facilitated a video study group of in-service teachers, who met once a month during a seven-month period to view and discuss the videos on the DVD. On this basis, they would choose aspects of SCM to try out in their own lessons. Videos of these try-outs were also viewed and discussed in the monthly group meetings, in whole-group sessions as well as in pairs of teachers. Both the preservice and the in-service trials involved mother-tongue education in Khmer and mathematics teaching. The underlying rationale was that by viewing and discussing video examples of SCM, the participating teachers would discover alternative approaches to instruction and then use them in their own lessons.

This project took place in the challenging context of a war-ravaged country, in which teachers – mostly female – lacked teaching resources and often had to work in second jobs and pursue family responsibilities. Also, the preservice teacher educators had received minimal training in working with the DVD. In the in-service setting, no Cambodian facilitator was available, so that Lok fulfilled that role herself. Finally, it was expected that cultural traditions, notably people's inclinations to defer to authority and avoid uncertainty, might hamper collegial exchange and discussion.

The preservice trial was studied using evaluative questions about the learning activities with the DVD and booklet, a post-intervention assessment of students' ability to identify SCM practices in the video and surveys measuring their self-perceived knowledge about and attitude towards SCM. Data were collected with these instruments in an intervention group of 68 students, 65% female and aged 22 years on average, and a control group of 56 students, 71% female and aged 21 years on average. The intervention group used the DVD videos and booklet, whereas the control group used written cases.

The findings of the preservice study showed that the students in the intervention group evaluated the video-supported learning activities positively. After the intervention, they scored slightly higher on self-perceived knowledge about and attitude towards SCM than the control group ($p < .01$). However, they did not score significantly higher on the assessment of their ability to identify SCM practices ($p > .01$).

The in-service trial was the object of three studies. The first involved pre- and post-intervention open-ended questions assessing the 21 participants' ability to describe SCM practices, self-rating scales about their knowledge of SCM and their use of SCM in the classroom and semi-structured interviews. In the second in-service study, six out of the seven video club sessions were filmed and audiotaped. These recordings were transcribed and the resulting transcripts translated and coded in order to discover any patterns in the eight participants' conversational acts. In the third in-service study, the development of one highly experienced and motivated teacher was traced using all the above instruments as well as pre- and post-intervention observations of her lessons. To secure the respondents' trust, data were collected anonymously whenever possible. Otherwise, data were analysed with the utmost confidentiality.

After participating in the video study group, the in-service teachers were slightly better able to describe SCM methods and rated their own knowledge accordingly (p < .01). Regarding using SCM in the classroom, the self-report survey did not show significant progress, but in their interviews, the teachers did report behaviour changes due to participation. However, they also mentioned obstacles to implementation, specifically a lack of time for lesson preparation due to a second job and/ or family responsibilities and a lack of money to make teaching materials available.

Interestingly, both the grouping of teachers during the monthly meetings and the type of video viewed influenced outcomes of the intervention (p < .01). After participating in whole-group discussions, teachers described more teaching approaches as student-centred than after working in pairs. Also, after viewing good-practice videos, teachers identified more teaching approaches as student-centred than after viewing videos of their own teaching (p < .01).

The analysis of the conversational acts during the group meetings showed that the teachers focussed their attention mainly on the behaviour of the teachers they viewed on video. There was a slight tendency for them, over time, to voice fewer opinions about and more descriptions of what they noticed in the lessons viewed. Efforts to initiate and structure the discussions came predominantly from the facilitator, even though she tried to encourage the teachers to also lead the discussions themselves.

Following the intervention, the teacher whose individual development was traced displayed and reported changes in her instructional behaviour. She came to activate pupils by asking more questions and using more resources and games in her teaching. She attributed these changes specifically to viewing good-practice videos and to the facilitator's questions and comments during the group meetings.

The studies summarised above allow tentative conclusions, primarily because of limited sample sizes and the predominance of self-report instruments. The pre-service intervention was moderately effective, as students appeared to develop a beginning understanding of SCM. Lok attributes this outcome to the fact that the video viewing and discussions were less intense than planned. Also, it would have been desirable to equip the teacher educators more thoroughly to implement the intervention fully (Lok, 2019, pp. 50–51 and 125). The in-service teachers' participation in the video study group increased their knowledge of SCM, made them aware of alternatives for instructional action and encouraged them to begin making changes in their instruction. There were indications that cultural traditions, notably deference to authority and uncertainty avoidance, caused a certain hesitance on the part of the participating teachers. Still, these phenomena appeared to be overridden by the substantive input they received, particularly by viewing and discussing good-practice videos in whole-group settings. These are encouraging outcomes in such a challenging context as Cambodian schools undoubtedly are.

Summary

When preservice teachers viewed video of experienced teachers at work, this promoted a deeper understanding of teaching (Docucases; CFS preservice) and increased the quality of their own lesson plans and their identification with the value of lesson planning (IPASS; VILMS). In an offline setting, video-based support intensified the communication between student and mentor teachers and appeared to shift its character from vertical to horizontal (VILMS). Web-based support intensified communication between student and mentor teachers (IPASS). When experienced teachers in a non-Western country viewed good-practice videos of other teachers in an offline setting, this encouraged them to consider alternative teaching approaches (CFS in-service).

When viewing video cases offline took place in a setting of collegial exchange and dialogue, this helped teachers develop a deeper understanding of teaching (Docucases, VILMS, CFS in-service). A plenary group setting and viewing good-practice videos appeared to be relatively effective conditions (CFS in-service).

Realism and authenticity in video representations of teaching and learning appeared to be influential features of the learning environment (Docucases). By creating cognitive conflict, videos showing teachers' dilemmas appeared to encourage preservice teachers to rethink ideas and beliefs (Didiclass).

Studying teaching and learning

Studying teaching and learning with the help of lesson recordings has become a widespread practice in groups of teachers, both in PTE and in PD. In this section, three approaches to this form of teacher learning, originating from the US and the francophone world, are described.

Learning to notice in video clubs

During the 1990s, the Educational Testing Service in the US carried out the Video Portfolio Project with the dual purpose of identifying highly accomplished mathematics teachers and of providing teachers with a procedure for examining and improving their teaching (Frederiksen, Sipusic, Sherin, & Wolfe, 1998). One interesting finding in this project was that teachers and researchers differed significantly in how they perceived teaching quality. The full reality of classrooms apparently displays such a wealth of phenomena that assessing them consistently amounts to an enormous challenge. One of the project members, Miriam Sherin of Northwestern University at Evanston, Illinois, concluded that teachers and researchers have a lot to learn from each other (Sherin, 2001, 2003).

Thus was born the initiative to organise "video clubs", a form of teacher collaboration in which teachers study video recordings of their lessons in ways that should help them "learn to notice" how pupils learn mathematics. The idea behind this is that teachers need to discover with what kinds of teaching behaviour they can foster active learning in their pupils and thus help them understand mathematics instead of blindly applying algorithms. The innovative teaching behaviours needed to achieve this ambitious goal are defined in official standards such as those defined by the NBPTS and the National Council of Teachers of Mathematics (NCTM). "Learning to notice" (henceforth abbreviated as LTN) should lead to "professional vision", i.e. the kind of expert perception (Goodwin, 1994) which detectives, archaeologists and judges bring to their respective professions. In the case of mathematics teaching, professional vision involves the ability to perceive when and how pupils understand or misunderstand subject matter, so that teachers may adjust their instruction and respond adequately to pupils' ongoing learning processes. Sherin, Van Es and colleagues refer to such teaching as "ambitious instruction".

A video club typically consists of a small group of experienced teachers who record and discuss their lessons during a period ranging between two and ten months. Usually, a researcher or an experienced teacher educator acts as a moderator or facilitator. The video fragments discussed and the viewing points or foci to guide the discussion are usually chosen by the facilitator, who aims to direct teachers' attention to aspects of pupils' learning in the subject involved.

Since 2001, a sizeable research programme has been conducted by Miriam Sherin and Elizabeth Van Es and colleagues of the School of Education at the University of California at Irvine (UCI), in which they investigated how video clubs function. Most of the studies in this research programme involve experienced teachers. Others were conducted in PTE settings. These studies were usually designed as fine-grained analyses of video recordings of video club sessions, in which teachers' utterances at the beginning and at the end of video clubs were quantified on the basis of predetermined categories, i.e. deductively and/or as they emerged from the data themselves, i.e. inductively. In the same ways, comments written by teachers before and after video clubs about video fragments from lessons were analysed. Both utterances and comments were coded with a minimal reliability of 80%. In some studies, interviews with teachers were used as additional data sources. Many of these data were collected in the context of licensure requirements that teachers had to fulfil in the context of the Performance Assessment of California Teachers (PACT).

The main findings from the UCI studies about LTN are summarised below, grouped under the following themes:

- how teachers view and interpret lesson recordings,
- how teachers' thinking develops over the course of a video club,
- what roles teachers take during video clubs,
- which conversational moves and strategies facilitators use to guide discussion and
- what impact video club participation has on instructional behaviour.

How teachers view and interpret mathematics lessons when they have no experience in a video club was studied by Colestock and Sherin (2009) in fifteen experienced middle and high school mathematics teachers. After viewing four three- to eight-minute clips of whole-class or small-group discussions of mathematical ideas, these teachers focussed their attention most frequently on aspects of pedagogy, classroom climate and classroom management. To interpret the classroom interactions they viewed, the teachers most frequently made comparisons to how they conducted their own lessons, took the perspective of how pupils probably experienced the lesson involved and considered how the teachers they viewed orchestrated instruction. In sum, these teachers did not attend foremost to pupils' understanding of mathematics, but to how they reacted to the teachers' instruction.

When teachers do participate in a video club, shifts in their perceptions tend to occur. Four studies by Van Es and Sherin (2002), Sherin and Han (2004), Van Es & Sherin, Russ, Sherin and Colestock (2008) and Tekkumru Kisa and Stein (2015) have yielded evidence of such shifts. The numbers of teachers in these studies ranged between four and twelve. In three studies, mathematics teachers were involved, in one biology teachers. In three studies, experienced teachers were involved, in one preservice teachers. The respondents were from both primary and secondary schools and viewed video clips of other teachers' as well as their own teaching. All four studies indicate that after video club participation, teachers shifted their perception towards noticing and interpreting pupils' thinking about the subject matter taught. In one study (Sherin & Han, 2004), the teachers also came to discuss alternatives for teaching action.

Three studies from the UCI research programme have produced evidence about the processes going on during the work of video clubs. The numbers of teachers in these studies ranged between five and seven. All were experienced mathematics teachers working in primary or secondary schools. They participated in ten to sixteen meetings, during which they viewed video fragments from their own lessons.

Two studies (Brantlinger, Sherin, & Linsenmeier, 2011; Van Es, 2012a) show which topics the teachers discussed most during their video clubs. Their conversations centred firstly on how to orchestrate learning and especially on the issue what techniques are suitable for facilitating discourse with and between pupils. Secondly, the teachers were concerned with the quality or level of such discourse. A third topic were contextual influences on their lessons, i.e. the type of pupils, curriculum requirements and the availability of resources.

Two studies (Van Es, 2009; Van Es, 2012a) show how teachers' roles changed over the course of the video clubs. They encouraged each other more to attend to the particulars of pupils' mathematics learning. They came to use evidence from the video fragments more as a basis for reasoning about instruction and their statements became more interpretive and tentative. Also, their interactions became more collaborative and collegial, i.e. over time, they listened more carefully to each other and their contributions to the conversation became more evenly distributed. In one study (Brantlinger et al., 2011), teachers explained what they particularly valued about the video club as a form of PD. What they appreciated was the opportunity it offered to exchange experiences with and developing their vision about mathematics teaching. This appreciation was enhanced when the teachers had the opportunity to set the agenda together with the facilitator and when the facilitator gave the discussions a relatively loose structure.

The roles facilitators and teachers take clearly influence how the discussion in a video club develops. This issue was researched in four studies of experienced and novice teachers, mostly of mathematics, working mostly in middle and high schools. The video clubs involved met between six and ten times and viewed mostly video clips from the participants' own classrooms.

One study by Van Es (2012b) shows that the contributions from facilitators and teachers tended to move the discussion in different directions. The facilitators stressed pupils' mathematical thinking, while the teachers addressed issues of lesson implementation. Apparently, different PD goals were implied here, which manifested themselves in how discussions evolved. As video clubs operate in different contexts and with different goals, the findings from studies comparing different video clubs are of interest. Van Es and Sherin (2006) show that the Mapleton club – a pseudonym for a video club from which they analysed data in several studies – developed more focussed and interpretive ways of analysing classroom video, while the Wells Park club – also a pseudonym – maintained diverse perspectives. This difference resulted probably from the fact that video clips and points for viewing and analysis were selected by the facilitator and the teachers themselves, respectively. Other differences influencing the development of these video clubs had to do with the periods during which they were active, the availability of transcripts of video fragments viewed and how strictly or loosely the discussions were structured.

The facilitation practices in video clubs were also studied in a comparison of the Mapleton club with the Atwood club – again a pseudonym. In these clubs, facilitators used a variety of conversation moves constituting four facilitation practices: "Orienting group to the video analysis task; Sustaining an inquiry stance; Maintaining a focus on the video and the mathematics; and Supporting group collaboration" (Van Es, Tunney, Goldsmith, & Seago, 2014, p. 347). Building on this work, Tekkumru-Kisa and Stein (2017, p. 4–15) have proposed the following seven facilitation practices: "Setting goals; Identifying PD tasks; Anticipating responses; Sequencing of videos and PD tasks structured around the videos; Monitoring responses; Selecting participant responses to share or highlight; and Connecting participants' responses to the big idea".

What the work in video clubs ultimately aims at is changes in teachers' instruction which strengthen pupils' learning with understanding. In this sense, the last four studies presented in this section represent the proof of the pudding. I have grouped them together because in all these studies, video recordings of participants' classroom instruction were analysed to explore if and what influence video club participation may have had on teachers' instructional behaviour. Between four and 26 secondary teachers were involved in this research, mostly experienced teachers in mathematics, but also in science. The number of video club sessions varies between five and ten.

The first three studies build on each other in explicating the types of instructional behaviours that teachers came to display more often in their classrooms during and shortly after video club participation. The main behaviour changes observed were: pausing during instruction to consider voluntary reactions by pupils; using wait time in order to give pupils opportunities to think about the subject matter; rephrasing pupils' ideas for the whole group; eliciting ideas from pupils; and asking pupils to explain how they reasoned while working on assignments (Sherin & Van Es, 2009; Sun & Van Es, 2015, p. 205; Van Es & Sherin, 2010). These instructional behaviours are all elements of responsive and dialogic teaching which teachers can use to foster learning with understanding (cf. the section *Quality learning and quality teaching* in Chapter 1).

The fourth study (Barnhart & Van Es, 2018) is one of the few from the UCI research programme in which teachers elucidated during interviews how shifts in perception related to changes in instruction. In this study, four experienced secondary science teachers were followed during participation in five video club sessions during one semester. During the first three meetings, published videos of other science teachers using practices for promoting evidence-based reasoning about science phenomena in pupils were analysed. In the last two meetings, the participating teachers viewed and discussed video clips showing attempts to enact such practices in their own classrooms. Analysis of the meeting transcripts showed that all four teachers shifted their perception in the direction of noticing more of pupils' thinking about science topics. However, their classroom instruction and interview statements indicated that two teachers began changing their instruction, while the other two did not. What the teachers who did change found especially demanding was reacting adequately to pupils' contributions to classroom discourse. The main difference between the two pairs of teachers was that those who changed their instruction had formulated more concrete personal goals for participating in the video club. Besides this difference, the teachers felt hindered by curricular and exam requirements. In addition, Barnhart and Van Es note that the duration of the video club may have been too short for the teachers to complete several cycles of experimentation and collegial discussion about their attempts at changing instruction.

In sum, the studies by Sherin, Van Es and colleagues have produced clear evidence showing that during video clubs, experienced teachers can develop their abilities to notice and interpret pupils' thinking about subject matter. It appears that while analysing lessons, experienced teachers tend to focus on relationships between teaching and learning, i.e. how they influence pupils' learning by orchestrating it within given curricular constraints, rather than on pupils' learning alone. Clearly fewer indications were found that participating in video clubs resulted in changes in instructional behaviour. Insofar as such indications were found, they suggest shifts in the direction of more responsive teaching practices. In addition, the studies by Sherin, Van Es and colleagues show that during video clubs, experienced teachers develop a more interpretive and tentative stance as well as increased collegiality. Finally, these studies have enabled explicating productive facilitation practices.

Developing lesson analysis abilities

While Sherin, Van Es and colleagues have mostly studied experienced teachers, another strand of research at the UCI School of Education involves predominantly preservice teachers. Since 2010, Rossella Santagata and colleagues have conducted a multi-year research project, in which prospective teachers were followed from the beginning of PTE into the third year of in-service teaching. This project's goal was to understand how preservice teachers develop the abilities needed to analyse and design lessons so that pupils will learn with understanding.

Important points of departure for this project were two findings from earlier research. Firstly, when planning and carrying out lessons, expert teachers consider what kinds of classroom events are likely to influence pupils' achievement. They design their lessons accordingly and adapt them flexibly on the spot when necessary (Sabers, Cushing, & Berliner, 1991). Secondly, experienced teachers' ability to analyse and design lessons has been shown to be subject-specific in nature and to relate to pupils' achievement. The mediating link between these two factors is the quality of teachers' instructional behaviour (Kersting, Givvin, Sotelo, & Stigler, 2010; Kersting, Givvin, Thompson, Santagata, & Stigler, 2012). The latter evidence was produced using Classroom Video Analysis (CVA), a validated measuring instrument in which teachers' comments on video clips of lessons are scored (Kersting, 2008; Kersting, Sherin, & Stigler, 2014).

Santagata's work is an attempt to guide preservice teachers towards observing those aspects of lessons that expert teachers attend to and to use these as the basis for analysing and planning lessons. The tool for doing so is the Lesson Analysis Framework (LAF), which distinguishes four essential aspects. The LAF framework assumes that after graduating from PTE, beginning teachers should be able to: 1. specify lesson goals and plan learning activities on the basis of expectations about how pupils will react; 2. while teaching, collect evidence about pupils' learning; 3. interpret the impact of their teaching on pupils' learning; and 4. formulate possible alternatives for instructional action (Santagata & Angelici, 2010; Santagata & Guarino, 2011).

To promote these skills, Santagata and colleagues have developed a course, variously entitled Learning to Learn from Mathematics Teaching, Learning from Mathematics Teaching and Learning to Learn from Teaching (henceforth abbreviated as LLT). Students participate in LLT parallel to teaching internships and proceed through three phases. They first study theory about subject-specific learning and instruction, then analyse published videos in which "ambitious instruction" can be observed and finally examine recordings of their own lessons in order to find ways to foster learning with understanding through their own teaching (Santagata & Yeh, 2016, p. 156; Yeh & Santagata, 2015, p. 24).

To investigate the impact of LLT, nine studies were conducted with the same methodology as the studies of teacher noticing by Sherin, Van Es and colleagues described in the previous section. However, the numbers of teachers in the groups studied by Santagata and colleagues are higher, varying between 24 and 59. In five studies, experimental groups participating in LLT were compared to control groups, which participated in traditional PTE methods courses. In two of these studies (Mohr & Santagata, 2015; Yeh & Santagata, 2015), students were randomly assigned to groups. In one exploratory study, three preservice teachers were followed after graduation (Santagata & Yeh, 2016). The studies involved mostly mathematics teaching, but also the teaching of science and other subjects. Half were carried out in primary schools and half in secondary schools. All but two studies involved viewing video of other teachers' lessons.

All nine studies have produced evidence about LLT's impact on preservice teachers' thinking, specifically on the levels of elaboration with which they commented upon videos of pupils' learning during lessons and the numbers of possible alternatives for instruction they proposed. In six out of these nine studies, the preservice teachers in experimental groups improved their lesson analysis abilities over time, mostly to degrees that were statistically significant ($p < .05$) (Mohr & Santagata, 2015; Santagata & Angelici, 2010; Santagata & Guarino, 2011; Santagata, Zannoni, & Stigler, 2007; Van Es, Cashen, Barnhart, & Auger, 2017; Yeh & Santagata, 2015). All five studies in which groups were compared showed that the experimental groups outperformed the control groups, again mostly with statistical significance ($p < .05$) (Barnhart & Van Es, 2015; Mohr & Santagata, 2015; Santagata & Angelici, 2010; Santagata & Yeh, 2014; Yeh & Santagata, 2015).

As mentioned, an important assumption behind the LAF is that developing preservice teachers' lesson analysis abilities should contribute to their lesson planning. From this perspective, one finding reported by Barnhart and Van Es (2015, p. 90) is particularly interesting. After preservice teachers' written comments on video clips of their own teaching were coded reliably for their level of sophistication (r ranging between .73 and .93), correlations showed that attending to and analysing pupil learning were significantly correlated (Kendall's tau = .387; p. = 003). Also, analysing and formulating intentions to respond to pupils' contributions during lessons were significantly correlated (Kendall's tau = .572; p. = .001). However, no clear correlation was found between attending and intentions to respond (Kendall's tau = .140; p. = 397). Apparently, attending is a necessary, but not a sufficient condition for formulating intentions to respond. Before preservice teachers can arrive at such intentions, they probably need to analyse pupils' thinking.

Two out of the nine studies by Santagata and colleagues have also yielded indications about LLT's impact on teaching behaviour. When video clips of LLT participants' teaching were compared to clips of non-LLT participants' teaching, the LLT students not only analysed the impact of their instructional behaviour on pupils' mathematics learning more deeply, but their teaching also received higher ratings (Santagata & Yeh, 2014). In addition, the three graduates who were followed into beginning teaching kept improving their lesson analysis abilities – albeit to differing degrees – but they also reported feeling pressure from the teaching cultures existing in their schools to conform to more traditional, transmission-oriented teaching (Santagata & Yeh, 2016).

In sum, the studies by Santagata and colleagues have produced similarly clear evidence as those by Sherin, Van Es and colleagues showing that preservice teachers can develop lesson analysis abilities by analysing video clips of other teachers' and their own teaching. Equally, fewer indications were found that participation in LLT resulted in changes in instructional behaviour. Insofar as such indications were found, they suggest that preservice and beginning teachers developed intentions to implement process-oriented teaching practices. In the case of beginning teachers, however, the teaching culture existing in their schools appeared to inhibit such practices.

Collaborative Video Learning Lab

In the francophone world, the collaborative study by teachers of digital video records of teaching and learning was developed in the 1990s by François Tochon. On the basis of projects carried out in Québec, Tochon (1999) introduced the concept of "video study groups". The theoretical perspective underlying this concept is semiotics, the study of meanings and how meaning-making takes place in human culture (Tochon, 2013). An important premise of semiotics is the unity of action, cognition and emotion. When applied to professionals' learning, this premise naturally leads to a focus on their personal experiences and concerns, in this case those of teachers.

This holistic approach characterises the Collaborative Video Learning Lab (CVLL), a PD approach applied and developed during projects in both primary and secondary schools and for preservice as well as in-service teachers (Lussi Borer, Gaudin, Roche, & Flandin, 2015). One CVLL project was undertaken in a middle school in a high-poverty area near Paris (Lussi Borer, Gaudin, Roche, & Flandin, 2015; Lussi Borer, Ria, Durand, & Muller, 2014; Lussi Borer & Ria, 2014). Its goal was to raise the effectiveness of beginning and experienced teachers' work. The participants taught diverse secondary school subjects. For the beginning teachers, the CVLL served as an induction programme, which in France, where PTE programmes provide few opportunities for student teaching, is a welcome form of support. For the experienced teachers, the CVLL was a platform for developing their work and share their practical knowledge with colleagues. By viewing and analysing video recordings of each other's lessons, the participants sought to access a wide range of possible approaches to teaching and try out instructional alternatives. The topics to be studied in this way were chosen by the teachers themselves together with the researchers and facilitators supporting the CVLL.

A central feature of CVLL design is the analysis of work activity in context. This feature was derived from ergonomics (Theureau, 2003) and made concrete in a working procedure to which all participants agreed. It relies on a willingness to suspend judgements and to compare the variety of teaching approaches available in the group. The procedure consisted of the following steps. To begin with, while the video-recorded teacher (VRT) remains silent, the other group members first describe in detail and then interpret what they observed in the lesson fragments viewed, taking into account the VRT's intentions and concerns. These accounts of what happened in the lesson are then confirmed or rejected by the VRT in such a way that the others can understand and relate it to her or his intentions. This step is followed by a discussion of the functionality of the lesson design, which then leads to proposals for alternative courses of action that should be realistic, feasible and in line with the VRT's intentions.

To study the CVLL, Lussi Borer and colleagues collected several types of video data over a period of two years. Data collection was planned for two more years. In addition to the participants' teaching and their group sessions, "self-confrontation interviews" were recorded (Theureau, 2002). These are sessions during which a teacher views her or his lesson together with a facilitator who asks questions aimed at making explicit her or his intentions, experiences, interpretations and conclusions. In the ensuing conversation, discrepancies between expectations and the actual course of the lesson take a prominent place. Also CVLL group sessions were recorded and reviewed in this way. Finally, group interviews with the CVLL participants were conducted. In total, 88 recordings were made, in which seventeen teachers were involved.

Initial data analysis was restricted to 37 recordings of four lower-secondary teachers. Two of these teachers were novices in their second year in the school. The two others had ten and thirteen years of experience and also took the role of CVLL facilitator. The topics these teachers examined during their CVLL participation were analysed by two dyads of researchers with the aim of characterising the participants' learning activities in terms of three levels. Referring to time spans of an increasing magnitude, these levels focussed the analysis on whether the teacher became able to (a) target a difficulty she or he had in teaching and to imagine alternative courses of action, (b) act differently during teaching and (c) incorporate new instructional approaches in her or his teaching repertoire, also as a basis for imagining new solutions in other situations. The researchers reached 82% agreement in characterising the data in terms of these levels.

The findings so far available show that the two novice teachers' main concern was classroom management. The focal question used in the CVLL to launch discussion of this issue was: "Do the students [pupils] work with or against the teacher?" (Lussi Borer et al., 2014, p. 68). During the first year of participating in the CVLL, the first novice teacher struggled to discover and implement other ways to start a lesson than the "stand up – be quiet – take off coats – get out the supplies routine" habitual in French schools. Then, in the second year, the video-based discussions in the CVLL helped him find new ways to start his lessons and justify these to his pupils (Lussi Borer et al., 2014, p. 69–70). The second novice struggled during her first year of participating to recognise an adversarial behaviour pattern between her pupils and herself. Then, in the second year, she began to identify and experiment with ways to approach pupils with more positive expectations.

The two experienced teachers made other discoveries. The first teacher recognised during a self-confrontation interview that she could display more confidence towards pupils. She then used this discovery while mentoring one of the novice teachers. The second experienced teacher began adopting the CVLL working procedure he experienced during his first year of participation while mentoring novice teachers during the second year.

These reconstructions of four participants' development suggest that analysing the work of teaching with the help of video helped them identify critical experiences, which brought them to view it in new ways. This was the starting point for searching and adopting alternative ways of acting, in itself a process that required time and effort. What appears to have set off and sustained these processes is the structured confrontation with colleagues' constructive feedback. What also appears to have promoted teacher learning in the CVLL was the deliberate use of diverse modalities of video viewing and analysis in diverse groupings. Novice and experienced teachers, researchers and facilitators engaged in video viewing and analysis in dyads and small as well as plenary groups, examining classroom teaching, pupils' learning activity and their own collaborative activity. This appears to have stimulated the comparison of different perspectives on teaching and learning and the generation of alternatives for teaching action (Mollo & Falzon, 2004; Lussi Borer & Flandin, 2016; Lussi Borer & Muller, 2016; Leblanc, 2018).

The initial findings of the CVLL project confirm the notion that teachers' professional learning is a long-term and gradual process, which can be driven forward when groups of teachers engage in video-supported study of their work with pupils. These findings also show that schools need to free working time and create and sustain organisational conditions to make teachers' collaboration in PD activities possible (Lussi Borer et al., 2014, p. 72–73).

Summary

All UCI studies, 25 in total, concern teachers' perception and thinking. Seven of these studies also concern teachers' instructional behaviour.

The studies of LTN by Sherin, Van Es and colleagues have demonstrated that viewing and analysing video of teaching and learning can support preservice and experienced teachers in attending to and interpreting pupils' mathematics learning. During video clubs, they tend to focus on relationships between teaching and learning rather than on pupils' learning alone and to develop increased collegiality. Protocols for collegial dialogue and facilitation practices helped teachers suspend judgements, develop a more tentative and interpretive stance and build trust.

The studies of LLT by Santagata and colleagues have shown that preservice teachers can develop lesson analysis abilities by analysing video clips of other teachers' and their own teaching. However, this research has also produced indications that as graduates move into beginning teaching, they experience pressure from the teaching cultures existing in their schools to conform to traditional, transmission-oriented teaching.

The evidence available about the impact of LTN, LLT and CVLL on changes in instructional behaviour suggests that it takes teachers more than one year to achieve such change. During CVLL, the provision of working time and collegial collaboration in examining and interpreting critical teaching experiences helped participants change their instructional behaviour.

Training teaching skills

The DV applications described in this section all aim at training specific skills essential to teaching. The first programme described is for training classroom management skills and the second for developing teachers' competencies in classroom discourse. The third aims at productive forms of interaction with learners.

Classroom Management Competencies

Making classrooms environments conducive to learning is one of the essential tasks for teachers. For beginning teachers, it is probably the most pressing concern. Still, many PTE programmes appear to lack provisions for effective training in classroom management. In order to fill this gap, the video-based programme Kompetenzen des Klassenmanagements (KODEK) or Classroom Management Competencies was developed for secondary teachers by Valentina Piwowar, Felicitas Thiel and Diemut Ophardt at the Freie Universität Berlin.

A first version of KODEK was developed for in-service teachers. The rationale behind it is that evidence-based knowledge about classroom management should be made available to teachers in explicit forms which they can relate to their daily work. To achieve this, three consecutive modules totalling 23 hours were developed. In Module 1, productive classroom management strategies derived from the work of Doyle (1986, 2006) and Kounin (1970) are presented through lecture and scripted videos (Piwowar, Barth, Ophardt, & Thiel, 2018), in which actors demonstrate preventive strategies such as mobilising and monitoring pupil behaviour as well as reactive strategies such as intervening and reprimanding. Discussion of these videos serves to make the principles behind the strategies explicit and to encourage the participating teachers to apply these principles in their own teaching and to work out alternative courses of action. During Module 2, they engage in MT and role-playing to reflect on their own routines, try out alternatives and receive feedback. In Module 3, the participants are recorded on video while teaching in their own work situation, select fragments from these recordings and discuss them in a "video circle" consisting of four colleagues and a coach, aiming to generate behavioural alternatives to try out in their own classrooms (Piwowar, Thiel, & Ophardt, 2013, p. 2–5).

The effectiveness of this programme design was investigated in a study involving 37 experienced secondary teachers, who divided themselves over an intervention group (IG) of nineteen teachers, aged 48 on average and 63% female, and a control group (CG) of eighteen teachers, aged 40 on average and 56% female. The intervention group participated in the whole KODEK programme, while the control group participated only in Module 1.

Several research instruments were used to assess the effectiveness of KODEK. Before and immediately after training, four instruments were administered in the IG and the CG. Firstly, teachers rated their own knowledge about seven proactive classroom management strategies (establishing rules; establishing procedures; time management; monitoring; creating and maintaining a working alliance with pupils; group mobilisation; and providing "clarity of programme of action" during lessons) and about two reactive strategies (dealing with disruption and handling conflicts among pupils). Secondly, the 666 pupils of the teachers in both groups rated their teachers' use of five of these strategies (time management; monitoring; group mobilisation; providing "clarity of programme of action"; and dealing with disruption). Thirdly, observers rated these same five strategies. Fourthly, observers used the standardised Munich Observation of Attention Inventory (MAI) to determine pupils' engagement and on-task behaviour during lessons (Helmke, 1988). Finally, the teachers in the IG rated after each training module to what extent they felt it encouraged them to reflect on their classroom management and to what extent they felt they could transfer what they learned to their own classrooms.

The findings showed that both IG and CG increased their self-rated knowledge about six of the eight classroom management strategies. About the other two strategies (time management and group mobilisation), the IG reported increased knowledge, but the CG reported decreased knowledge. Overall, the IG reported greater increases than the CG, but this trend was not statistically significant (p > .05). According to the pupils, the IG teachers improved their use of all five strategies rated, outperforming the CG teachers significantly (p < .05). However, the observer ratings confirmed this pattern only for the preventive strategies of group mobilisation and monitoring. The observer ratings also showed non-significant trends in pupils' behaviour: their off-task behaviour decreased more in IG than in CG teachers' classes, while their engagement increased more in IG than in CG teachers' classes. Finally, the IG teachers' self-reported reflection and their appreciation of the transferability of what they learned during KODEK increased significantly over time (p < .05), especially after Modules 2 and 3, i.e. after engaging actively in video-supported learning (Piwowar, Thiel, & Ophardt, 2013, p. 4–9).

In drawing conclusions from these findings, we have to consider that the participating teachers could select themselves in either the IG or the CG. Also, the post-intervention measures were limited to outcomes assessed immediately after training. No follow-up data about the sustainability of these outcomes are available. Even so, this study has yielded several indications that participating in the KODEK training did improve teachers' knowledge as well as behaviour in the domain of classroom management. For a training programme totalling no more than 23 hours, this is an encouraging result. Similarly positive learning outcomes were apparent from studies of KODEK's effectiveness in beginning teachers (Piwowar, Ophardt, & Thiel, 2013). Effects on perception were also found in a study involving student teachers (Barth, Piwowar, Kumschick, Ophardt, & Thiel, 2019).

Dialogic Video Cycle

Dialogic Video Cycle (DVC) is a programme for in-service secondary teachers in the Science, Technology, Engineering and Mathematics (STEM) subjects intended to train competencies in classroom discourse needed to foster learning with understanding. In order to support teachers in activating pupils cognitively, Ann-Kathrin Pehmer, Katharina Kiemer, Alexander Gröschner and Tina Seidel of the Technical University of Munich (TUM) adapted a training design called the Problem Solving Cycle developed by Borko, Jacobs, Eiteljorg and Pittman (2008). The rationale behind this design is that to change their instruction, teachers need to go through two or more cycles, each of which consists of three steps: making a lesson plan; carrying out the lesson and recording it on video; and discussing the recordings during workshops with a facilitator and colleagues focussing on specific aspects of their teaching behaviour. The DVC focussed on how teachers can use questioning and feedback in order to encourage cognitive elaboration in pupils. Cognitive elaboration means that pupils acquire concepts, differentiate aspects and come to understand general principles which help them explain STEM phenomena.

In the DVC, features of effective PD (see the section *Professional development* in Chapter 1) were implemented as follows. During one school year, three mathematics and three science teachers participated, during a total of 22 hours, in two iterations of the cycle of activities described above. Each cycle consisted of three workshops. In the first workshop, the teachers designed lesson plans which included opportunities for classroom dialogue. In these plans, the teachers prepared ways to engage pupils in conversation, to ask open questions aiming to encourage them to reason about and elaborate on the subject of the lesson as well as giving them concrete and constructive feedback. After their lessons were recorded on video, the workshops were devoted to group discussions about fragments from recordings selected by the facilitator (Gröschner, Seidel, Pehmer, & Kiemer, 2014, p. 7–9).

To evaluate the DVC, quasi-experimental studies were conducted. The intervention group (IG) participating in the DVC was compared to a control group (CG) of one mathematics and three science teachers, who participated in an "advanced traditional programme" (ATP). There were two main differences between the IG and the CG. During the school year, the IG had seven meetings, while the CG met three times. The CG teachers also discussed information about activating discourse practices, but did not engage in video analyses of their own lessons. The teachers participating in the studies could choose for themselves in which group they wanted to participate, the IG or the CG. The six teachers in the IG were aged 40 on average and four of them were women. The four teachers in the CG were aged 37 on average and three of them were women.

Besides background data, pre- and post-intervention surveys were conducted among teachers and pupils. To find out if and how the teachers in the IG and the CG changed their teaching after participating and if they differed in the discourse competencies targeted, also surveys were conducted among 226 of their pupils, aged 15.7 years on average, 136 in the IG and 90 in the CG. In addition, teachers' lessons and group meetings were recorded on video. The video recordings were transcribed and coded with sufficient reliability. Collecting data from both teachers and pupils was meant to ensure that not only the nature of the teachers' classroom behaviour could be determined, but also how pupils reacted to it.

Analysis of the lesson videos showed no clear changes in IG and CG teachers' questioning behaviour over the course of the school year. However, in their feedback behaviour, the IG teachers outperformed the CG teachers. The IG teachers decreased simple feedback – i.e. only saying if pupils' answers or solutions were right or wrong – and increased constructive feedback – i.e. elaborating on pupils' contributions. Among CG teachers, the reverse pattern was found (Pehmer, Gröschner, & Seidel, 2015a). For the IG teachers, changing the type of feedback given to pupils from simple to constructive appeared to be easier than developing a type of questioning suited to fostering cognitive elaboration (Kiemer, Gröschner, Pehmer, & Seidel, 2015).

Analysis of the pupil surveys showed that the IG teachers' pupils felt equally activated in their learning over the course of the school year, whereas the CG teachers' pupils experienced a decrease in this respect. The teachers' use of strategies to encourage cognitive elaboration showed a different pattern: while the IG teachers' pupils – especially those with a high reported self-efficacy – experienced an increase, the CG teachers' pupils experienced a slight decrease (Kiemer et al., 2015). The development of one teacher during her participation in the IG was reconstructed by Schindler, Gröschner and Seidel (2015). This teacher, who experienced the DVC very positively, achieved a high degree of behaviour change compared to colleagues. When the video codings quantifying her instructional behaviour were compared to her pupils' self-reported experience of classroom learning, similar patterns were found. Especially during the second half of the school year, the behaviour changes achieved by the teacher appeared to be "mirrored" in the pupils' experiences (Schindler et al., 2015, p. 25–29).

Further analysis of how IG pupils' and teachers' interaction developed over the school year did not reveal clear changes in pupils' utterances indicative of cognitive elaboration. In the development of IG teachers' classroom behaviour, considerable interindividual differences were found (Pehmer, Gröschner, & Seidel, 2015b). Group differences were found in the IG and CG teachers' appreciation of the learning activities they engaged in. While the IG teachers' appreciation of video-supported learning activities increased during the second half of the school year, the CG teachers decreased their appreciation of the workshop activities without video in which they participated (Gröschner et al., 2014, p. 15–21).

In conclusion, the above studies of the DVC approach are valuable because of their meticulous examination of possible effects on classroom interaction and pupils' learning experiences. However, mostly because of their small sample sizes and the preponderance of quantitative data analysis, the effectiveness of the DVC could not be determined definitively. Even so, trends in favour of the IG teachers' video-supported learning were found. At the same time, changing instructional routines, especially asking questions to foster cognitive elaboration, turned out to be quite a challenge for teachers.

Interactional and instructional skills in early childhood education and care

Changing behaviour in the professional interaction with clients — not only by teachers, but also by counsellors, therapists and physicians — has been the object of video-supported learning since the invention of the video recorder. The effectiveness of viewing and analysing recordings of one's own interaction with clients has been studied in a meta-analysis of experimental research by Fukkink, Trienekens, and Kramer (2011). Their main findings are that video feedback is about equally effective regardless of professionals' amount of experience. Furthermore, the effects of training programmes were clearly strongest when they aimed at behavioural targets explicitly stated in observation forms and protocols. The meta-analysis also yielded indications that training was more effective for targets formulated in positive than in negative terms. When using video, in other words, learning appeared more effective than unlearning.

In the field of early childhood education and care (ECEC), the quality of caregivers' interaction is of great importance for developing children's capabilities for later learning. While this influence is acknowledged internationally, it is also known that ECEC teachers are often stronger in interactional than in instructional skills (Jilink, Fukkink, & Huijbregts, 2018, p. 278–279). This is why Ruben Fukkink and colleagues of the University of Amsterdam have conducted experimental studies of training programmes in the ECEC field aiming at both types of skills.

Fukkink and Tavecchio (2010) studied the effectiveness of Video Interaction Guidance (VIG), a training method practised in several European countries and the US which is based on Bandura's theory of social cognition (Bandura, 1997) and hence places emphasis on developing professionals' sense of self-efficacy. The VIG training studied consisted of four 30-minute sessions spread over a period of sixteen weeks, in which trainers and trainees viewed and discussed in depth ten-minute video fragments of trainees' practice. These sessions focussed on aspects of sensitivity and emotional support and related aspects of verbal stimulation, such as making eye contact and acknowledging children's actions and intentions.

95 ECEC teachers, all female and aged 28 years on average, were randomly assigned to an experimental group which participated in the VIG training (n = 52) and a control group which did not (n = 43). Standardised and validated observation instruments were used (Arnett, 1989; Rimm-Kaufman, Voorhees, Snell, & La Paro, 2003) for rating of video recordings in the respondents' work situation made at the beginning and at the end of the intervention. In addition, the VIG group was filmed again three months after the intervention to find out to what extent any effects of training were sustained over time.

Analyses of variance showed that the VIG training produced significant effects in the experimental group (p < .05) for the interactional skills of stimulating caregiving, sensitive responsivity, verbal stimulation, making eye contact, verbal reception, letting children take a turn and acknowledging children. Three months after training, most of these skills were slightly weaker than at post-test, but still stronger than at pre-test.

In a subsequent study, Jilink et al. (2018) compared the development of inter-actional with instructional skills in an experimental study of 72 ECEC teachers, 99% female and aged 46 on average. In this pre-test and post-test study, four con-ditions were involved. One group of seventeen teachers followed the in-service Early Childhood Education (ECE) programme, which focussed on three com-ponents: children's development; offering an attractive learning environment for children; and educational activities. This programme included eleven 2.5-hour ses-sions during one ten-month school year. During the same period, the participants received on-the-job coaching, in which experienced coaches on 22 locations provided them with individual feedback on their work. In the second condition, sixteen ECEC teachers participated in the VIG training described above. In the third condition, eighteen teachers participated first in the VIG training and then the ECE programme. The fourth condition was a control condition without any form of training, which included 21 teachers. In all conditions, the Caregiver Interaction Profile (CIP), a standardised and validated observation instrument (Helmerhorst, Riksen-Walraven, Fukkink, Tavecchio, & Gevers Deynoot-Schaub, 2017) was administered.

Multivariate and univariate analyses showed that teachers who participated in either the ECE programme, the VIG training or both showed higher levels of CIP skills at post-test than the control group. These differences were partly significant effects ($p < .05$) and partly trend effects ($.05 < p < .10$). In addition, evidence emerged indicating that the ECE programme and the VIG training had differen-tial effects on participants' interactive skills. The teachers in the ECE programme developed stronger skills in verbal communication and developmental stimulation, while the teachers in the VIG training developed stronger skills in fostering peer interactions between children.

In sum, the well-controlled studies by Fukkink and his research group justify the conclusion that training programmes for in-service ECEC teachers in which video feedback plays a central role can foster interactional and instructional skills. These are part-time programmes lasting between four and fourteen months which combine on-the-job coaching with explicit information about domain-specific professional behaviours. What makes these studies also noteworthy is that they have produced indications for specific effects. Fukkink and Tavecchio (2010) found evi-dence for the retention of training effects after three months. Jilink et al. (2018) found evidence for differential effects of different interventions.

Summary

Teachers in intervention groups who engaged in active video-supported learn-ing reported a more positive PD experience than control teachers who did not (KODEK; DVC). Video-supported training promoted changes in teachers' knowl-edge (KODEK) and instructional behaviour (KODEK; DVC; ECEC). What was effective in KODEK was the combination of evidence-based scripted videos with teachers' active DV-supported learning.

Video platforms for teachers

The introduction of video streaming has given rise worldwide to an ever-changing supply of video platforms for teachers (for a selective overview see the section *Video platforms for teachers* in Chapter 9). I define such platforms as public web sites which are dedicated exclusively to supporting teachers and accessible at no cost. Although much video material about teaching is available on portals such as YouTube and Vimeo, I focus here on dedicated platforms because of three distinctive features.

Most importantly, dedicated platforms concentrate on offering videos showing "good" or "best" teaching practices, so that teachers may get ideas and inspiration for their own work. Secondly, these videos are presented in relation to issues and resources relevant to teaching. Finally, video platforms for teachers provide users with structure and navigability to help them benefit from the content offered.

In this section, I describe three video platforms from the UK, the Netherlands and France, about which evaluative research is available.

Teachers TV

Teachers TV was developed with funding from the British Department for Education with the aim of contributing to increasing the quality of education. It was first presented through TV channels, then also on the Internet. Its active existence lasted from 2004 till 2011, when it was discontinued for financial reasons. For a while, the 3.500 videos produced and part of the related materials were still available on two licensed web sites. Unfortunately, however, these resources are no longer accessible.

Links on the opening pages of both web sites made their contents accessible categorised by school types, school subjects, users' roles in schools and by topics. The topics were subdivided in a fine-grained way. One of the web sites also included a search function. The videos available within a category were shown with a clickable title, a content summary and a video thumbnail. The videos themselves were designed as minidocumentaries showing teachers in different career stages.

For example, in a video entitled "Primary English writing activities", three activity formats for writing lessons were presented by showing pupils' learning activities in class, alternated with interview fragments with the teacher, who described the rationale behind the approach and her intentions with it. Voiceovers by a narrator introduced and further described the approach. A prominent element in Teachers TV were series about special topics, for instance "Bailey on Behaviour", in which expert John Bailey could be seen analysing recordings of teachers' classroom management behaviour in conversation with them. As a viewer of these videos, one could observe not only the classroom events discussed, but also how the teacher and the expert discussed them. For example, the video "Establishing the ground rules" showed how expert teacher Libby established rules for behaviour in the first lessons of a school year. In conversation with John Bailey, she explained why she did what she did. Other videos showed how newly qualified teachers (NQTs) handled the challenge of classroom management and how Bailey spoke with them about their performance. These conversations were of direct interest for beginning teachers. They also illustrated what is exemplary coaching. Bailey recognised the NQT's effort and concerns, took the time to analyse and interpret what happened during the lesson, wove insights from theory and research into the conversation and concluded the session by outlining two or more viable alternatives for instructional action.

How Teachers TV reached teachers, how they experienced the service and what impact it had on the work of schools was researched in three policy-oriented evaluation studies. A qualitative study, in which 60 school leaders, experienced as well as beginning teachers and teaching assistants, were interviewed (Counterpoint Research, 2006) and an analysis of traffic and survey data by Brainbox Research (2010) produced similar findings. These studies showed that teachers used Teachers TV on an individual basis as well as during collaborative PD activities. Once they became familiar with it, they felt it helped them develop their practitioner knowledge by enabling them to see other teachers at work. Watching the service on TV had a predominantly orientating function, while the overview and the search facilities available online promoted more active use. However, important barriers to effective use were teachers' lack of time and when their schools had no policy or took no initiatives to use Teachers TV as a resource for PD activities. An important additional outcome of the Counterpoint study had to do with the opportunities for user control offered by Teachers TV. The interviewees in this study emphasised that accessibility and navigability had a decisive influence on how intensively they used the service.

The third study of users' experience with Teachers TV is a series of case studies by the London Institute of Education (Bourdillon, 2007). Over a period of two years, teachers from 38 schools in primary, secondary and special education were surveyed and interviewed about the impact of their use of Teachers TV during continuing professional development (CPD) activities. These case studies led to the following conclusions and recommendations.

The majority of teachers perceived Teachers TV as offering a wide range of relevant resources from which they could benefit in their teaching practice. Teachers TV could promote this impact by presenting practical knowledge about teaching in easily accessible ways, which supported teachers' collaboration in their local work context (cf. the section *Professional development* in Chapter 1). "Video of teachers at work brings practitioner knowledge into focus in a way text materials cannot do. As such, Teachers TV is a unique learning support for CPD" (Bourdillon, 2007, p.16). As one CPD leader phrased it:

> One thing we've found with our CPD is the use of video … it takes away [the] 'it's a great idea but it will never work with our kids' argument, because we've got members of staff who are trying these things … they're being videoed, they're coming back and they're talking and saying it is working with our kids … people can actually see that it does work, that's the really powerful thing about it. Teachers TV is also powerful in that it comes across as being

'authentic' and the one thing teachers want is to be able to see and observe other teachers at work in classrooms they can relate to.

(Bourdillon, 2007, p. 16)

At the same time, to achieve and sustain an impact of Teachers TV on PD, not only the service, but also the schools should fulfil certain conditions. While Teachers TV would need to keep its contents up to date, accessible and navigable, schools should pursue an active PD policy both locally and regionally. Specifically, they should develop strategies for using Teachers TV as a resource, for example commissioning one teacher as PD leader, who could track the supply of online video, select relevant clips and organise teacher groups discussing them.

In sum, Teachers TV has developed a prototypical video platform for teachers, which has demonstrated its potential to contribute to teachers' professional learning in practically useful ways.

Leraar24

In the Netherlands, the example set by Teachers TV has been followed by Leraar24, a government-funded platform which has been on air since 2006. This platform aims to make available anytime anywhere "practical and expert information" to teachers in primary, secondary, special and occupational education which they "can directly apply" (https://www.leraar24.nl/over-leraar24/).

The information offered on Leraar24 is structured in six themes – Curriculum, Pedagogy, Instruction, Media, The Teaching Profession and School Organisation – each divided in several subthemes. By clicking on these subthemes, but also through highlights and a search function, users reach dossiers about topics. Information about specific school subjects can be found through the search function. A dossier consists of an introductory text and one or more video clips. These clips mostly show lesson fragments and explanations by teachers about their goals and experiences with teaching approaches such as cooperative learning and formative assessment. Some dossiers also contain links to practice-oriented research, research reviews and teaching materials developed by other schools.

In 2013, the Open University of the Netherlands undertook an online survey among 503 teachers about their user experience of Leraar24 (Brouwer & Kreijns, 2014). Among those surveyed, 289, or 57.4%, were acquainted with the platform. Those unacquainted were significantly older, longer employed and less skilled in IT use ($p < .001$). Of the teachers acquainted with Leraar24, 21% visited the platform often, 29% did so once or twice, 46% sometimes and 4% never.

Interesting contrasts emerged between the intended and actual use made of the platform. Of the 289 teachers acquainted with Leraar24, 31.8% never used it, whether they had intended to or not. Of those who intended to use the platform, 10% actually did not. On the other hand, of those who did not intend to use the platform, 28.7% did use it sometimes or regularly. Apparently, the platform did have a certain attractiveness. Still, just 12.1% of those acquainted with Leraar24 became regular users.

Of the 277 teachers who visited Leraar24, 31% mostly found what they searched for, 57.8% sometimes and 11.2% hardly. The visitors evaluated the platform with an average score of 7.05 on a ten-point scale. This score was about equal for the different aspects of layout, navigability and the quantity and quality of video clips and dossiers. When asked to what extent the platform had helped them get better in their work, 34.3% of the visiting teachers felt they had benefitted a lot, 45.8% a little and 19.9% hardly or not at all. 197 teachers responded that they had used Leraar24. 153 or 77.7% of these teachers stated that they had been able to apply certain topics in their work.

The survey also included questions about the role Leraar24 played in schools. Of the 289 teachers acquainted with the web site, 32.5% discussed the platform with colleagues. 35.6% reported that in their schools, Leraar24 was considered useful. 13.1% preferred it as a form of professional development over other forms. 5.2% reported that in their schools, a group of colleagues engaged themselves with Leraar24 and 3.5% participated in such a group.

Finally, the 277 visitors of Leraar24 were asked to suggest improvements for the web site. 29.6% of them gave 82 comments regarding four issues. 15.9% of the comments were about the amount and specificity of the platform's contents, 29.2% about their navigability, 19.6% about their practical relevance and 35.3% about their quality.

The teachers felt that the amount and variety of information on Leraar24 could well increase. What they desired in particular was information more specific to the various sectors of education, especially to learning domains and school subjects. Typical suggestions were: "more information for occupational schools" and "more information about teaching young children" or "Please pay more attention to learning domains" and "Also refer to learning material for pupils".

Secondly, the teachers voiced a need for more structure and easier navigation. Typical comments were: "more overview in categories" and "Improve the search function".

Thirdly, the teachers felt that the practical relevance of Leraar24 could improve. They wanted "more examples", "more good practice" and "more directly applicable material".

Finally, most comments were given about quality. The teachers wanted to see contents on the platform that were more up to date and had a higher level and better knowledge base. Some teachers wanted more innovative and future-oriented information, for example about activating instruction. One teacher commented: "Keep following new developments and assess critically what opportunities they have to offer." Typical comments about the level of the contents were: "Contents of the clips look good, but are too superficial", "There is more talk than in-depth discussion" and "Avoid promotion activities by vague commercial providers". As to the knowledge base of the contents, teachers suggested: "Select content more strictly", "higher content quality for the video clips with a relevant underpinning" and "Please give teaching professionals access to scientific research".

In sum, Leraar24 has succeeded in building up an audience among teachers. More than half of the survey respondents knew about the platform. Almost two fifths actually used it, and almost one fifth did so regularly. The users of the platform evaluated it mostly positively. Even so, they rated its utility for reconsidering and changing their own teaching less favourably. A gap is apparent between the promise teachers perceived in Leraar24 and the operational benefits they actually drew from it. There is clearly room for improvement. The main recommendations emerging from the survey are firstly to improve navigability and secondly to ground the video material and related information more strongly in theory and research. It should be noted that teachers appeared to use Leraar24 predominantly on an individual basis. The conditions prevailing in Dutch schools apparently offer few opportunities to teachers to study and discuss the information and video clips on the platform in collaboration with colleagues.

Néopass@ction

PTE programmes in France consist of two phases. Prospective teachers first complete a five-year university programme of disciplinary studies, which includes two or three internships in public schools during which they observe experienced teachers at work for one or two weeks. Then, after passing a national examination, they begin to work half-time as a probationary teacher under the supervision of a cooperating teacher. The other half of each week is spent studying at the university (Gaudin, Flandin, Ria, & Chaliès, 2014, p. 25). Given this type of PTE programming, it is not surprising when beginning teachers encounter practice shock (cf. the section *Preservice teacher education* in Chapter 1). This problem was even aggravated after the "Masterisation" of French teacher education in 2010 (Picard & Ria, 2011, p. 2). At the time of this reform, the opportunity to build stronger links between practice and theory into PTE programmes was missed (Leblanc & Ria, 2011, p. 42).

It is against this background that Luc Ria of the Institut Français de l'Éducation, École Normale Supérieur de Lyon and colleagues studied the problems of French beginning teachers (e.g. Ria, Sève, Saury, Theureau, & Durand, 2003). Parallel to this research, they studied the possibilities of media production to support schools and teachers in deprived areas. Campaigning on the basis of these studies eventually resulted in the funding and development of Néopass@ction, a video platform designed to support beginning teachers as they develop their teaching competence during entry into the profession.

Néopass@ction intends to address the needs of beginning teachers in all sectors of education and in all school subjects. Its design centres on the typical problems that beginning teachers experience in practice. The platform is used in different settings: during PTE courses, online by beginning teachers individually and in PD initiatives such as the CVLL (see the section *Studying teaching and learning* above). The organisation behind Néopass@ction supports these uses online as well as through user conferences in France and francophone dominions worldwide. Some resources on the platform are available not only in French, but also in English, Spanish and Catalan (http://neo.ens-lyon.fr/neopass/connexion.php).

The overarching structure of Néopass@ction consists of four tabs: Welcome, Resources, Videos and Development. In the Welcome tab, aims and contents of the platform are explained. The Resources tab contains links to reading material and podcasts for further study, while the Development tab provides background materials for teacher educators, PD leaders and researchers.

For beginning teachers, the central tab is Videos. This is structured around themes, i.e. typical problems encountered by beginning teachers, such as "Having pupils enter the classroom and putting them to work", "Rituals and assignments in preschool", "Supporting pupils while working and learning" and "Handling incidents". These themes are produced in collaboration with schools.

Each theme consists of a "development film strip", i.e. a series of videos exemplifying stages through which beginning teachers proceed over time while mastering specific challenges (Leblanc & Ria, 2011, p. 40). In the first theme, "Having pupils enter the classroom and putting them to work", this challenge is how to bring pupils to enter the classroom in an orderly way and engage without delay in the learning activities planned by the teacher. The first video in this theme shows beginning teacher Romain waiting helplessly while pupils boisterously enter the classroom. The second video shows beginning teacher Séverine in the same situation, but beginning to negotiate with pupils. In the third video, teacher Nora uses an individual writing activity that will keep pupils quiet as a bargaining chip. If the pupils complete this quietly, she will let them watch a film as a reward. In the fourth video, teacher Rémy hands out an assignment for a writing task to pupils already at the classroom door while they are entering. The fifth video shows how teacher Lucie greets each pupil individually at the door and instructs them as a group to move to their seats, sit down and take out their papers so that she can start the homework review. The sixth and last video shows how experienced teacher Cécile uses minimal nonverbal behaviours signalling to pupils that it is normal and rewarding for them to come into the classroom quietly and cooperate in a writing activity.

Each video is accompanied by subordinate tabs giving access to a description of what is at stake in the teaching situation shown, a series of perceptive clues that viewers can look for and formulations of teacher concerns and professional knowledge relevant to the situation shown. In addition, video examples of other teachers as well as comments on video by experts are provided. An important element of each theme, finally, is a self-confrontation interview with the teacher, in which the interviewer and the teacher look back together on the classroom events shown. During these interviews, the teacher voices the intentions and concerns involved for her or him personally.

The rationale behind these design features of Néopass@ction is that the viewer should be enabled to step into the shoes of the teachers shown, to relive their experience and thereby make connections with their own experience (Leblanc & Ria, 2011, p. 43–49). While the classroom video shows, as it were, the outer side of the teacher's experience, the self-confrontation interview opens up its inner side. The effect intended with the video material is what Lussi Borer and Muller (2016) call "mimetic engagement", the phenomenon described similarly by Laurillard (1993, p. 114) with the word "vicarious". The function of the accompanying texts is to frame the events shown by the video in a more general understanding of teaching and learning. In the first theme on Néopass@ction, this understanding is about the need to establish efficient behavioural routines in a learning group and how to achieve such routines.

Just as with the CVLL, the design of Néopass@ction and the research into it stand in the tradition of francophone ergonomics (cf. Durand, 2013; Filliettaz & Billett, 2015). The research is therefore predominantly exploratory and qualitative. The effects on users identified by research are summarised by Leblanc and Ria (2011, p. 49) as follows:

> (a) reassurance and removal of guilt among beginning teachers thanks to their new awareness of the more or less inevitable passages they must go through to acquire skills in this occupation, (b) spontaneous recall of real experiences favoured by video-based classroom situations possessing a "*family resemblance*" with their own ways of exercising the profession, (c) comparison of users' real experiences, not only with experiences presented in classroom videos but also with "*professional experience*" videos and/or "*commented*" videos, allowing them to evaluate their own practices as they see themselves through the eyes of others, and (d) projection into the future leading to the anticipation of as-yet unknown scenarios, and foreseeing other possible ones to be tested in one's own classroom, while drawing from experience acquired by peers.

In a later study of six beginning teachers aged 23 to 25 years and teaching different secondary school subjects, the influence of their individual viewing activity of Néopass@ction videos on their classroom teaching was explored (Flandin & Gaudin, 2014; Gaudin et al., 2014). The teachers first viewed the film strip "Having pupils enter the classroom and putting them to work" described above. Then, lessons they taught themselves were recorded. Finally, their retrospective statements about these lessons were recorded during self-confrontation interviews. Content analyses of these data showed that the beginning teachers concretely related the intentions and actions of the teachers viewed to their own teaching experiences. Their mimetic engagement led them to consider and elaborate alternative teaching practices that they saw as viable options for their own teaching. This impact occurred especially, when what the beginning teachers viewed "resonated" with concerns they had about their own teaching. However, the teachers found implementing the alternative practices viewed on Néopass@ction sometimes hard when they could not communicate about this with colleagues.

The data sources of this study were further analysed in the dissertation research by Flandin (2015; Flandin & Ria, 2015). In this research, also recordings of the respondents' browsing activity on Néopass@ction were analysed. This showed that the beginning teachers engaged in two kinds of sequences. During opening sequences, they explored and identified couplings between instructional issues and practices which they felt could address their personal concerns. This exploratory activity then led to inquiry sequences, during which the beginning teachers evaluated what instructional practices were viable and desirable for them to adopt or adapt in their own lessons. "Echoes" of these deliberations could be traced in the instructional behaviour they displayed in their own lessons.

In sum, Néopass@ction appears to elicit the kinds of uses that its design aims for. The available evidence indicates that the platform is able to support teachers by offering them a window on alternatives for instructional action and encouraging them to judge for themselves if and how they will engage in similar teaching practices.

Summary

Video platforms appear capable of supporting teachers in reconsidering and changing their teaching, when they offer visual and verbal information that they experience as practically relevant (Néopass@ction).

Both substance and form of video platforms influence how teachers use them. Substantive features promoting such use appear to be the specificity and quality of the information provided (Leraar24, Néopass@ction). Form features promoting the use of video platforms are their structure, accessibility and navigability (Teachers TV, Leraar24) as well as opportunities to experience other teachers' classroom behaviour vicariously (Teachers TV, Néopass@ction). In addition, school context factors contributing to the actual use of video platforms as a PD resource are the availability of working time for teachers (Teachers TV, Leraar24) and opportunities for collaboration with colleagues (Néopass@ction).

Computer-supported collaborative learning around video

Since the introduction of electronic learning environments enabling computer-supported collaborative learning (CSCL), a host of software platforms has been developed that teachers can use for professional collaboration. A specific variety of these platforms centres on the use of video. These applications usually include opportunities for viewing and editing video clips, downloading and uploading study resources and communicating with colleagues, teacher educators and other professionals. Access is usually restricted to groups affiliated with educational institutions.

In this section, I describe a selection of such applications from the US, the UK and Switzerland.

Video Interactions for Teaching and Learning

Video Interactions for Teaching And Learning (VITAL) is a CSCL platform developed at Teachers College of Columbia University, New York (http://ccnmtl.columbia.edu/vital/nsf/index.html). VITAL grew from a course entitled "Development of Mathematical Thinking," created and taught for master's students in early childhood education by professor Herbert Ginsburg. In his course, Ginsburg had been using a collection of analog video home system (VHS) tapes built up during twenty years of research. VITAL was developed in order to make this video material more widely and more flexibly available in a way that could contribute to raising the quality of early childhood mathematics education.

To achieve this goal, a development project was funded by the National Science Foundation (NSF), which was driven by three assumptions. Firstly, by enabling prospective teachers to observe concrete examples of pupils' learning and to interpret these carefully, they would learn to use evidence to understand learning. Secondly, this ability would increase their willingness to base professional judgement and decision-making on sound pedagogical theory. These short-term outcomes would, thirdly, promote their teaching competence in the long term (Moretti & Ginsburg, 2009).

In order to further these outcomes, the VITAL learning environment was designed as follows. A course in VITAL contains – besides the usual electronic syllabus in which students find all necessary course information – a library of video clips and a series of viewing assignments linked to reading materials. The video library is a digitised update and expansion of Ginsburg's VHS tapes. The clips in this library show clinical interviews and classroom lessons during which young children engage with mathematics topics such as number, shape and patterns. Clinical interviewing is a method, derived from Piaget's developmental psychology, which makes it possible to understand what a child knows and how it learns at a given moment (Ginsburg, 1997; Ginsburg, Jacobs, & Lopez, 1998). In addition, VITAL provides users with a video viewer, a video editor and a personal writing space. They use these tools not only during course sessions, but also anytime anywhere, as part of individual study. A video clip about the VITAL interface is available at: http://ccnmtl.columbia.edu/vital/nsf/environment.html.

The learning activities that prospective teachers undertake in VITAL are based on the principle of "guided viewing". This means that they do not just view the clips in the video library. This is only a first step. Students prepare each weekly course session by closely examining specific events in assigned video clips. To help them do so, VITAL provides detailed prompts and rubrics. Students view the clips first as a whole and then with pauses. In response to prompts such as "What mathematical concepts are the children exploring?" they must annotate specific moments in the video with tagged comments (Lee, Ginsburg, & Preston, 2007, p. 9). In one clip about number conservation, for example, a boy is shown repeatedly counting building blocks. However, when the blocks are covered, he cannot yet remember how many blocks there were. The prospective teachers observing this clip are required to write notes describing how they analyse and interpret the child's thinking and to point out – by editing and tagging clip segments – on which evidence they base their notes. They synthesise this work in a multimedia essay of maximally 350 words, which they upload in VITAL and about which they receive feedback from the course instructor and fellow students. Student teachers conclude their course participation with a final project, in which they analyse video recordings of their own teaching activities during field placements.

The results of the VITAL development project include the dissemination of the software and research evidence. The software is available for distribution to educational institutions and has been applied in curricula for social work, dentistry, film and dance. Besides exploratory research about users' experiences with VITAL, an experimental study of learning effects on students has been reported.

Four exploratory studies conducted by Cornelia Brunner yielded the following indications. Five course instructors were enthusiastic about the usability of the VITAL software. Content analysis of 74 students' reflection assignments showed that at the beginning of the course, 35 were in doubt about the pedagogy advocated. At the end, however, they had shifted their attitudes in a positive direction. Content analysis of 34 students' final project reports showed that half of them referred to the pedagogical theory offered in the course, which suggests that some students succeeded better in relating teaching practice to theory than others. Another finding was that when students' video clips made pupils' learning well visible, this promoted critical thinking about their own teaching (Moretti & Ginsburg, 2009, p. 11–20). Content analysis of 87 critical incident reports produced by 57 students from two courses showed that they experienced the features of VITAL as efficient, especially for creating arguments in course assignments. Over time, the comments in their reports shifted significantly from VITAL's efficiency towards what their use of it contributed to their own learning (p < .05) (Moretti & Ginsburg, 2009, Appendix D).

Learning effects of working with VITAL were studied in a randomised controlled experiment by Michael Preston. 60 student teachers in early childhood or elementary mathematics from ten colleges and universities around the US were randomly and blindly assigned to one of three conditions. Twenty students in a "guided video group" participated in seven VITAL sessions during which they viewed and analysed lesson fragments about the topic of number. After each fragment, they answered a question requiring them to describe or interpret the behaviour of the child shown, hypothesise about what the child knows, predict what will follow or suggest further questions, tasks or strategies for teaching. Twenty students in an "unguided video group" viewed the same video material, but unsegmented and without prompting questions. Twenty students in a control group engaged in no video-supported activities and only completed the same pre- and post-tests as administered to all groups.

The pre- and post-tests consisted of a transfer task to analyse an unsegmented video clip about a different early mathematics topic, understanding pattern. Participants had to respond to two summative questions about the child's knowledge and about how to continue teaching her or him. The respondents' 120 essays were coded reliably (r > .80) in four categories. It was assessed how they (1) substantiated claims, (2) used observable behaviours as evidence, (3) interpreted these behaviours and (4) displayed intellectual modesty through qualifying statements showing awareness of what they felt they could or could not conclude from the available evidence. Between- and within-group comparisons were conducted by means of ANOVA.

The results showed that neither the unguided video group nor the control group progressed over time on any of the four categories. However, the guided video group did significantly improve in interpretive skill and intellectual modesty (p < .01). The implications of these findings are that by using the guided viewing approach as developed in the VITAL project, teacher educators can promote prospective teachers' interpretive abilities and their awareness of the boundaries of their observations of pupil learning (Moretti & Ginsburg, 2009, p. 20–23; Preston, 2010).

In sum, the developers of VITAL have carefully designed, purposefully implemented and successfully disseminated well-functioning CSCL software for video-supported professional education. There is positive evidence of short-term learning effects on prospective teachers' observation and interpretation skills. An open question remains what improving professional judgement and decision-making in this way contributes to teaching competence in the long term.

IRIS Connect

IRIS Connect is a commercial platform developed in the UK, which offers a package of DV facilities designed specifically for the purpose of teachers' professional learning (www.irisconnect.com/uk/). This package includes both hardware and software for capturing, editing and sharing footage of classroom teaching. The hardware consists of two iPads mounted on tripods for simultaneous recording of the teacher and pupils. The software allows footage to be uploaded immediately after recording to a secure online platform. Teachers, mentors and teacher educators – within and/or outside the school involved – can then edit it and view and comment the resulting clips. As in VITAL, these comments can be tagged to the exact clip sections to which they pertain. Additional features include in-ear coaching and the use of smart phones. IRIS Connect can be used by teachers in all school subjects and educational sectors.

The philosophy behind IRIS Connect is to enable teams of teachers to collaborate in PLCs with a focus on improving instructional behaviour. The platform is therefore not intended to be used for teacher appraisal. It is, instead, designed to give teachers full control over all recordings of their own teaching. Only the teacher decides with whom she or he shares any video and IRIS Connect takes elaborate care to safeguard confidentiality.

IRIS Connect has provided on its web site three evaluation studies of teachers' use of the platform. The first is an exploratory survey among 99 teachers in 30 British schools (31% primary and 69% secondary schools), who used IRIS Connect for one month or longer (Preston, 2013). Following are modal findings about how they used IRIS Connect, how they experienced the collegial collaboration it supported and what impact they felt this had on their work.

Before using IRIS Connect, 66.7% of the teachers in this survey had never seen themselves teaching. 67.4% had sometimes shared their lessons or had lessons shared with them using IRIS Connect. The platform was used most for self-review and reflection (94%), peer review and coaching (68%) and sharing best practice with colleagues in the school (58%).

66.3% of the teachers felt that using IRIS Connect had a positive impact on collaborative practice in their school. 79.5% thought that as a consequence of using IRIS Connect there had been an increase in teachers talking to teachers about teaching. 67.7% thought that using IRIS Connect had increased the level of collaboration among colleagues in the school. 75% felt that using IRIS Connect had a positive impact on their confidence as a teacher. 74.7% felt that using IRIS Connect had a positive impact on their teaching. 52.8% felt that using IRIS Connect had promoted an improvement in pupil outcomes.

In the second study (Davies, Perry, & Kirkman, 2017), the experiences were explored of 92 British teachers in eleven primary schools, who used IRIS Connect during projects to develop their skills in dialogic teaching. During a six-month period, the participating teachers recorded their teaching, selected and shared clips with their colleagues on the platform and discussed these in monthly group meetings focussing on aspects of dialogic teaching.

The following dependable findings emerged from metrics data provided by IRIS Connect and from retrospective surveys among the participating teachers and project leaders. Considerable variation existed between the schools in the amount of working time they assigned to teachers for participating. Differences also existed in how teachers were selected for participation. In five schools, teachers were selected by the school management. In three schools, teachers volunteered, whereas in the three remaining schools, all teachers participated. Five schools had prior experience with IRIS Connect, while six schools had not.

During collaboration, the teacher teams in four schools were considerably more active than those in the other schools. On average, 2.7 clips per user were created with an average duration of 1.36 minutes. An analysis of videos shared with the researchers showed that the audibility of pupil talk in classroom recordings was sometimes insufficient. During their group activity, 71.7% of the teachers viewed clips from group members once or more times. 67.4% viewed clips from other schools once or more times. 45.7% collaborated in planning, teaching and reviewing lessons – as in Lesson Study (Dudley, 2015) – once or more times.

The project leaders reported that over time, it was generally a functional sequence for the participating teachers to first view clips of other teachers and then of their own teaching. An important issue while facilitating the discussion about these clips was how much structure to introduce. In the experience of the project leaders, a more open style of facilitation appeared to promote more transfer among participants, in the sense of applying insights gained to other aspects of instruction than those momentarily discussed. Most project leaders made a positive cost–benefit analysis of using IRIS Connect and all but one of them said they would use IRIS Connect again in the future.

Also a majority of the participating teachers stated that they would use IRIS Connect again. They clearly experienced benefits from using IRIS Connect. However, they felt that the purpose and focus of collegial collaboration for PD should be clear and that school management should consider carefully how to orga-nise it. In particular, they saw as important whether participation is voluntary or not and how much working time is assigned for participation. Concerning outcomes in their practice, 87% of the teachers responded positively to the open-ended question if IRIS Connect had helped them make changes in their instruction. In descending order of frequency, they reported changes specifically in their questioning behav-iour, in how they gave pupils feedback and in how they used instructional language. Furthermore, they felt that their participation had raised their level of reflection and awareness and helped them identify professional learning needs.

The third evaluation is a case study of the use of IRIS Connect in a South African context (Simons, 2017; the references in the remainder of this section are to pages in this report). Six schools in township areas in the Ekurhuleni South District near Johannesburg were involved, which were facing challenges in pupils' school participation and mathematics performance. Six pairs of lower-secondary teachers, half of them newly qualified and half more experienced, participated in a six-month collaboration endeavour during which they were mentored by two British teacher educators. The teachers participated on a voluntary basis and were motivated to develop their teaching. The main project goals were to increase teachers' awareness of how pupils learn mathematics and the ability to assess pupils' understanding of mathematics as well as developing their use of questioning and differentiation dur-ing instruction.

The intervention consisted of three phases. First, the schools' management and teachers were introduced to the project during on-site visits, followed by an online induction session during which the teachers learned how to use the IRIS Connect platform. Then, a one-week on-site contact session took place in each school in order to develop engagement and rapport between the teachers and the British teacher educator assigned to their school. During this phase, the project goals were further specified to fit the teachers' personal learning needs. The third and main phase con-sisted of online video mentoring sessions, during which each teacher was requested to send in biweekly a minimum of three video reflections. The teachers could choose by themselves which lessons fragments they found relevant to share. Consequently, clips from different parts of lessons and of different lengths were uploaded.

The project was studied with a mixed-methods design. The data sources included pre- and post-project questionnaires and evaluation forms, diaries written by the British teacher educators during the contact sessions, telephone interviews and an analysis of recorded footage. The respondents were the participating teachers and their heads of department. The response percentages for these data sources ranged between 58% and 100%. The findings indicate how the contact sessions and the online mentoring sessions were conducted, what benefits the teachers experienced from their participation and how they developed their instruction (p. 14–62).

During the one-week contact session, the teachers learned to use IRIS Connect and built a working relationship with their mentor. However, Internet connection was frequently unavailable or intermittent. This seriously hampered the project and was probably one reason why, during the second phase of online mentoring sessions, not all teachers succeeded in completing the three intended cycles of recording, sharing and reflecting on instances of their classroom teaching. Eventually, at the end of the project, six teachers had completed three such cycles, three teachers two cycles and three teachers were active in their first cycle. The problems with Internet connection also prevented the teachers from sharing video and verbal information via the IRIS Connect platform as much as intended. Even so, all the teachers found the recording equipment and the platform easy to use.

The British teacher educators found the teachers' mathematics content knowledge to be sound, so in substance, the project was henceforward focussed on mathematics pedagogy (p. 28). Looking back on the benefits they experienced from participation, "80% of the teachers 'agreed' or 'strongly agreed' that they would recommend this training to others" (p. 60). About the outcomes of participation, 80% "'agreed' or 'strongly agreed' that the training had helped to develop their teaching practice" (p. 29). This response was especially positive among those teachers who completed more reflection cycles. Also 80% "'agreed' or 'strongly' agreed that the project had helped improve their learners' behaviour in class" in the sense of participation and engagement during the lessons (p. 34).

The outcomes found in teachers' instructional behaviour related to the following aspects. 80% "of the teachers 'agreed' or 'strongly agreed' that the project had helped them improve their classroom organisation" by placing their pupils more evenly in the classroom and having them keep their desks more orderly (p. 42). They also felt they came to understand differentiation better, put more work into lesson planning including learner activities and "moving away from textbooks and using other resources" (p. 33–41). Last, but not least, teachers began changing their questioning behaviour. The mentors' classroom observations during the contact sessions had shown that pupil passivity and choral responses to closed teacher questions of the type "Right or wrong?" were the prevailing pattern during lessons. As indicated by analysis of the shared classroom footage, six of the teachers had, by the end of the project, made some modest steps towards activating their pupils. They mainly did so by including questions to pupils during whole-class instruction and having them work on the board (p. 32–46).

The three studies reviewed above indicate that IRIS Connect is a complete package that teachers can learn to use within a month or so, whether in Western or non-Western contexts. The available evidence suggests that when its use is facilitated and supported in a collaborative context, this can promote reflection and behaviour change in teachers. The benefits reported by the teachers in these studies are clearly positive. However, these studies do not allow firm conclusions about the impact of teachers' work with IRIS Connect on pupils' learning.

Science Teachers Learning from Lesson Analysis

Initiatives to utilise DV for teacher learning have more than once grown from large-scale research projects in which it was used as a method for studying teaching. In the US, the Third International Mathematics and Science Study (TIMSS) was initiated, a pioneering comparative study funded by the OECD, in which video records of mathematics teaching in Australia, the US, Hong Kong, Japan, the Czech Republic, the Netherlands and Switzerland were analysed (Hiebert et al., 2005). These records have been made publicly available, first on compact disc (CD) and later on the web site www.timssvideo.com.

In their book *The Teaching Gap*, James Stigler and James Hiebert, two leading TIMSS researchers, argue on the basis of the project's video analyses that improving pupil achievement is not so much a matter of reorganising schools and raising the stakes of accountability as it is of enabling teachers to collaborate on making their instruction more effective (Stigler & Hiebert, 1999). Teaching, Stigler and Hiebert argue, is a cultural practice, which as such differs between countries. Accordingly, efforts at improving teaching must take into account how teachers are used to doing their work and how they interpret it.

TIMSS became the forerunner of LessonLab, a PD provider which developed Visibility, a CSCL platform designed to support groups of teachers in improving their instruction. Visibility was an environment for online and blended learning with video records of teaching as the central element. It enabled users to view other teachers' teaching and study the underlying lesson plans, related teaching materials and other relevant documents. Users could also upload and annotate video clips, share their tagged comments and communicate about them. LessonLab developed and provided courses for mathematics and science teachers, in which trained facilitators used Visibility to encourage groups of collaborating teachers to analyse their instruction and make it more effective. The features of Visibility are generic, which in principle made the platform usable for teachers in all school subjects and sectors of education. LessonLab was eventually bought by Pearson Education and – unfortunately – discontinued.

Science Teachers Learning from Lesson Analysis (STeLLA) is a PD programme developed by LessonLab for primary teachers teaching science topics in the upper grades. It was first carried out with teachers in California, then on a larger scale in Colorado. Both programmes, STeLLA-I and STeLLA-II respectively, were based on the consensus in the literature about the features of effective PD (see the section *Professional development* in Chapter 1). A fundamental assumption was also that teachers' thinking about lesson content, i.e. their science content knowledge, is deeply intertwined with their view of how pupils learn, i.e. their pedagogical content knowledge (PCK). This is why STeLLA operated from a conceptual framework providing teachers with a combination of two "lenses" for analysing science teaching.

The "Science Content Storyline" lens comprises teaching strategies to "create a coherent science content storyline" such as "Select content representations matched to the learning goal and engage students in their use". The "Student Thinking" lens comprises teaching strategies "to reveal, support, and challenge student thinking", such as "Engage students in interpreting and reasoning about ideas data and observations" (Taylor, Roth, Wilson, Stuhlsatz, & Tipton, 2017, p. 245; see also the overviews in Roth et al., 2017, p. 21–22). Structured video analysis tasks focussed on these two kinds of teaching strategies were used by trained facilitators to support teachers in analysing video cases of physics teaching, first cases of exemplary teaching by other teachers, then recordings of their own teaching. Characteristic prompts from the lesson analysis protocol used are the following: "What do students seem to understand (or not) about the sun's effect on climate and seasons?" and

> Point to a specific place in the video transcript lesson plan, or student work that supports your claim. Connect your claim and evidence with reasoning based on STeLLA Strategies, research on learning, your teaching experience, or scientific principles. Also look for evidence that challenges your claim. Consider an alternative interpretation or explanation.
>
> (Roth et al., 2017, p. 12)

STeLLA-I and STeLLA-II were both programmed in three phases. Teachers participated voluntarily. They first received science content instruction from university scientists and engaged in analysing videos of teaching practice during a summer institute lasting three and two weeks, respectively. Then, during the first half of the subsequent school year, the participants taught lesson plans provided by the PD programme themselves alongside monthly 3.5-hour group meetings in which they analysed videos of each other's teaching and their pupils' learning. Finally, during the second half of the school year, the participants developed and taught plans of their own for series of lessons about other science topics, again alongside monthly 3.5-hour group meetings for analysing videos of teaching and learning in each other's classrooms. In total, these PD activities amounted to 102 and 88.5 hours, respectively (Roth et al., 2011; Taylor et al., 2017).

The impact of the two STeLLA programmes has been researched in two quantitative experimental studies in which data were collected not only from teachers, but also from pupils. Outcome data were compared between as well as within groups. The teachers in the control groups who did not participate in the STeLLA PD programmes experienced a "content deepening programme" involving only science content, but no video analysis activities. In STeLLA-I, this programme for the control group was provided only during the summer institute. In STeLLA-II, it was continued during the school year.

The research instruments used were standardised tests measuring teachers' science content knowledge ($r = .95$) and ability to analyse lessons (based on the work of Kersting, 2008 and Kersting et al., 2014; $r = 85\%$ or higher), observation instruments regarding teaching practices with "at least a moderate degree of inter-rater agreement" (Roth et al., 2011, p. 126–127) and tests of pupils' science content learning ($r =$ at least .74) (Taylor et al., 2017, p. 258).

The data of both studies were analysed by means of ANOVA and hierarchical linear modelling (HLM). In the STeLLA-I study, knowledge gains were compared between 32 teachers who did and sixteen teachers who did not participate in the PD programme. For the participating teachers, also changes over time in lesson analysis abilities and the use of teaching strategies were analysed. In addition, the learning outcomes were compared of one cohort of 725 pupils taught by teachers before their participation in STeLLA and another cohort of 765 pupils after these teachers' participation.

The main outcomes of the STeLLA-I study are the following. The teachers in the experimental group increased their science content knowledge and lesson analysis abilities during the summer institute to a significantly higher degree than those in the control group. During the subsequent school year, these levels declined, but remained still higher at the end of the school year than in the control group ($p < .05$ or lower; Roth et al., 2011, p. 130). The STeLLA teachers also significantly improved their classroom use of teaching strategies ($p < .05$ or lower) with one exception, i.e. asking elicitation questions. On average, they asked one elicitation question per lesson before as well as after participation (Roth et al., 2011, p. 134). Asking such questions is apparently difficult for teachers.

The pupils taught after teachers' participation in STeLLA-I reached significantly higher achievement levels than those taught before it ($p < .05$ or lower). HLM analyses were carried out to find out if pupils' learning gains could be attributed to particular teaching strategies used by their teachers. These models indicated that the pupils' gains in science learning were significantly associated with the teachers' science content knowledge ($p = .075$), their lesson analysis abilities ($p = .001$) and their use of four Science Content Storyline strategies: linking activities to the learning goal, providing opportunities for students to use content representations matched to the learning goal, linking science content ideas with activities and linking science content ideas with other content ideas ($p < .001$ or lower; Roth et al., 2011, p. 133–135).

The outcomes of the STeLLA-II study confirm the patterns found in the STeLLA-I study. Again, statistically significant effects on teachers were found (Roth et al., 2017, p. 5). Pupil achievement levels in STeLLA-II were compared between 1,485 pupils whose teachers did and 1,338 pupils whose teachers did not participate in the PD programme. The STeLLA teachers' pupils significantly outperformed the pupils of the teachers in the control group (Taylor et al., 2017, p. 262–263).

The studies of the STeLLA programme have a special significance in several respects. Findings on outcomes of video-based learning extending to relatively large numbers of teachers *and* their pupils are scarce. The HLM analyses conducted in the STeLLA studies have yielded important indications that improvements in specific instructional behaviours can, in turn, exert a positive influence on pupils' learning achievement. These indications confirm the evidence produced in the research by Kersting et al. (2010, 2012) that the quality of teachers' instructional behaviour is a mediating factor, which can enhance or detract from pupil learning (cf. the section *Developing lesson analysis abilities* above).

Roth and colleagues conclude that the STeLLA studies confirm the consensus in the literature about the features of effective PD. Looking back on STeLLA, they add to this conclusion by pointing out which features of the programme were, in their experience, particularly effective. These were, firstly, the clarity and specificity of the programme's goals and the depth with which they were addressed.

Indispensable features were, secondly, the video-based analysis and scaffolding of effective teaching practice. Thirdly, the combination of content knowledge and PCK and how it was adjusted to the participating teachers' specific work situation and, finally, the support by expert PD leaders contributed to the programme's effectiveness (Roth et al., 2017, p. 20). As the researchers note, further research accounting for the mechanisms involved in teachers' PD is indeed necessary (Roth et al., 2017, p. 3). Clarification of these mechanisms requires also qualitative inquiry.

Summary

Teachers judge CSCL software facilitating viewing, annotating and communicating about classroom video as learnable and usable (VITAL, IRIS Connect). This software can be implemented in institutional contexts to support teachers' PD (IRIS Connect). When it is, guided and focussed viewing of classroom video can help teachers interpret pupil learning (VITAL, STeLLA) and support them in changing their instructional behaviour in the direction of activating pupils (IRIS Connect, STeLLA). There is also empirical evidence that content-focussed video-based teacher PD in a blended learning environment supported by CSCL can raise the quality of teachers' instruction and thus contribute to raising pupils' learning achievement (STeLLA).

Online support of classroom teaching

Most of the applications described above involve teachers working together in groups in local settings. One exception are online video platforms, which can be used in groups, but also on an individual basis. In this section, two applications are described in which video is used as a medium for supporting teachers individually through online video use. Both were developed in the US.

Best Foot Forward

In 2012, the Center for Education Policy Research (CERP) of Harvard University started a project with the aim of making the existing procedures in schools for evaluating teachers' performance more efficient and more useful for teachers' professional learning. The idea behind this project was that teachers should get more opportunities to show their administrators what are their best classroom practices as well as the challenges involved in them, in other words to put their Best Foot Forward (BFF). The BFF project introduced an approach to substitute administrators' in-person lesson observations by video records serving as a basis for conversations between teachers and administrators. This could also help solve the problem that schools' organisation can make it difficult to conduct classroom visits during instructional hours. The BFF strategy should be usable for teachers and administrators in all subjects and school types.

In the BFF approach, teachers choose and record lessons which they feel show the best of their professional competence. They send these videos to the observer through a secure, password-protected platform. The observer then views the videos and provides the teacher with feedback, which can but must not include ratings on specific aspects of teaching. Finally, the teacher and observer meet to discuss the video, the feedback and possible next steps. To support schools, BFF has made available a *Video Observation Toolkit* containing resources in four areas covering how to 1. use video for teacher development, 2. cultivate trust and guarantee privacy in conducting video observations, 3. implement the necessary technology effectively and 4. gauge a school's readiness for and success in using BFF (https://cepr.harvard.edu/video-observation-toolkit). During the CERP project, also training for administrators and instructions for teachers were available.

Two studies have been carried out in which the experiences of teachers and administrators with BFF during the first and second year of implementation are described (Kane, Gehlbach, Greenberg, Quinn, & Thal, 2015 and Quinn, Kane, Greenberg, & Thal, 2018 respectively). In both studies, surveys were conducted among participants in four states, Colorado, Delaware, Georgia and California. The respondents were randomly assigned on the school level to treatment groups using BFF and control groups using in-person lesson observation. In the first-year study, 347 teachers in different school types were involved, 162 in the BFF condition and 185 in the control condition. In the second-year study, 295 elementary teachers were involved, 148 in the BFF condition and 147 in the control condition. Below, the most conspicuous findings are summarised. Where differences found between treatment and control groups are involved, these are differences larger than five percentage points and have a statistical significance $p < .05$.

In the first year of implementation, video-supported observation enabled administrators in the treatment group – as intended – to view and give feedback on teachers' classroom work during non-instructional hours. Two thirds of the administrators logged in during those hours (Kane et al., 2015, p. 21).

In order to check how representative the videos submitted by the teachers in the treatment group were for their regular classroom work, the researchers had a random sample of video recordings that were or were not submitted for BFF assessed by external raters. These raters used the standardised classroom observation instrument CLASS (Pianta & Hamre, 2009; see for more information the next section). It was not known to the raters if the videos they assessed had been submitted or not. The outcome was that for "two-thirds of teachers, the average score on the submitted lesson was higher than the non-submitted lessons. However, … the teachers who scored better on their submitted lessons also tended to score higher on their unsubmitted lessons" (Kane et al., 2015, p. 10). Another finding about the nature of the video material in the BFF project was that the administrators in the treatment group found teacher activities better visible than pupils' activities (Kane et al., 2015, p. 23).

The use of video appeared to influence teachers' perception of their classroom behaviour. The teachers in the treatment group tended to be more critical of their own teaching than those in the control group, notably regarding time management, classroom management and assessing pupils' mastery of content (Kane et al., 2015, p. 19). Also, the teachers in the treatment group found the classroom observation process fairer and more productive than in-person observation. They found their observer more supportive and they identified more changes in their teaching practice as a result of feedback from their administrator. Finally, they shared video of their teaching more with colleagues (Kane et al., 2015, p.17). This last finding also surfaced in the second year of BFF implementation (Quinn et al., 2018, p. 20).

In sum, the evidence available about the implementation of BFF suggests that video use in a setting of teacher evaluation can help shift its emphasis from a summative into a formative direction. However, these studies do little more than bring a possible trend to light. BFF does appear to have encouraged the communication among teachers and administrators about professional issues, but this is just one of the conditions conducive to teacher development.

MyTeachingPartner

MyTeachingPartner (MTP) is an online coaching system developed on the basis of theory and research by Robert Pianta, Bridget Hamre, Joseph Allen and colleagues of the Center for Advanced Study of Teaching and Learning (CASTL) at the Curry School of Education and Human Development of the University of Virginia. MTP is marketed internationally through Teachstone (https://teachstone.com).

Conceptually, MTP is based on the Teaching Through Interactions (TTI) framework. Pianta, Hamre and Allen developed this framework to fill the gap they saw in theory and research about effective teaching. Large-scale multilevel research into pupils' learning achievement in the United States has demonstrated that teachers' classroom behaviour is by far the strongest predictor of achievement. This research, however, has not identified the concrete teacher behaviours responsible for the production of learning. This leaves unaddressed the issue which teaching behaviours should be improved or changed to better foster learning gains in pupils (Pianta, Hamre, & Allen, 2012). This gap is what the CASTL team sought to remedy in the TTI framework. This framework assumes that the quest for effective teaching behaviours should focus on systematic observation of the daily interaction between teachers and pupils in the classroom, rather than on outcome measures of learning or teacher self-reports. The reason for this focus is that classroom interaction is the central or mediating factor influencing pupils' engagement and achievement in learning (Pianta & Hamre, 2009). This interactionist perspective stems from an ecological or systems paradigm (Bronfenbrenner, 1979; Pianta et al., 2012).

Given these arguments, the next step in the CASTL team's work was to operationalise the Classroom Assessment Scoring System (CLASS), a system for observing effective classroom interaction (Pianta, La Paro, & Hamre, 2008). The TTI framework and CLASS categorise effective teaching practices in three interwoven domains: Emotional Supports, Classroom Organisation and Instructional Supports.

Each domain is subdivided in dimensions and indicators which observers and teachers can use. Emotional Supports refers to interactions supportive of a positive classroom climate and respectful communication, teachers' sensitivity and regard for pupil perspectives. This domain is theoretically grounded in attachment theory (Ainsworth, Blehar, Waters, & Wall, 1978; Bowlby, 1997) and self-determination theory (Ryan & Deci, 2000). Classroom Organisation refers to behaviour management conducive to learning, maintaining efficient routines during learning activity and the use of diverse groupings and formats for activating learners. Instructional Supports refers to general and content-specific teaching strategies that foster content knowledge, analysis and reasoning, knowledge of procedures and skills as well as teacher feedback behaviour and instructional dialogue aiming at learning with understanding (Stuhlman, Hamre, Downer, & Pianta, 2007). The latter two domains are grounded in process-product research into effective teaching (Brophy & Good, 1986; Dunkin & Biddle, 1974).

Different versions of CLASS were and are being developed for use in different educational sectors and countries. Evidence for the ability of these standardised observation instruments to capture teaching behaviours suited to fostering learning gains, in other words for the content validity of CLASS, was found in several large-scale studies. These were carried out first in 4,341 preschool to elementary classrooms (Hamre et al., 2013), then in 1,482 and 37 secondary classrooms (Allen et al., 2013; Hafen et al., 2015). In particular, the studies in secondary education produced evidence that specific teaching behaviours promoted learning achievement in adolescents.

> In the Emotional Support domain, teachers' ability to establish a positive emotional climate (Positive Climate), their sensitivity to student needs (Teacher Sensitivity), and their structuring of their classroom and lessons in ways that recognize adolescents' needs for a sense of autonomy and control, for an active role in their learning, and for opportunities for peer interaction (Regard for Adolescent Perspectives) were all associated with higher relative student achievement, after covarying baseline levels of such achievement. Similarly, use of instructional learning formats that encouraged active participation by students and that provided variety in classroom approaches (Instructional Learning Formats) was also predictive of student achievement, as were lessons that required high levels of analysis and problem solving by students (Analysis and Problem Solving). ... Notably, two of the domains of teacher–student interaction quality that were assessed, emotional and instructional support, were more strongly related to achievement in smaller as opposed to larger classrooms. One explanation for these findings is that qualities such as sensitivity to student needs or provision of high-quality feedback to students might have the greatest effect when they are concentrated among relatively fewer students. Conversely, the effect of these factors might be relatively diluted in very large classrooms.

(Allen et al., 2013, p. 14)

These effects were more pronounced when class sizes were smaller.

MTP was developed on the basis of the theoretical and empirical groundwork described above. MTP consists of three components: a video library with examples of best practice; a three-credit college course focussed on developing teachers' knowledge about effective interactions and their skills in identifying and applying these in their own classrooms; and web-mediated individualised coaching. Teachers usually work with MTP during one school year. During this year, they record their work in the classroom every two weeks on video and discuss it with a licensed coach during online conferences. During their collaboration, the teacher and the coach follow the five-step MTP cycle. The teacher (1) records a sample of her or his teaching and sends the footage through a secure connection to the coach, who (2) analyses it using selected indicators from CLASS and (3) gives the teacher feedback in the form of prompts. Then, during their online conference, the teacher and coach use these prompts to (4) discuss the teacher's practice and (5) derive an action plan for the next cycle aimed at raising the effectiveness of the teacher's practice. Over the course of a number of these cycles, the focus of collaboration shifts to different teaching behaviours, while the initiative in choosing these behaviours shifts from the coach to the teacher (see for more information https://curry.virginia.edu/myteachingpartner and for resources for practitioners on using CLASS https://curry.virginia.edu/classroom-assessment-scoring-system).

Just as the validity of CLASS, the impact of using MTP has been researched in large numbers of classrooms. The studies involved employed randomised controlled trials and standardised measures. To measure teacher behaviour and pupil engagement, mostly observation instruments were used. To measure pupil achievement, standardised tests were used. The data were analysed using multilevel techniques and significance testing. Three studies were conducted in preschool and primary classrooms and five studies in secondary classrooms. Below, I first describe one illustrative study in a preschool setting and one illustrative study in a secondary setting. Then, the main findings from all eight studies are summarised. All findings described pertain to statistically significant differences between trial and control groups.

Pianta, Mashburn, Downer, Hamre and Justice (2008) studied the impact of using MTP on the quality of pre-Kindergarten teachers' interaction with pupils. 61 teachers were randomly assigned to a Consultancy condition, in which they had access to video clips exemplifying high-quality interactions and received web-mediated MTP consultation. 52 teachers were randomly assigned to a Web-Only condition, in which they had access to video clips only. The interaction quality displayed by the teachers during their classroom work was rated using CLASS. The teachers in the Consultancy condition

> showed significantly greater increases in independent ratings of the quality of interactions than did those only receiving access to a website with video clips. The positive effects of consultation were particularly evident in classrooms with higher proportions of children who experienced economic risks
>
> (Pianta, Mashburn, et al., 2008, pp. 431 and 441–445)

The authors of this study draw the tentative conclusion that MTP has the potential for widespread use by teachers as an effective PD application. They also suggest further research into the impact of different combinations of intervention features. Impacts on teachers could differ depending on whether and how they relate the viewing of video clips of exemplary teaching to implementation efforts in their own lessons (Pianta, Mashburn, et al., 2008, p. 445–447).

Allen, Hafen, Gregory, Mikami, and Pianta (2015) and Gregory et al. (2016) studied the impact of using MTP in a sample of 86 lower-secondary, predominantly urban classrooms totalling 1,194 pupils of diverse socioeconomic backgrounds. Because of teachers' challenges and workload in this context, a modified version of MTP was implemented. Teachers participated during two school years instead of one and completed MTP coaching cycles once every six instead of two weeks. This allowed for a more extended PD experience. Teachers in the MTP condition were shown to achieve significantly higher achievement in their pupils than teachers in the control condition. This outcome was upheld in both school years and in different classrooms and school subjects (Allen et al., 2015). Significant outcomes were also evident in the social-emotional domain. Even in the year after coaching was discontinued, the number of discipline referrals of black pupils in the MTP teachers' classrooms was reduced. Specific teacher behaviours were shown to be responsible for these outcomes. The MTP teachers

> increased skills to engage students in high-level analysis and inquiry [and] exposed [their pupils] to rigorous, engaging curricula and to high expectations for engagement and achievement. A proactive, prevention-oriented approach to discipline, therefore, is a means to reduce racial disproportionality in exclusionary discipline.
>
> (Gregory et al., 2016, pp. 1 and 17–18)

In the three MTP impact studies in preschool and primary classrooms, 166 teachers and 1,159 pupils on average were involved. In the studies in secondary classrooms, 85 teachers and 1,544 pupils were on average involved. Statistically significant improvements in the quality of classroom interaction were found in one preschool study (Pianta, Mashburn, et al., 2008) and three secondary studies (Allen, Pianta, Gregory, Mikami, & Lun, 2011; Gregory, Allen, Mikami, Hafen, & Pianta, 2014; Gregory et al., 2016). Statistically significant cognitive achievement gains in pupils were found in one preschool study, i.e. improved language and literacy (Downer et al., 2011), and in two secondary studies (Allen et al., 2011, 2015). Statistically significant social-emotional outcomes in pupils resulting from changed teacher behaviours were found in one preschool study, i.e. greater social competence in children (Hamre, Pianta, Burchinal et al., 2012), and in three secondary studies, i.e. an improvement in positive peer interactions (Mikami, Gregory, Allen, Pianta, & Lun, 2011), higher student behavioural engagement (Gregory et al., 2014) and a reduction in black pupils' discipline referrals as mentioned above (Gregory et al., 2016). In the three most recent studies, evidence was found for the mediating function of teaching behaviour engaging pupils in active, higher-order learning (Allen et al., 2015; Gregory et al., 2014; Gregory et al., 2016).

In sum, the large-scale and rigorous studies into the impact of MTP have produced empirical evidence for both social-emotional and cognitive outcomes in classroom interaction and pupil learning. This research shows that using MTP for their PD enables teachers in diverse school subjects and settings to make school learning more interesting and relevant for pupils, in particular for adolescents.

Summary

Video-based web-mediated coaching of individual teachers can be cost-effective and scalable. When this type of coaching is grounded in theory and research about effective teaching and directly targets teachers' individual instructional practice and their concerns about it, it can help them become more effective and promote pupils' learning. This, in turn, can contribute to raising pupils' social-emotional competence and learning achievement (MTP). When teacher evaluation becomes video- and web-based, its emphasis may shift from a summative into a formative direction (BFF).

Functions and features of digital video applications

Together, the nineteen applications reviewed above represent the wide variety of situations in which DV is used to develop teaching competence. Evidence about these applications was summarised on the basis of 69 studies in total. Before drawing conclusions from this evidence, it will be useful to create some overview and structure in the variety of DV uses found. In this section, therefore, I first introduce concepts and terminology with the aim of determining main functions and features of DV use for teacher learning. Then, using this terminology, I distil some general trends which characterise the applications reviewed.

Concepts and terminology

DV applications can serve different functions in three domains: Orientation, Support and Assessment. As stated in Chapter 1, this book addresses the first two domains.

The domain of Orientation includes applications that enable prospective teachers to develop a concrete idea of what the teaching profession entails by viewing videos exemplifying the work of experienced teachers. Some applications aim to show the manifold ways in which teachers do their work. I call this function Illustration. Others aim to present ways in which teachers handle specific tasks such as preparing lessons or organising group work. I call this function Demonstration.

In the domain of Support, video can serve the functions of Training and Reflection. Training involves cycles of three consecutive types of activity: Instruction, Practice and Feedback. For example, programmes to develop skills in classroom management, questioning or encouraging thinking skills and social behaviour engage teachers first in instruction and study about research-based insights and examples of target skills, then in practising those skills themselves and finally in receiving and discussing feedback on their practice. The function of Reflection predominates in DV applications aiming to promote understanding of different aspects of teaching such as how teachers influence pupil learning and how they can improve their instruction.

Table 2.1 contains an overview of the applications reviewed, categorising them according to these domains and functions. None of the applications can be assigned exclusively to one function, as they usually serve more than one function at a time. Their place in Table 2.1 only indicates which function predominates in the application concerned.

Table 2.1 also characterises each application in terms of six features. The first feature, Career Phase, shows to which group or groups of teachers an application is addressed: preservice teachers, ACP candidates, beginning teachers and/or experienced teachers. The second feature, Activity Cycles, specifies which types of activities in the cycle underlying teachers' work play an explicit part in an application: preactive, interactive and/or postactive (see the section *Quality standards for teacher learning* in Chapter 1). The third feature, Setting, shows if and how computers support teachers' communication, i.e. whether they collaborate exclusively offline or online or in a combination of both, in other words in a blended setting. In each of these settings, teachers can be grouped differently, i.e. individually, in dyads and/or in larger groups. These possibilities constitute the fourth feature, Grouping. This influences how teachers cooperate and consequently, how they learn. Equally influential is the fifth feature, Video Type, which distinguishes the three types of video introduced earlier: model videos, trigger videos and action videos (see the section *Self-modelling* above). While model and trigger videos involve viewing other teachers, action videos can involve viewing both others and oneself teaching. These two options constitute the sixth feature, *Viewing*. They were termed "Other-viewing" and "Self-viewing" by François Tochon and defined as: "Process of observation, evaluation, and professional development based on the screening of others' experiences [or] on video feedback on individual experience recorded on video in a work setting", respectively (Tochon, 1999, p. 147–148).

General trends

From the description of DV applications in the previous section and the overview in Table 2.1, the following general trends can be distilled.

DV uses occur in all school types and in an increasing number of school subjects, although originally, they were often developed in mathematics and science. This is probably because governments tend to perceive and emphasise the economic relevance of educating the working population in these subjects, especially in secondary education. Similar considerations underlie the development of DV applications for promoting the teaching of literacy.

Most DV applications are directed at teachers in their preservice and experienced career phases. Those applications addressing preservice teachers predominantly

TABLE 2.1 Video functions and features

Domain	Function	Application	Career Phase: Preservice / Alternative / Beginning / Experienced	Activity: Cycles / Preactive / Interactive / Postactive	Setting: Offline / Online / Blended	Grouping: Individual / Dyad / Group	Video Type: Model / Trigger / Action	Viewing: Other / Self
Orientation	Illustration	Docucases	Pres	Pre	Off	G	M	O
		Didiclass	Pres + Alt	Pre + Post	Off + On	G	T	O
		Teachers TV	All	Pre + Post	On	I	A	O
		Leraar24	Pres + Beg	Pre	Off	G	A	O
	Demonstration	IPASS	Pres	All	Bl	I + G	M	O
		VILMS	Pres	Pre	Off	D	M	O
		Child-friendly school	Pres + Exp	Pre + Post	Off	G	M	O + S
Support	Training:	KODEK	Beg + Exp	All	Off	I + G	A	O + S
	- Instruction	Dialogic Video Cycle	Exp	All	Off	I + G	A	S
	- Practice	ECEC	Exp	All	Off	I + D	A	S
	- Feedback	STeLLA	Exp	All	Bl	I + G	M	O + S
	Reflection	Learning to notice	Pres + Exp	All	Off + Bl	I + G	M + A	O + S
		LLT	Pres + Beg	All	Off + Bl	I + G	M + A	O + S
		CVLL	Exp	Post	Off	G	A	O
		Néopass@ction	Beg	Pre + Post	On	I	A	O
		VITAL	Pres	Pre + Post	Bl	I + G	A	O + S
		IRIS Connect	All	Post	Bl	I + G	A	O + S
		Best Foot Forward	Exp	Post	Bl	I + D	A	S
		MyTeachingPartner	Alt + Exp	All	On	D	A	S

have an orientation function, while applications with a training function primarily address experienced teachers. It is characteristic for DV applications with a training function that they comprise complete activity cycles, in which preactive, interactive and postactive learning activities follow upon and influence each other.

Online and blended settings occur by definition in the use of video platforms and CSCL.

Viewing and analysis almost always take place in groups of two or more teachers, with the exception of Teachers TV and Néopass@ction, which address teachers individually. Cooperation with colleagues does tend to be combined with individual feedback when the functions of training and reflection are pursued. This is probably because feedback is often given in the context of coaching.

The three types of model, trigger and action videos appear to occur in all functions, although model videos, by definition, play a prominent part in demonstration and training.

The nature of video viewing tends to differ between domains. Other-viewing predominates in the domain of orientation, while in the domain of support, it is usually combined with self-viewing. This happens typically in the sequence of first viewing others, then oneself.

Conclusions

In this section, the three questions guiding this review are answered. The conclusions presented should be considered above all as statements about the potential of video use for supporting teacher learning. As stated in the *Method* section, the selection of sources was not exhaustive. Rather than generalising on the basis of all the available research, I aim here to formulate what kinds of "proof of existence" can be derived from the studies reviewed. In other words, the conclusions below delineate what kinds of outcomes may be expected of VTL (review question I), what kinds of processes are involved in it (review question II) and which conditions need to be fulfilled for these outcomes and processes to be realised (review question III).

Before presenting the answers to each of the review questions in separate sections, I first address different assumptions underlying the research reviewed. The main conclusions are listed in Boxes 2.1 through 2.3.

What we know and how we know it

What knowledge one may or may not derive from research depends in part on the assumptions researchers make about their object of study, in other words on the paradigm or world view within which studies are situated. Paradigmatic assumptions influence the methodology used and consequently, what different studies can contribute to explanation.

VTL is studied, broadly speaking, on the basis of three paradigms: cognitivist, interpretive and sociocultural. Each of these approaches entails its own specific interests, emphases, strengths and limitations. Below, I first characterise these three paradigms briefly. Then, following an overview of the respondents and methods involved in the studies reviewed, I illustrate how different assumptions behind their methodology influence the findings and the conclusions that may be drawn from them.

Cognitivist, interpretive and sociocultural paradigms

Historically, the cognitivist paradigm has its roots in behaviourism, which proclaimed a prohibition on studying unobservable, "internal" aspects of human behaviour. Instead, behaviourism favoured external description and studying causation through quantitative and/or experimental research designs as customary in physics. These tendencies are still recognisable in studies conducted on the basis of the cognitivist paradigm, for example those about LTN and the DVC. Today, cognitivism has moved with the times. The ban on studying internal aspects has been lifted and more research is based on the notion that knowledge development is always situated in local contexts (Brown, Collins, & Duguid, 1989). In this vein, the developers of IPASS assume that student teachers acquire applicable knowledge through "cognitive apprenticeship", i.e. engaging deeply in the type of thinking that is inherent in a specific context such as teaching (Collins et al., 1989).

The interpretive paradigm, in contrast to cognitivism, emphasises human experience and its subjectivity. Approaches such as ethnography and semiotics (Tochon, 2013) can be situated within this paradigm. Studies based on it show a preference for using qualitative methods, often in small samples. Research interest tends to focus on the processes involved in perception and meaning-making. Examples of interpretive approaches to VTL can be found in the design of Docucases and Didiclass and in the studies of the CVLL and Néopass@ction. Another example of an interpretive approach is "camera ethnography" (www.kamera-ethnographie.de), in which video is used to examine and interpret the interaction between children and adults in-depth in unique local situations (Hare, Mohn, Vogelpohl, & Wiesemann, 2019).

The socio-cultural paradigm considers human learning as principally situated in a historical and societal context. In this paradigm, influences on learning are assumed to operate on different levels: the macro-level of society at large, the meso-level of institutions and/or the micro-level of individuals. Such an ecological approach entails a focus on how teachers interact with learners in learning environments and how this interaction influences the development and outcomes of learning. Important topics in sociocultural approaches are the uses made of symbol systems and cognitive tools (Blanton, Moorman, & Trathen, 1998; Engeström, Miettinen, & Punamäki, 1999; Jonassen & Rohrer-Murphy, 1999). Elements of a sociocultural approach can be found in the studies of the CVLL, STeLLA and MTP. Also my own research fits within the sociocultural paradigm. In my view, learning can only be explained by studying the relations between its development and its outcomes, and this is best done through mixed-methods designs (Brouwer, 2010).

Whichever choices researchers make, there are two methodological issues to be solved. Firstly, a balance has to be struck between breadth and depth, i.e. not only the frequency or prevalence of phenomena needs to be determined, but also their quality or nature (Berger, 1974). Studies are often stronger in breadth and weaker in depth or vice versa. The knowledge they produce is therefore either predominantly nomo-thetic, capturing breadth and contributing to generalisation, or idiographic, capturing depth and contributing to understanding (Holzkamp, 1972, p. 35–75). In this respect, the studies reviewed in this chapter are no exception. This is evident from the following data about the numbers of respondents involved and the methods employed.

Respondents and methods

As far as could be retrieved, the number of teachers studied per intervention ranged considerably, namely between four and 503. Two interventions were researched in three studies – those from France – involving fewer than ten teachers. Eleven interventions were researched in 46 studies involving between ten and 50 teach-ers. 27 of these studies were from UCI, sixteen regarding LTN and none regarding LLT. Seven interventions were researched in nineteen studies involving more than 50 teachers. The largest numbers of teachers were involved in the research about Leraar24, BFF and MTP. Data from pupils were included in thirteen studies, in which the number of pupils ranged between 226 and 2,823. Eight of these studies were MTP impact studies. These figures mean that the greatest generalisability and robustness can be attributed to the knowledge produced by the UCI studies and the MTP impact studies.

As to the type of methods used, data collection and data analysis should be distin-guished. Data collection was wholly qualitative in the research about five interven-tions, while for four interventions, it was wholly quantitative. In the research about four interventions, qualitative and quantitative data were collected side by side. In the research about five interventions, a mixed-methods strategy was followed, i.e. qualitative and quantitative data were collected in relation to each other.

What is also important from a validity point of view is that most, namely thirteen interventions were studied with self-report instruments. Eleven interventions were studied with observation instruments. Standardised tests and assessments were least used, namely in the research about six interventions. The studies about KODEK, STeLLA and MTP should be noted for their strength in combining teacher and pupil data as well as using standardised instruments. The use of standardised class-room observation instruments makes the research into ECEC similarly strong.

Data analysis was carried out far more often with quantitative than with qualita-tive methods. Data analysis was wholly qualitative in the research about two inter-ventions, while it was wholly quantitative for twelve interventions. Qualitative and quantitative data were analysed side by side in the research about two interventions. Qualitative and quantitative analyses were combined in a mixed-methods strategy in the research about three interventions. Data analysis was thus predominantly quantitative. This is because in many studies, notably those from UCI, qualitative data were quantified through coding before they were analysed. In many of these cases, further qualitative analysis was omitted. In these cases, data analysis is limited to categorising series of events, which makes it difficult to grasp the underlying processes or mechanisms.

How assumptions influence findings and conclusions

Studies based on the cognitivist paradigm tend to consider individual teacher learning in isolation from its social context. Thus, the studies about the DVC and LTN are characterised by a singular concentration on teachers' perception, in particular their conscious perception. What the interventions aim at, almost exclusively, is to boost teachers' selective attention to and interpretation of pupils' cognitive learning. Scheiner (2016, p. 231–234) criticises the LTN studies for reducing the complexity involved in teacher learning, especially through their coding procedures. This, he argues, leads to a disregard for how teachers develop "situation awareness", i.e. being cognisant of the whole perceptual field in which they find themselves.

For prospective teachers, coming to realise what they are inclined *not* to see is at least as important as learning to focus on specific aspects of pupils' learning. It is known from research that inexperienced teachers overlook relevant signals in pupil behaviour when it comes to classroom management (Van den Bogert, 2016) and that cultural backgrounds can predispose them towards "attentional blindness" (cf. Miller & Zhou, 2007). "Interdependencies between individual and environment" (Scheiner, 2016, p. 234–235) should therefore remain within researchers' vision. Otherwise, it becomes difficult to explain how teachers' thought and action are related.

Cognitivist VTL research appears to assume a unidirectional relationship between thought and action, implying that training the perception of instruction should by itself enable teachers to enact effective instruction. This assumption is in line with the "theory-to-practice" approach to PTE programming, whose ineffectiveness was demonstrated by the research into practice shock. The phenomenon of counter attitudinal action causing discrepancy experiences explains why changes in perception do not necessarily lead to changes in action. The influence of occupational socialisation in daily school practice is probably far stronger than perception training on a university campus (cf. the section *Preservice teacher education* in Chapter 1). As Kelman (1974, p. 324) summarises, what is at play in attitude-discrepant action are

> interactions, both between deliberate choice and external constraints, and between action and attitude change. [This case] shows most clearly the engagement of attitude and action in a continuing, reciprocal, circular process. Not only is attitude an integral part of action, but action is an integral part of the development, testing and crystallization of attitudes.

A marked contrast to the cognitivist approach is provided by the research based on francophone ergonomics. The R&D work involved in the CVLL and Néopass@ction shows its interpretive character in how it takes teachers' personal concerns about teaching practice as its point of departure. In this work, noticing pupil thinking is not so much a purpose as a means towards developing teachers' competence and dispositions to act in the classroom (Flandin & Ria, 2015, p. 5). While in the R&D work at UCI the goals of teacher learning are driven by official standards and innovation mandates, teachers' personal experiences take centre stage in the French work. In practice, this difference manifests itself in the issue who decides which fragments and foci are used for video analyses. In the CVLL and Néopass@ction, this is done foremost by the teachers themselves. Gaudin et al. (2014) articulate this difference as "developmental" vs. "normative approaches". The studies about these applications reconstruct teachers' development in detail, also over longer periods than one year. The number of respondents, however, is small, which limits generalisability.

The relation between teachers' thought and action is a recurring issue in VTL research, more often implicitly than explicitly. This can be seen in the type of outcome variables used in the studies reviewed. In the research about nine interventions, outcomes were operationalised in terms of teacher thought only. In the research about two interventions – ECEC and MTP – outcomes were operationalised exclusively in terms of teacher action. In the research about seven interventions, aspects of both teacher thought and action were operationalised in the outcome variables.

The studies of the STeLLA and MTP interventions manifest most clearly an ecological approach, in which due attention is given to the macro-, meso- as well as micro-aspects of teacher learning. Not only psychological, but also sociological perspectives enter into the research questions asked and the research design. The multilevel methodology used enables examination of how the contextual factors of school organisation and school culture shape teachers' development in the profession and their agency in it. This situates these studies in the sociocultural paradigm.

Elements of this paradigm are also recognisable in studies of other interventions. Notably, the IRIS Connect evaluation studies have yielded descriptive data about how teachers' DV use was embedded in school contexts and collegial collaboration in teacher groups figures prominently in the CFS, KODEK and CVLL studies.

Outcomes: What do teachers learn when using digital video?

In 2003, reviewing the evidence available about the effectiveness of DV use in PTE, Wang and Hartley (2003, p. 129) concluded "that the effects of video technology in supporting teacher education reform are more often assumed than carefully documented". Meanwhile, researchers have produced more knowledge about the effects of VTL on both preservice and in-service teachers. However, as noted in the previous section, more studies address the effects on teachers' thought than on their action in the classroom. In their more recent literature review, Gaudin and Chaliès

(2015, p. 54) are right in calling this a paradoxical point, given the need for research to underpin practical recommendations.

The review of DV interventions in this chapter shows that these interventions aim at changing teaching behaviour in the two broad areas of classroom instruction and interaction. Specifically, they aim to encourage teachers to adjust the way they teach to the way pupils learn by increasing the variety of their instructional approaches, promoting pupils' cognitive activation and encouraging higher-order learning. The ultimate goal behind the intended changes in instruction was to increase pupils' engagement in learning as a condition for cooperation and achievement.

Most of the interventions reviewed address teaching in the foundational subjects of language and mathematics in primary and secondary education. However, also interventions addressing generic aspects of teaching such as Docucases, Didiclass and KODEK involve showing subject-specific teaching. This is inherent in the medium of video and facilitates teachers in developing their PCK. As noted above, teachers' lesson-analysis abilities and their PCK are related (Kersting et al., 2010, 2012).

The empirical evidence found shows that VTL can produce outcomes not only in teachers' professional thought and action, but also in pupils' learning.

Where effects on teachers' thought are concerned, engaging in VTL helped preservice teachers develop a deeper understanding of teaching (Docucases, CFS preservice, LTN). It helped beginning and experienced teachers consider alternative instructional practices (CFS in-service, CVLL, KODEK, Néopass@ction, IRIS Connect, STeLLA, MTP). The findings indicate that viewing and analysing video of lessons – both others' and their own lessons – can modify how teachers interpret the influence they exert within the instructional triangle. Viewing and analysing classroom video together with colleagues can bring teachers to increase their interest in how they influence pupils' learning. The resulting insights can then lead teachers to change their intentions for teaching. This, in turn, can have consequences for detailing and improving lesson plans (IPASS, VILMS, CFS in-service, LLT).

Where effects on teachers' action is concerned, differences appear to exist between preservice and beginning teachers on the one hand and experienced teachers on the other. While for preservice and beginning teachers, engaging in VTL served foremost to build a repertoire of instructional skills, the benefits to experienced teachers lay mainly in strengthening and expanding or modifying their repertoires of instructional behaviours.

There are indications that achieving changes in instructional behaviour takes preservice and beginning teachers more than one year (LTN, LLT, CVLL). This probably has to do with the issue of occupational socialisation. In the UCI studies, it is recognised that teaching experience is an important influence on teachers' learning (Yeh & Santagata, 2015, p. 33) and that during the transition from preservice to beginning teaching, graduates from PTE programmes risk "falling back" to transmission-oriented practices (Mohr & Santagata, 2015, p. 116). Also, Barnhart and Van Es (2018, p. 70) note that the school context can keep teachers from changing their instructional practice. However, the reports about the UCI studies do not elaborate on how video-supported learning activities and teaching practice combine to influence teachers' instructional behaviour. It appears, though, that reality shock is alive and kicking. This is also apparent in the study of the CVLL. Here, attention is explicitly directed to the gaps that beginning teachers experience between their expectations and the realities of school life (cf. the section *Preservice teacher education* in Chapter 1 about "discrepancy experiences").

The research into interventions addressed at experienced teachers also shows that engaging in VTL was helpful in changing instruction. Participating teachers changed existing instructional practices in the direction of dialogic teaching and cognitive and social-emotional activation of pupils (KODEK, DVC, ECEC, STeLLA, MTP). CSCL software facilitating viewing, annotating and communicating about classroom video supported teachers in doing so (IRIS Connect, STeLLA).

Finally, experienced teachers' participation in VTL can have an influence on pupils' learning. Through their scale and rigour, the studies of STeLLA and MTP have clearly shown that teachers' instructional action has a mediating function in improving pupils' learning. This provides empirical support for a central assumption of the process-product research into teaching and learning carried out in the 1960s and 1970s (Dunkin & Biddle, 1974; Pianta et al., 2012). Engaging in VTL has thus been shown to help teachers make their classroom instruction and interaction more effective and, as a consequence, promote pupils' learning. This was apparent from increases in pupils' social competence (MTP) as well as their achievement (STeLLA, MTP). The outcomes in teachers and pupils resulting from both interventions can be attributed to a combination of features. STeLLA was effective because of the combination of video-supported blended learning with the provision of PCK based on theory and research. MTP was effective because it combined web-mediated, individualised coaching with video analysis of teachers' own lessons grounded in theory and research about effective teaching. Both interventions directly targeted teachers' instructional practice and their personal concerns about it.

The above conclusions, listed in Box 2.1, imply that VTL is a feasible way for teachers in different career phases to discover possibilities for raising the quality of their instruction and to implement changes in it. This synthesis is in line with the conclusions drawn by Gaudin and Chaliès about the impact of DV use on teachers' thought and action. In their review, these authors found that the main effects of DV use on teacher thought were that it enhanced preservice and experienced teachers' selective attention, helped them interpret other teachers' intentions and pupils' understanding of subject matter and reassured them about their own performance. The main effects on teacher action found by Gaudin and Chaliès (2015, p. 53–55) were that teachers redeployed behaviours seen in videos of colleagues in their own teaching, provided that these behaviours were relevant to their own concerns.

The findings about the outcomes of VTL in teachers, as reviewed by Gaudin and Chaliès and in this chapter, point in the same direction. The evidence suggests that engaging in VTL can help teachers translate thought into action, as I call it. This is a complex process for preservice, beginning and experienced teachers alike. Just how this process takes place, however, remains partly shrouded, because most

BOX 2.1   OUTCOMES OF VISUAL TEACHER LEARNING IN TEACHERS AND PUPILS

Aims

- The DV interventions reviewed aim at encouraging teachers to change their classroom instruction and interaction by
  - increasing the variety of instructional approaches,
  - promoting pupils' cognitive activation and
  - encouraging higher-order learning.
- Most of the interventions address teaching in the foundational subjects of language and mathematics learning in primary and secondary education.

Teacher outcomes

- VTL is a feasible way for teachers in different career phases to discover possibilities for raising the quality of their instruction and to implement changes in it. VTL can help
  - preservice teachers develop a deeper understanding of teaching and acquire instructional skills,
  - beginning and experienced teachers consider and introduce alternative instructional practices and
  - experienced teachers make their classroom instruction and interaction more effective.

Pupil outcomes

- When teachers raise the quality of their instruction by enaging in VTL, this has a mediating function in promoting pupils' learning.

VTL research takes teacher perception and thought as its end point. What happens in between teachers' viewing of classroom video and their changing of instruction needs to be better clarified. A neglected point, in my view, is that while viewing classroom video, teachers not only attend to and interpret aspects of the interplay between teaching and learning. They also judge what they see. I assume that judgement is the basis for instructional decision-making and planning new lessons. These cognitions mark the transition from postactive to preactive teacher thinking, i.e. the transition from a past teaching cycle to a future teaching cycle. How VTL may influence these specific processes is addressed in the next section.

Processes: How do teachers learn when using digital video?

In answering the second review question, two issues are at stake: how teachers become aware of how they influence pupils' learning and how they draw conclusions and consequences from this experience. The studies reviewed clarify that these processes depend to a large extent on how perception and cognition take place during teachers' collegial collaboration. Below, I first discuss the evidence found about perception and cognition, then the evidence about teachers' collaboration.

Perception and cognition

A large majority of studies shows that viewing and analysing classroom video can increase teachers' understanding of the interplay between teaching and learning. During their participation in video clubs, preservice and experienced teachers develop their abilities to notice and interpret pupils' thinking about subject matter. While doing so, they tend to focus their attention on relationships between teaching and learning rather than on pupils' learning alone (LTN). These conclusions are also supported by the evidence from the research on the CVLL, KODEK, STeLLA and MTP. Teachers also develop a more interpretive and tentative stance (LTN) or intellectual modesty (VITAL). In addition, by analysing video clips of other teachers' and their own teaching preservice teachers can develop lesson analysis abilities (LLT).

The American studies of in-service teachers' LTN and the development of preservice teachers' lesson analysis abilities show two commonalities with the French study of the CVLL. In both cases, the video-supported examination of how lessons unfold encouraged teachers to stand back and shift attention from their own teaching behaviour towards how it interacts with pupils' actions and reactions. This then became the basis for discovering, deliberating about and formulating intentions to implement alternatives for instructional action. Also the research about other interventions indicates that teachers' increased understanding of the interplay between teaching and learning can pave the way for changing teaching (CVLL, KODEK, STeLLA, MTP).

What remains unclear in many studies, especially quantitative studies in the cognitivist paradigm, is how the transitions from video viewing and analysis to judgement and decision-making and then to changing instruction take place. In a review of the research into mathematics teachers' perception, interpretation and decision-making, Stahnke, Schueler, and Roesken-Winter (2016), p. 24) speak of a "missing link between … teachers' knowledge … and their performance". The mechanisms and processes involved in the transitions between teachers' video viewing and analysis, judgement, and instructional decision-making have been conceptualised in an interesting study by Chan (2003; Chan & Harris, 2005). Chan asked a sample of six experienced elementary teachers, all female, to think aloud while viewing video records of literacy teaching embedded in a multimedia environment (Harris et al., 2001). From the resulting transcripts, he derived the Cognitive Development Process Model (CDPM). This model specifies six categories of cognitive activities during teachers' video viewing: Awareness, Comprehension, Acceptance, Rejection, Connection and Desire to act.

These categories provide a conceptual map of what happens in teachers' minds while viewing classroom video. This can be interpreted as a decision-oriented assessment from a pedagogical perspective, in which teachers seek answers to different types of questions:

- interpretive questions: Do I understand what is happening here? ("Comprehension");
- normative questions involving the judgement of pedagogical value: Do I agree with this or not? ("Acceptance vs. Rejection") and: Do I consider this a worthwhile thing to do? ("Connection");
- decision-oriented questions related to their own teaching intentions: Do I want to do this myself? If yes, how can I do this? ("Desire to act").

How video viewing and analysis influence teachers' instructional understanding, judgement and decision-making probably depends on different types of factors, i.e. viewers' personal characteristics and goals, the instructions with which the viewing is framed and the nature of the video material itself.

Miller and Zhou (2007, p. 323–326) have shown in several studies that teachers filter their perceptions and interpretations on the basis of their cultural backgrounds. Just like other people, they have the habit of confirming existing beliefs through rapid impression formation. Thus, when viewing lessons on video, American teachers tend to attribute how teaching and learning unfold to the teacher's personal characteristics, whereas Chinese teachers rather attribute what they see to how pupils engage with the subject matter. In the TIMSS studies comparing mathematics teaching in the US, Japan and Germany, Stigler and Hiebert (1999) found similar differences in teachers' perceptions. Such culturally determined impressions can be quite persistent.

In another study, Miller and Zhou (2007, p. 326–329) found that providing college students with instructions for viewing produced changes in perception. Explicit instructions to attend to specific instructional aspects caused the respondents to change their ratings of the teaching behaviour viewed both during and after viewing. Although this study was conducted with college students, not teachers, it does suggest that providing instructions can help viewers examine specific aspects of teaching and learning. Also the studies of CFS suggest that viewing instructions can encourage teachers to examine cultural traditions in their work.

The research reviewed confirms, then, that it is possible to guide teachers' viewing and analysis of teaching and learning. In particular, focussing viewing and analysis by means of instructions helps teachers examine aspects of teaching, such as explaining and questioning, which are related to effects on learners. The evidence shows that the following factors contribute to the effectiveness of video use.

The benefits that teachers derive from video viewing and analysis depend on both substance and form of the video material involved. Specifically, these benefits are increased when the substance is grounded in theory and research about effective teaching (VILMS, KODEK, DVC, VITAL, STeLLA, MTP) and directly targets teachers' personal concerns about instructional practice (CVLL, KODEK, Néopass@ction, MTP). The benefits to teachers also increase when in form, the video material is clearly structured, accessible and navigable, and it offers opportunities to experience other teachers' classroom behaviour vicariously (Teachers TV, Leraar24, Néopass@ction).

Collegial cooperation

One strand runs conspicuously through the research findings reviewed in this chapter. How teachers learn from using video is closely connected with the opportunities provided to them for collegial exchange and dialogue. Teachers' thinking about professional practice is strongly mediated by their interaction with colleagues. Collegial exchange and dialogue supported by viewing video cases encourage a deeper understanding of teaching (Docucases, VILMS, CFS in-service). The benefits teachers experience during collaboration are increased when they face comparable and therefore recognisable challenges and questions, whether subject-specific or generic (VILMS, CFS in-service, LTN, CVLL, KODEK). Following protocols for collegial dialogue and purposeful facilitation practices helped them suspend rapid judgements and develop a more tentative and interpretive stance (LTN). Similar approaches and experiences are described by Calandra (2015) and Rich (2015). When teacher evaluation becomes video- and web-based, its emphasis tends to shift from a summative into a formative direction (BFF).

Together, these findings indicate that exchange and dialogue are powerful drivers of teachers' collaborative learning. They encourage social meaning-making about shared concerns regarding the interplay between teaching and learning. Viewing and discussing examples of each other's teaching can change teachers' ideas about their own work, notably their intentions for instruction and their lesson planning (Docucases, IPASS, VILMS, KODEK, CVLL, Néopass@ction). In addition, collegial exchange and dialogue can encourage teachers to change teaching practices (CVLL, KODEK). This is a gradual process, which, as noted above, can last longer than one year (LTN, LLT, CVLL).

Both other-viewing and self-viewing can contribute to teachers' reconsidering and changing their teaching. In the DV applications reviewed, engaging first in other-viewing, then in self-viewing was clearly the prevailing sequence (CFS in-service, KODEK, STeLLA, LTN, LLT, CVLL, IRIS Connect). Researchers have asked what has a stronger impact on teachers, other-viewing or self-viewing.

From research among experienced teachers, Seidel, Stürmer, Blomberg, Kobarg and Schwindt (2011), p. 259) concluded that "Teachers who analyzed their own teaching experienced higher activation", while Kleinknecht and Schneider (2013, p. 13) concluded that "teachers viewing videos of other teachers are more deeply engaged". Since studies directly comparing both types of viewing are few and far between, this issue remains unsettled. The review in this chapter suggests, rather, that other-viewing and self-viewing function in different ways.

The studies based on francophone ergonomics have yielded indications that other-viewing arouses mimetic experiences – the types of "as if" experience which Laurillard (1993, p. 114) calls "vicarious" – and that these experiences, in turn, lead teachers to compare colleagues' instructional performance with their own. Such comparison appears to encourage teachers to examine their own teaching (cf. Gaudin & Chaliès, 2015, p. 45–47 and 50–51). Several studies reviewed above suggest that during other-viewing, the power of good examples is at work by suggesting alternatives for instructional action to teachers (CFS in-service, CVLL, KODEK).

Several other studies suggest that also self-viewing can bring teachers to change their instruction (KODEK, DVC, ECEC, STeLLA, MTP). These studies have made the processes involved less clear, however. Drawing on my experiences as a teacher educator, I hypothesise that self-viewing can bring teachers to engage in an examination of strong and weak points in their performance. This can touch on feelings of professional confidence and self-worth, which shows how important it is to build and maintain a climate of trust in teachers' learning environment. An important mechanism involved in self-viewing is probably that the visual representation of oneself in action can cause shifts in viewers' thinking. This experience can be emotionally disturbing, but also reassuring. Whether in slight shock or with unexpected relief, the teacher who sees herself or himself in action wonders "Is this what I am doing?" I think it is this experience which brings teachers, when they want to be frank with themselves, to change their professional self-image and then to judge and decide which of the behaviours in their instructional repertoires they should omit, replace, change or expand. Such considerations can even be made visible, as the self-confrontation interviews on the Néopass@ction web site testify. It takes some courage to engage in these cognitions, but I think this is necessary before a teacher can and will plan and use new teaching practices.

The mechanism described above may explain what happens during self-confrontation. I think it is an important part of the special affordances of DV. As Miller and Zhou (2007, p. 322) write, "Video cases are perhaps the ultimate in vivid secondhand experience, because however selected and edited the material shown to viewers might be, they are seeing it for themselves. Thus, it is not surprising that video cases are persuasive."

How other-viewing and self-viewing function cannot be considered in isolation from the settings in which they occur. Studies among preservice teachers by Kleinknecht and Gröschner (2016) and Weber, Gold, Prilop and Kleinknecht (2018) show that the settings in which they receive feedback – methods courses or coaching and supervision – matter as well as the sources from which they receive feedback – peers and/or experts. In these studies, teacher learning supported by video – as opposed to journal writing – and feedback from peers and experts – as opposed to feedback from peers only – were shown to be the most effective. All these aspects have to do with how teachers collaborate.

The final feature that emerges from the studies reviewed as influencing VTL is how often teachers engage in complete cycles of preactive, interactive and postactive activities. When they do so repeatedly, this encourages them to change their instructional behaviour. As noted in the section *Functions and features of digital video applications*, the four programmes with a training function, KODEK, DVC, ECEC and STeLLA, had this feature in common.

Still, these programmes also differed in their effectiveness. Although no programme achieved all its aims, the DVC appears to have resulted in the fewest outcomes. Possibly, DVC target skills – notably asking elaborative questions – were more difficult to implement, but another explanation may lie in the programme's duration and the nature of the learning activities. The number of cycles teachers went through in the DVC was lower than in KODEK and ECEC. The participants in KODEK viewed, analysed, redesigned and retaught their lessons during the second and third programme modules at least three times. The teachers participating in ECEC had four repeated opportunities for these activities. Also, KODEK and ECEC combined opportunities for teachers to role-play new behaviours and practice them in their own work situation within a four-month period. This created a situation comparable to the principle of swift reteaching in MT. In the DVC, active learning through MT and role-play was lacking.

BOX 2.2 PROCESSES OF VISUAL TEACHER LEARNING

Perception and cognition

- Viewing and analysing classroom video can increase teachers' understanding of the interplay between teaching and learning.
- Guiding and focussing teachers' viewing and analysis of teaching and learning by means of instructions helps teachers examine aspects of teaching which are related to effects on learners.
- By analysing video clips of other teachers' and their own teaching, preservice teachers can develop lesson analysis abilities.
- Teachers' increased understanding of the interplay between teaching and learning can pave the way for changing instruction.
- The benefits that teachers derive from video viewing and analysis are increased when:

- the substance of the video material is grounded in theory and research about effective teaching and
- directly targets teachers' personal concerns about their instructional practice;
- in form, the video material is clearly structured, accessible and navigable and
- offers opportunities to experience other teachers' classroom behaviour vicariously.
- Protocols for collegial dialogue and purposeful facilitation help teachers suspend rapid judgments and develop a more tentative and interpretive stance.

Collegial cooperation

- How teachers learn from using video is closely connected with the opportunities provided for collegial exchange and dialogue.
- Collegial exchange and dialogue can encourage teachers to reconsider and change teaching practices.
- Other-viewing and self-viewing appear to contribute in different ways to teachers' reconsidering and changing instruction.
  - Other-viewing leads teachers to compare colleagues' performance with their own and consider alternatives for instructional action.
  - Self-viewing may bring teachers to engage in an examination of strong and weak points in their performance.

Cyclical learning

- When teachers engage repeatedly in complete cycles of preactive, interactive and postactive activities, this encourages them to change their instructional behaviour.

Conditions: In what kinds of learning environments do teachers learn when using digital video?

Different kinds of conditions influence what and how teachers learn when using DV. Four types stand out in the studies reviewed. Firstly, teachers' learning environments are shaped by the school context within which teachers operate. Secondly, the design of PTE programmes and PD interventions influences VTL. Thirdly, the nature of the available video material influences what and how teachers can learn. Finally, the DV software implemented and its affordances influence VTL.

School organisation and culture play vital roles in making VTL possible. An explicit finding in several studies is that when schools make sufficient time available – in quantity as well as duration – and offer opportunities for collegial cooperation, this contributes to enabling teachers to derive new insights and ideas from video analyses and to use these insights for changing their instruction (CVLL, Teachers TV, Leraar24). In addition, when a school's culture is characterised by an ethic of collaboration, this favours collegial exchange and feedback (CVLL, Néopass@ction).

The evidence from the research reviewed shows that two design features of programmes and interventions for VTL (see the section *Functions and features of digital video applications* above) influence to a considerable extent in what kind of learning environment it takes place: its setting – offline, online or blended – and how teachers are grouped. Different combinations of these features determine what and how teachers can learn. When VTL takes place offline in dyads, this can be an effective setting for coaching, as illustrated by VILMS. However, individual coaching can also be effective online, as in IPASS and MTP. The MTP impact studies also show that online coaching can be cost-effective and scalable. When video cases become available in offline settings, blended learning can give teachers the best of both worlds. As VITAL, STeLLA and IRIS Connect show, viewing, annotating and communicating about classroom video are affordances which can be implemented in institutional contexts to support teachers' PD. Viewing model videos in plenary groups appears to be relatively effective, whether offline (CFS in-service, KODEK) or in blended settings (STeLLA, VITAL).

The nature of the video material used during VTL influences how teachers perceive and interpret it. As concluded in the section *Perception and cognition*, VTL outcomes depend in part on the extent to which and the respects in which the substance of the video material is evidence-based. In addition, form features are influential. Notably, realism and authenticity – as in the Docucases videos – contribute to the effects on viewers. Trigger videos – as in Didiclass – encourage preservice teachers to rethink ideas and beliefs by creating cognitive conflict.

How DV software and its affordances are implemented and used in teachers' learning environments determines what teachers can learn. Notably, usability online and facilities for annotating video can increase the benefits teachers experience from VTL (IPASS, Teachers TV, Leraar24, Néopass@ction, VITAL, IRIS Connect, MTP). Video repositories and electronic learning environments enable teachers to share visual artefacts displaying their work and can thus benefit workplace learning and professional collaboration (Smith, 2003). However, to realise this potential, certain conditions need to be fulfilled.

To begin with, funding is necessary to keep video platforms for teachers functioning and up to date. As the example of Teachers TV shows, they can be hit

BOX 2.3   CONDITIONS OF VISUAL TEACHER LEARNING

School organisation

- When schools, in their organisation, make sufficient time available – in quantity as well as duration – and offer teachers opportunities for collegial cooperation, this contributes to enabling them to derive new insights and ideas from video viewing and analysis and to use these insights for changing their instruction.

School culture

- When a school's culture is characterised by an ethic of collaboration, this favours collegial exchange and feedback.

Design features: setting and grouping

- Viewing model videos in plenary groups appears to be relatively effective, whether offline or in blended settings.

Nature of video material

- The nature of the video material used during VTL – notably the extent to which it is evidence-based, realistic and authentic – influences how teachers perceive and interpret it.

Software use

- How DV software and its affordances are implemented and used in teachers' learning environments determine what teachers can learn.
  - The implementation of DV software is facilitated, when teachers judge it as learnable and usable.
  - Online DV uses based on streaming require sufficient bandwidth.
  - Facilities for annotating video can increase the benefits teachers experience from VTL.
- Funding is necessary to keep video platforms for teachers functioning and up to date.
- Teachers' appreciation of video platforms is enhanced when
  - their structure is accessible,
  - their navigability is fine-grained enough to allow teachers to quickly find topics that interest them and
  - they provide not only classroom videos, but also related information explaining the rationale behind the teaching practices shown.

by budget cuts. Another platform in the Netherlands, Palet, disappeared from the Internet after millions of euros were invested in its development. What also helps is when schools encourage teachers to use video platforms as a resource during collaborative PD activities (Teachers TV, STeLLA, CVLL, IRIS Connect). Moreover, specific design features of video platforms affect the experience and the appreciation of the teachers visiting them. The latter are enhanced when a platform's structure is accessible and its navigability is fine-grained enough to allow teachers to quickly find topics that interest them (Teachers TV, Leraar24). Once teachers view videos, it serves their practical concerns when they not only see colleagues at work in the classroom, but also find related information which helps them understand the rationale behind the teaching practices shown (Teachers TV, Leraar24, Néopass@ction). The implementation of DV software is facilitated, when teachers judge it as learnable and usable (VITAL, IRIS Connect). The importance of this concern is diminished as smart phones continue to conquer the world. Still, as the experiences with IRIS Connect in South Africa show, online DV uses based on streaming require bandwidth that the available Internet infrastructure not always – or not yet always – provides.

Finally, issues of privacy and data protection are of course of utmost importance in VTL. These issues are addressed in the section *Data protection* in Chapter 9.

What we need to know more

The empirical evidence synthesised in this chapter points to the following gaps in the existing research and issues for future R&D work.

Identifying effective teaching

In educational research, effective teaching is often defined on a generic level, but in everyday practice, teaching and learning always take place in relation to specific subjects and content. A number of subject-specific pedagogies, however, is under-researched. This state of affairs is mirrored in VTL research. The majority of VTL studies has been conducted in the areas of mathematics and science, some in relation to literacy and few or none in other school subjects. This is beginning to change (Riegel & Macha, 2013), but more R&D work in less-served subjects is needed. A common challenge in such work will be to define operationally what are subject-specific teaching strategies and skills suited to promoting higher-order learning (see the section *Quality learning and quality teaching* in Chapter 1) and to find out how VTL can contribute to developing them. Programmes on a generic level similarly face the need to operationalise what are effective teaching behaviours. A good example of how this can be done is the approach taken by KODEK to derive effective classroom management skills from the available research evidence and visualise these in scripted videos.

School context

In quite a few studies of preservice teachers'VTL, little attention is paid, at least in the reports published, to the PTE programmes within which it takes place, in particular to the amount, sequencing and organisation of student teaching. However, these features have a considerable influence on student teachers' occupational socialisation (see the section *Preservice teacher education* in Chapter 1). It is therefore advisable to include them in research design. Studies of experienced teachers' VTL more often address context influences, in particular schools' organisation and work culture. Important topics to pursue in future research have to do with the potential influence of changes in teachers' instruction following participation in VTL on pupils' learning. The first is how PD goals are chosen, in particular if and on what grounds evidence-based knowledge about teaching is fed into teachers' collaboration (Hiebert, Gallimore, & Stigler, 2002; Stigler & Thompson, 2009). The second is whether and how schools facilitate teachers' collaboration during all activity phases in the teacher work cycle: the preactive phase of lesson planning, the interactive phase of lesson observation and the postactive phase of collegial feedback and consultation. These aspects are included in the case study I report in Chapter 6.

How teachers translate thought into action

As noted in the above conclusions, how VTL affects teachers' judgement, decision-making and planning regarding instruction receives little attention in VTL research. These thought processes in teachers were investigated by Chan and Harris (2005) and conceptualised in their CDPM. In Chapter 4, I report a replication study aimed at finding out how generalisable the CDPM is. As most VTL studies take teacher perception and thought as their end point, also less evidence is available about its impact on teachers' instructional behaviour. This impact is addressed in the case study I report in Chapter 5. How teacher thought and action influence each other and how VTL may affect this relationship are issues of decisive relevance to teaching practice and raising the quality of instruction.

Differences depending on career phase

From research on expertise in pedagogy, it is known that experienced teachers perceive and interpret classroom events differently than novices. Experienced teachers have already built a more differentiated frame of reference about instruction (Carter, Cushing, Sabers, Stein, & Berliner, 1988; Berliner, 2004). It may therefore be assumed that the outcomes, processes, concerns and preferences involved in teachers' VTL will differ depending on their career phase – whether they are prospective, beginning or experienced teachers. However, these differences are rarely the direct object of VTL research. An exception in this respect is a study by Jacobs,

Lamb, Philipp and Schappelle (2011), who found that with growing PD experience, teachers were better able to notice and respond to children's understandings. There is clearly a need for more such research.

Long-term effects

Of the studies reviewed, just two have produced evidence about the impact that teachers' participation in VTL had on learners, i.e. those of STeLLA and MTP. These studies covered a time span of at least one year. Similarly few studies were designed to follow teachers' VTL longitudinally, notably those of the development of pre-service and beginning teachers by Santagata and Yeh (2016) and Lussi Borer et al. (2014). More such studies are needed to understand how VTL may support teachers in improving their instruction in the long run and what factors can promote the sustainability of VTL outcomes. The case study I report in Chapter 6 includes follow-up data which throw some light on these issues.

Tool use

As noted (in the introduction to the above section *Digital video use*), the new affordances introduced by DV technology have given rise to profound changes in tool use. There is still relatively little research available showing how teachers use the video platforms developed for their benefit and how they collaborate in electronic learning environments built around video. More knowledge about these issues should inform the design of these new tools. Amongst other topics, it would be fruitful to know more about how teachers can benefit from the use of video annotation tools and mobile devices. Both possibilities hold promise for enabling teachers anywhere anytime to connect across institutional, regional and national boundaries and make their collaboration local and global at the same time, or "glocal".

Video production

In most studies, the nature of the video material used during VTL is taken for granted. However, what there is to be seen in lesson videos in the first place considerably influences teachers' reception of them. As Miller and Zhou (2007) note, what video selection and editing allow teachers to see and interpret are critical issues. Selection and editing create the framing of what viewers perceive. They therefore play an important role during the production of video, not only when it is produced for online distribution through video platforms, but also when teachers themselves select and edit footage from lesson recordings for local use. Research should address how different types of lesson videos – model, trigger and action – are produced, perceived and interpreted. Guidelines for visualising teaching and learning based on user research should benefit video production. I elaborate on these issues in Chapter 7.

Visual Teacher Learning, a model

The review in this chapter makes clear that teacher learning supported by video use is influenced by a host of factors, which can interact in different ways. In order to synthesise the evidence from the review, I have included these factors in the Visual Teacher Learning model, depicted in Figure 2.2. This model is intended as a conceptual map or heuristic for understanding how video use can help teachers relate practice and theory and raise the quality of instruction.

The VTL model comprises the following nine components:

- teachers' biographies and personal learning goals,
- the learning environment in which their professional learning takes place,
- the learning activities they undertake in cooperation with colleagues,
- the perceptual processes involved in these activities,
- the kind(s) of feedback they receive,
- the reflection processes involved in the foregoing,
- the consequences they draw for instructional action,
- how changes in teachers' enactment of instruction affect pupils' learning and
- the further development of teachers' professional competence and motivation.

How VTL evolves can be explained in terms of relationships between these model components. The reasoning behind the VTL model is as follows.

When teachers enter into VTL, they do so with individual biographies characterised by their cultural backgrounds and earlier experiences as learners and teachers. Relevant entry characteristics they bring with them are gender, age and the amount and nature of their teaching experience. These characteristics shape teachers' current practices, knowledge and views regarding teaching, which, in turn, affect the personal learning goals they will embrace as well as what and how they will learn while participating in VTL. This is indicated by the forward arrow on the left.

What and how teachers learn during VTL is determined not only by their biographies and personal goals, but also by the learning environment that PTE programmes or schools offer them. For preservice teachers and ACP candidates, their programmes' design and the opportunities these provide for learning from practice are influential determinants. For beginning and experienced teachers, the amount of working time and resources made available for collegial collaboration and the culture of instruction in their schools have a potent impact. Both groups' learning will also be shaped by goals set on institutional levels.

The learning environment determines the context for teachers' learning activity. It is this activity which directly influences their experience with VTL. Teachers' learning activity takes place in two different spheres of interaction, i.e. their collaboration with colleagues – depicted by the three overlapping circles on the left – and their interaction with pupils or the interplay between teaching and learning – depicted by the two overlapping circles on the right. The model components in the circles are detailed below. The dotted lines between the circles indicate that the teacher learning

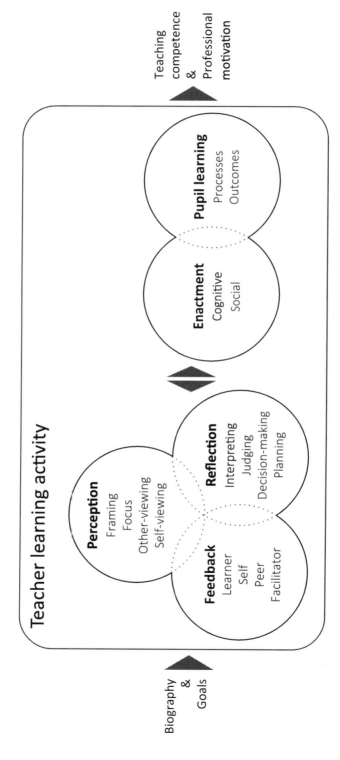

FIGURE 2.2 The Visual Teacher Learning model

processes specified within each component are not isolated from each other. On the contrary, I assume that these processes fundamentally influence each other.

As indicated by the arrows in the middle, the two spheres of interaction mutually influence each other. The interplay between teaching and learning sets the stage for teachers' collegial collaboration. During this collaboration, the kinds of VTL activities teachers undertake and how these activities are organised and supported shape how teachers view and analyse teaching and learning. Video viewing and analysis, in turn, shape what consequences teachers will draw from their VTL experiences for how they interact with their pupils during instruction.

How teachers perceive video of teaching and learning depends first of all on how the content-focussed interaction between teacher and learners is framed through selection and editing. Secondly, teachers' perception is influenced by whether and what kinds of focus are provided or chosen in the form of observation points, analysis questions or protocols. Thirdly, perception appears to serve different functions depending on whether teachers view videos of colleagues or of themselves teaching.

When teachers view video, especially of their own teaching, their learning is also influenced by the sources from which they receive feedback. During teaching, pupils' actions and reactions continually provide teachers with feedback (learner feedback). Additional sources of feedback can be the self as when a teacher alone views a recording of a lesson given by herself or himself (self feedback), colleagues (peer feedback), and/or a teacher educator or PD provider (facilitator feedback).

Perception and feedback together influence teachers' reflection about their work. As discussed along the lines of the CDPM presented by Chan and Harris (2005), video viewing brings teachers to engage in different cognitive activities, i.e. interpreting, judging, decision-making and planning. I assume that these cognitions are the basis upon which teachers draw consequences from VTL and translate thought into instructional action.

Teachers' enactment of lessons and pupils' learning together constitute the interplay between teaching and learning. When teachers introduce changes into their instruction, this changes their interaction with pupils. In other words, when teachers enact their lessons in different ways than they were used to, this has cognitive and/or social consequences for what and how pupils learn, i.e. the processes and outcomes of learning. This is an essential assumption of the VTL model, which it shares with process–product research and for which the MTP impact studies have provided empirical corroboration. Teachers' enactment of lessons functions as a mediator of pupils' learning.

For teachers, participating in VTL may lead to outcomes in the longer term. I expect that examining and changing instruction during VTL can affect how teachers' professional competence and motivation develop over the whole of their careers. This is indicated by the forward arrow on the right.

To conclude this chapter, I use the components of the VTL model and the potential relations between them as a guide to the chapters that follow. The literature review in Chapter 3 focusses on what changes in instruction can result from VTL. While the studies reported in Chapters 4 and 5 deal primarily with the Perception, Reflection and Enactment components, the case study in Chapter 6 addresses all model components. The guidelines for video production presented in Chapter 7 are relevant to how teachers may perceive videos of teaching and learning. Chapter 8 addresses the use of video for developing teaching and learning in dialogue with pupils.

3

CHANGING INSTRUCTION THROUGH VISUAL TEACHER LEARNING

Niels Brouwer

Visual Teacher Learning (VTL) can contribute to raising the quality of instruction. So much has become clear from the overview of DV applications and the related research evidence presented in Chapter 2. Still, we need to know more about the issue *how* VTL can help teachers make their instruction more effective. In this chapter, I therefore present an up-to-date systematic review of empirical research carried out since 2000, focussing specifically on the effects of VTL on teachers' instructional behaviour.

First, the questions guiding this review are introduced. Then, I describe the method employed and present the findings. On this basis, I synthesise which outcomes from participating in VTL the studies reviewed have brought to light in teachers as well as pupils. Finally, I draw conclusions about the processes and conditions involved.

Introduction

The evidence about the nineteen DV applications reviewed in Chapter 2 collectively amounts to proof of existence for the potential of VTL to help teachers raise the effectiveness of their instruction. Increased understanding of the interplay between teaching and learning can lead teachers to discover and implement alternatives for instructional action which, in turn, will help raise pupils' achievement. When schools' organisation and culture encourage collegial collaboration, this supports teachers in benefitting from VTL (see for more detail the conclusions summarised in Boxes 2.1 through 2.3).

Surprisingly, the great majority of VTL studies takes teacher perceptions and cognitions regarding teaching and learning as its end point. This is apparent in the wide array of terms used in the published research. I found the following terms, in alphabetical order: analysis; awareness; beliefs; conceptions; confidence; considering; (self-)efficacy; insight; (practical) knowledge; noticing; perspective(s); rationale;

DOI: 10.4324/9780429331091-3

(ways of) reasoning; reflection(s); reflective practice; self-concept; thought(s); (conceptual) understanding; views; (professional) vision.

Far less evidence is available about how teachers' participation in VTL influences their instructional action and if and how VTL-induced changes in instruction affect pupils' learning. This is apparent from the limited number of terms used in the published research. I found the following terms, in alphabetical order: action; behaviour; competence; performance; practice; teaching; (use of) (teaching) strategies.

This skewed state of affairs is due, I think, to the fact that the research about teacher learning is dominated by a "theory first" or a "theory to practice" perspective (cf. Chapter 1, in particular the sections *Preservice teacher education* and *Professional development*, and the section *What we know and how we know it* in Chapter 2). Underlying this perspective is the assumption that first teachers' thinking and then their action should or does change. The implication for teacher education and PD is that once teachers get the desired theory in their heads, competent teaching will follow effortlessly. Understandably, then, reproduction of theory remains the dominant goal of teacher education and PD.

A similar diagnosis is found in the review of case-based learning in teacher education presented a quarter century ago by Katherine Merseth (1996, p. 729; cf. p. 737–739):

> Ideally, one would like to read research that links classroom effectiveness to study and work with cases. However, there is only limited research on the influence of case-based instruction on classroom performance. Instead, researchers appear to emphasize teacher thinking rather than teacher action in their work. This emphasis implicitly suggests that cognitive abilities of teachers, including flexibility, are a proxy for classroom performance. Appropriately, many teacher educators question this leap of faith.

Putting theory before or above practice creates a "deductivist bias", as I call it. This bias seems to lead a persistent, if not obstinate life. The research about teachers' perceptions and cognitions in connection with VTL has, in my opinion, reached saturation point. It has become a case of "normal science", producing more of the same knowledge (Kuhn, 1970). I cannot help wondering why this is the case. Is it because academia is in denial of reality? Is it because it is easier to measure perceptions out of context than to observe behaviour in context (cf. Kelman, 1974, p. 311)?

Whatever the reason, this deductivist bias remains deeply problematic, because the overriding challenge for teachers is not to master theory, but to put instructional intentions into practice. This is what I call translating thought into action. Concomitantly, the main driving force behind teacher learning is practical experience. These are the reasons why we need to know more about how teachers' participation in VTL may influence their instructional action and their pupils' learning. A fine-grained understanding of the issues involved here is required as a foundation for designing effective learning environments and activities for VTL. Such understanding is a necessary step towards an evidence base for effective uses of VTL, i.e.

uses which contribute to raising the quality of teaching and learning (cf. the section *Quality learning and quality teaching* in Chapter 1).

The review reported below, then, focusses specifically on the effects of VTL on teachers' instructional behaviour and their pupils' learning. I have deliberately formulated the questions guiding this review so as to reverse the deductivist "theory to practice" perspective into an "inductivist," "practice to theory" perspective which reflects the primacy of practical experience in teacher learning. The review questions are:

When teachers change their instructional action as a result of participation in VTL,

I. what is the nature of these changes?   TEACHER OUTCOMES
II. do these changes influence pupils' learning and   PUPIL OUTCOMES
   if so, in which respects?
III. which processes of teacher learning contribute PROCESSES
   to changes in instruction?
IV. which conditions in teachers' learning support CONDITIONS
   or obstruct changes in instruction?

The subclause preceding these four questions presupposes that teachers can and do change their instruction after participating in VTL. The evidence presented in Chapter 2 includes ample indications for this assumption. Especially the survey research about Science Teachers Learning from Lesson Analysis (STeLLA) and the impact studies of MyTeachingPartner (MTP) (see the eponymous sections in Chapter 2) have uncovered relationships between participation in VTL, changes in instruction and increases in pupil learning. The STeLLA and MTP studies show that teachers' action in the instructional triangle is the prime factor driving pupil learning. Review question I therefore focusses on the outcomes of teacher participation in VTL. It is meant to clarify what kinds of changes in instruction are induced by VTL. The consequences of such changes for processes and outcomes of pupil learning are the object of review question II.

Review questions III and IV then turn to the antecedents of the outcomes of VTL in teachers and pupils. Question III focusses on those processes of VTL which contribute to changes in instruction. This question is specifically meant to clarify the mechanisms involved in VTL. Question IV focusses on the conditions in teachers' learning environments which support or obstruct changes in their instruction while and after they engage in VTL.

In terms of the VTL model, the strategy behind this review is to reason backwards, as it were, from outcomes – teachers' enactment of teaching, its influence on pupils' learning and the development of teachers' professional competence and motivation – to antecedent processes – teachers' learning activity, perception, feedback and reflection – and conditions in their learning environments. In short, teachers' instructional action takes the central position of mediator between outcomes of teacher and pupil learning on the one hand and conditions, activities and processes of VTL on the other.

Method

The review in this chapter builds on an earlier review published in a theme issue of the Swiss journal *Beiträge zur Lehrerinnen- und Lehrerbildung* (Brouwer, 2014). In comparison to the earlier review, this chapter is not only an update, but it also has different emphases. While the present review focusses more exclusively on teachers' instructional action, it also extends the 2014 review by including effects on pupil learning.

In this section, I describe which procedures were followed to search the research literature, which criteria were used to select sources relevant to the review questions and how the sources selected as relevant were analysed.

Search procedure

As in the 2014 review, the search for sources was conducted firstly through search systems provided by university libraries in the Netherlands, Germany and the US, as well as Google Scholar. The search terms used were: "video" AND "teach★" AND "practic★". While searching in German databases, the equivalent terms "Video" UND "Lehr★" UND "praktik★" were used. Secondly, those journals which had yielded the most sources for the 2014 review were systematically searched for more recent publications. These 33 journals are listed in Box 3.1.

BOX 3.1 JOURNALS SYSTEMATICALLY SEARCHED

American Educational Research Journal
British Journal of Educational Technology
Cognition and Instruction
Contemporary Issues in Technology and Teacher Education
Early Childhood Research Quarterly
The Elementary School Journal
International Journal of Educational Research
Instructional Science
Journal of Computing in Teacher Education, renamed *Journal of Digital Learning in Teacher Education*
Journal of Early Childhood Teacher Education
Journal of Mathematics Teacher Education
Journal of Music Teacher Education
Journal of Research on Computing in Education, renamed *Journal of Research on Technology in Education*
Journal of Research on Educational Effectiveness
Journal of Teacher Education
Learning and Instruction
Professional Development in Education

Psychology in the Schools
School Psychology Review
Teaching and Teacher Education
Teacher Development
Teacher Education and Special Education
Teacher Education Quarterly
Technology, Pedagogy and Education
Teachers and Teaching, Theory and Practice
Unterrichtswissenschaft
ZDM Mathematics Education
Zeitschrift für Erziehungswissenschaft
Zeitschrift für Pädagogik

Thirdly, sources were selected from 22 reviews about VTL published by Bacevich (2010), Baran (2014), Blomberg, Renkl, Sherin, Borko and Seidel (2013), Fukkink, Trienekens and Kramer (2011), Gaudin and Chaliès (2015), Gobeil-Proulx (2015), Hall and Wright (2007), Hixon and So (2009), Loera-Varela, Flores and Del Campo (2018), Major and Watson (2018), Marsh and Mitchell (2014), Martin and Siry (2008), Meloth, Good and Sugar (2008), Nagro and Cornelius (2013), Fabiola and Chavez (2007), Rook and McDonald (2012), Sacher (2008), Stahnke, Schueler and Roesken-Winter (2016), Tripp and Rich (2012), Wang and Hartley, 2003, Yousef, Chatti and Schroeder (2014) and Yung, Yip, Lai and Lo (2010).

Fourthly, the databases resulting from literature searches performed separately by my colleagues Alexander Gröschner and Marc Kleinknecht at the Technical University of Munich and by myself were compared. This comparison yielded a list of non-overlapping references, part of which were selected for this review.

Fifthly, all sources used for the review in Chapter 2 were included.

Finally, after the sources found in the above ways were examined according to the criteria described in the next section, the reference lists in those publications selected as relevant were inspected for further sources. In this way, some additional sources were identified.

Selection criteria

The studies reviewed in this chapter were selected on the basis of four criteria: relevance to the review questions, methodological quality, period and geographical origin.

Relevance

The prime criterion for a study to be included in the review was that empirical findings were reported about the influence of a VTL intervention on teachers' instructional action – as required by review question I. To fulfil this criterion, such influence had to be explicitly addressed by the research question(s) and/or targeted by the research design. This means in particular that measures and/or descriptions of intervention outcomes were operationalised as instructional behaviours observable in classroom interaction. The operationalisations used should preferably refer to teaching behaviour "in the field". The data should, in other words, rather be proximal than distal in nature.

Studies were further eligible for inclusion when findings were reported about the influence of a VTL intervention on pupil learning. This means in particular that a study had produced evidence indicating relations between teacher and pupil behaviour – as addressed by review question II.

Thirdly, studies were included when findings were reported about relationships between outcomes of VTL and/or pupil learning on the one hand and processes involved in teacher learning on the other – as addressed by review question III.

Finally, studies were included when findings were reported about relationships between outcomes of VTL and/or pupil learning on the one hand and conditions in teachers' learning environments on the other – as addressed by review question IV.

Methodological quality

Guarantees for methodological quality were sought in the following ways. First, to be included in the review, a study had to be published in a peer-reviewed journal or book. Secondly, studies should conform to methodological standards. It did not matter within what paradigm a study was situated, nor what kind of research design was used, quantitative, qualitative or mixed-methods. Instead, I have required that a study should provide a sufficiently clear description of the VTL intervention studied and of the methods used.

Regarding the latter, I attended specifically to the following standards. The report of a study should provide a justification for a minimum of generalisability. This means that the report had to provide sufficient information about sampling, response rates and representativeness and that findings had to exceed anecdotal description. Also, the operationalisations chosen should have sufficient validity to meet the criterion of relevance to the review questions as described in the previous section. Finally, the procedures for data collection and analysis had to be clearly described.

Period

Only studies published in 2000 or later were included, as by far the most VTL research began to appear from that year onwards.

Geographical origin

Finally, I have sought to include studies from as many different countries as possible. As most peer-reviewed journals are in English or German, a bias towards

English- or German-speaking countries can easily occur. However, R&D work in the area of VTL also takes place in French- and Spanish-speaking countries and in non-Western countries generally.

Analysis

Performing the initial search according to the procedure described above resulted in a pool of 303 potentially relevant publications. From this pool, 79 sources fulfilled the four selection criteria. For each of these sources, I typed the characteristics and contents of the studies involved into a database in the form of an Excel spread sheet, using the categories listed in Table 3.1.

The database containing the final pool of sources provides information about the publications selected and the VTL-based programmes or interventions about which findings are reported.

For each intervention, the country where it took place was registered as well as the school type in which it was situated. School type was characterised by level of general education (primary or secondary). When other sectors were involved (special education or ECEC), this was also specified. In addition, the career phase(s) of the teachers studied were registered. Career phase was subdivided as either prospective (referring to participants in a PTE programme or an ACP), beginning (teachers with 0–5 years of experience) or experienced (teachers with more than five years of experience). For each source, the school subject or subject domain involved was noted, as far as this information was reported.

In order to be able to retrieve the necessary information about the design and implementation of the interventions studied, I summarised the descriptions of them as reported. Where the duration of interventions was concerned, information should ideally be available about three different factors: the total number of hours spent, the time span within which VTL activities took place and the frequency of preactive, interactive and postactive teacher learning activities (see the section *Duration* in Chapter 1). However, reasonably complete information was reported only about time span. This factor could therefore be quantified. I did so in months, counting one school year as ten months. Finally, the IT settings in which the interventions took place (offline, online or blended) was registered, as far as reported.

About the studies reviewed, the database contains the following information. When research goals and questions were explicitly stated, they were copied literally. In some cases, however, either research goals or research questions were not explicit. I then summarised or paraphrased them.

In addition, I characterised the research designs used in two ways: firstly, by the type of knowledge produced – using labels such as descriptive, experimental, follow-up and longitudinal – and, secondly, by the type of methods predominantly used – quantitative, qualitative or mixed-methods. Furthermore, the numbers of teachers and pupils studied were registered. The kinds of data collection instruments were specified, i.e. questionnaires, interviews, written comments on video images viewed, assessment instruments (standardised or not), observations on the basis of video

TABLE 3.1 Analysis categories for systematic literature review

Publication	
Source	publication reference
Project	title of VTL intervention studied
Intervention	
Country	country where intervention took place
School type	primary education
	secondary education
	special education
	early childhood education and care
Career phase	prospective, preservice teacher
	prospective, alternative certification candidate
	beginning teacher
	experienced teacher
School subject	subject or domain
Intervention description	intervention characteristics
Time span in months	length of period during which intervention took place
IT setting	offline
	online
	blended
Research goal and questions	
Research goal	research goal as stated
Research question(s)	research question(s) as stated
Research design	
design type	type of knowledge produced
	type of methods predominantly used
N teachers	number of teachers studied
N pupils	number of pupils studied
Instruments	types of data collection instruments used
Qualitative analysis	types of qualitative analysis methods used
Quantitative analysis	types of quantitative analysis methods used
Reliability ≥	lowest rate found in reliability analyses
Findings	
VTL model components	Biography & Goals
	Learning environment
	Teacher learning activity
	Perception: Framing, Focus, Other-viewing and/or Self-viewing
	Feedback: Learner, Self, Peer and/or Facilitator
	Reflection: Interpreting, Judging, Decision-making and/or Planning
	Enactment: Cognitive and/or Social aspects
	Pupil learning: Processes and/or Outcomes
	Teaching competence & Professional motivation
Evidence	main findings
Interpretation and conclusions	interpretation and conclusions warranted by evidence
Limitations	limitations resulting from methods use

recordings (coded or not), think-aloud protocols and/or other kinds. Similarly, the kinds of data analysis techniques were specified, i.e. descriptive statistics, analysis of (co)variance, factor analysis, correlational, regression and/or HLM techniques. Finally, when reliability analyses were reported, the minimum rates found were registered.

About the findings of the studies reviewed, the database contains the following information. I first categorised the findings in terms of the review questions, i.e. whether they pertained to changes in teachers' instructional action only or also to impact on pupil learning, processes of teacher learning and/or conditions in teachers' learning environments. In addition, I noted to which components of the VTL model the findings explicitly referred (see Figure 2.2). Then, I copied and/or summarised the main findings as reported and formulated the interpretation and conclusions insofar as I judged them to be warranted by the evidence presented. Finally, I noted limitations resulting from the methods as used.

Most information entered into the database is verbal in nature. In addition, I coded this information in order to determine which of the categories in Table 3.1 are applicable to each source. For instance, in the category School type, the characteristics "primary education" and "secondary education" were coded as applicable or not applicable. Another example is the VTL model component Perception. For this category, I coded whether or not a study's findings pertain to the elements of Framing, Focus, Other-viewing and/or Self-viewing. Four categories in the database contain quantitative information on a ratio level, i.e. interventions' time span, the numbers of teachers and pupils studied and the minimum reliability rates reported.

These different types of information were analysed as follows. In order to uncover general trends in the research reviewed, I first determined frequencies for the main characteristics of the interventions studied and for the studies' methodological characteristics. Then, I focussed the analyses on answering the review questions. To do so, I used the components of the VTL model as a guide (italicised below).

To answer review question I about the nature of changes in teachers' instructional action, I first selected all those studies coded as relevant to cognitive aspects of teachers' *Enactment*. Then, I examined the findings from these studies to discover commonalities between them. Findings displaying such commonalities were grouped together under a limited number of headings, and the findings under each heading were further differentiated. This inductive procedure made it possible to synthesise which evidence the studies together have produced. This same procedure I then applied to those studies coded as relevant to social-emotional aspects of teachers' *Enactment* as well as those relevant to the development of *Teaching competence* and *professional motivation*.

To answer review question II about the possible impact of changes in teachers' instruction on pupil learning, I separately selected those studies relevant to processes and outcomes of *Pupil learning*. I then analysed the findings from these studies according to the same inductive procedure described above.

To answer review question III about teachers' learning processes, I separately selected and inductively analysed the findings from those studies relevant to the components of *Perception*, *Feedback* and *Reflection*.

To answer review question IV about the conditions in teachers' learning environments, I separately selected and inductively analysed the findings from those studies relevant to the components of teachers' *Biography* and *Goals* as well as their *Learning environment*.

Given the nature of these studies and how I analysed them, the review findings presented below are predominantly of a factual and conceptual nature. Given the search procedure followed, I am reasonably confident that these findings are representative of the current state of VTL. The research now available about the impact of VTL on teachers' instructional action is quite diverse and the field therefore appears in need of comprehensive and structured interpretation.

Findings

This section opens with an outline of general trends in the scope and the methodology of the studies reviewed. Then, against this background, the findings regarding each of the review questions are presented.

Scope

The VTL interventions and the 79 studies about them contained in the final database are quite heterogeneous in several respects.

The research originates from twelve different countries. Most studies were carried out in the United States (51 or 65%), followed by the Netherlands (nine or 11%), Germany (six or 8%), the Czech Republic (four or 5%) and France (two or 3%). Australia, Cambodia, Cyprus, Jamaica, Sweden, Switzerland and the UK are each represented with one study (1.3%). The preponderance of studies from the US is perhaps due to the fact that funding for educational research there is often motivated by an economic interest in developing the "basic" school subjects. At any rate, more than half the VTL studies from the US are in literacy, mathematics and science.

The level of general education in which interventions were carried out was reported in 67 or 85% of the studies. Little more than half (35) were carried out in primary education. Slightly less than half (32) were carried out in secondary education. Seven studies or 9% were carried out in special education and six or 8% in the ECEC sector.

The school subjects or domains in which interventions were carried out were reported in 51 or 65% of the studies. Of these 51 studies, fifteen or 29% were carried out in science subjects, thirteen or 25% in mathematics and nine or 18% in literacy. In six studies or 12%, findings were reported about interventions in several different subjects. Social studies, economics and physical education were each represented with two studies (together 12%) and history and music each with one study (together 4%). These figures reflect the fact that VTL studies are most frequently funded in the basic subjects which form the core of school learning.

The large majority of studies selected for this review, i.e. 49 or 62%, involved experienced teachers. The next largest group of studies, i.e. fourteen or 17.7%, involved preservice teachers. In eight studies or 10.1%, beginning as well as experienced teachers participated. Four studies or 5.1% were of preservice and experienced teachers. Three studies were of beginning teachers, while one involved alternative certification candidates.

The time span of the interventions is reported in 58 or 73% of the studies. The average time span was 8.7, the mode as well as the median being 10. This time span was found in 28 out of these 58 studies. This suggests that almost half the interventions were undertaken over the course of one whole school year. In sixteen out of the 58 studies, i.e. 28%, a time span of less than one school year was reported. On the other hand, interventions lasted longer than one school year in eight out of the 58 studies, i.e. 14%, the maximum being 22 months. On the lower end of the spectrum, time spans ranging between three days and two months were reported in six out of the 58 studies, i.e. 10.3%. The interventions involved here were designed as short training trajectories.

As noted above, the total number of hours spent on teacher learning activities and the number of cycles within which they took place could not be quantified because data about these factors were lacking in most studies. This means that in this review, conclusions about the intensity or dosage of VTL interventions can only be drawn on qualitative grounds.

The IT settings in which the interventions took place is known from 60 or 76% of the studies. This resulted in a clear ranking. Most of the interventions were undertaken offline, i.e. 30 out of 60, exactly half. Nineteen out of 60 interventions or almost one third, took place in a blended learning environment. Eleven out of 60 interventions, almost one fifth, took place exclusively online.

Method use and the issue of causation

The 79 studies in this review are not only heterogeneous with respect to the interventions studied. They also diverge in terms of paradigm and methodology. To assign them unequivocally to any one underlying paradigm (see the section *Cognitivist, interpretive and sociocultural paradigms* in Chapter 2) is difficult. The research designs and methods used are quite divergent.

Predominantly descriptive findings were reported in more than half the studies, i.e. 43 or 54%. 37 studies or 47% had an experimental design, in all but three cases with random assignment of subjects. Data were mostly collected at two or more time points, i.e. in 47 or 60% of the studies, usually at the beginning and at the end of interventions. Follow-up data were collected in very few, i.e. in seven or 9% of the studies. When such data were collected, this happened on average 10.9 months after the interventions concerned. The number of teachers studied ranged from eight to 142. The average number was 83.

The number of teachers studied was reported in all but two studies. The average number of teachers in a study was 48, the minimum being 1 and the maximum 486. Most often, i.e. in 34 or 44% of the studies, the number of teachers fell between 1 and 10. In ten studies or 13%, this number fell between eleven and 30. In twelve studies or 16%, the number of teachers fell between 30 and 50. Higher numbers, ranging between 51 and 486, occurred in 21 or 27% of studies. The median number of teachers in a study was 23. These figures mean that currently, the majority of studies on the impact of VTL on teachers' instructional action can be characterised as small-scale research. This finding is visualised in Figure 3.1.

Pupils were involved in seventeen out of the 79 studies, i.e. 22% or less than a quarter. The average number of pupils studied was 1,207, the minimum being 4 and the maximum 2,823.

Data collection took place mostly with a combination of direct observation and self-report instruments. Observations were made in 58 or 73% of the studies. Standardised assessment based on observations occurred in 30 or 38% of the research. Two studies or 2.5% employed think-aloud protocols. The self-report methods used included questionnaires, interviews and comments written by teachers in response to video fragments viewed. Questionnaires were used in 24 or 30% of the studies, interviews in 21 or 27% and written comments in seven or 9%.

Reliability information about quantitative instruments was provided in 52 or two thirds of the research reports. Reliabilities of .80 or higher were reported in 23, i.e. 44% of these reports. In fifteen studies or 29%, minimum reliabilities were between .70 and .80. In the fourteen remaining reports, i.e. 27%, minimum reliabilities fell below .70.

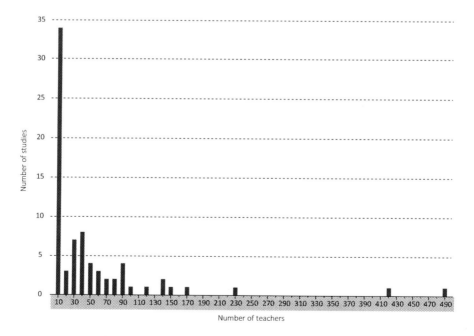

FIGURE 3.1 Numbers of teachers in studies

In data analysis, quantitative methods clearly predominated.

Qualitative data analysis methods were used in just 26 or one third of the studies. Content analysis of interview statements or written comments occurred in seven or 9% of the studies and discourse analysis of video club meetings in eight, i.e. one tenth of the studies. Crosscase analysis occurred in twelve or 15% of the studies, within-case analysis in seven or 9% of the studies. Combination of both these strategies occurred also in seven studies or 9%.

Quantitative data analysis methods were used in the large majority of studies, i.e. in 68 or 86%. In addition to descriptive statistics, between-groups and/or within-groups comparisons were reported in 43 or 54% of the studies. Correlational methods were used in 24 or 30% of the studies.

What I find rather striking is that in most studies, data analysis was either only qualitative or only quantitative. In eleven or 14% of the studies, both qualitative and quantitative data were collected, but the qualitative data were coded and analysed numerically, so that only quantitative results were reported. The reverse did not occur. Combinations between qualitative and quantitative data analysis did occur in eighteen or 23% of the studies. The above figures reflect that truly mixed-methods designs were clearly in a minority. The essence of a mixed-methods design is that qualitative and quantitative data are analysed in a deliberate relation to each other so as to answer the research questions.

The above trends in the methodology of the studies reviewed have consequences for the interpretation and the explanatory power of their findings. As a researcher, one wants ideally to be able to determine not only *if* any effects occur after teachers' participation in VTL, but also *how* and *why* this happens. We touch here on the issue of causation in educational research. Which methodological characteristics of studies make it possible to attribute learning outcomes in teachers and pupils to specific causal factors? In interpreting the studies reviewed I have used the following criteria for accepting causal inferences.

In connection with review questions I and II about learning outcomes in teachers and pupils, I have examined in particular how relationships between antecedents and outcomes were determined. In the case of quantitative research, I consider causal inferences possible when a basic experimental or quasi-experimental design is used, i.e. when pre-intervention as well as post-intervention measures are administered in one or more intervention groups and one or more comparison groups. In addition, I consider causal inferences possible, when dependent variables are regressed onto independent variables, as in multivariate regression and HLM designs. In the case of qualitative research, I consider causal inferences possible, when researchers describe how they reconstructed teachers' learning processes and this reconstruction clarifies to what outcomes these processes led and in what ways.

In connection with review questions III and IV about processes and conditions involved in VTL, I have examined in particular to what extent studies clarified the mechanisms underlying learning and how these were encouraged or constrained by contextual conditions. Such clarification, in my view, ideally requires mixed-methods research (Brouwer, 2010).

Changes in teachers' instructional action

The 79 sources selected for this review provide the evidence base for answering the first review question about the nature of changes in teachers' instructional action as a result of participating in VTL. Together, they show that after participating in VTL, teachers change cognitive as well as social-emotional aspects of their instructional action. Where the cognitive aspects are concerned, changes were found in how teachers sequence the contents and the learning activities during their lessons, in how they engage in discourse with their pupils and in how they diagnose and respond to pupils' learning. As to the social-emotional aspects, teachers make changes in their instructional routines and classroom management, shift their interaction with pupils in the direction of two-way communication and develop greater sensitivity in their contact with pupils. Some studies have yielded indications about the extent to which these teacher outcomes persist after VTL interventions end, in other words about their sustainability. Other studies have explored the role of teaching experience and individual differences in the outcomes of teachers'VTL. In this section, the above types of teacher outcomes are detailed and illustrated with salient examples.

Table 3.2 shows how many and which sources of the review are relevant to each of these types of outcomes. The sources have been ordered by descending number of teachers studied. This helps in judging the generalisability of the findings concerned. Using N = 15 – about the average group size of a PTE or PD group – as a demarcation, it can be seen that the majority of relevant studies involved more than fifteen teachers. This strengthens the generalisability of the evidence synthesised below. Generally, the findings from studies with N > 15 have more breadth, while those from studies with N < 15 have more depth. They thus complement each other.

Sequencing lesson content and learning activities

Participating in VTL has effects on how teachers structure their lessons, both when teaching and when planning them. They pay more attention to how they can sequence contents and organise learning activities in ways that require more cognitive effort from pupils than in traditional teacher-directed, transmission-oriented instruction.

This type of teacher outcomes is well illustrated by the STeLLA project. In the second version of this project (STeLLA-II), 71 experienced primary teachers in the US used the CSCL platform Visibility for focussed analysis of video records of their own and colleagues' teaching and then for planning and implementing alternatives for instruction in their own lessons. Research with standardised instruments showed that the participating teachers not only increased their science content knowledge and lesson analysis abilities (Roth et al., 2017; Taylor et al., 2017), but also changed their instruction by sequencing lesson contents and orchestrating learning activities on the basis of an explicit storyline (Roth et al., 2019).

TABLE 3.2 Types of teacher outcomes

Source	N of teachers	Sequencing lesson content and learning activities	Discourse practices	Diagnosing and responding to pupil learning	Instructional routines and classroom management	Two-way communication	Sensitivity and stimulation	Sustainability of teacher outcomes	Differences depending on career phase	Individual differences
Early et al., 2017	486				•					•
Hamre, Pianta, Burchinal et al., 2012	440		•	•						
Hamre, Pianta, Mashburn, & Downer, 2012	223						•			
Downer et al., 2011	161	••								
Roth et al., 2017	144	••								
Taylor et al., 2017	144	••	•							
Kraft & Hill, 2020	142	•								•
Mashburn et al., 2010	134	•								
Jacobs et al., 2011	131			••			•	•	•	
Pianta et al., 2008	113							•		
Fukkink & Tavecchio, 2010	95		•			•				
Mikami et al., 2011	88							•		
Gregory et al., 2014	87	•	•			•		•		
Allen et al., 2015	86		•		•	•		•		
Gregory et al., 2016	86				•	•		•		
Allen et al., 2011	78		•			•		•		
Jilink et al., 2018	72		•			••	•			
Roth et al., 2019	71	••	•		•		••		•	
Werner et al., 2018	64									

(Continued)

TABLE 3.2 (Continued). Types of teacher outcomes

Source	N of teachers	Sequencing lesson content and learning activities	Discourse practices	Diagnosing and responding to pupil learning	Instructional routines and classroom management	Two-way communication	Sensitivity and stimulation	Sustainability of teacher outcomes	Differences depending on career phase	Individual differences
Downner et al., 2009	62									
Christ, et al., 2014	57	●●					●			●
Baumgartner, 2018	56									
Wright et al., 2012	51		●		●					
Ely et al., 2014	49		●							
Roth, 2009	48	●								
Roth et al., 2011	48	●	●		●					
La Paro et al., 2011	46		●						●	
Sun & Van Es, 2015	38		●							
Hylton, 2000	37				●●					
Piwowar et al., 2013	37	●●			●●					
Kersting et al., 2012	36	●●								
Cain et al., 2007	35					●●				
Osborne et al., 2019	35	●●	●	●●						
Kuntze & Reiss, 2006	32	●●	●	●						
Van de Pol et al., 2014	30		●●	●						
Schildwacht, 2012	26	●	●●	●●						
Brock & Carter, 2015	25	●	●							
Lee et al., 2012	25	●	●							
Matsumura et al., 2019	25		●●							
Santagata & Yeh, 2014	24	●			●				●	
Voerman et al., 2015	23								●	●
Reisman & Enumah, 2020	21		●						●	

Study	Count
Kohen & Borko, 2019	18
Koellner & Jacobs, 2015	13
Sherin & Van Es, 2009	11
Browning & Porter, 2007	10
Kiemer et al., 2015	10
Pehmer et al., 2015a	10
Pehmer et al., 2015b	10
Williams, 2004	8
Gaudin et al., 2018	8
Harlin, 2014	8
Lok, 2019	8
Šed'ová et al., 2016	8
Shernoff & Kratochwill, 2007	8
Snoeyink, 2010	8
Van Es & Sherin, 2010	7
Damhuis et al., 2009	6
Brown & Kennedy, 2011	6
Barnhart & Van Es, 2018	4
Hemmeter et al., 2011	4
Lussi Borer et al., 2014	4
Robinson, 2011	4
Santagata & Bray, 2016	4
Šed'ová, et al., 2014	4
Tekkumru-Kisa & Stein, 2017	4
Van de Pol et al., 2012	4

(Continued)

TABLE 3.2 (Continued). Types of teacher outcomes

Source	N of teachers	Sequencing lesson content and learning activities	Discourse practices	Diagnosing and responding to pupil learning	Instructional routines and classroom management	Two-way communication	Sensitivity and stimulation	Sustainability of teacher outcomes	Differences depending on career phase	Individual differences
Walker et al., 2019	4		●							
Capizzi et al., 2010	3		●							
Charalambous et al., 2018	3	●								
Damhuis & De Blauw, 2008	3		●							
Hawkins & Heflin, 2011	3				●					
Oliveira, 2010	3		●			●				
Rich & Hannafin, 2009b	3	●								
Santagata & Yeh, 2016	3	●								
Stephenson et al., 2011	3		●			●				
Šed'ová, 2017a	1		●							
Šed'ová, 2017b	1		●							
Schindler et al., 2015	1		●							
Number of sources with N > 15	43 54%	15 19%	20 25%	5 6%	9 11%	8 10%	5 6%	7 9%	5 6%	4 5%
Number of sources with N < 15	36 46%	10 13%	17 22%	2 3%	8 10%	5 6%	1 1%	2 3%	1 1%	4 5%
Total number of sources	79 100%	25 32%	37 47%	7 9%	17 22%	13 16%	6 8%	9 11%	6 8%	8 10%

Notes:
● Relevant source.
●● See text.
Rounded percentages based on N = 79.

These findings confirm the relationships between lesson analysis ability and instructional quality reported by Kersting, Givvin, Thompson, Santagata, & Stigler 2012). These researchers demonstrated that teachers who analysed video records of teaching with the help of specific viewing points were better able during their mathematics teaching to develop concepts, make appropriate use of representations to explain algorithms and connect concepts and topics.

That participating in VTL encourages teachers to employ activating learning formats as a part of deliberate instructional strategies is also apparent from a study by Downer et al. (2011) among 161 experienced primary teachers in the US. The teachers in the experimental group who viewed model videos and participated in online coaching on the MTP platform implemented effective activities in their own language/literacy teaching as defined by evidence-based conceptual frameworks. Comparable outcomes were reported by Christ, Arya, & Chiu (2014), who found that nine preservice and 48 experienced primary teachers applied teaching methods in their literacy instruction which they had viewed and discussed with colleagues during peer coaching.

VTL-induced changes in instruction involving the move towards activating learning formats were also found in other countries than the United States. In Jamaica, Williams (2004) showed that eight preservice secondary science teachers, who studied collaborative learning as an instructional strategy during their PTE programme in a multimedia case-based learning environment, implemented the cooperative learning principles of individual accountability, face-to-face interaction and monitoring groups as defined by Johnson and Johnson (1991) in their own lessons, even in the face of difficult working circumstances.

In Germany, Kuntze and Reiss (2006) showed that 32 experienced upper-secondary mathematics teachers provided their pupils with more activating learning tasks, organised more open forms of cooperation between them and encouraged them to present their learning results after participating in three training weekends focussing on video-based analysis of classroom situations conducted parallel to two implementation phases.

Discourse practices

Participating in VTL induces changes in teachers' discourse practices. They change their verbal communication with pupils in the following ways. During classroom teaching, teachers talk less themselves and encourage their pupils to talk more about lesson content. Teachers come to ask fewer closed questions eliciting reproduction in favour of more open, probing and follow-up questions aimed at cognitive elaboration. These changes go hand in hand with an increase in the amount of feedback they provide to their pupils as well as the levels on which they give feedback. This means that teachers' verbal communication shifts from being unilateral – proceeding mainly from teacher to pupils – towards becoming more bilateral and triadic – proceeding between the parties. In sum, VTL participation helps teachers move in the direction of dialogic discourse practices.

Encouraging pupil talk has become an important goal of PD efforts in the field of literacy instruction. Research suggests that involving pupils in focussed dialogue about the meaning of text enhances their understanding. To achieve this, instructional techniques have been developed called "Questioning the author" and "Accountable talk". Teachers using the first technique ask questions and engage pupils in dialogue about the meaning of difficult parts in a text (Beck & McKeown, 2006). The second technique involves encouraging pupils to voice arguments and explanations and connect ideas in a text to phenomena in the wider world (Michaels, O'Connor, & Resnick, 2008). To increase the quality of teachers' classroom text discussions, Matsumura and colleagues developed "a six-week online workshop (approximately 24 hours of professional development), followed by individual, video-based coaching sessions" (Matsumura et al., 2019, p. 194). After 25 beginning and experienced primary teachers in the US participated in this intervention, their classroom instruction was rated with the Instructional Quality Assessment (IQA) instrument (Matsumura, Garnier, Slater, & Boston, 2008; Matsumura, Garnier, & Spybrook, 2013). It was found that during the work-shop as well as the subsequent coaching, the teachers increased their use of both techniques. This increase, in turn, was followed by a rise in the quality of pupils' contributions to classroom dialogue.

Similarly, effects of VTL participation on teachers' as well as pupils' classroom behaviour were found in a small-scale study in the Czech Republic. Four experi-enced and motivated lower-secondary teachers in civics and mother-tongue educa-tion volunteered to participate in seminars and individual coaching about dialogic teaching. The participants then increased their use of discourse practices which placed higher cognitive demands on pupils and encouraged them to give more open and longer replies to questions. As a result, the number of instances when pupils themselves initiated communication increased. The researcher concluded that as teacher communication methods change, a change in pupils' communication pat-terns follows (Šeďová, Švaříček, Sedláček, & Šalamounová, 2014).

How classroom communication unfolds depends to a large extent on how teach-ers ask questions. Several studies show that VTL participation leads to changes in teachers' questioning behaviour. After VTL, they generally ask fewer closed ques-tions and more open questions. This effect was found for example by Damhuis, (De Blauw, Tammes, & Sytema, 2009) after three preservice and three experienced Dutch primary teachers analysed video footage of their own classroom discourse during team meetings about dialogic teaching combined with individual coaching over a period of six months.

Classroom discourse is also the arena in which pupils receive feedback from their teachers. Research by Pehmer, Gröschner and Seidel (2015a) illustrates how VTL can influence teachers' feedback behaviour. After participating in two itera-tions of the Dialogic Video Cycle (see the eponymous section in Chapter 2), six experienced lower-secondary science teachers in Germany decreased their simple feedback, i.e. only saying if pupils' answers or solutions were right or wrong, and increased constructive feedback, i.e. elaborating on pupils' contributions.

Diagnosing and responding to pupil learning

Participating in VTL helps teachers become aware of and change how they interact with pupils. They begin to base their communication more on how pupils react to them. However, while engaging more in dialogue with their pupils, they meet new challenges. When they elicit reactions from pupils by asking more open questions and giving more elaborate feedback, it then becomes a challenge how to respond to those reactions. What is even more challenging for teachers is to diagnose pupils' current understandings and make their responses contingent on those understandings. It is possible to train this ability, but the average classroom setting does not lend itself well to the type of individualised communication which contingent teaching requires (see the section *Contingent teaching* in Chapter 1).

How teachers may learn to respond to what children say about lesson content was studied by Jacobs, Lamb, Philipp and Schappelle (2011) in a cross-sectional study of 131 experienced primary mathematics teachers in the US, who took part voluntarily in a PD programme based on the Cognitively Guided Instruction (CGI) approach (Carpenter, Fennema, Franke, Levi, & Empson, 1999; Carpenter, Franke, & Levi, 2003). During five full days of workshops per year, these teachers analysed classroom video and their own pupils' work, focussing on how children (learn to) think mathematically and on how this can inform their own instruction. 36 of the PD participants were prospective primary teachers, 31 were "initial participants", i.e. teachers beginning PD, 31 were "advancing participants", i.e. teachers with two years of PD experience and 33 were "emerging teacher leaders", i.e. teachers with at least four years of PD experience.

These different groups of respondents viewed a two-part video of a one-on-one problem-solving interview between a teacher and a kindergartner once and wrote a comment to a prompt after each part. These written comments were coded and rated by means of two scales: one for how teachers decided to respond and one for how they attended to children's mathematical strategies. The statistical analyses of differences between the subgroups indicated that "increased experience with children's thinking was related to increased engagement with children's thinking". Teachers' "expertise in deciding how to respond on the basis of children's understandings … grew with two years of professional development and again when teachers had engaged in four or more years of professional development and leadership activities". The researchers conclude that "expertise in attending to children's strategies is foundational to deciding how to respond" and that "developing expertise in deciding how to respond is challenging but can be achieved with engagement in PD that is sustained over many years" (Jacobs et al., 2011, p. 109–111).

Three other studies about the development of teachers' discourse practices yielded similar indications that for teachers, learning to respond to and stimulate pupils' thinking is relatively difficult, but possible.

Osborne et al. (2019) distinguished six discourse practices that teachers and/or learners could use during dialogic science teaching: Ask, Press, Link, Explain/claim, Co-construct, Critique. 35 experienced primary science teachers in the US participated in a summer institute and four follow-up sessions during the subsequent school year, during which they analysed video records of colleagues' and their own teaching. Quantitative analyses of video observations of their lessons showed that the PD participants performed best in Asking questions. However, the practices of Link and Critique proved difficult to sustain.

Similarly, in a small-scale study of four experienced secondary science teachers in the US who participated in five video club sessions, Barnhart and Van Es (2018) found that two of them changed their instructional behaviour, but found it especially difficult to react adequately to pupil reactions.

Finally, Van de Pol et al. (2014) in the Netherlands studied seventeen experienced lower-secondary social studies teachers who studied theory and video cases about contingent teaching, i.e. teaching adapted to learners' current understandings and providing learning activities and feedback on appropriate levels of challenge (see the section *Higher-order teaching* in Chapter 1). They then attempted to implement such teaching themselves and recorded and analysed their instructional action with the support of an expert facilitator and each other over a period of eight weeks. Observations showed that in contrast to a control group, most of the participating teachers

> significantly improved the quality of their diagnostic strategies (eliciting demonstrations of understanding instead of just claims), the quality of their checks of students' learning (eliciting demonstrations of understanding instead of just claims), and the quality of their support (adapting their degree of control contingently to students' understanding and in taking up students' ideas in the ongoing conversation …).
>
> (Van de Pol et al., 2014, p. 640)

Instructional routines and classroom management

As most pupils and experienced teachers know, clear and justifiable routines of classroom behaviour are a necessary condition for learning. This is one of the ways in which cognitive aspects of instruction and social-emotional aspects of classroom management are related. By engaging in VTL, preservice teachers can learn about and begin to implement basic routines and classroom management behaviours which contribute to effective instruction. Experienced teachers can develop these routines and behaviours further by refining the types of discourse they use. By doing so, they improve the establishment of positive behavioural routines in their classrooms and promote cooperative working relationships with their pupils.

Preservice teachers can develop their competence in classroom management through other-viewing as well as self-viewing. Hylton (2000), in the US, compared how an experimental group of nineteen student teachers learned compared to a control group of eighteen student teachers. The experimental group viewed videos of expert teachers modelling classroom management behaviours, engaged in guided group discussion of these model videos and received instruction on implementing the techniques shown. The control group experienced traditional lecture, discussion and role-playing. These activities took place during a twelve-week period during which weekly group seminars and student teaching in schools ran parallel. Classroom observations showed that in their classroom management behaviour, the student teachers in the experimental group more frequently acknowledged appropriate pupil behaviours and displayed a greater variety of and flexibility in teaching behaviours. Survey instruments also showed that they developed less controlling and interventionist attitudes regarding instruction and people management.

In another American study, Snoeyink (2010) followed eight preservice teachers during their student teaching over a period of one semester. The students were filmed on four consecutive occasions with two cameras, one focussed on them, one focussed on their pupils. They then analysed the recordings focussing on classroom management behaviours as conceptualised in Kounin's concept of "withitness" (Kounin, 1970). Additional data were collected with self-rating scales, weekly written reflections and a group focus interview. To trace students' development over time, "dissonance scores" were calculated indicating the difference between student teachers' self-ratings and the researcher's ratings of the consecutive videos of their teaching. The findings indicate that the student teachers became more effective in classroom management in the following respects. They came to see themselves from the students' perspective, reduced annoying mannerisms and became better able to notice how well students understood and more aware of their own reflection-in-action. For four participants, dissonance scores were reduced over time, while two of them already had realistic images of their classroom management behaviour at the start of the intervention.

Effects on student teachers' instructional routines and classroom management behaviour were also shown in a VTL intervention of shorter duration. Browning and Porter (2007) studied ten student teachers in the US who participated in an online observation training focussing on eye contact during music teaching. They were videotaped while teaching before and after using the computer observation programme eMirror.

> eMirror allows observers to view and control QuickTime and mpeg4 video segments directly within the software package, stores a time-based record of every instructional event, and quantifies and summarizes these events. … participants were able to view the statistical results of this observation and were required to submit a printout of the summary report to the instructor.
>
> (Browning & Porter, 2007, p. 66–67)

Each participant handed in fifteen-minute video recordings from the middle part of two different lessons. Analysis of these data showed that over time, the preservice music teachers showed an increase in eye contact with their pupils. Also, the ratio of performance to instructional time in their lessons changed to the benefit of performance.

In Germany, Piwowar, Thiel and Ophardt (2013) showed how in-service teachers can refine their classroom management behaviours. Nineteen teachers participated in a training programme totalling 23 hours which consisted of three modules. In Module 1, productive classroom management strategies derived from the work of Doyle (1986, 2006) and Kounin (1970) were presented through lecture and scripted videos (Piwowar, Barth, Ophardt, & Thiel, 2018). During Module 2, they engaged in MT. In Module 3, they discussed video recordings of their own teaching with four colleagues and a coach (see for more detail the section *Classroom Management Competencies* in Chapter 2). Analysis of observer ratings showed that compared to the control group, which participated only in Module 1, the teachers in the experimental group improved their use of preventive classroom management strategies, notably how they mobilised groups of pupils and monitored their behaviour.

Two-way communication

In general education as well as special education, VTL-supported training can help teachers within a relatively short time span to use specific communicative abilities, notably giving pupils general and specific praise and catching and keeping children's attention. These abilities help teachers establish and maintain rapport with individual pupils. In group settings, they help teachers foster two-way communication with and between pupils.

In a study by Cain, Rudd and Saxon (2007), sixteen beginning and experienced childcare providers working in childcare centres in disadvantaged areas in the US received two half days of training and three coaching visits over a period of three months. The goal of this intervention was to increase the use of a pivotal skill in interaction called Joint Attention Engagement (JAE), i.e. forms of speech suited to stimulating children's cognitive and social development, as operationalised in the "Focus–Follow–Talk" technique. "Focus" means that the childcare provider directs her attention to "objects to which the child has already chosen to attend". "Follow" means that she follows "the child's lead. That is … engage[s] with the child and with what the child is attending to. … The final step is to Talk (or Teach) about the object in ways that will promote language development" (Cain et al., 2007, p. 170). After an introduction into the Focus-Follow-Talk technique, each childcare provider was filmed on site during her everyday interaction with children and received video-supported feedback from the visiting coach. Analysis of the video recordings based on standardised observation instruments showed that, compared to a control group, the participants in the intervention significantly increased the number of their Focus–Follow–Talk statements and JAE support statements to children. Also, in contrast to the childcare providers in the control group, the training participants' interactional behaviours became more suited to stimulating children's language development. When talking with children, they more often addressed their activities instead of using directive forms of speech.

In the UK, six experienced teachers in primary special education participated in two workshops over a period of twelve weeks, during which they studied videos of educative types of dialogue with children with learning difficulties and identified areas for improvement in their own classroom interaction. In addition, they analysed videos of their own classroom interaction during three individual reflection sessions with an educational psychologist. The intervention concluded with a final workshop in which the teachers exchanged their learning experiences and planned for future collaboration (Brown & Kennedy, 2011). The video recordings of the teachers' classroom interaction at the beginning and the end of the project were rated on the following aspects: building on children's ideas; supporting cooperation between children; children's involvement in conversation. The findings showed that after the intervention, the participating teachers generally talked less and children talked more. Also, teachers' talk became more educative, i.e. they talked less about their own agenda, spent less time giving information and making requests, used more linking statements within conversation and spent more time and focussed more on inputs from children.

Increases in teachers' communicative abilities as an effect of VTL is particularly apparent from a study by Jilink, Fukkink and Huijbregts (2018) among 72 experienced ECEC teachers in the Netherlands. These teachers were divided over three experimental groups and one control group. The experimental groups participated in different video-supported training programmes, which focussed on three components: children's development; offering an attractive learning environment for children; and educational activities. Participants received on-the-job coaching, in which experienced coaches provided them with individual feedback on their work. Coaching consisted of eleven 2.5-hour sessions during one school year. Observations with standardised instruments showed that compared to the control group, participants in experimental groups developed stronger skills in verbal communication, developmental stimulation and in fostering peer interactions between children (for more detail, see the section *Interactional and instructional skills in early childhood education and care* in Chapter 2).

An original study of teachers' development is reported from Sweden by Eva-Marie Harlin (2014). This researcher proceeded from the idea that self-viewing of their work in the classroom can launch cycles of surprise, reflection and action in teachers. She therefore engaged 43 teachers during their preservice education in analysing video records of their classroom interaction. Then, two years into in-service teaching, Harlin randomly selected out of this group fifteen graduates, of whom eight volunteered to participate in a follow-up study. The respondents were asked to analyse a video recording of their current teaching and report if and what changes in teaching habits they had developed since their student-teaching days. The reflective comments they had written as student teachers and their current lesson recordings were used as a stimulus for semi-structured interviews. Content analysis of their responses showed that over time, seven out of eight teachers had refined existing teaching habits and developed new ones. Their teaching had developed in the direction of more learner-oriented instruction characterised by reduced teacher control. During classroom discourse, they had created more opportunities to speak for their pupils and this had allowed them to build better relationships. The teachers felt that making these changes had been triggered by self-viewing, as this had led them to discover discrepancies between their classroom behaviour and personal values.

Sensitivity and stimulation

When VTL-supported individual coaching focusses on well-defined and evidence-based behaviours, this can encourage both preservice and experienced teachers to develop their sensitivity to the needs of children and their ability to stimulate cognitive and social-emotional development. These outcomes were found predominantly in Dutch research in the ECEC sector (see the section *Interactional and instructional skills in early childhood education and care* in Chapter 2) and in the MTP impact studies in the US (see the section *My TeachingPartner* in Chapter 2).

In the Netherlands, the Video-feedback Intervention to promote Positive Parenting and Sensitive Discipline (VIPP-SD) was developed for use in families with children in the preschool age (Juffer, Bakermans-Kranenburg, & Van IJzendoorn, 2014). This intervention was adapted by Werner, Vermeer, Linting and Van IJzendoorn (2018) for use in childcare centres. 34 childcare providers participated in this adapted version during periods between twelve and 24 weeks. Trained coaches visited each of them six times in their work settings, filmed their interaction with children during both structured and unstructured play situations and gave them feedback on their interaction behaviour regarding aspects of sensitivity such as contact seeking and empathy and aspects of discipline such as distraction and limit setting. Standardised observation scales were used to measure the caregivers' behaviours. Data analysis comparing the participants in the adapted VIPP-SD to a control group of 30 childcare providers showed that "after the intervention, observed sensitivity increased … only in the intervention group … the structured play situations accounted for the increase in sensitivity over time." After the training, the participants also "showed a more positive attitude towards caregiving and limit setting than the control group" (Werner et al., 2018, p. 100). They "evaluated the video-feedback intervention very positively, indicating that the training was informative, interesting and useful to them" (Werner et al., 2018, p. 101).

Sustainability of teacher outcomes

To which extent do the teacher outcomes synthesised above persist after VTL interventions end? This question is obviously of vital importance. However, as can be seen in Table 3.2, only nine out of the 79 studies reviewed, i.e. 11%, have produced evidence about it. Seven of these studies include follow-up data (see also the above section *Method use and the issue of causation*), while in two studies, subgroups of teachers were compared – by Barnhart and Van Es (2018) on the basis of growth profiles and by Jacobs et al. (2011) on the basis of teachers' career phase.

Together, the findings from these nine studies point in the same direction as the outcomes reported in the preceding sections. The studies cover all the types of teacher outcomes distinguished and thus suggest that after the end of interventions, teachers retain at least part of the changes in instructional action induced by VTL participation. However, given the low number of studies involved, this evidence can be considered only tentative.

Differences depending on career phase

The influence of differences in teachers' career phase on the outcomes of VTL is equally difficult to determine. Explicit findings about this issue are reported in only six or 8% of the studies reviewed and these findings are mixed. On the one hand, the study by Jacobs et al. (2011) suggests that the more experience teachers have with children's thinking and the more they engage with VTL in this area, the better they will be able to respond to how pupils learn mathematics (see the section *Diagnosing and responding to pupil learning* above). Also, Reisman and Enumah (2020) report indications that beginning and experienced teachers' discourse practices were influenced by their prior learning. In the domain of social-emotional behaviours, Werner et al. (2018) report that participation in VTL-supported training encouraged experienced teachers in ECEC to increase their caregiver sensitivity (see the section *Sensitivity and stimulation* above), while Harlin (2014) found changes in beginning teachers' instruction towards more open relationships with learners following self-viewing (see the section *Two-way communication* above). On the other hand, no indications for systematic differences depending on career phase were found in teachers' social-emotional behaviours after VTL participation in the studies by La Paro et al. (2011) and Voerman et al. (2015).

Individual differences

Explicit findings about the influence of individual differences on teacher outcomes are reported in only eight or 10% of the studies reviewed. However, most of these studies indicate that such differences do play a role in outcomes as well as processes of VTL.

Early, Maxwell, Ponder and Pan (2017) found that teachers with lower initial qualifications and teachers in metropolitan areas increased their instructional and emotional support of pupils relatively strongly as they engaged in online coaching through the MTP platform. Both Šeďová and colleagues (Šeďová, Sedláček, & Švaříček, 2016; Šeďová et al., 2014) and Brown and Kennedy (2011) found considerable differences in the changes that individual teachers made in their discourse practices after participating in VTL. In addition, these researchers as well as Pehmer, Gröschner and Seidel (2015b) and Downer, Locasale-Crouch, Hamre and Pianta (2009) found individual differences in the nature and timing of teachers' change trajectories. Downer and colleagues found that older teachers and teachers reporting relatively high levels of self-efficacy spent more time on viewing model videos and on consultation. Also, teachers who showed relatively high levels of positive emotional and instructional support to their pupils at the beginning of the school year were rated by their consultants as more responsive to support through MTP.

Impact on pupil learning

To answer the second review question about the possible impact of changes in teachers' instructional action on pupils' learning, 27 empirical sources are available, i.e. 34% of the 79 sources in the whole review. In these sources, findings relevant to pupil learning are reported. This evidence base is considerably smaller than the one about teacher outcomes. At the same time, these 27 studies do cover the whole causal chain extending from teachers' instruction through their interaction with pupils to the processes and outcomes of pupil learning.

The studies described in this section rest on direct observations of teachers' and pupils' classroom interaction and/or on standardised assessments of pupils' learning processes and/or achievement. Research reports based only on teacher self-report have been excluded here in order to counter the risk of findings being biased by wishful thinking. As can be seen in Table 3.3 – laid out in the same way as Table 3.2 – most sources involve studies of more than fifteen teachers. When data were collected

TABLE 3.3 Types of pupil outcomes

Source	N of teachers	N of pupils	Activation and engagement	Improved classroom behaviour
Hamre, Pianta, Mashburn, & Downer, 2012	223	980		●
Roth et al., 2017	144	2823	●	
Taylor et al., 2017	144	2823	●	
Mashburn et al., 2010	134	134	●	
Pianta et al., 2008	113			●
Mikami et al., 2011	88	1423		●
Gregory et al., 2014	87	1669	●●	
Allen et al., 2015	86	1194	●	●
Gregory et al., 2016	86	1195		●●
Allen et al., 2011	78	2237	●	
Roth et al., 2019	71		●	
Downer et al., 2009	62			●
Roth, 2009	48	1490	●	
Piwowar et al., 2013	37		●	●
Cain et al., 2007	35			●●
Lee et al., 2012	25		●	
Matsumura et al., 2019	25		●	
Kiemer et al., 2015	10	226	●●	
Šed'ová et al., 2016	8		●●	
Shernoff & Kratochwill, 2007	8	13		●
Brown & Kennedy, 2011	6		●	
Hemmeter et al., 2011	4			●
Robinson, 2011	4	4		●
Šed'ová et al., 2014	4		●●	
Šed'ová, 2017a	1		●	
Šed'ová, 2017b	1		●	
Schindler et al., 2015	1		●●	
Number of sources with N > 15	17	22%	11	14%	8	10%
Number of sources with N < 15	10	13%	7	9%	3	4%
Total number of sources	27	34%	18	23%	11	14%

Notes:
● Relevant source.
●● See text.
Rounded percentages based on N = 79.

directly among pupils, the numbers of pupils involved have been included. In fourteen studies, pupil data were part of observations of their interaction with teachers.

The studies of teacher samples larger than fifteen are mostly based on quantitative analysis, while those of smaller samples predominantly involve qualitative analyses of classroom interaction and teachers' experiences with it. It is important to note that both types of studies indicate that processes and outcomes of pupil learning relate to specific types of teachers' instructional action. In other words, the evidence summarised below specifies to some extent in what ways teachers' instructional action promotes pupil learning.

Teachers' VTL participation has been shown to result in achievement gains in pupils, both in science – as evident from the STeLLA studies – and in literacy – as evident from the studies by Mashburn et al. (2010) and Matsumura et al. (2019). Several MTP impact studies, notably Allen, Hafen, Gregory, Mikami and Pianta (2015), Downer et al. (2009), Hamre, Pianta, Mashburn, and Downer (2012), and Mikami Gregory, Allen, Pianta and Lun (2011) as well as other studies such as the one by Cain et al. (2007) also show that teachers' VTL participation has the potential to produce improvements in pupils' social-emotional engagement and competence. These pupil outcomes are promoted when VTL participation encourages teachers to increase their content knowledge and lesson analysis abilities, to put more effort into lesson planning, to change their discourse practices and to shift towards two-way communication with pupils (see the previous section about these teacher outcomes).

The following examples clarify the interaction processes involved.

Activation and engagement

As noted earlier, cognitive and social-emotional aspects of classroom teaching and learning are closely related (see the section *Instructional routines and classroom management* above). Detailed evidence about how this relationship operates and how it can change when teachers participate in online video-supported coaching comes from a study by Gregory, Allen, Mikami, Hafen and Pianta (2014). 87 experienced secondary teachers teaching 1,669 pupils in the US completed nine coaching cycles through the MTP platform during one school year. It was found that their

> focus on analysis and problem solving during instruction and their use of diverse instructional learning formats … acted as mediators of increased student engagement. … intervention teachers had significantly higher increases, albeit to a modest degree, in student behavioral engagement in their classrooms after 1 year of involvement with the program compared to the teachers in the control group.
>
> (Gregory et al., 2014, p. 143)

It is worth quoting here at length how the authors discuss their findings:

> This study is among the first experimental studies to establish the efficacy of a teacher professional development program in changing adolescent

behavioural engagement in the classroom. It is striking that the program was able to significantly and positively shift engagement, albeit to a modest degree (explaining 4% of the variance), across a diverse range of middle and high school classrooms, whether high and low achieving, more or less ethnically diverse, or more or less economically disadvantaged.

(Gregory et al., 2014, p. 156–157)

About the mechanisms of change, they write:

For the intervention teachers, changes in a dimension in the Classroom Organization domain (Instructional Learning Formats) and in the Instructional Support domain (Analysis and Problem Solving) were associated with increased engagement from the start of the year to the end of the year. As measured by Instructional Learning Formats, intervention teachers were better able to structure their interactions with adolescents—they improved in their presentation of material and the provision of interesting lessons and materials. They communicated learning objectives, provided clear summaries, and sequenced material logically. The teachers learned to present information in multiple ways, using different materials and modalities (e.g., hands-on activities, peer collaboration). They became more skilled at actively facilitating student involvement by asking students questions, and scaffolding and extending their learning. As measured by observed Analysis and Problem Solving, these teachers also improved in their facilitation of students' use of higher level thinking skills, such as reasoning and synthesis through the application of knowledge and skills. Teachers improved in how they interacted with students through their instruction. Specifically, they structured learning so students had opportunities to gain a deep level of understanding of the material. For instance, teachers used lessons that offered complex tasks, in which students needed to independently problem solve, generate, and test hypotheses, as well as examine relationships among ideas and synthesize material. Finally, improved teachers typically encouraged "thinking out loud" (meta-cognition) so that students reflected on their own process of learning. Taken together, classrooms high on these dimensions of the CLASS-S reflect a developmentally appropriate instructional context for adolescents.

(Gregory et al., 2014, p. 157–158)

Pupils apparently perceive and react to the nature of their teachers' instructional action. In the German Dialogic Video Cycle (DVC) project (see the eponymous section in Chapter 2), researchers sought to find out how changes in teachers' discourse practices aiming at cognitive elaboration influenced their pupils. While six experienced lower-secondary science teachers participated in the DVC, their 136 pupils – especially those with a high reported self-efficacy – indeed experienced an increase in their teachers' use of these instructional strategies (Kiemer et al., 2015). In a case study of one high-performing teacher, Schindler, Gröschner and Seidel (2015) coded video records of her instructional behaviour and compared these to her pupils' self-reported experiences during classroom learning. They found that especially during the second half of the school year, the behaviour changes achieved by the teacher appeared to be "mirrored" in the pupils' experiences (Schindler et al., 2015, p. 29).

In their action research project in the Czech Republic, Šeďová et al. (2014) found similar indications of a correspondence between changes in teachers' instructional action and pupils' classroom experiences. Four experienced and motivated lower-secondary teachers of Czech and civics voluntarily participated in seminars about dialogic teaching and discussed video recordings of their teaching with a researcher over a period of nine months. As the study was based on a mixed-methods design, quantitative analyses of video codings were combined with content analysis of the teachers' interview statements. It was found that as teachers placed higher cognitive demands on pupils by changing how they asked questions, their pupils began giving longer and more open answers and more frequently initiated communication themselves.

In a sequel to this study, Šeďová et al. (2016) involved eight teachers in workshops and other-viewing of model videos alternating with video-based discussions of their own teaching, focussing on four criterion behaviours derived from theory and research about enacting effective classroom discourse during dialogic teaching. The study's findings were again based on quantitative analyses of the video recordings of the participants' teaching combined with content analysis of interview statements. Regression analyses of the relative influence of the four criterion behaviours showed that as teachers increased their number of utterances promoting thought and reasoning – i.e. using argumentative talk, encouraging open discussion, building on previous speakers' remarks and asking questions of high cognitive demand – this promoted their pupils' participation in classroom dialogue.

Šeďová and colleagues "observed that when teacher communication methods change, a change in student communication patterns follows". They conclude from their studies that there exists an "interdependence of teacher and student communicative actions [which] is extremely important. ... To maximize student learning, it is necessary to make students more involved in communication" (Šeďová et al., 2014, p. 37). It is equally important that teachers can change this interdependence by studying what higher-order teaching entails and by using video analysis of their instruction to develop such teaching in their own work (Šeďová et al., 2016, p. 21–22).

Improved classroom behaviour

How teachers' instruction and pupils' social-emotional behaviour are related surfaces again – and impressively – in another study by Gregory and colleagues (Gregory et al., 2016). In a randomised controlled trial, 44 experienced secondary teachers of 659 predominantly black adolescents in the US were assigned to an experimental condition in which they participated in five to six MTP coaching cycles over a period of two school years, while 42 teachers of 536 pupils experienced PD in a form described as "business as usual" (Gregory et al., 2016, pp. 27

and 6, respectively). Building on the earlier MTP impact study by Allen et al. (2015), Gregory and colleagues sought to determine if changes in instruction made by the teachers in the coaching condition had any influence on pupils' classroom behaviour after coaching was ceased. In the third year after coaching began, standardised observations with the CLASS instrument showed that

> in classrooms where teachers showed greater improvement in Teacher Sensitivity and Analysis and Inquiry across two years of the study, Black students were less likely to be issued a disciplinary referral than their peers in classrooms where teachers showed less improvement on these two CLASS-S dimensions. … The degree to which teachers were observed as facilitating higher level thinking skills, problem solving, and metacognition was significantly linked to their equitable and infrequent use of discipline referrals. In classrooms observed as high on Analysis and Inquiry, students appeared to carry the "cognitive load." Teachers created opportunities for students to evaluate, synthesize, or engage in challenging problems. Examples include teachers a) asking students to formulate the history of an imaginary country based on its geography, b) supporting small groups in developing a plan to reduce pollutants from entering the stream behind the school c) facilitating student experiments to test how plants respond to different environmental stimuli, and d) helping students apply existing knowledge to new applications such as writing out word problems based on their solved mathematical equations.
>
> (Gregory et al., 2016, p. 13–15)

As teachers raised the quality of their instructional action, their working relationship with their pupils apparently improved. Indications of a comparable phenomenon were observed by Cain and colleagues in their study of the effects of ECEC teachers' use of Focus–Follow–Talk and JAE (see the section *Two-way communication* above):

> Anecdotally, children in the classroom appeared to respond positively to the phenomenon of joint attention engagement when it was occurring. Children were observed to be drawn towards a childcare provider who was practicing Focus–Follow–Talk.
>
> (Cain et al., 2007, p. 178)

Processes of teacher learning

In almost half the sources selected for this review, i.e. 39 or 49%, evidence is reported not only about the outcomes of teachers' VTL, but also about the processes contributing to changes in instruction. This is the issue addressed by the third review question. This specific evidence about process influences fulfils one or more of the criteria that I formulated for acceptable causal inference (see the section *Method use and the issue of causation*). The evidence presented below can therefore serve as a basis for answering the third review question aimed at clarifying which VTL processes contribute to changes in instruction.

The available evidence points towards three overarching relationships between processes and outcomes of VTL. Firstly, when teachers engage repeatedly in cycles of learning activities, this helps them choose which changes they want to make in their instruction and implement those changes. Secondly, when viewing and analysing classroom video are embedded in cooperation and dialogue with colleagues, this helps teachers examine their instruction in light of concepts and theories. Thirdly, the fact that classroom video makes the complex interplay between teaching and learning visible helps teachers perceive and understand their role in it.

The studies reviewed contain a wealth of valuable detail about the relationships between VTL processes and outcomes. This is reflected in the structure of the following sections. The evidence about each of the three relationships is presented separately and within each section, several aspects are further distinguished. This subdivision is also present in Table 3.4.

Table 3.4 shows that the evidence below rests mostly on studies of more than fifteen teachers. As in the sections about the first and the second review questions, this strengthens its generalisability. However, there is one exception here. While the effectiveness of engaging in repeated activity cycles is demonstrated by several large-scale studies, the findings about its impact on teachers personally stems – understandably – from small-scale studies of fewer than fifteen teachers.

Engaging in repeated activity cycles

An essential element of teacher learning is its cyclical character. Both the general literature about teacher learning (see the section *Quality standards for teacher learning* in Chapter 1) and evidence about VTL (see the conclusions in the section *Processes: How do teachers learn when using digital video?* in Chapter 2) make clear that teachers develop professional competence by engaging repeatedly in activities involving sequences of performance, feedback, reflection and planning. Explicit findings confirming this come from ten or 13% of the sources selected for the review in this chapter. MTP impact studies as well as other studies indicate that the more time teachers spend on viewing, analysing and discussing videos and the more activity cycles teachers complete, the stronger their VTL outcomes become. The researchers interpret these indications by pointing out that teachers' learning is incremental and therefore gradual in nature.

At the same time – as noted already in the section *Individual differences* above – considerable variation exists in how teachers proceed through cycles of VTL activities. What and how teachers learn by engaging in these activity cycles is highly personal. 21 or 27% of the available sources reveal something about this issue.

The first MTP impact studies not only demonstrated VTL outcomes in teachers and pupils (Downer et al., 2009 and Pianta, Mashburn, Downer, Hamre, & Justice 2008; see the sections *MyTeachingPartner* in Chapter 2 and *Impact on pupil learning* in this chapter, respectively). They also brought to light interesting details about how these outcomes

TABLE 3.4 Process influences

Source	N of teachers	Engaging in repeated activity cycles — Planning > Performance > Feedback > Reflection	Personal learning	Cooperation and dialogue — With peers	With experts	Using resources	Visibility — Other-viewing	Self-viewing	Comparing perspectives
Early et al., 2017	486	●							
Hamre, Pianta, Burchinal et al., 2012	440	●							
Mashburn et al., 2010	134					●			
Pianta et al., 2008	113		●		●	●			
Jilink et al., 2018	72		●		●				
Downer et al., 2009	62	●●							
Christ et al., 2014	57	●		●●					
Baumgartner, 2018	56						●	●●	●
Wright et al., 2012	51		●					●	●●
Ely et al., 2014	49						●●		
LaParo, 2011	46	●							
Sun & Van Es, 2015	38						●		
Hylton, 2000	37		●	●●			●		
Piwowar et al., 2013	37	●	●					●	
Kersting et al., 2012	36	●	●	●●					
Schildwacht, 2012	26	●	●		●	●●			
Brock & Carter, 2015	25		●				●		
Lee et al., 2012	25		●						
Matsumura et al., 2019	25		●	●	●				
Santagata & Yeh, 2014	24								●
Voerman et al., 2015	23								
Browning & Porter, 2007	10							●	

Source	Total
Gaudin et al., 2018	8
Harlin, 2014	8
Lok, 2019	8
Shernoff & Kratochwill, 2007	8
Snoeyink, 2010	8
Damhuis et al., 2009	6
Lussi Borer et al., 2014	4
Robinson, 2011	4
Santagata & Bray, 2016	4
Van de Pol et al., 2012	4
Walker et al., 2019	4
Charalambous et al., 2018	3
Hawkins & Heflin, 2011	3
Rich & Hannafin, 2009b	3
Stephenson et al., 2011	3
Šeďová, 2017a	1
Šeďová, 2017b	1

Number of sources with N > 15	21	27%	7	9%	8	10%	4	5%	4	5%	4	5%	7	9%	2	3%	4	5%
Number of sources with N < 15	18	23%	3	4%	13	16%	2	3%	5	6%	0	0%	5	6%	2	3%	3	4%
Total number of sources	39	49%	10	13%	21	27%	6	8%	9	11%	4	5%	12	15%	4	5%	7	9%

Notes:
- Relevant source.
- See text.

Rounded percentages based on N = 79.

depended on the ways in which teachers and consultants used the MTP platform. Consultants significantly influenced the number of activity cycles teachers completed and the amount of time they spent in online discussion with their consultant.

Other process influences pointing to the personal nature of VTL are the following. VTL impact was shown to occur when interventions were tailored towards teachers' personal practice by giving them opportunities to determine viewing points and goals during coaching (Piwowar et al., 2013; Stephenson, Carter, & Arthur-Kelly, 2011; Wright, Ellis, & Baxter, 2012). VTL outcomes were also promoted when teachers' participation was driven by active, goal-directed effort and when interventions encouraged identifying and becoming aware of critical experiences (Charalambous, Philippou, & Olympiou, 2018; Lussi Borerr, Ria, Durand, & Muller, 2014). Last but not least, what challenged and helped teachers were attempts to link their instructional practice to theory (Downer et al., 2009; Pianta et al., 2008; Rich & Hannafin, 2009b; Van de Pol, Volman, & Beishuizen, 2012).

What such attempts may involve for teachers is exemplified in case studies by Klara Šeďová of two Czech teachers who participated in the action research project she initiated to promote dialogic teaching (see the section *Activation and engagement* above). Using interviews and observations, Šeďová reconstructed the efforts undertaken by teacher Daniela to introduce and establish in her lessons the five discourse practices aimed at in this project: encouraging open discussion; asking open questions of high cognitive demand; promoting uptake, i.e. encouraging speakers to build on what others have said previously; eliciting pupils to voice their reasoning; and ask questions of their own. Over time, Daniela encountered tensions and discrepancies between her intentions for enacting the elements of dialogic teaching and how their enactment actually played out during classroom teaching. In particular, conflict and disharmony between different elements posed challenges, which she only overcame by engaging in repeated cycles of video-supported reflection in dialogue with the researcher (Šeďová, 2017a). How to combine different instructional behaviours is a familiar challenge, which was also encountered in the project carried out by Damhuis and colleagues in the Netherlands (Damhuis et al., 2009).

In the second case study, teacher Hana's efforts to introduce and establish triadic interaction in her lessons, i.e. "a communication structure where students respond immediately to other classmates" were traced (Šeďová, 2017b, p. 225). For Hana, changing her instruction in this way was not a straightforward, but a stepwise process in which she encountered dilemmas and setbacks. While trying to use triadic interaction she felt that this was at odds with achieving the intended lesson goal of text interpretation. Only gradually did she come to reconcile this conflict by recognising that increasing communication between pupils about lesson content is furthered, not obstructed by triadic communication.

Cooperation and dialogue

It has already become clear that collegial cooperation and dialogue have a positive influence on the outcomes of VTL (see the conclusions in the section *Processes: How do teachers learn when using digital video?* in Chapter 2). The sources selected for the review in this chapter point to three specific kinds of processes underlying this influence. As outcomes of VTL, changes in instruction are promoted firstly when teachers, during peer collaboration, connect viewing and analysing classroom video with collegial discussion – as evident from six or 8% of the available sources. Secondly, changes in instruction are promoted when teachers receive individualised feedback based on evidence-based viewing points from experts – as evident from nine or 11% of the sources. Changes in instruction are promoted thirdly when teachers access and study web-based resources – as evident from four or 5% of the sources.

When teachers discuss video records of each other's teaching, this leads them to discover and interpret aspects of their work which had formerly remained implicit. This dialogue, during which they also receive suggestions for lesson improvement from colleagues (Kersting et al., 2012), then encourages changing their lessons (Gaudin, Chaliès, & Amathieu, 2018; Lussi Borer et al., 2014). In the study of peer coaching with video by Christ et al. (2014), for example, 48 preservice and nine experienced primary teachers of literacy in the US reported from which sources – video, discussion and study materials – they derived ideas to apply during instruction. The teachers felt that their pedagogical learning was supported for 50% by video and for 45% by discussion. They "were 48% more likely to report applying ideas that were based on both video and discussion [which] suggests the importance of using video and discussion in combination" (Christ et al., 2014, p. 369).

The benefits to teachers of individualised expert feedback based on evidence-based viewing points have become evident not only from several MTP impact studies, but also from other studies, notably those by Jilink et al. (2018) (see the sections *Interactional and instructional skills in early childhood education and care* in Chapter 2 and *Two-way communication* above) and Walker, Douglas and Brewer (2019).

In the latter study, which builds on the work by Brock and Carter (2015), one special education teacher and three paraprofessionals in the US participated in a training consisting of a workshop, video modelling and coaching with performance feedback in order to learn to implement "constant time delay" (CTD) while teaching three pupils with multiple disabilities. CTD means that the teacher, after each instructional move, waits for pupils' reaction and decides how to proceed. This intervention was based on a train-the-trainer model, as the special education teacher was first trained during one session by a university supervisor and then, in turn, trained the paraprofessionals during two to three coaching sessions over a period of six weeks. It was found that "[a]ll paraprofessionals implemented the systematic instructional procedures with high levels of fidelity and accuracy after training" (Walker et al., 2019, p. 1). The authors conclude that a video-based training model for paraprofessionals in special education is feasible, but they caution that after initial training, coaching including observation and performance feedback may be necessary to ensure that paraprofessionals' instructional action retains sufficient quality (Walker et al., 2019, p. 14).

Accessibility of evidence-based resources as a factor contributing to changes in instruction is evident from several MTP impact studies, notably Pianta et al. (2008), Mashburn et al. (2010), Hamre, Pianta, Mashburn and Downer (2012) and Lee, Kinzie and Whittaker (2012). Lee and colleagues investigated the influence of blended teaching supports including video and workshops during one year of MTP use in 25 experienced primary teachers of mathematics and science and their pupils. Eleven teachers in an experimental group experienced blended supports focussed on teacher questioning, while fifteen teachers in a control group did not. Standardised observations, surveys and assessments showed that in contrast to the control group, the teachers in the experimental group used more open questioning and their pupils responded with significantly more complex sentences. The authors conclude that "[t]he results corroborate the mediating role of teachers' questioning practice between web-based questioning-specific supports and [pupil]s' use of complex sentences" (Lee et al., 2012, p. 574–575). Similar findings are reported by Matsumura et al. (2019; see the section *Discourse practices* above).

Visibility

The affordances of DV (see the section *The special affordances of digital video* in Chapter 2) play a role in teachers' other-viewing as well as self-viewing. Twelve or 15% of the sources in this review indicate that in settings where teachers can practice and/or experiment with teaching themselves, viewing and analysing model videos of other teachers – more experienced colleagues or expert teachers in other schools – provide them with ideas to try out in their own lessons. Interpreting and discussing such videos appear to encourage teachers to connect their own implementation efforts to wider conceptual frameworks. This "power of good examples" also surfaced in the MTP impact studies (see the previous section).

Four or 5% of the sources indicate that self-viewing encourages teachers to become aware of how their own instructional action influences pupils' learning. Seven or 9% of the sources indicate that self-viewing can deliver the impetus to change one's instruction, when the video material reveals discrepancies between a teacher's ideas about her or his teaching practice and how this practice actually plays out. Such discrepancies apparently have the potential to challenge teachers to bring their practice more into line with their intentions.

The power of good examples combined with conceptual information and perspectives is illustrated by R&D work carried out by Ely, Kennedy, Pullen, Williams and Hirsch (2014) in the US. Ely and colleagues developed multimedia materials consisting of model videos and "Content Acquisition Podcasts" (CAPs), which demonstrate and explain vocabulary teaching practices. The intent behind this "video plus CAP" approach was to make not only these teaching practices, but also their underlying rationale easily accessible to preservice primary teachers. 24 student teachers were randomly assigned to a video plus CAP condition and 25 to a text-only condition, in which they studied written materials about vocabulary instruction. "In summary, the video plus CAP group used significantly more vocabulary practices than the reading group when teaching" (Ely et al., 2014, p. 41). The authors attribute this outcome to the dual opportunity that the experimental group had to see and understand the relevant instructional behaviours modelled as well as actively trying them out in their own student-teaching classes.

Effects of self-viewing during student teaching were studied by Baumgartner (2018) in a group of 56 Swiss preservice secondary teachers teaching physical education. 24 student teachers examined and discussed during four sessions with peers and teacher educators video recordings of how they gave feedback to their pupils, while nine students studied text-based cases and 23 students in a control group experienced neither type of cases. Pre- and post-intervention video vignettes of the student teachers' feedback-related instructional behaviour were rated by experts. The findings show that both the video- and text-based groups improved their feedback behaviour. However, the video-based group made most progress, while the control group did not improve. Baumgartner attributes the success of the experimental group to the fact that the complexity of teaching in field settings was directly visible to the student teachers. This probably enabled them to consider, choose and try out alternatives for instructional action.

The potential of self-viewing to unveil discrepancies between instructional intentions and actual teaching practice was studied in-depth by Rich and Hannafin (2009b) in three American women who volunteered to document their learning process during a one-month student-teaching practicum in primary education. Each participant completed five cycles of lesson planning, enactment and analysis of video records of their teaching using viewing points derived from individual study. In addition to the video records, they wrote reflection papers, gave interviews and completed pre- and post-surveys in order to reconstruct how their teaching changed over time. A within-case comparative content analysis of all qualitative data served to "examine how the proposed, intended, or perceived changes took shape from iteration to iteration" (Rich & Hannafin, 2009b, p. 133). Although the participants were "never told ... to look for ... discrepancies" between their recollections of teaching and the video records of it, this is what their video analyses drew attention to (Rich & Hannafin, 2009b, p. 142). Discovering these discrepancies brought the student teachers to "step back" "to see their teaching from another perspective" and to enact purposeful changes in their instruction (Rich & Hannafin, 2009b, p. 137).

Conditions in teachers' learning environments

Regarding the fourth and last review question, nine or 11% of the sources selected for this review contain specific findings about the influence – supportive or obstructive – of conditions in teachers' learning environments. As shown in Table 3.5, this is quite a small number, but the available sources do illustrate different kinds of influences operating at the meso-level of teacher education institutions' and schools' organisation.

Preservice teachers' competence development is promoted when teacher education institutions cooperate with schools to achieve and maintain congruent learning environments. When such cooperation makes blended learning possible, this constitutes a favourable condition for teacher learning. When evidence-based resources including DV and other multimedia are available online for teachers to study and

TABLE 3.5 Influences of conditions

Source	N of teachers	Supportive conditions		Obstructive conditions	
		Boundary crossing	Interaction with web-mediated resources and expert coaching	Material shortages	School culture and organisation
Hamre, Pianta, Burchinal et al., 2012	440		•		
Hamre, Pianta, Mashburn, & Downer, 2012	223		•		
Matsumura et al., 2019	25		••		
Voerman et al., 2015	23	••			
Williams, 2004	8		•	••	
Gaudin et al., 2018	8	••			
Lok, 2019	8			••	
Barnhart & Van Es, 2018	4				••
Santagata & Yeh, 2016	3				••
Number of sources with N > 15	4 5%	1 1%	3 4%	0 0%	0 0%
Number of sources with N < 15	5 6%	1 1%	1 1%	2 3%	2 3%
Total number of sources	9 11%	2 3%	4 5%	2 3%	2 3%

Notes:
• Relevant source.
•• See text. Rounded percentages based on N = 79.

when they can discuss their concerns and ideas with an expert coach, this supports their experimentation with instructional approaches new to them.

Barriers to VTL arise firstly when teachers have to cope with material shortages of time, money and resources. Secondly, curricular and exam requirements, a short duration of interventions and a transmission-oriented teaching culture in schools can obstruct teachers engaging in VTL in changing their instruction.

Supportive conditions

Two examples – one from PTE, one from PD – show in different ways how VTL can be promoted when providers of teacher development and schools cooperate in order to bridge institutional boundaries between and within them.

An example of such boundary crossing is reported from France by Gaudin et al. (2018). These researchers studied the learning experiences of eight preservice teachers in physical education, who participated in a one-month PTE course designed to demonstrate and explain teaching strategies to them as well as providing opportunities to practice those strategies themselves. As a preparation for their student teaching, the participants witnessed demonstrations of these strategies by a university supervisor, viewed action videos of teachers unknown to them instructing pupils for assignments, analysed the teaching skills involved with the help of worksheets and role-played them themselves. Two to four days later, they practised these skills during their own practicum lessons and were video-recorded while doing so. During self-confrontation interviews, they finally reviewed their performance and voiced their reflections about it in dialogue with a researcher (see for more information about this procedure the section *Collaborative Video Learning Lab* in Chapter 2).

Analysis of the video and interview data showed that seven out of the eight student teachers enacted the teaching strategies targeted in the intervention. Their statements also revealed that they attributed their performance to a variety of learning experiences. Most influential – in decreasing order – were past student teaching experiences, own role-playing experiences, experiences with analysing the experienced teachers' action videos and the demonstrations and explanations by the university supervisor. The authors conclude that during PTE courses, preservice teachers need opportunities to discuss and judge the merits of both other, experienced teachers' and their own teaching, before they can attempt to use advocated teaching strategies themselves. Only on the basis of understanding and judgement will they adopt and adapt teaching strategies current in the profession for themselves. This process of competence development takes place in incremental steps. To facilitate such teacher learning, university supervisors and school mentors should collaborate to create a congruent learning environment enabling continuous learning trajectories for student teachers.

How the design of teachers' learning environment shapes their actual VTL experience becomes apparent also from a PD intervention in the Netherlands. 23 experienced lower-secondary teachers engaged in Feedback-Theory into Practice (FeTiP), a trajectory aiming "to help teachers to expand their feedback behavior in the classroom to provide more, and more effective (i.e. learning-enhancing), feedback" (Voerman et al., 2015, p. 990). Over a period of six months, five types of interventions inside and outside the classroom – providing theory, demonstration, practice, video coaching in a collegial support group and feedback – were combined on three organisational levels – individual teachers, the collegial support group and the whole school team (Voerman et al., 2015, p. 990–991). Analysis of video recordings of the participants' pre- and post-intervention classroom interaction showed that over time, they came to provide significantly more, more specific and more positive feedback to their pupils. The authors conclude that combining support for teachers and school leaders was an important success factor in FeTiP.

One condition favouring VTL is the availability of web-mediated resources and expert coaching. As described in the section *Cooperation and dialogue* above, these two resources together create opportunities for teachers to relate their thinking about instruction to more general concepts and frameworks. The study by Matsumura et al. (2019) illustrates how teachers can benefit from VTL when these conditions are present in a blended learning environment. Collaborating in such an environment 25 beginning and experienced teachers in the US succeeded in increasing text-discussion quality in their classrooms (see the section *Discourse practices* above). The researchers conclude that individualised online coaching "opens up a universe of exciting possibilities with respect to creating fully online productive working relationships among teachers – novice and expert – that can support instructional improvement". Working in such an environment can become even more effective, they suggest, when teachers "view the video clips and reflective questions posed by the coach in advance of a post-[lesson-]conference" (Matsumura et al., 2019, p. 210).

Obstructive conditions

Two studies from non-Western countries show that material shortages of time, money and resources can obstruct VTL. Teachers participating in the Child-friendly School project in Cambodia (see the eponymous section in Chapter 2) lacked time for lesson preparation due to a second job and/or family responsibilities as well as money to make teaching materials available. These shortages were serious obstacles to implementing changes in instruction. In Jamaica, the preservice teachers studied by Williams (2004) felt hampered in their attempts at introducing cooperative learning by large class sizes, noise from surrounding classes and the urgency to complete lessons within allocated time frames (see the section *Sequencing lesson content and learning activities* above).

Also school culture and organisation can obstruct VTL. In the study by Barnhart and Van Es (2018), curricular and exam requirements made it difficult for the participating teachers to learn to respond adequately to pupil reactions over the course of five video club sessions (see the sections *Learning to notice in video clubs* in Chapter 2 and *Diagnosing and responding to pupil learning* above). The three beginning teachers studied by Santagata and Yeh (2016) were held back in their ambitions with process-oriented mathematics teaching by transmission-oriented beliefs and practices existing among colleagues (see the section *Learning to notice in video clubs* in Chapter 2).

Conclusions

What is there to be learned from the research findings reviewed above about the influence of VTL on teachers' instructional action? What does this review contribute to a knowledge base that can inform VTL interventions suitable for raising the quality of instruction? In this final section, I present my answers to the four review questions formulated at the outset of this chapter. I discuss first the outcomes found in teachers and pupils, then the conditions and processes influencing them.

The status of my conclusions is provisional, as all scientific conclusions must be. At the same time, it should be remembered that they rest on a systematic review procedure (described in the section *Method*) and that the underlying findings clarify causation in different ways (see the criteria specified in the section *Method use and the issue of causation*). This is why I feel justified in attributing the VTL outcomes found in the 79 studies reviewed to the processes and conditions involved. Where relevant, I indicate which findings confirm and/or add to the conclusions of the review in Chapter 2 and which issues remain under-researched. I conclude each section by formulating consequences for the design of learning environments for teachers and future perspectives.

Teacher and pupil outcomes

The main conclusion about the outcomes of teachers' engaging in VTL is that this helps them change how they orchestrate pupils' learning. "Orchestrating" refers to both cognitive and socio-emotional aspects of teaching and learning. As detailed in the *Findings* section, when teachers engage in VTL, they change how they sequence lesson contents and learning activities and they shift their discourse towards more and deeper dialogue with their pupils. They also make their instructional routines and classroom management more effective, their interaction with pupils becomes more bidirectional and they display greater sensitivity in their contact with them. In these ways, teachers activate their pupils more, improve their working relationship with them and as a result encourage them to learn with understanding. Importantly, these VTL-induced changes in instructional action lead to changes and increases in pupils' learning. In other words, engaging in VTL strengthens how teachers' instructional action mediates pupil learning.

These conclusions mean that engaging in VTL has the potential to raise the quality not only of instruction, but also of pupils' learning and achievement. Teachers thus develop their professional competence in the direction of higher-order teaching and learning – as characterised in the section *Quality learning and quality teaching* in Chapter 1.

The changes teachers make in their instruction as a result of engaging in VTL are at least partly sustained after VTL interventions end. This conclusion is tentative, because the evidence available about the sustainability of VTL outcomes is scarce.

Compared to the direct influence of VTL activity on teachers' outcomes, their personal backgrounds and characteristics appear to have a moderating influence. The available evidence about the influence of teachers' career phase is inconclusive, but there are indications that over the course of the career span, a certain sequence is at work in teachers' competence development. The research by Jacobs, Šeďová and Van de Pol and colleagues, in particular, suggests that preservice and beginning teachers first need to acquire effective instructional routines and master basic classroom management skills, before they can develop a flexible ability to engage pupils in active learning and content-focussed dialogue. Especially responding adequately to pupils' reactions after having elicited them appears to be a relatively difficult skill. This conclusion corresponds to the developmental stages found in the large-scale survey research conducted by Kyriakides, Creemers and Antoniou (2009). These researchers found that effective differentiation is a competence which manifests itself relatively late in a teacher's career, if at all.

These conclusions are a refinement of the VTL outcomes that emerged from the review in Chapter 2 (see the section *Outcomes: What do teachers learn when using digital video?*). The underlying evidence indicates that teaching competence develops quite gradually. At the same time, how teachers develop their professional competence differs considerably between individuals. All in all, however, the evidence shows that for teachers, engaging in VTL is a rewarding strategy to acquire, develop and refine a variety of complex skills, notably providing activating instruction, creating and maintaining a constructive classroom climate and conducting forms of content-focussed dialogue with pupils suitable for promoting learning with understanding.

In sum, raising the quality of teaching and learning is possible through VTL. However, the success of this endeavour will depend on the functionality of the VTL processes teachers engage in as well as on the extent to which their learning environments provide the conditions favouring them. These processes need to unfold, and these conditions need to be given during all phases of teachers' careers.

Processes

The causal evidence about process influences gathered in this review confirms and strengthens the conclusions about teachers' collegial collaboration and the visualisation of teaching and learning drawn in Chapter 2 (see the section *Processes: How do teachers learn when using digital video?*).

Collegial exchange and dialogue during repeated activity cycles are the main drivers of VTL which promote changes in instructional action. It is only in combination with professional dialogue that teachers' viewing and analysis of classroom video – whether of their own or colleagues' lessons – will impact their teaching. For changes in instruction to occur, it is essential that teachers engaging in VTL alternate video analysis with experimentation in the classroom and that they do so in successive activity cycles. Otherwise, they will not find enough opportunities to strengthen and expand, build and refine their professional competence.

Given these opportunities, collegial collaboration will be considerably enhanced when the video records used display the interactions taking place within the instructional triangle. Analysing these interactions during other-viewing is what produces insight in how other teachers promote their pupils' learning. During self-viewing, understanding the interactions in the instructional triangle gives teachers insight in what their own actions add to or detract from their pupils' learning and specifically in how they can help pupils solve misconceptions and overcome stumbling blocks.

Collegial collaboration will further benefit teachers engaging in VTL when feedback from peers and experts combined with evidence-based resources provides them with foci for reflection and enactment. The effectiveness of VTL will be increased when viewing guides or other means for structured video viewing are underpinned with valid theory and research about subject-matter content and pedagogy, not only in science, technology, engineering and mathematics (STEM) and literacy, but in all school subjects. This would be a feasible way of putting a knowledge base for the teaching profession to practical use (cf. Hiebert, Gallimore, & Stigler, 2002).

One finding that has consistently emerged from the reviews in both this and the previous chapters is that teachers benefit more from VTL when they have control over the targets pursued. It is therefore a little odd that the role of the self as a source of feedback to teachers is the object of so few VTL studies. Teachers undoubtedly reflect about their work in private and when they view video recordings of their lessons by themselves, they engage in self-review leading to new personal learning. Feedforward videos as developed by Dowrick and colleagues in therapeutic settings (cf. the section *Self-modelling* in Chapter 2) could be an effective tool to bring such learning forward. Such video use, however, does not seem to be widespread among teachers. Another practice seemingly escaping attention is the consultation of learners as a source of feedback. Except in a number of MTP impact studies and the research about KODEK and the DVC (see the pertinent sections in Chapter 2), pupils' experience of their teachers' instruction and of changes in it is virtually disregarded in VTL research. This suggests, in philosophical terms, that the research suffers from a certain neglect of human subjectivity, whether teachers' or pupils' subjectivity is involved.

Neglect of human subjectivity is perhaps also one of the reasons why the issue how teachers translate their instructional thought into action and the role of their judgement, decision-making and planning in this process remain under-researched (as noted in the sections *Outcomes: What do teachers learn when using digital video?* and *How teachers translate thought into action* in Chapter 2). In my earlier review of VTL research (Brouwer, 2014), I developed the hypothesis that analysing video of one's own and others' teaching during collegial collaboration leads teachers to compare and judge different approaches to teaching. This, I presume, then arouses the development of new intentions for their own instructional action, followed by the design and planning of altered or completely experimental lessons and their enactment.

In combination with collegial exchange and dialogue, another main driver of VTL is visualisation. Using video adds objectification and explication to teachers' professional learning. The special affordances of DV (see the eponymous section in Chapter 2) confront teachers with a direct representation of the complex interplay between teaching and learning. This brings them to sharpen their perception of their mediating role in this interplay and to explicate how they interpret this role (cf. Tochon, 1999). Despite the popularity of DV as a medium, what also remains under-researched in VTL studies are the ways in which framing through different video types may differentially influence teacher learning. What is shown and how it is shown in classroom video determines what and how teachers can learn from viewing and analysing it (cf. the sections *Tool use* and *Video production* in Chapter 2).

The above findings and conclusions about the processes involved in VTL allow deriving some general consequences for the design of learning environments for teachers. Four such consequences stand out.

Firstly, effectiveness of VTL is promoted when opportunities for cyclical learning and instructional experimentation are built into PTE programmes and PD efforts. In order to encourage teachers to connect professional thought and action, practical and theoretical elements should preferably be sequenced inductively (see the section *Quality standards for teacher learning* in Chapter 1).

Secondly, it is clearly advisable for the designers of any VTL intervention to create ample opportunities for collegial exchange and collaboration between the participants. The overview of interventions in the section *Digital video use* in Chapter 2 provides a range of ideas for doing so.

An important guideline appears to be, thirdly, to seek a balance between providing ideas, concepts and viewing points based on research and theory on the one hand and respecting teachers' personal judgement and decision-making on the other. It should always be clear to VTL participants how expert input relates to their personal work experience. Likewise, they should always be free to shape and prioritise their own learning goals.

Fourthly, the review in this chapter clearly shows that using video records for self- and other-viewing encourages teachers to examine and change their instruction. Capitalising on the special affordances of DV is therefore a sensible ingredient of teacher development. Collegial collaboration during VTL opens the perspective of transforming how teachers' competence development and occupational socialisation unfold. Such collaboration can make the long lamented professional isolation of teachers, brought to the fore by Waller (1932) and Lortie (1975), avoidable. Perhaps – and hopefully – such isolation will one day even become unnecessary. Teachers can employ collaborative VTL to master core challenges of their profession such as classroom management. "Withitness" can be trained in PTE, as the studies by Hylton (2000) and Snoeyink (2010) illustrate. This can help take the shock out of practice shock, so to speak. Experienced teachers can employ VTL to improve their working relationship with pupils, as the studies by Piwowar, Thiel and Ophardt (2013) and Gregory et al. (2014, 2016) show. More generally, teachers can employ collaborative VTL to make their instruction more activating and thus develop higher-order teaching and learning.

Conditions

In the research reviewed, little attention is paid to the influence of organisational conditions on VTL. This influence, however, is huge. The lack or availability of resources for educating teachers and promoting their professionalism originates on the macro-level of politics. The resulting conditions then constrain schools and providers of teacher development on the meso-level of school organisation. In an ideal world, the current underfunding of teacher development would be replaced by consistent and systemic opportunities for evidence-based teacher learning. Until that time, it remains an urgent challenge for teacher education institutions, PD providers and schools to free all resources possible for raising the quality of education. These parties should cooperate to create congruent learning environments for teachers and to make learning activities possible encouraging them to relate practice and theory (cf. Feiman-Nemser, Schwille, Carver, & Yusko, 1999; Korthagen, Kessels, Koster, Lagerwerf, & Wubbels, 2001).

VTL is a valuable strategy for strengthening teacher development. The effectiveness of this endeavour probably depends not only on the extent to which the activities and processes discussed in the previous section actually take place, but also on how they are combined in a specific PTE programme or PD effort. If teachers are to change their actions in the classroom in ways that demonstrably improve pupil achievement, a host of necessary conditions apparently needs to be fulfilled simultaneously. Foremost among these conditions are that teachers receive working time and material support for collaboration *and* experience models of alternatives for instructional action *and* participate in video-supported coaching *and* engage in redesigning lessons *and* purposefully enact step-by-step changes in their instruction over a prolonged period.

As Voerman et al. (2015) conclude on the basis of her research, there is wisdom in combining multiple intervention components on different organisational levels (see the above section *Supportive conditions*; cf. also Joyce & Showers, 2002). It is ideally for teacher educators, school leaders and teacher teams together to decide which combination of activities and resources is feasible to implement and promising for achieving the specific goals relevant to their situation. The chances of success in reaching those goals are probably increased when all the parties involved know and understand each other's possibilities and concerns. For decision-making about intervention design, the quality standards for teacher learning presented in Chapter 1 can be of help.

In analog times, teacher education and PD took place in local environments and knowledge was imparted mostly through oral presentation and the study of written materials. In this day and digital age, web-based multimedia and video are becoming available worldwide. Teachers' benefits from VTL increase when they access and use evidence-based resources to examine and inform their teaching practice. It is especially effective when these resources come in the form of web-based hypermedia and when model videos exemplify explanations of instructional strategies and the rationales underlying them.

When the conditions outlined above should be fulfilled, I imagine a perspective for the future of teacher learning in which teachers anywhere in the world view and analyse each other's work with learners. In that case they would engage in a form of "glocal" collaboration amounting to collective professional self-help.

Coda

What the review in this chapter adds to our knowledge is summarised in Box 3.2.

What we now know better is, first of all, which specific types of VTL-induced changes in instructional action promote pupil learning. Secondly, the review has clarified how outcomes in teachers and pupils depend on VTL processes and conditions. Finally, the findings confirm the central assumption behind the VTL model (see Figure 2.2) that teachers' video-supported professional learning unfolds in two related spheres of interaction. Teachers are normally absorbed by their daily work

BOX 3.2 REVIEW CONCLUSIONS

Outcomes

Teacher outcomes

- Engaging in VTL helps teachers change cognitive and socio-emotional aspects of how they orchestrate learning.

Cognitive aspects

- Teachers sequence lesson contents and learning activities in ways that activate pupils more,
- shift their discourse towards more and deeper dialogue with pupils and
- make their instructional routines and classroom management more effective.

Socio-emotional aspects

- As teachers' interaction with pupils becomes more bidirectional and
- they display greater sensitivity in their contact with pupils,
- they improve their working relationship with their pupils.

Pupil outcomes

- The changes in teachers' instructional action mediate changes in pupils' learning which lead to higher achievements.

Sustainability

- The VTL-induced changes in teachers' instruction are sustained in part after VTL interventions end.

Moderating factors

- As teachers' career phases advance, a number of them appear to increase their competence in responding adequately to pupils' cognitive development.
- How professional competence develops during VTL participation differs considerably between individual teachers.

Processes

Collegial collaboration

- Exchange and dialogue during successive activity cycles are the main drivers of VTL which promote changes in instructional action.
- Analysing the interactions within the instructional triangle provides teachers with insight

- during other-viewing in how other teachers promote learning and
- during self-viewing in what their own actions add to or detract from pupil learning.
- Feedback from peers and experts combined with evidence-based resources provides teachers with foci for reflection and enactment.
- The role of the self as a source of feedback to teachers is the object of few VTL studies.
- The role of teachers' judgement, decision-making and planning in how they translate their instructional thought into action remains under-researched.

Visualisation

- Video use adds objectification and explication to teachers' professional learning.
- The ways in which framing through different video types may differentially influence teacher learning remains under-researched.

Conditions

- The effectiveness of VTL interventions depends considerably on how activities and processes are combined.
- There is wisdom in combining multiple intervention components on different organisational levels.
- Teachers' benefits from VTL increase when they access and use evidence-based resources in order to examine and inform their teaching practice.

with pupils, but this fast-paced sphere of interaction is put between brackets, as it were, when they engage in VTL with colleagues. When the latter sphere of interaction becomes part of teachers' work, it helps them examine their instruction, open up alternatives for instruction, redesign their instruction and move it in the direction of higher-order teaching and learning.

At the same time, some gaps remain in our knowledge of VTL. In the following three chapters, which cover my own research, I contribute to closing these gaps. Chapter 4 addresses how a teacher education institution and the schools it serves can collaborate to implement VTL effectively without needing special or additional resources. Chapter 5 delves into the under-researched issue of teachers' processes of judgement and decision-making during VTL. In Chapter 6, I report a comprehensive case study of a four-year intervention in which one school's management and teachers joined forces to raise the quality of instruction. As the participating teachers could be followed for up to six years after the intervention ended, this study reveals to what extent and through which processes the participating teachers succeeded in introducing and sustaining changes in their instruction.

4

THE POWER OF VIDEO FEEDBACK WITH STRUCTURED VIEWING GUIDES

*Niels Brouwer, Eric Besselink and
Ida Oosterheert*

Quality of instruction is a key factor influencing the contribution a country's education system can make to its economic prosperity and cultural vitality (OECD, 2005; Hattie, 2009). One of the great challenges facing teacher education and professional development (PD) is to promote the shift from teacher-dominated and reproduction-oriented learning towards active, higher-order learning, in which pupils develop an understanding of foundational, transferable concepts. Such higher-order learning is increasingly being demanded by technological developments in industrialised as well as industrialising countries. In this area, teacher education and PD have a multiplier function to fulfil. Both influence generations of teachers, who, on their part, influence generations of learners.

Success in learning to read and write in primary school can have a considerable influence on pupils' later learning. For instance, ample print exposure helps children develop good reading habits (Mol & Bus, 2011) and growth in reading proficiency promotes text comprehension in the longer term (Verhoeven & Van Leeuwe, 2008). Evidence from longitudinal studies suggests mechanisms of reciprocal causation, i.e. either positive or negative spirals characterise reading development. Such "Matthew effects" can widen achievement gaps over time (Bast & Reitsma, 1998). Reading and writing, then, are foundational domains of learning, in which it is crucially important for learners to have teachers who possess an outstanding instructional competence (Neuman & Cunningham, 2009, p. 535–536). Therefore, educational research should clarify not only what are effective teaching behaviours, but also how teachers can develop and apply them in the classroom.

It is with these purposes in mind that we designed, conducted and evaluated three interventions aiming to improve teachers' instructional competence in reading and writing lessons. The core element in these interventions is that teachers receive video feedback on their classroom behaviour structured by means of observation items describing domain-specific effective teaching behaviours.

DOI: 10.4324/9780429331091-4

Introduction

In this chapter, insights derived from research into features of effective teacher education and PD and into the potential of video use for teacher learning are first summarised. On this basis, the design of the interventions is accounted for and the aim and questions of this study are formulated. After specifying the interventions' contexts and goals, we describe the method and findings and present the conclusions and implications. Finally, limitations and suggestions for further research are discussed.

Features of effective teacher education and professional development

How can teachers acquire and strengthen high-level instructional competence in specific domains of learning? During the last decades, research has yielded evidence about features of teacher education and PD which are effective in promoting such instructional competence.

To encourage transfer between knowledge construction and competence development in preservice teacher education (PTE), it is effective to systematically provide preservice teachers with opportunities to move back and forth between action and reflection in collaborative settings (Brouwer & Korthagen, 2005, p. 197–199). When PTE programmes are designed as activity sequences in which inductive learning from practical experiences alternates with deductive learning from theory, this helps preservice teachers develop varied repertoires of innovative teaching behaviours (Brouwer & Korthagen, 2005, p. 158, 186, 190–196 and 213–214; cf. Boyd, Grossman, Lankford, Loeb, & Wyckoff, 2009; Dann, Cloetta, Müller-Fohrbrodt, & Helmreich, 1978; Darling-Hammond, 2000; Korthagen, Kessels, Koster, Lagerwerf, & Wubbels, 2001; Müller-Fohrbrodt, Cloetta, & Dann, 1978). In the PD literature, there is a consensus that effective interventions are coherent with in-service teachers' current knowledge, beliefs and daily practice as well as with school, district and state policies (Desimone, 2009; Garet, Porter, Desimone, Birman, & Yoon, 2001). They are clearly focussed on subject-matter content and pedagogy and not only on generic aspects of teaching (Kennedy, 1998). Participating teachers are engaged in active learning and do so in collegial collaboration. Finally, effective PD has a duration not of "one-shot experiences", but extends over sustained periods of time (Borko, Jacobs, & Koellner, 2010; Guskey, 1986 and 2000; Van Veen, Zwart, & Meirink, 2012).

The quality features of PTE and PD summarised above have two commonalities. The first is that teacher learning takes place in the course of repeated cycles in which action alternates with reflection. The second is that teachers collaborate in collegial groups. We assume that when these features are in place, it becomes possible to support teachers in developing their instructional competence.

Professional vision and teacher behaviour change

To be able to promote learning it is crucial for teachers to "learn to notice" how their teaching behaviour influences pupils' learning. This is the rationale behind the research and development work aiming at "professional vision" in teachers as originated by Sherin and Van Es (Sherin & Van Es, 2005; Van Es & Sherin, 2002). The term professional vision was borrowed from Goodwin (1994) and refers to the type of perception characteristic of experts in specific professional domains. As applied to teaching, this concept encompasses selective attention and knowledge-based reasoning (Sherin, Jacobs, & Philipp, 2011). Guiding attention towards pupil learning processes should help teachers examine those aspects of their instruction which impact pupils' learning. Asking focussed questions about how teaching influences learning should help teachers reason about their work in knowledge-based ways, i.e. justify and decide about alternatives for action on the basis of accountable judgement (Santagata & Guarino, 2011).

Digital video (DV) is a medium with considerable potential for developing professional vision. This can be attributed to the following affordances (see the section *The special affordances of digital video* in Chapter 2). Because of its vividness, video can focus teachers' attention on the complex interactions between the content of learning, their learners' (re)actions and teachers' own (re)actions. The concreteness of video images invites teachers to make the analysis of teaching and learning subject-specific. The user-friendliness of digital video enables repeated analysis from different perspectives without the need for immediate action. And last but not least, moving images invoke vicarious experience (Laurillard, 1993, p. 114) and emotional response.

As conceptualised in the Visual Teacher Learning (VTL) model (see Figure 2.2), behaviour change in teachers may ensue from focussed perception and interpretation of visual representations of teaching supported by feedback. However, relatively little is known about whether and how teachers actually put into practice what they discover through examining video records of their teaching. A review of the research of the last fifteen years into video use for teacher development has shown that most studies of "professional vision" have taken teacher perception and thought as their end-point (see the section *Outcomes: What do teachers learn when using digital video?* in Chapter 2).

The evidence available about behaviour change under the influence of VTL indicates that VTL can help teachers make their content-focussed interaction with learners more cognitively activating (see the section *Teacher and pupil outcomes* in Chapter 3). Teachers firstly take more initiative to engage pupils in active learning. They achieve this by acquiring, developing and/or sustaining basic skills in direct instruction, by talking less oneself and by using more open and probing questioning, thus eliciting learners to engage with and talk about the lesson content. These behaviour changes in teachers result in increased on-task behaviour in learners on higher levels of cognitive activation. A second effect of video-enhanced reflection is that teachers provide their learners with greater amounts of feedback and with more focussed feedback. Thirdly, teachers act and react more adaptively while teaching. Finally, video-enhanced reflection encourages teachers to target and try out effective teaching behaviours (cf. Gaudin & Chaliès, 2015, p. 54–55).

These changes in teaching behaviour are of the type needed to deepen dialogue and discourse with learners. It has been shown that such behaviour plays a key mediating role in fostering performance, retention and transfer (Palincsar & Brown,

1984, p. 157, 166–169; Resnick, Asterhan, & Clarke, 2015, p. 1). We therefore expect that VTL is particularly suited to encouraging those forms of teaching which foster higher-order learning.

Intervention design

While video can help teachers analyse their work in the classroom, several authors caution that lesson viewing in itself will not automatically bring about the development of pedagogical content knowledge and/or more effective teaching (Brophy, 2004; Erickson, 2011; Goldman, Pea, Barron, & Derry, 2007). Heuristics for the design of VTL in preservice teacher education have been proposed (Blomberg, Renkl, Sherin, Borko, & Seidel, 2013) as well as "a continuum of video use in PD from highly adaptive to highly specified [to] consider the affordances and constraints of different approaches" (Borko, Koellner, Jacobs, & Seago, 2011, p. 175). In designing the interventions reported here, we have built on this work.

We reason that when teachers' attention is directed towards effective teaching behaviours, this may trigger them to extend their professional frames of reference beyond prior belief and intuitive speculation (Oosterheert & Vermunt, 2003) and serve as a starting point for developing teaching behaviours suited to the cognitive activation of learners. We therefore decided to design an intervention combining video feedback on teaching behaviour with structured viewing guides (SVGs). SVGs are lists of "viewing points", i.e. observation items describing domain-specific teaching behaviours and pupil reactions, subdivided in categories. The following features characterise the intervention design.

Structured

From their review of studies about video feedback in education and training, Fukkink, Trienekens, & Kramer (2011, p. 56–57) conclude that the use of structured observation forms focussing on positive target behaviours makes video feedback particularly effective for achieving behaviour change, regardless of participants' level of development. They attribute this to the fact that such "forms enable participants … to zoom in and focus on the professional target behavior". Accordingly, we used SVGs to provide teachers with concrete foci for learning from practice. To make these foci easily accessible, they were grouped in a limited number of categories. In a review of studies of how teachers used video for analysing their own teaching, Tripp and Rich (2012) found that "when there were too many items, teachers felt overwhelmed and found less utility in video-facilitated reflection" (p. 681).

Evidence-based and domain-specific

If teaching is to promote pupil learning, the content of SVGs should be derived from available evidence about the impact of specific teaching behaviours. How teachers analyse their work and choose between alternatives for action should ideally be informed by such evidence not only on a generic, but also on a domain-specific level (Kennedy, 1998; West & Staub, 2003). The viewing points in the SVGs were therefore selected on the basis of literature reviews about specific domains of learning, in this case reading and writing.

Focussed on classroom behaviour and interaction

Teaching and learning unfold in the age-old "instructional triangle", i.e. in the interaction between teacher, learners and content (Reusser, 2019). The viewing points in the SVGs therefore focus on how teacher behaviour affects pupils' progress through particular activities such as instructing and questioning and through shifting roles such as activator, guide and coach (Palincsar & Brown, 1984, p. 119–124). The viewing points, then, describe observable teacher behaviours that have the potential to promote pupils' learning as well as pupil reactions. Viewing points were formulated in short sentences, i.e. main clauses in the active voice and the present tense such as "During the whole lesson, the teacher keeps the purposes of reading assignments available on the blackboard" and "The teacher walks through the classroom and gives comments on the structure of the stories that pupils are writing".

Personally relevant

Because of the above three features, the SVGs can be situated on the dimension from "highly adaptive" to "highly specified" introduced by Borko et al. (2011) towards the specified end. In a quasi-experimental study, we found evidence that such SVGs helped preservice teachers reduce judgemental reactions and take a more analytical stance while viewing others' lessons (see Chapter 5). However, Tripp and Rich (2012) note in their review that "a few studies reported that teachers preferred to select their own reflection focus" (p. 683). On this basis, the authors suggest "allowing teachers to select the focus of their reflection and then helping teachers to narrow the focus to a structured framework" (p. 687). We therefore invited the participating teachers to make their own selection from the target behaviours formulated in the SVGs and to add viewing points of their own, if they wished.

We assume that professionals learn most when they pursue goals that they consider relevant for their personal competence (Fuller, 1969 and 1974). In addition, local settings for providing and discussing feedback were created by instructing teachers and observers to use peer consultation. We expect that in such settings, teachers can shape their own professional learning with a maximum of autonomy and a minimum of resources (Ackland, 1991).

Procedure

The procedure followed during the interventions was that each participating teacher first studied the teaching behaviours in the SVGs and decided which behaviours she or he wanted to develop. Then, the teacher was observed and filmed by a fellow student, mentor or colleague as was feasible in the given local situation. As soon as possible after the lesson, the teacher viewed the video footage together with the observer, who provided feedback on the teaching behaviours targeted.

In sum, the rationale of the intervention design is that structured video feedback in terms of domain-specific effective teaching behaviours should encourage teachers to analyse and improve their teaching in collegial collaboration.

Research aim and questions

The aim of this study was to evaluate the effectiveness of video feedback with SVGs for developing teaching competence. The research questions were the following:

I.   Can video feedback combined with structured viewing guides support teachers in raising the quality of instructional behaviour during reading and writing lessons for pupils aged 10–11?
II. Which changes in teachers' instructional behaviour occur after video feedback with structured viewing guides?
III. What kinds of learning experiences can video feedback with structured viewing guides engender?

In the following sections, the intervention context and goals are first described. Then, the methodology is accounted for, and the findings are presented. Their implications for theory, practice and research are discussed in conclusion.

Three interventions: contexts and goals

The three interventions studied were based on the same design, but their contexts and goals varied. These variations are described below. The interventions were carried out by a PTE college in cooperation with schools in a rural area in the Netherlands. Consent from schools and parents was obtained for filming in classrooms and for using the resulting images in non-public settings for purposes of teacher education and PD.

Among the reasons for embarking on these interventions were indications that literacy achievement in Dutch primary education has been declining since 2001. The most recent findings from the Progress in International Reading Literacy Study (PIRLS) show that in international comparison, the large majority of Dutch pupils are good readers. However, the percentage of excellent readers is diminishing and the percentage of weak readers is rising (Meelissen, Netten, Drent, Punter, Droop et al., 2012; Vernooy, 2006). The PIRLS findings also show that "Higher average reading achievement was … related to engaging instruction, as well as having reading teachers with specialised education in language or reading, more experience, and greater career satisfaction" (IEA, 2011). Research has raised similar concerns about the quality of education in writing (Koster, Tribushinina, De Jong, & Van den Bergh, 2015).

For these reasons, the college of education where this study was carried out embarked on a policy to develop both its preservice curriculum and its PD services with respect to reading and writing. To this end, it organised regional cooperation bringing together the different types of expertise available from teachers, subject specialists, teacher educators and mentors in settings allowing for both formal and informal cooperation (cf. Ronfeldt, Farmer, McQueen, & Grissom, 2015; Shanklin, 2007). A core element in this drive to improve teachers' competence in literacy instruction was the use of coaching. Several comprehensive evaluations have shown that literacy coaching for teachers can raise the quality of instruction and that this is an important mediator benefiting pupil achievement (Biancarosa, Bryk, & Dexter, 2010; Matsumura, Garnier, & Spybrook, 2013; Neuman & Cunningham, 2009).

The three interventions undertaken were prepared by project groups coordinated by the second author, which consisted of teachers from the participating schools, preservice teachers and teacher educators. The project group members were mostly experienced staff with a specific interest and expertise in both reading and writing instruction and mentoring. These groups studied professional publications aiming at identifying teaching behaviours characterising effective instruction in reading and writing. This work formed the basis for the contents of the SVGs used.

Reading comprehension

The first intervention took place in the domain of reading comprehension in an experimental group of 23 first-year preservice teachers. During the weeks before practice teaching, they carried out the following assignment in groups of four: study the literature compiled by the project group, present a critical assessment of the viewing guide it produced and propose additional viewing points elaborated on the basis of your own insights. This assignment was given to encourage the preservice teachers to develop their own professional judgement (cf. Danielowich, 2014). All presentations were given and discussed during plenary "confrontation meetings" in which the preservice teachers, mentors, project group members and researchers participated. Also before practice teaching, the preservice teachers attended three training workshops totalling twelve hours, in which they learned to use Windows Live Moviemaker to cut and sequence video fragments on a timeline and insert captions and subtitles.

Then, the SVG about reading comprehension was used during a full-time six-week practice-teaching period, in which the preservice teachers cooperated in groups of mostly two or three with their mentors. They were instructed to choose a limited number of teaching behaviours to practise in their lessons. If they wished, preservice teachers and mentors could add viewing points of their own. The viewing points chosen shifted over time, depending on how the preservice teachers' personal concerns developed. Mentoring sessions of at least one hour took place at least once a week, during which the mentors and preservice teachers analysed fragments from their recent lessons from the perspective of the viewing points chosen. The format mostly used for post-lesson conferences was the ALACT reflection model developed by Korthagen (2001, p. 44–45).

After practice teaching, all preservice teachers selected and edited fragments from their lessons in a video clip in order to show to each other how they had practised the teaching behaviours chosen. At the beginning of each fragment, they inserted the relevant viewing point as a caption. The instruction for producing these video clips was to "show the best of your teaching" (cf. the section *Best Foot Forward* in Chapter 2). The preservice teachers showed their video clips to each other and discussed them in subgroups as part of a plenary peer consultation meeting with the aim of making their intentions for future teaching concrete.

Table 4.1 contains the full SVG produced by the project group for the reading comprehension intervention. This group studied mostly Dutch-language publications such as Vernooy's summary of the international state of the art in reading research (Vernooy, 2012, p. 35–109). Through this channel, features of quality instruction in reading comprehension found their way into the SVG, i.e. notably

TABLE 4.1 Reading comprehension viewing guide

Content	Items
Quality of own instructional behaviour	
Clear expectations	When I teach reading comprehension, I make clear what I expect from pupils.
Motivation	During my reading comprehension lessons, I succeed in motivating pupils to do the best they can.
Involving pupils	I succeed in motivating my pupils to participate actively in my reading comprehension lessons.
Predicting	During my lessons, I regularly let pupils predict the text content.
Illustrations	During my lessons, I often use illustrations, photos or video clips.
Recapitulating last lesson	At the beginning of a lesson, I always let pupils tell what the last lesson was about.
Making concrete	If possible, I make the meaning of difficult words concrete.
Achieving learning goals	In my lessons, I succeed in having the children achieve the learning goals within the time given.
Cognitive activation of learners	
Examples	During reading comprehension lessons, I always let pupils present their own examples.
Think all	While questioning, I always take care to give all children enough opportunity to think for themselves.
Multimedia as trigger	In my lessons, I regularly use multimedia sources that triggger children.
Asking higher-order questions	I find it easy to find ways of asking questions that challenge children to think.
Encouraging text analysis	During my reading comprehension lessons, I encourage children to ask questions about the text themselves.

(*Continued*)

Table 4.1 (Continued). Reading comprehension viewing guide

Content	Items
Speaking in whole class	I take care to give many children opportunities to speak in whole-class settings.
Giving compliments	During my reading comprehension lessons, I give task-oriented compliments like "That's a clever solution, I think".
Constructive response from learners	
Enthusiasm	When I introduce the lesson, children are always enthusiastic to tell their own stories about the theme.
Topics	During my lessons, pupils often present topical examples.
Finding out more	After my lessons, some children have become so interested that they want to find out more about the topic.
Main issues	Through my questions, I achieve that children can distinguish well between major and minor issues.
Original solutions	During my reading comprehension lessons, children often contribute original solutions.
Thinking aloud	During my lessons, children are willing to demonstrate while thinking aloud how they arrived at a solution or answer.
Promoting anticipatory reading	
Asking about pictures	At the beginning of a lesson, I often ask questions about pictures alongside the text, so that children can predict a little in which direction the text will go.
Predicting remaining text	I always have children make predictions about how the text will continue.
Promoting cooperative learning	
Sharing ideas	I often use the opportunity to have children share opinions and ideas in groups.
Discussion	I encourage children to arrive at different solution strategies through discussion.
Strategy	I deliberately ask children "how" they solve problems and challenge them to have a dialogue together about those solutions.
Dialogue and discussion	My lessons are mainly lessons in which I have dialogues and discussion with the children.

providing goal clarity and explicit strategy instruction (through modelling, thinking aloud and scaffolding); clarifying text structure, summarising, visualising and questioning about text content; having pupils predict text content; guiding and monitoring peer work; and gradual release of responsibility (cf. Duke & Pearson, 2002, p. 235 and Palincsar & Brown, 1984, p. 119–122).

In a control group, the video activities described above did not take place. The preservice teachers in the control group also studied literature about reading comprehension, but during practice teaching, they received only verbal feedback on their lessons.

Writing instruction

The second intervention involved an experimental group of sixteen in-service teachers working in three schools, focussing on instruction for writing tasks. These teachers received the SVG about writing instruction, were filmed during writing lessons and received video feedback on their instructional behaviour at the beginning and at the end of a four-month period. In addition to the SVG, these teachers received model lesson plans designed to suggest how they could practise the teaching behaviours specified. Filming and feedback were provided by colleagues from their own school and/or preservice teachers from the college.

Table 4.2 contains the full SVG produced by the project group for the writing instruction intervention. Features of quality instruction in writing were derived from Bonset and Hoogeveen (2009 and 2015), Hoogeveen (2012), Hoogeveen and van Gelderen (2015) and Rijlaarsdam, Van den Bergh, Couzijn, Janssen, Braaksma et al. (2011), i.e. goal setting; strategy instruction; text structure instruction; peer assistance; feedback from teacher and peers; evaluation; grammar instruction; revision; prewriting activities and planning-writing-revising. Evidence for the effectiveness of these features of instruction is presented in the review by Koster et al. (2015, p. 255–257 and 262–269).

TABLE 4.2 Writing instruction viewing guide

Content	Items
Orientation	
Using books for warming up	When I assign writing tasks I use non-fiction and fiction books to bring children into an atmosphere for writing.
Using film fragments	When I start the lesson I use film fragments to motivate children for their writing task.
Following the textbook	I follow the textbook method.
Creating own writing tasks	I create writing tasks myself that fit in with a theme that the class is already working on.
Creating a rich writing environment	During the writing activity I create a writing environment, for instance by installing a reading table or exhibiting images relevant to the task.
The writing task fits in a meaningful context	
Meaningful tasks	The children experience my writing tasks as meaningful.
Complete writing tasks	I always offer complete writing tasks, i.e. the writing activity should lead to a complete text.
Naming a theme	When children get a writing task, I explicitly name the theme about which they are going to write.
Functional use of texts	My pupils make functional use of the texts they write, for instance they send a letter or they write a report read by other children.
Clarifying audience	When children begin to write, it is always clear for whom they write.

(*Continued*)

TABLE 4.2 (Continued). Writing instruction viewing guide

Content	Items
The writing task is clear and process-oriented	
Assessment criteria	I always tell my pupils what counts when I assess their work.
Thinking aloud	I demonstrate, while thinking aloud and considering different choices, how a writing task can be tackled, for instance on my whiteboard.
Giving writing tips	I always give my pupils writing tips.
Making writing tips visible	After my instruction, the children can always see which writing tips are important for the activity at hand.
Using formats	When I give writing instructions I always use formats.
Help during writing	
Mutual support	During the writing lesson I give children the opportunity to support each other.
Constructive atmosphere	I succeed in creating a pedagogical atmosphere in which children react respectfully and critically to each other's texts.
Using children's texts	In my lessons I use text fragments from my pupils as good examples.
Commenting form and spelling	While the children are writing, I walk around and give comments on form and spelling.
Commenting content	While the children are writing, I walk around and give comments on the contents of their texts.

In a control group, the video activities in writing instruction described above were not carried out.

Writing feedback

In the third intervention, an experimental group of fourteen in-service teachers from the same three schools as the reading instruction intervention participated, focussing on giving feedback during writing tasks. These teachers received the SVG about giving feedback on writing tasks and model lesson plans suggesting how to provide feedback to their pupils during writing tasks, were filmed during writing lessons at the beginning and at the end of a four-month period and received feedback on their feedback behaviour with the help of the SVG.

Table 4.3 contains the full SVG produced by the project group for the writing feedback intervention. For this SVG, the same sources were used as for the writing instruction SVG.

Again, in a control group, the video activities in giving feedback on writing tasks as described above were not carried out.

Method

In this section, the research design, the participants and their response, as well as the instrumentation, data collection and data analysis, are described.

TABLE 4.3 Writing feedback viewing guide

Content	Items
Writing tips	
Providing writing tips	When my instruction is complete, there is a list of writing tips on the board which the children can use during writing.
Pointing out core writing tasks	At the end of my instruction, I summarise for the children what they should pay special attention to during writing.
Stressing main points for assessment	At the end of my instruction, I tell the children what I will especially look for when assessing their texts.
Spelling, punctuation and layout	During instruction, my tips focus on spelling, punctuation and layout.
Text organisation	During instruction, my tips focus on text organisation, for example how sections are ordered and subdivided.
Exploring the task	
Brainstorming	Before they begin to write, I give the children a little time to brainstorm together.
Looking back	Before they begin to write, I let the children tell each other if they have written a similar text before and what they learnt from this.
Drawing up a writing plan	Before they begin to write, I encourage the children to draw up a writing plan first.
Determining success criteria	Before they begin to write, I let the children determine for themselves when they will be satisfied with the text they are going to write.
Anticipating text use	Before they begin to write, I ask the children to think about how they want the text to be used.
Teacher help	
Giving space for problem-solving	While children are writing, I do not interfere. I do my best to give them space to solve problems by themselves.
Giving support during writing	As soon as the instruction is complete, I walk through the classroom and try to support children at the right moment when they encounter problems during writing.
Giving suggestions to attend to spelling and layout	Once children are writing and I am walking around, I give them suggestions that help them attend to spelling and layout.
Asking questions to encourage progress	While children are writing, I try to ask questions that promote the writing process, for example "How far are you now?" or "Do you know already how you will continue the story?"
Matching feedback to text type	In my lessons, feedback is determined by the type of text children are writing. When they write a letter, my feedback is clearly different from when they write a comic strip.

(Continued)

TABLE 4.3 (Continued). Writing feedback viewing guide

Content	Items
Thinking aloud together	When children get stuck during writing, I try to think aloud with them how we can get it going again.
Asking about progress	While walking around, I ask about the progress of the text.
Reminding of writing tips and tasks	While giving feedback, I remind the children of the writing tips and the writing tasks we agreed on during instruction.
Feedback among children	
Peer feedback among children	In my writing lessons, I let children give feedback on each other's texts.
Focussing feedback	When children give each other feedback on their texts, they know what it should focus on.
Using writing tips to guide peer feedback	I use the writing tips during instruction as a guide for peer feedback among children.
Training how to give feedback	I deliberately taught children how they can give feedback on each other's texts.
Using feedback	The children use the feedback they receive to write a new text.
Writing comments	The feedback that children give each other consists of comments under the text.
Placing feedback in specific spots	Feedback that children give each other is placed in specific spots in the text.
Giving feedback orally	When children give each other feedback, they do so orally, for example in a dialogue.
Annotating	When giving suggestions during feedback, children use the options offered by computers and tablets, for example by marking, circling or annotating
Reading aloud to the group	Children take the initiative to read texts or fragments they are proud of aloud to the group
Giving compliments	Children compliment each other with "cool sentences".
Assessing	
Assessing text form	When assessing my pupils' work I give feedback on the text form (spelling and punctuation).
Grading	When assessing my pupils' work I assign grades.
Reacting to text content	When assessing my pupils' work I react to the contents of their texts, for example by asking a question or making a remark.
Telling about personal reading experience	When assessing my pupils' work I also write about my own reading experience, for instance: "Your story made me laugh a lot!"
Giving special attention	Special achievements get special attention.

Research design

As the interventions took place in the natural settings of schools, a mixed-methods, quasi-experimental design was used in order to trace changes in teaching behaviour (Bronfenbrenner, 1979). Pre- and post-intervention measurements were conducted in experimental and control groups. To increase validity, teacher self-assessments of their classroom behaviour were combined with observations of their lessons.

The same research design and the same types of instruments were used in the three similarly designed interventions in an attempt to replicate outcomes. Comparing the outcomes of several interventions makes it possible to assess their reproducibility (Open Science Collaboration, 2015). This increases the number of respondents and thus the robustness of findings. This approach is valuable not only in direct, but also in conceptual, replications, because the latter allow for exploring "the stability of a phenomenon across different content domains" (Carpenter, 2012, p. 1561). We see our study as a conceptual replication, in which different groups of participants are involved.

Participants

Table 4.4 shows the numbers of teachers participating in the experimental and control groups for the three interventions. Also, the pre- and post-intervention response frequencies and percentages are specified for the teacher surveys. Finally, because repeated measures were analysed, the numbers of respondents are given for whom complete score pairs were available.

The response rates achieved are satisfactory. Only the post-intervention response in the control group in the third intervention is relatively low. This is possibly due to attrition, as most teachers in this group (86%) worked in schools which had participated in the second intervention and non-response was concentrated among teachers who already served as controls in the second intervention. The experimental and the control groups are comparable where prior experience and gender are

TABLE 4.4 Participants and response

Intervention	Exp/ Ctrl	n teachers	Pre-intervention		Post-intervention		Score Pairs	
			freq.	%	freq.	%	freq.	%
Reading	Exp	23	22	95.6	17	73.9	17	73.9
(preservice)	Ctrl	140	94	67.1	117	83.6	61	43.6
	Total	163	95	58.3	134	82.2	78	47.8
Writing	Exp	16	16	100	15	93.8	15	93.8
instruction	Ctrl	23	23	100	16	69.6	16	69.6
(in-service)	Total	39	39	100	31	79.5	31	79.5
Writing	Exp	14	14	100	11	78.6	11	78.6
feedback	Ctrl	21	21	100	8	38	8	38
(in-service)	Total	35	35	100	19	54.3	19	54.3

concerned. The preservice teachers in the first intervention had by definition no formal teaching experience and the amount and nature of prior teacher education courses attended by the experimental and the control groups were similar. The in-service teachers in the second and third interventions had, on average, twenty years of teaching experience with a minimum of one and a maximum of 41 years. This average did not differ significantly between the experimental and the control groups.

The distribution of men and women was 17.4% versus 82.6% in the first inter-vention, 30.8% versus 69.2% in the second and 25.7% versus 74.3% in the third. This skewed distribution represents the feminisation in primary teacher education found in many countries. In none of the interventions did significant differences in gender distribution exist between the experimental and the control groups.

Observation data were collected only in the experimental groups. The response percentages for these data were 47.8% in the first intervention, 93.3% in the second and 78.6% in the third.

Data collection

To be able to answer the first and second research questions about the interven-tion outcomes, the teachers in the experimental and the control groups completed self-assessments of their instructional behaviour at the beginning and the end of all interventions. In these self-assessments, the viewing points in the SVGs (Tables 4.1 through 4.3) were used as criterion measures. The teachers rated on five-point scales the frequency with which the behaviours described in these items occurred during their lessons (5 = often; 4 = regularly; 3 = sometimes; 2 = hardly ever; 1 = never).

To explore the validity of self-assessments in this study, two senior teacher educa-tors rated video clips produced by eleven preservice teachers from the experimental group of the first intervention on whether and how well they actually practised the teaching behaviours targeted. For these ratings, the questions in Table 4.5 were used

TABLE 4.5 Rater prompts

Visibility and audibility
Are pupils' reactions and input visible and audible enough to be comprehensible?

Camera position
Was the camera in a fixed or a moving position?

Selection of viewing points
Which viewing points were selected by the students?

Evidence
Did the students really display in their lessons the behaviours described in the viewing points chosen?

Relevance
Which teacher and/or pupil behaviours in each clip are relevant for the viewing points chosen?

Pedagogical quality
In which respects is the teaching behaviour shown suited to encourage substantive learning by pupils?

TABLE 4.6 Prompts for open comments and learner reports

Statements to comment upon
The video helps me develop a *command of the teaching profession.*
Self-viewing challenges me to think about *how I design my lessons.*

Sentences to complete
To develop my instruction, my *new personal learning goal(s)* is/are ...
The peer consultation has given me the *idea* to ...
Through the peer consultation I have *discovered* that I ...
Because of the peer consultation I am now *better able* to ...
The peer consultation has given me the *feeling* that ...

---

as prompts. The raters were asked to assess through discussion and consensus how visible and audible the preservice teachers' interaction with pupils was in these clips and from which camera positions their interaction with pupils was filmed, i.e. fixed or moving, because we assume that these factors strongly influence what viewers absent in the teaching situation represented will comprehend (see about this and related issues Chapter 7). The raters were asked to determine the preservice teachers' selection of viewing points, because we wanted to know what were their personal concerns while learning to teach. The last three prompts in Table 4.5 were meant to evaluate whether the preservice teachers understood and actually enacted the viewing points chosen and what was the pedagogical quality of their teaching behaviour.

In the second and third interventions, preservice teachers were trained to observe whether or not the in-service teachers in the experimental groups practised the instructional behaviours in Tables 4.2 and 4.3 during their lessons. The observers also wrote down specific descriptions of these behaviours. These observations took place in the teachers' classrooms, both at the beginning and the end of the respective interventions.

To be able to answer the third research question about learning experiences, the preservice teachers in the experimental group of the first intervention were asked to write open comments in reaction to two statements and learner reports by completing five sentences. Learner reports are semi-structured response formats in which learners describe their learning experience in their own words (Haanstra, 2008; Van Kesteren, 1993). Table 4.6 shows the wording of the statements and sentences used. Responses to these prompts were received from fifteen out of 23, i.e. 65% of the preservice teachers in the experimental group.

Data analysis

The validity of the instruments was examined as follows. Firstly, the homogeneity of the items in the SVGs was evaluated by calculating Cronbach's alphas for each SVG as a whole and for each category of viewing points separately. Secondly, the expert ratings of preservice teachers' video clips were analysed to answer the questions in

Table 4.5. Thirdly, the observations of the in-service teachers were compared with their self-assessments by calculating for which percentages of viewing points the teachers and observers agreed that over time, the behaviours described increased in frequency.

To answer the first and second research questions about the intervention outcomes, the pre- and post-intervention criterion measures were analysed as follows. For each intervention, descriptive statistics were calculated for the experimental and control groups separately.

Then, the means found in the experimental and control groups were compared through t-tests for independent samples. These between-group analyses were carried out separately for the pre-intervention and the post-intervention measures. The comparisons between the pre-intervention means served to determine if and what initial differences existed between the control and the experimental groups. The comparisons between the post-intervention measures served to determine if and what changes in the experimental groups could be attributed to the intervention.

To determine which changes occurred over time, t-tests for paired samples were carried out on the available pairs of repeated measures. These within-group analyses show which learning gains the teachers achieved over time. Also, these analyses were carried out separately for the control and the experimental groups, so that it could be determined if these groups differed in how the teachers' use of the criterion behaviours changed over the course of the interventions.

All t-tests were performed in two-sided fashion and with significance levels of $p <$ .05. For all comparisons, effect sizes were calculated (Grissom & Kim, 2005, p. 48–70).

Finally, in order to assess the influence of the three interventions in relation to each other, we calculated the percentages of viewing points for which significant and non-significant learning gains were found. These percentages were then compared across the interventions.

In addition, cross-case content analyses were conducted on all observations in the second and third interventions. The first author summarised which types of teaching behaviours the observers had described using the viewing points in Tables 4.2 and 4.3. These summaries were then checked and found correct by the third author.

To answer the third research question about learning experiences, cross-case content analyses were performed on the preservice teachers' open comments and learner reports. Their responses to the prompts in Table 4.6 were summarised and categorised by the first author, checked and found correct by the third author.

Validity checks

Three validity checks were conducted on the data. These are reported below.

Homogeneity of teacher self-assessments

The homogeneity of the teachers' pre- and post-intervention self-assessments on the viewing points in the SVGs was satisfactory, Cronbach's alphas respectively being .89 and .86 for reading comprehension, .83 and .88 for writing instruction and .67

and .91 for writing feedback. When calculated for the viewing points within each category, Cronbach's alphas ranged between .70 and .91 for eight out of the twelve categories in the three SVGs before the intervention and for seven categories after the intervention. The teachers apparently considered most SVG categories as coherent descriptions of classroom behaviour.

Expert rating of video clips

The expert rating of preservice teachers' video clips (see the section *Data collection* above) yielded the following results. In the experts' judgement, teacher–pupil interaction in five out of the eleven clips analysed was visible and audible enough to be comprehensible to viewers. Among these were all three clips produced with a moving camera position.

The viewing guide about reading comprehension as elaborated by the preservice teachers (cf. the section *Reading comprehension*) contained 37 viewing points divided over six categories. For their practice teaching, they targeted sixteen viewing points regarding three instructional challenges, i.e. activating pupils' prior knowledge, relating lesson content to pupils' experience and involving them actively in the lesson. The experts determined that the teaching behaviours involved were visible in twenty out of 22 lesson fragments distinguished in the video clips. They also judged that in all but two fragments, the preservice teachers actually displayed the teaching behaviours chosen. In the two fragments in which this was not the case, different behaviours were visible and/or the preservice teachers had labelled the behaviours shown incorrectly.

Four out of the five clips assessed on evidence, relevance and pedagogical quality (the last three prompts in Table 4.5) show that the preservice teachers activated pupils' prior knowledge by giving instructions for reading and writing tasks, by asking for word meanings and by using representations of content such as reading texts and word webs on the whiteboard. Two preservice teachers encouraged pupils to predict text content by showing them a reading text and asking questions about it. Two preservice teachers asked starting questions and elaborated on pupils' answers or reactions from other pupils. Four preservice teachers activated their pupils by using forms of cooperative learning.

Regarding the extent to which the preservice teachers' behaviour was suited to encourage pupils' substantive learning, the experts noted that especially asking starting and elaborating questions raised the quality of the lessons. They also noted that four preservice teachers' interaction with pupils was characterised by forthcoming behaviour and an inviting attitude. In their judgement, this had a positive impact on the quality of the lessons.

Behaviour changes as reported by teachers and observers

For the writing instruction and feedback interventions, the frequencies of behaviour change as registered by the participating teachers themselves and by their observers were compared. For 71% and 67% of the viewing points in the respective SVGs, the teachers and observers agreed that over time, the behaviours described increased in frequency. Thus, the teacher self-assessments and the observations predominantly point in the same direction.

Findings

In this section, the findings bearing on the first and second research questions about changes in teachers' instructional behaviour are presented and compared across the three interventions, followed by those concerning the third research question about learning experiences.

Changes in instructional behaviour

As described in the section *Data analysis*, independent t-tests were carried out to determine differences in instructional behaviour between the teachers in the experimental and the control groups. T-tests of repeated measures served to determine learning gains over time. Table 4.7 gives an overview of the statistically significant between-group and within-group differences found in all three interventions. The columns in Table 4.7 show from left to right for each category in the SVGs how many viewing points it contained, in how many of the criterion behaviours the teachers in the experimental groups showed significant post-intervention differences from their colleagues in the control groups and for how many of these behaviours significant learning gains over time were found in the experimental groups. These results are summarised in subtotals of criterion behaviours for each SVG and in total numbers of criterion behaviours for all the SVGs.

All significant differences in Table 4.7 indicate positive intervention outcomes, i.e. the teachers in the experimental groups developed the teaching behaviours in the SVGs to a greater extent than their colleagues in the control groups. Below, these findings are specified for each intervention. When significant initial differences existed between experimental and control groups, this is taken into account. For all results, group means, effect sizes and p values are presented. When the observations provided additional information to the teacher self-assessments, this is summarised.

Reading comprehension

After the reading comprehension intervention, most significant outcomes concerned the quality of the preservice teachers' instructional behaviour.

The preservice teachers in the experimental group succeeded better than those in the control group in making the meaning of difficult words concrete ($M = 3.71$ vs. 3.14; $ES = .17$; $p = .03$). In this respect, their learning gains were significant (M changed from 3 to 3.71; $ES = .2$; $p = .04$). They also felt they progressed considerably in making clear what they expected from pupils (M changed from 3.44 to 3.88; $ES = .18$; $p = .02$), in making them distinguish between major and minor issues (M changed from 2.75 to 3.44; $ES = .21$; $p < .00$) and in using illustrations, photos or video clips (M changed from 3.12 to 3.88; $ES = .21$; $p = .023$).

TABLE 4.7 Significant post-intervention differences

Category	Numbers of		
	criterion behaviours / viewing points	significant post-intervention group differences	significant within-group learning gains
READING INSTRUCTION			
Quality of own instructional behaviour	8	1	4
Cognitive activation of learners	7	1	1
Constructive response from learners	6	2	2
Promoting anticipatory reading	2	0	0
Promoting cooperative learning	4	0	0
Subtotal	27	4	7
WRITING INSTRUCTION			
Orientation	5	2	3
The writing task fits in a meaningful context	5	1	2
The writing task is clear and process-oriented	5	0	1
Help during writing	6	1	2
Subtotal	21	4	8
WRITING FEEDBACK			
Writing tips	5	1	1
Exploring the task	5	1	1
Teacher help	9	2	0
Feedback among children	11	7	5
Assessing	5	1	0
Subtotal	25	12	7
Total	73	20	22

The preservice teachers in the experimental group cognitively activated their pupils by having them present examples of their own significantly more often than the control teachers ($M = 4.18$ vs. 3.21; ES $= .3$; $p < .00$). In this respect, the experimental group's learning gains were significant (M changed from 3.06 to 4.18; ES $= .3$; $p < .001$). When pupils in the experimental group's classes presented examples, these were significantly more often about topics from their own lives than was the case in the control teachers' classes ($M = 4$ vs. 3.34; ES $= .23$; $p < .00$). Also in this respect, the experimental group's learning gains were significant (M changed from 3.24 to 4; ES = .25; p < .005).

The preservice teachers in the experimental group succeeded more often than the control teachers in eliciting a constructive response from their pupils, i.e. these pupils were significantly more enthusiastic to tell their own stories about the theme at hand than the control teachers' pupils (M = 4.06 vs. 3.63; ES = .14; p = .04). The preservice teachers in the experimental group felt they significantly progressed in motivating their pupils to participate actively in their reading lessons (M changed from 3.21 to 3.71; ES = .22; p = .014). In this behaviour, they even departed from a significantly lower baseline than the control teachers (M = 3.02 vs. 3.43; ES = -.13; p = .043).

The above findings are in line with what the experts noted when rating pre-service teachers' video clips, i.e. that pupils' learning especially benefitted from the teachers' questioning behaviour and was encouraged by the teachers' forthcoming and inviting attitudes.

In sum, the preservice teachers' main learning outcomes were in giving clear instructions to their pupils and bringing them to engage actively with reading comprehension.

Writing instruction

After the writing instruction intervention, most significant outcomes concerned the way in which the in-service teachers oriented their pupils towards writing activities.

The teachers in the experimental group used books to bring children into an atmosphere for writing significantly more often than those in the control group (M = 3.47 vs. 2.75; ES = .24; p = .014). The observers noted that they did so mainly by reading aloud or telling stories themselves and having the pupils engage in role-play. To motivate children for writing tasks, they also used film fragments at the start of lessons significantly more often (M = 3.57 vs. 2.06; ES = .38; p < .00). In both these respects, the experimental teachers felt they progressed significantly in the course of the intervention (M changed from 2.81 to 3.47; ES = .21; p < .006 and from 2.06 to 3.57; ES = .36; p < .000 respectively). They also reported significant learning gains in creating a writing environment, for instance by installing a reading table or exhibiting images relevant to the writing task (M changed from 2.13 to 3.03; ES = .25; p < .003).

While providing writing tasks for pupils, the experimental teachers had them make a functional use of their texts, for instance by sending a letter or writing a report for other children, significantly more often than did the control teachers (M = 4.30 vs. 3.56; ES = .22; p = .027). In this respect, the experimental teachers also reported significant learning gains over time (M changed from 4.3 to 3.63; ES = .24; p < .004). As noted by the observers, children read their texts aloud to each other or sent them to addressees through email or to a poetry web site. In addition, the experimental teachers significantly increased the use of formats when giving writing instructions (M changed from 2.63 to 3.87; ES = .28; p = .011). In this respect, they even departed from a significantly lower baseline than did the control teachers (M = 2.63 vs. 3.57; ES = −.24; p < .009).

While giving help during writing, the experimental teachers walked through their classrooms and commented on the content of pupils' texts significantly more often than the control teachers (M = 4.53 vs. 3.88; ES = .20; p = .04). In this respect, they reported significant learning gains over time (M changed from 3.88 to 4.53; ES = .2; p = .014). As noted by the observers, the teachers' comments consisted mostly of suggestions, compliments, help and instructions. The experimental teachers also felt that over time, they significantly increased the opportunities they gave pupils to support each other (M changed from 3.3 to 4.1; ES = .24; p < .003). Also in this respect, they departed from a significantly lower baseline than the control teachers (M = 3.3 vs. 3.68; ES = −.12; p = .023). The observations showed that mutual support by pupils usually took place in small groups of two or more children during different parts of a lesson.

In sum, the in-service teachers participating in the writing instruction intervention particularly changed their classroom behaviour in the direction of creating context-rich learning environments and supporting pupils in writing substantive messages directed at specified audiences.

Writing feedback

After the writing feedback intervention, most significant outcomes concerned the ways in which the in-service teachers instructed and supported their pupils in giving each other feedback.

To prepare for this, the teachers in the experimental group took significantly more care than those in the control group to make sure that at the end of their instruction, a list of writing tips was available on the board for children to use (M = 4.55 vs. 2.63; ES = .67; p < .00). In this respect, the experimental teachers reported significant learning gains over time (M changed from 2.82 to 4.55; ES = .52; p < .00). They also asked their pupils significantly more often to think, before beginning to write, how they wanted their texts to be used than did the control teachers (M = 3.27 vs. 2.13; ES = .27; p = .04).

While the pupils were writing, the experimental teachers tried significantly more often than the control teachers to ask questions promoting the writing process, such as "How far are you now?" or "Do you know already how you will continue the story?" (M = 3.64 vs. 2.88; ES = .28; p = .02). They also matched their feedback significantly more often to the types of texts children were writing, for instance a letter or a comic strip (M = 4.45 vs. 3.25; ES = .31; p = .046).

To encourage pupils to give feedback to each other, the experimental teachers employed the following range of behaviours significantly more often than the control teachers: allowing children to give feedback on each other's texts (M = 3.82 vs. 2.5; ES = .39; p < .003); making sure that when children give such feedback on each other's texts, they know what it should focus on (M = 4.18 vs. 2.25; ES = .65; p < .00); using the writing tips given during the instruction as a guide for peer feedback among children (M = 4.18 vs. 2.38; ES = .5; p < .00); and teaching children how to give feedback on each other's texts (M = 3.36 vs. 2.13; ES = .32; p = .012). Significant learning gains over time occurred in the experimental group for allowing children to give feedback on each other's texts (M changed from 2.73 to 3.82; ES = .28; p < .006) and teaching children how to give feedback on each other's texts (M changed from 2.18 to 3.36; ES = .31; p < .007).

In reaction, the experimental teachers' pupils used the feedback they received for writing a new text significantly more often than the control teachers' pupils (M = 3.09 vs. 2.25; ES = .25; p = .049), even though initially, the experimental teachers lagged significantly behind the control teachers (M = 1.57 vs. 2.1; ES = −2.1; p = .02). Also, the feedback the experimental teachers' pupils gave each other consisted significantly more often of comments written under a peer's text than the feedback given by the control teachers' pupils (M = 2.73 vs. 1.63; ES = .36; p = .012). For both aspects, significant learning gains were found in the experimental group (M changed from 1.64 to 3.09; ES = .45; p < .003 and from 1.55 to 2.73; ES = .3; p < .005, respectively). Also, over time, the experimental teachers' pupils complimented each other with "cool sentences" significantly more often than the control teachers' pupils (M changed from 2.09 to 3; ES = .2; p = .01). When giving each other feedback, the experimental teachers' pupils significantly more often did so orally, for example in a dialogue (M = 2.91 vs. 2; ES = .29; p = .026). Finally, the experimental teachers gave special attention at the end of their writing lessons to special achievements by pupils significantly more often than the control teachers (M = 4.09 vs. 3; ES = .26; p = .04).

The observations largely confirmed the above findings and clarified the nature of the experimental teachers' behaviour change, i.e. in the course of the intervention, they gave more specified assignments for cooperation between pupils, asked more pointed questions about and voiced more positive appreciations of the contents of pupils' writing.

In sum, the in-service teachers participating in the writing feedback intervention particularly changed their classroom behaviour by instructing and encouraging their pupils more specifically towards giving each other feedback on their writing.

Comparison of intervention outcomes

Figure 4.1 visualises how the teachers in the experimental and control groups developed over time. The upper pair of horizontal bars specifies the learning gains found after the reading intervention, the middle pair those after the writing instruction intervention and the lower pair those after the writing feedback intervention. The bands within each bar show on the right-hand side the percentages of criterion variables which increased significantly and non-significantly over time. On the left-hand side, these bars show the percentages of criterion variables which decreased significantly or non-significantly (see legend).

When one compares the performance of the experimental and control groups across the interventions, it can be seen that the experimental teachers achieved

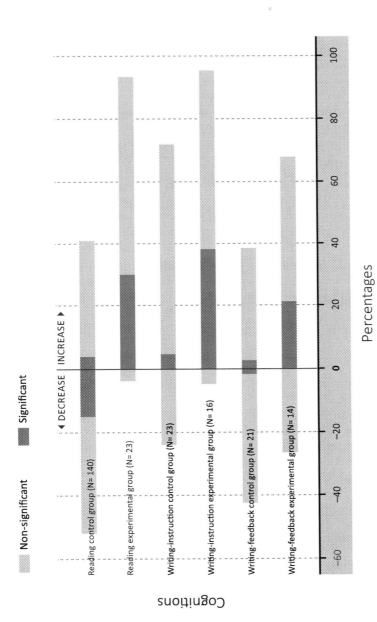

FIGURE 4.1 Learning gains compared

significant learning gains in more criterion behaviours than the control teachers. The same contrast is apparent for the amounts of non-significant learning gains, except in the writing instruction intervention. The inverse pattern is found, when one compares across the interventions the percentages of criterion variables which decreased significantly and non-significantly over time. In none of the experimental groups did significant decreases occur, whereas among the control teachers in the reading and writing feedback interventions they did. In addition, the amounts of non-significant decreases were lower among the experimental than among the control teachers.

The above synthesis of findings means that the learning gains achieved by the teachers receiving video feedback with SVGs consistently exceed those achieved by the teachers who did not receive such feedback. The percentages of criterion variables in which pre-post intervention decreases were found even suggest that the control teachers' classroom performance remained on initial levels or fell behind.

It should also be noted that the effect sizes found are relatively small. On average, the effect sizes for the significant differences between the experimental and control groups were .20 in the reading intervention, .26 in the writing instruction intervention and .38 in the writing feedback intervention. The average effect sizes for the significant learning gains within the experimental groups were .22, .25 and .32, respectively.

Preservice teacher learning experiences

The open comments and learner reports written by the preservice teachers during the reading intervention (see the prompts in Table 4.6) revealed what kinds of learning experiences their use of video had engendered. The response to the open comments was 65%. Learner reports were received from 78% in response to the fifth prompt and from 83% to the remaining prompts. Below, the findings are summarised and illustrated with one quote for each prompt. Because for these results N = 23, frequencies are only reported where more than 25% of responses were about similar topics.

All preservice teachers felt that giving and receiving video feedback had helped them develop proficiency in teaching. The main reason they gave for this is that using video had enabled them to analyse the stronger and weaker points in their teaching and to identify points for improvement. "You become more aware of how you face the group, how you react to pupils and what sort of language you use." The preservice teachers also felt that self-viewing had challenged them to think about how to design their lessons. "Yes, in this way you see which way of teaching is the best to get attention from the pupils."

The goals for improvement the preservice teachers mentioned most often had to do with how they designed their lessons, carried out instructions and presentations (30%), engaged groups of pupils in learning activities and managed their classroom interaction with them. "My goal is to allow everyone to contribute, also those children who do not raise their fingers."

From their participation in peer consultation with video, the preservice teachers had derived several ideas for the future, i.e. to film their own lessons more often, discuss them with fellow students (30%) and look for specific points for improvement while doing so. "I got the idea to use the viewing guides more often and talk about it together."

The preservice teachers reported having discovered that they had a better command than they previously thought of aspects of teaching such as designing and conducting reading lessons and engaging pupils in learning activities (30%). "I have a command of more viewing points than I had expected at first." Again, they noted that through video use and peer consultation, they had become better able to analyse the stronger and weaker points in their teaching and identify points for improvement (48%). "I can learn a lot from my lessons by filming myself and looking back on them."

The peer consultation had given the preservice teachers the feeling that the quality of their teaching had improved (39%). They also noted again that they had a better command of (specific aspects of) teaching than they had previously thought. "Peer coaching has given me more self-confidence."

Discussion

Below, answers to the research questions are formulated and their implications are discussed. Then, limitations of this study are described in relation to suggestions for further research.

Conclusions and implications

Three similarly designed interventions were evaluated in which preservice and in-service primary school teachers received video feedback using SVGs in order to improve the instructional quality of reading and writing lessons for pupils aged 10–11.

The findings show that both the preservice and the in-service teachers in the experimental groups made significantly more progress than those in the control groups in acquiring and developing the teaching behaviours targeted. The group differences as well as the learning gains found within the experimental groups have made it possible to specify which changes in teachers' behaviour occurred after receiving video feedback with SVGs. The greatest learning gains by the preservice teachers were in making the contents of their lessons concrete and bringing their pupils to engage actively with the subject matter by clarifying lesson goals and activities, questioning and encouraging cooperative learning. Expert ratings of pre-service teachers' video clips indicate that their classroom behaviours corresponded to a considerable extent to the types of teaching intended in the SVGs. The open comments and learner reports from the preservice teachers suggest that explicating and visualising domain-specific teaching behaviours can motivate them to analyse strengths and weaknesses in their teaching and to engage in continued efforts to enact effective classroom behaviours. The greatest gains by the in-service teachers were in contextualising and structuring children's writing tasks, giving them active support during writing and encouraging them to help each other.

The comparison of the outcomes across the three interventions strengthens the evidence indicating the effectiveness of video feedback with SVGs. The between-group differences and the within-group trends occurred consistently in all three interventions. The control groups' instructional competence remained on initial levels or even decreased over time. This phenomenon suggests that when the impetus to develop effective teaching behaviours is lacking, these behaviours may wane or even wither. Conversely, as the teachers in the experimental groups consciously targeted and made focussed efforts to enact effective teaching behaviours, this apparently raised the quality of their instruction. The changes found after the interventions occurred for relatively large numbers of teaching behaviours, while the effect sizes were relatively small. We interpret this to mean that the criterion behaviours targeted developed at a modest rate and in relation to each other. This interpretation is supported by the relatively high interrelations between the criterion measures.

The most important implication of the evidence found is that focussing video feedback through domain-specific SVGs can be a powerful contribution towards raising preservice as well as in-service teachers' quality of instruction as enacted in the classroom. These findings point in the same direction as the review of video feedback research by Fukkink et al. (2011, p. 56–57). As noted in the introduction, most studies of "professional vision" in teachers take perception as their end point. The specific contribution of this study is that video feedback with SVGs can affect professional behaviour. It is important to note that in this study, the forms of teaching and learning promoted by video feedback with SVGs were characterised more by responsiveness and dialogue than by direct instruction alone. This confirms the outcome of the literature review in the previous chapter that VTL can encourage teachers to develop the type of teaching behaviours suited to the cognitive activation of learners.

Even so, caution is needed in interpreting the findings. Although the outcomes were reproducible in three interventions, these interventions took place in different contexts and with different scenarios. How generalisable the findings are and how scalable their implementation probably depends to a large extent on factors in the local sociocultural contexts where VTL takes place. The prevalent culture of collaboration is one of these factors (Matsumura, Garnier, & Resnick, 2010). One strength of this study was that in the absence of sizeable additional funding, different groups of stakeholders – teacher educators, preservice and in-service teachers, mentor teachers and researchers – pooled their resources and expertise in regional collaboration.

Another factor that may affect the outcomes of future trials of video feedback with SVGs is the availability of evidence-based knowledge in a range of learning domains. Until now, video use in teacher education and PD has been developed largely in mathematics education. Developing SVGs for other domains (about DV use for developing literacy teaching, see Ortlieb, McVie, & Shanahan, 2015) could and should contribute to a knowledge base for teaching that local teams of teachers and teacher educators can draw upon (Gallimore, Ermeling, Saunders, Goldenberg, 2009 & Hiebert, Gallimore, & Stigler, 2002). Also, there is a trade-off to consider between the precision of SVGs on the one hand and practical feasibility in using them on the other. How many categories and viewing points can one include without overwhelming teachers and teacher educators (cf. Tripp & Rich, 2012, p. 681) or limiting them in pursuing personal concerns (cf. Danielowich, 2014)?

Thirdly, intensity and fidelity of implementation may influence intervention outcomes. As an approach situated in daily work situations, it would seem that video feedback with SVGs can be easily practised by teachers in order to expand and modify their repertoires of professional behaviour. However, the availability or lack of resources, especially in terms of working time, will affect how intensive VTL work can be. Finally, teachers and teacher educators will need training in the use of SVGs for facilitating teacher learning (Van Es, Tunney, Goldsmith, & Seago, 2014).

Limitations and further research

From the validity checks performed in this study, we infer that the data have a realistic bearing on teachers' actual classroom behaviour. Also, the reproducibility of the findings strengthens the conclusions. Still, caution is warranted about their generalisability because of the following limitations.

Firstly, this study is one instance of replication. Additional replications could shed more light on the power of video feedback with SVGs. Conducting such studies with teachers in different domains and career stages could clarify if and how the structure and content of SVGs should vary on the continuum from "adaptive" to "specific" (Borko et al., 2011). Prospective and beginning teachers may need more structure and/or different content in SVGs than more experienced teachers, as they have had fewer earlier opportunities to develop professional frames of reference. As reported in the section *Differences depending on career phase* in Chapter 3, there are hardly any studies in which outcomes of VTL among teachers in different career phases were directly compared. Just one study indicates that beginning and in-service teachers were better able than preservice teachers to respond to pupil reactions during classroom learning (Jacobs, Lamb, Philipp, & Schappelle, 2011).

Secondly, the resources available for this study only allowed process data to be collected among preservice teachers. More process data are needed, also among in-service teachers, to clarify the influence of factors influencing the intensity of intervention such as the frequencies of viewing, reviewing and discussing lesson recordings with colleagues and the types of viewing points preferred. Investigating these factors can help explain in what ways teachers transform insights gained from video analysis and feedback into new and modified classroom behaviours.

Finally, no data could be collected in this study among pupils. Further investigations are desirable into the conditions favouring teacher behaviour change and how this, in turn, may affect pupils' learning and achievement (cf. Allen, Pianta, Gregory, Mikami, & Lun, 2011; Kiemer, Gröschner, Pehmer, & Seidel, 2014; Koster, Bouwer, & van den Bergh, 2017; Pehmer, Gröschner, & Seidel, 2015a).

Quality of instruction is one of the levers teachers can and should use to foster children's learning. As an approach suitable for raising the effectiveness of teaching and learning, video feedback with SVGs deserves further development. It can help teachers discover what in their professional behaviour hinders or fosters children's learning.

5

IN SEARCH OF EFFECTIVE GUIDANCE FOR PRESERVICE TEACHERS' VIEWING OF CLASSROOM VIDEO

Niels Brouwer and Fokelien Robijns

Since the digitisation of video, video platforms are being established in PTE and PD (see the section *Video platforms for teachers* in Chapter 2).Video records of teaching and learning are attractive to teachers and teacher educators, because video is a suitable medium to make the interactions within the instructional triangle concrete and vivid and thus connect practice with theory.Video enables viewers a vicarious experience of the teaching situation (cf. Laurillard, 1993) and can involve them both cognitively and emotionally. This added value is often assumed to be self-evident. It would, however, be valuable to examine empirically how video viewing impacts teachers. In the practice of teacher education, it is quite a challenge to make prospective teachers understand the relationships between teaching and learning, as thorough observation, analysis and reflection are not skills and habits that they bring with them of their own accord. The same can sometimes even be said of mentors and teacher educators. It is therefore a reasonable assumption that teachers need training in observing and analysing teaching and learning processes, if they are to develop an eye for the manifold ways in which learners learn (cf. Brophy, 2004).

What do teachers perceive, when they view video records of lessons? How do they interpret what they see? Do they draw consequences from their observations for their own teaching and if so, what consequences? Which kinds of support in viewing teaching and learning help teachers develop a subtle understanding of the relationships between teaching and learning? Since the 1990s, a theoretical as well as empirical basis for such support systems is being developed internationally, especially in the US (Sherin, Jacobs, & Philipp, 2011; Stigler & Hiebert, 1999), Switzerland (Krammer, 2014) and Germany (Blomberg, Stürmer, & Seidel, 2011; Kobarg, 2009; Schwindt, 2008; Seidel, Stürmer, Blomberg, Kobarg, & Schwindt, 2011).

The purpose of this study is to clarify which characteristics viewing guides should have in order to support student teachers in understanding the teaching skills with which they can effectively promote children's learning.Viewing guides are lists

DOI: 10.4324/9780429331091-5

of "viewing points", i.e. observation items regarding effective teaching behaviours, subdivided in categories. These viewing points are selected on the basis of evidence from empirical research into effective teaching in a specific subject (see Chapter 4). The wider goal of our research is to contribute to evidence-based knowledge about the conditions in which DV use can promote teacher learning. Such knowledge is relevant for designing, implementing and upscaling video use in PTE.

Introduction

This study is informed by the VTL model introduced in Chapter 2 and the underlying literature review. It builds on a study by Chan and Harris (2005), who investigated six language teachers' thinking *while* they viewed video records of colleagues' lessons. In contrast to studies analysing teacher comments on video records written *after* viewing (Kobarg, 2009; Schwindt, 2008), think-aloud protocols can be assumed to offer more direct access to teachers' cognitions. To categorise these, Chan and Harris have introduced the Cognitive Development Process Model (CDPM).

This model comprises two main categories, Awareness and Reflection, based on the assumption that a person can only reflect on what she or he perceives with a certain degree of consciousness. The meaning of the category Awareness and the subcategories under Reflection is illustrated below. The whole model and further distinctions within it can be seen in Table 5.1.

Awareness: "The pupils are listening."
Comprehension: "She now begins with guided practice and makes a round through the classroom."
Acceptance: "She integrates the excursion in her maths activities. That's nice, a creative idea."
Rejection: "She explains a lot, but she doesn't show it. I think that's a pity."
Connection: "The noise level is rather high, but they are meant to discuss their work together, so then that's allowed, I guess."
Desire to Act: "I'd like to know what brought her to give this assignment, when she designed the lesson."

The study by Chan and Harris deals not only with teachers' perceptions, but also with how they are linked to their judgement, actions and intentions. Chan and Harris (2005, p. 367) formulate the assumption that during their observation, teachers proceed linearly through the cognitions specified in the CDPM. However, there are reasons to doubt this. Miller (2011) and Erickson (2011) point out that teachers are inclined to split-second judgements. The findings of Chan and Harris suggest that when teachers view video records of colleagues' lessons, their perceptions tend to be coloured by ethical or pragmatic considerations. Notably, their respondents often combined their perceptions of the teaching fragments shown with the consideration whether this style would be desirable or feasible in their own work.

TABLE 5.1 Cognitive Development Process Model and interview questions

	Awareness			Reflection — Comprehension			Acceptance			Rejection			Connection			Desire to act	
	Basic noticing	Advanced noticing	Recalling	Interpreting	Expressing uncertainty	Assuming	Agreeing	Liking	Judging positively	Disagreeing	Not liking	Judging negatively	Sharing Belief	Comparing	Sharing Experience	Applying	Requesting more
Opening questions	1. What was most striking to you in this maths lesson?		[not applicable]	3. Please describe in your own words what happened in this lesson.			5. What is your opinion about this lesson?						8. Please mention a number of things that the children can learn from this lesson. Please explain.			10. If you could speak with this teacher, what would you ask her?	
Follow-up questions	2. Wat makes this interesting to you?		[not applicable]	4. [Referring to description and/or interpretation:] What do you mean by ... [quote]?					6. What, do you think, is good about this lesson?			7. What, do you think, should the teacher improve in this lesson?		9. Did you teach a maths lesson like this yourself? Please tell me about it.		11. Would you teach this maths lesson in the same way? [If yes:] How would you go about this lesson yourself? [If no:] In what other way?	

In this chapter, we describe how Dutch prospective primary-school teachers viewed a compilation of fragments from a mathematics lessons, which reactions this elicited from them and in which respects these reactions differed depending on the conditions in which they viewed the video images shown to them.

The research questions are the following:

I.   Can the Cognitive Development Process Model developed by Chan and Harris (2005) be used to make explicit Dutch second-year student teachers' thoughts during their viewing of video clips of a mathematics lesson?

II. What kinds of thoughts do these prospective primary-school teachers report while they are viewing video clips of a mathematics lesson?

III. Do their reactions differ depending on the conditions of perception, i.e. whether they were provided with no viewing guide, one with categories only or one structured by means of viewing points?

Research design

As far as we know, the study by Chan and Harris has not yet been replicated. In order to test the CDPM, we conducted a pilot study with four student teachers of Iselinge College of Primary Teacher Education in Doetinchem, the Netherlands. In the subsequent main study, a condensed version of this category system was used with twelve student teachers. We studied if think-aloud protocols could be reliably coded with this version (research question I), in which subcategories the student teachers' statements fell (research question II) and if their reactions differed depending on the viewing conditions (research question III).

Pilot study

In the pilot study, four student teachers viewed the case Fantasialand from the video platform Didiclass (see the eponymous section in Chapter 2). This material is about a mathematics lesson in which a prospective primary-school teacher has pairs of children in her classroom make budgets for buying drinks, sweets and fruits during an excursion to the amusement park Fantasialand.

Data collection in the pilot study

Each student teacher viewed the video material under different conditions. Three student teachers viewed a 3½-minute compilation of lesson fragments, in which particularly the student teacher's instruction and her interaction with the children were visible. The first student teacher was provided with neither a viewing guide nor captions in the video compilation (condition A). The second student teacher was given a viewing guide in which only categories referring to the phases of direct-instruction lessons – introduction, instruction, guided practice, debriefing and summary – were mentioned and no captions in the video compilation (condition B).

The third student teacher received a structured viewing guide, i.e. one in which aspects of direct instruction were specified in the form of viewing points as well as captions in the video compilation (condition C). Examples of viewing points used are the following. "The teacher explains what the goal of the lesson is" (during the introduction). "The teacher demonstrates the learning activity and thinks aloud while doing so" (during instruction). "The teacher checks if the children understand what they must do and how" (during guided practice). "The teacher summarises what the children have learned" (during debriefing and summary).

A possible objection against the research design chosen was that in conditions A through C, the context of the whole case is lacking. For this reason, we included in the pilot study a condition D, in which the student teacher could view the unchanged fragment of the mathematics lesson and the related interviews with the teacher, her mentor and two pupils.

All four participants received the instruction to stop the video whenever they felt they could voice thoughts, associations and ideas relating to what they saw. They had the opportunity to view the images in a non-linear sequence, i.e. peruse them at will. They were also told that only their thoughts were of interest, in other words that correct or false answers were not at issue. While they were viewing and thinking aloud, the researcher present only asked short informative questions, mostly after student teachers had stopped the video themselves. Immediately after the think-aloud session, interview questions were asked in order to get to know more about the types of cognitions as distinguished by Chan and Harris.

Video recordings were made of both the think-aloud sessions and the subsequent interviews.

Data analysis in the pilot study

The recordings of the think-aloud sessions in the pilot study were examined to find out whether such sessions were realisable and whether the interview questions following them elicited sufficient information. On this basis, the data collection protocol used in the main study was generated. Also, a qualitative content analysis was performed on the think-aloud and interview statements in condition D in order to find out to what extent reactions during viewing of the whole case differed from those in conditions A through C.

Main study

In the main study, twelve second-year student teachers selected at random viewed the 3½-minute compilation from the mathematics lesson in the Fantasialand case. Two women and two men were placed in each of three conditions: no viewing guide, a guide with categories only and a guide structured by means of viewing points.

Data collection in the main study

Immediately after the think-aloud sessions, the participants in the main study were asked the interview questions derived from the CDPM. These were divided into opening questions and follow-up questions (see in Table 5.1 the numbers 1 through 11). The interview was concluded with retrospective questions about the student teachers' own experiences with learning and teaching mathematics and about working with viewing guides. The latter questions were asked only in the conditions in which viewing guides were provided (B and C).

Data analysis in the main study

The video recordings of the twelve think-aloud sessions were completely transcribed, segmented according to explicit rules and coded using the categories developed by Chan and Harris. The coding was carried out by six raters. To achieve sufficient reliability, all protocols were first analysed by two raters. If their ratings differed, the statements involved were coded by a third rater. If possible, final codings were determined by a majority of two raters. Any remaining divergences were discussed and resolved in consensus.

Statistical analysis began with determining the frequencies of the codes in each subcategory for the whole group of participants. Then the frequencies in the different conditions were compared and tested for significance using one-way ANOVA. In addition, effect sizes were calculated pairwise for the differences between the conditions A–C, B–C and A–B. Effect sizes < .50 were considered small, effect sizes > .50 < .75 moderate and effect sizes > .75 large (Grissom & Kim, 2005, 98-117). On the participants' interview statements, a crosscase content analysis was performed.

Findings

In this section, we describe in which form and with which outcomes the CDPM turned out to be applicable in a Dutch PTE context.

Response

The response rate was 100% both in the pilot and the main study. The student teachers in the main study had an average experience in teaching mathematics of 19.7 hours with a minimum of ten and a maximum of 35. They rated their own ability to teach mathematics with an average of 7.9 on a scale ranging from 1 to 10 and gave their own liking for learning and teaching mathematics average ratings of 4.17 and 3.82 respectively on five-point scales.

Condensed version of the Cognitive Development Process Model

From the pilot study, it became clear that the research design consisting of think-aloud sessions and subsequent interviews was realisable. These methods were then used in the main study. After the first round of ratings, the percentage of identically coded statements was 51. The addition of third raters increased this percentage to 82. Consensus had to be sought predominantly in the subcategories Awareness and Comprehension.

To characterise Dutch student teachers' think-aloud statements, the categories in the CDPM were surprisingly usable. The student teachers made an average of 15.17 separate statements per protocol with a maximum of 34 and a mode of 11. No more than 1.2 statements on average – or 8% of all statements – were not scorable. No statements were made in the subcategory Desire to Act. Consequently, all but one of the subcategories in the model turned out to be replicable.

Also the distinctions within the subcategory Comprehension were replicable. However, the distinctions between Basic and Advanced noticing and those within the subcategories Acceptance, Rejection and Connection could not be coded with sufficient reliability. Where Noticing, Acceptance and Rejection are concerned, this is probably because in these subcategories, differences in intensity or level are at stake rather than qualitative differences. In the condensed version of the model used in the main study, those distinctions which could not be replicated were pooled within their respective subcategories.

Statements about the mathematics lesson

The think-aloud sessions and the subsequent interviews showed in different ways which thoughts the video compilation elicited in the student teachers.

Think-aloud statements

The think-aloud statements by the twelve student teachers in the main study were distributed over the subcategories as follows. They mostly made statements indicating that they noticed and interpreted aspects of the mathematics lesson (19.8% and 20.1%, respectively). Almost as many remarks had to do with sharing beliefs and experiences (16.9%). The student teachers more often accepted than rejected what they saw (15.4% vs. 8%). Considerably fewer statements expressed uncertainty or assumptions (6.7% and 5%, respectively).

Interview statements

In the interviews, the student teachers clarified to which aspects of the mathematics lesson they paid attention. They attended in the first place to the teacher's instructional behaviour. Secondly, they focussed on how the teacher encouraged and motivated the children through her sequencing of activities, her enactment of group work, the way she conducted whole-group discussions and the compliments she voiced. A clear majority of student teachers judged the lesson as satisfactory till strong, in particular because the teacher created a positive learning climate and offered the children help. However, they were more critical about the learning outcomes of the lesson. They found its contents – adding up till a given limit – rather simple and felt that the teacher could have probed the assignment more deeply during the whole-group discussions. Asked what they found educative in the lesson they predominantly mentioned instructional aspects of a general nature such as working in groups.

In contrast to the think-aloud sessions, the student teachers connected what they saw during the interviews to their own actions. Out of a total of 28 remarks about this issue, eighteen referred to the consecutive phases of the lesson. Most of all, the student teachers were interested in getting to know the motives behind the teacher's lesson planning. They asked, for instance, why she enacted the introduction the way she did, why she ruled out certain alternatives from the shopping list that the children had to draw up, why she encouraged them to do group work and in which cases she should have continued or interrupted the lesson because of unrest. Ten remarks were phrased in the form of "Why didn't she do (more) … ?", after which the student teachers mentioned behavioural alternatives that they themselves preferred. Seven student teachers noted that they would follow the direct instruction model more closely, i.e. they would communicate the goal of the lesson more clearly and place more emphasis on the instruction. They also preferred demonstrating the learning activity more, debriefing it more thoroughly in whole-group discussion and concluding the lesson in a more explicit way.

Differences between conditions

Before examining if and what differences between conditions occurred in the student teachers' cognitions during video viewing, we checked for possible influences from the background variables number of mathematics lessons given and liking for learning and teaching mathematics. No significant differences in these respects were found.

Figure 5.1 shows that the frequencies of student teachers' cognitions clearly differed between conditions. Within the stacked bars, rounded percentages show how the student teachers' think-aloud statements in each condition were divided over the subcategories in the condensed CDPM.

It can be seen in Figure 5.1 that the student teachers in the most structured condition C made considerably more noticing and interpreting statements. At the same time, they made fewer statements in the subcategories Acceptance, Rejection and Connection. Most non-scorable statements were made by the student teachers in condition A without viewing guide. Still, the one-way ANOVA yielded only one significant difference, i.e. in the subcategory Interpreting ($F = 8.793; p = .01$). Three student teachers in condition A and four student teachers in condition B made an average of 8% and 10% interpreting statements respectively, while the four student teachers in condition C made an average of 39% interpreting statements. These effects are of a moderate size (.69 in the comparison between conditions C and A; .61 in the comparison between conditions C and B).

The comparisons between the conditions yielded only small effect sizes in the subcategories Noticing (varying between .03 and .19), Rejection (varying

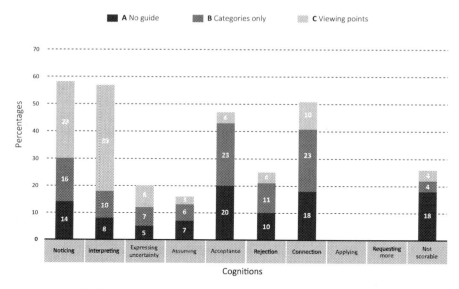

FIGURE 5.1   Think-aloud statements in three viewing conditions

between −.33 and .03) and Connection (varying between −.4 and .08). Clearly, differing effect sizes were found for the frequencies of accepting statements. The student teachers in condition C made an average of 4% accepting statements, while those in conditions B and A made 23% and 20% of such statements, respectively. The effect sizes involved are large and moderate, i.e. −1.94 and −.55, respectively. For the comparisons between conditions A and B, only small effect sizes were found.

In sum, the student teachers who received the viewing guide structured by means of viewing points made more think-aloud statements. Their statements were of a predominantly noticing and interpreting nature and less characterised by elements of acceptance, rejection or connection. This is in clear contrast to the statements made by the student teachers who received no viewing guide or a guide existing of broad categories only.

The use of viewing guides

In the interviews, most student teachers expressed positive opinions about working with viewing guides. Five out of the eight student teachers in the conditions with a viewing guide (B and C) felt that they had noticed more aspects with the viewing guide than they would have done without one. In this respect, the student teachers in the most structured condition C were most outspoken. The student teachers who received the viewing guide with categories only (condition B) found it helpful that they were provided with explicit points to attend to. Seven out of the eight student teachers interviewed expected that viewing guides such as the SVG used in the main study would help them during internships and PTE generally to formulate targets for improving their own teaching.

The student teachers gave the following recommendations for using viewing guides:

- Make it possible to add your own items.
- Watch a clip, watch the viewing guide, talk about it, pause and repeat this procedure.
- Use viewing guides to think about *why* things happen in the classroom as they do.
- Use viewing guides to make the transition from reviewing one lesson to preparing the next.
- Both student teacher and mentor can perform the above learning activities, independently and/or together.

Conclusions and recommendations

We first answer our three research questions and conclude with recommendations for PTE and PD and for future research.

Conclusions

The first research question was if the CDPM developed by Chan and Harris (2005) can be used to make explicit Dutch second-year student teachers' thoughts during their viewing of video clips of a mathematics lesson. It was indeed possible to code Dutch student teachers' reactions reliably on the level of the subcategories in this model. Distinctions within subcategories, however, were only possible for Comprehension and Desire to Act. Distinctions within the remaining subcategories appear to be possible only insofar as they constitute clear substantive differences. This is the case in the condensed version of the model used in our main study.

Regarding the second research question we conclude that the prospective primary-school teachers in our study did indeed demonstrate the cognitions distinguished in Chan and Harris' model. The majority of their think-aloud statements indicated Noticing, Interpreting, Acceptance and Rejection. This means that the student teachers not only attempted to comprehend what went on during the lesson fragments shown, but simultaneously formed a judgement about this. The interviews following the think-aloud sessions made clear that the moving images viewed elicited a considerable number of concrete comments, discussion themes and ideas for their own teaching.

Most student teachers attended to aspects concerning interaction rather than subject-specific instruction. One reason for this may be that the viewing guide offered was formulated on a general instructional level. The student teachers appeared inclined to assess the quality of the lesson in terms of interaction: when the teacher behaved towards the children in a friendly manner, they found it a good lesson. Only a minority made critical remarks about the extent to which the lesson challenged the pupils cognitively. The student teachers appeared little inclined to consider the material from perspectives other than those they brought with them from their own accord. As a group, however, they produced a rich array of thoughts.

An important aim of this study was to find out if viewing guides can influence prospective teachers' reactions to video records of a lesson. The quantitative results regarding this third research question yield clear indications for such an influence. The ANOVA showed that the student teachers in the most structured condition made the greatest number of think-aloud statements and that these statements were more interpretive and less judgemental in the sense of acceptance or rejection than those from the student teachers in the less structured and the unstructured conditions. The more structured the viewing guide was, the more statements the student teachers made and the more they attempted to interpret the lesson shown. This process went hand in hand with the expression of positive or negative judgements. In other words, the student teachers viewed the lesson more critically to the extent that the available viewing guide was structured. It made little or no difference whether they received no guide or one in which only categories were named.

In combination with the student teachers' retrospective interview statements, these findings lead us to conclude that viewing guides can have a noticeable influence on the number and nature of student teachers' perceptions during classroom video viewing. Specifically, the more explicit and structured viewing guides are, the more they can encourage student teachers to notice and distinguish between relevant aspects of teaching and learning, recognise relationships, attend to details of pupils' learning and suspend judgements. It is encouraging that the results from both the think-aloud sessions and the interviews point in this direction. Offering a viewing guide is in itself a simple intervention. It is surprising, then, that this can exert so much influence.

Recommendations

The findings of this study confirm the idea that video records of authentic lessons are a suitable medium to import the reality of the classroom into the PTE curriculum. Viewing moving images of real lessons can help teacher educators connect practice and theory when they encourage student teachers at the same time to analyse these images in a structured and goal-directed way. On this basis we formulate the following recommendations for developing and using video materials and viewing guides in teacher education.

Whether and what prospective teachers learn from video material depends not only on the availability and the content of viewing guides and how they are used, but also on the nature of the video material itself. As stated in the introduction, the content of viewing points should be based on empirical evidence and/or plausible theory about what constitutes effective teaching. Viewing guides may take a general instructional angle – as in this study – or be formulated in terms of specific subject domains. In the latter case, the use of viewing guides becomes explicitly content-focussed (cf. West & Staub, 2003). It can then attain a maximum concreteness and specificity. This may increase the likelihood of contributing to raising the quality of instruction. An equally important issue is which characteristics video clips should have if they are to offer teachers opportunities to understand the relationships between teaching and learning. The most important characteristic in our view is that the content-focussed interaction between teachers and learners is made visible (cf. Roelofs, 2007). When viewing guides and video materials fulfil the above requirements, we expect that these tools can encourage teachers to pay explicit attention to the question what makes their own professional behaviours functional or effective in terms of student learning and achievement (cf. Reusser, 2019).

To maximise the usability of viewing guides, we would like to make the following suggestions about their form (cf. the section *Intervention design* in Chapter 4). In our experience, viewing guides can become more accessible to teachers when one attempts to translate or merge the expert language of educational research into teachers' craft language. Viewing points should furthermore be formulated in terms of observable behaviour and as short sentences in the active voice and the present tense, for example "The teacher walks through the classroom and comments on the writing activities going on". In our experience, a parsimonious structure can also make viewing guides more usable, i.e. when not too many viewing points are grouped within a limited number of categories. When viewing guides are in digital form, it is a good idea to make them navigable and clickable on different levels of specificity. Such features could be built into video annotation tools (cf. Rich & Hannafin, 2009a).

Finally, using viewing guides for analysing lessons is something that student teachers, teacher educators and mentors should train themselves in. A suitable approach is first to view video records of lessons in a broad exploratory way and then engage in repeated viewing with the help of viewing points selected from specific perspectives and/or on the basis of teachers' personal concerns.

A limitation of this study is its small number of respondents. We suggest carrying out further research into the use of viewing guides with larger samples, different populations and a greater variety of video materials. Such "user research" would be possible in online video environments and allow drawing more generalisable conclusions about the factors influencing what teachers perceive in and can learn from video records of teaching and learning. One such factor is the setting in which viewing takes place. We expect that the processes and results of analysing video records of lessons with the help of viewing guides will differ depending on whether other-viewing or self-viewing takes place, how many teachers take part and how many years of teaching experience they have (cf. Tochon, 1999). In all such studies, due attention will of course have to be given to the reliability of the coding systems used.

6

ACTIVATING LEARNERS

The impact of peer coaching with video on teaching and learning

Niels Brouwer and Harmen Schaap

It is a consistent finding from educational research that the quality of teachers' instruction is positively related to learners' achievement (Hanushek, 2005; Hattie, 2009). Quality of instruction is a key factor influencing the contribution that a country's education system can make to its economic productivity and cultural vitality. In this area, teacher education and PD have a multiplier function to fulfil. Whether, in which respects and how PD efforts influence teachers' daily work in the classroom are therefore vital issues for research.

In this chapter, we report the evaluation of PD efforts by in-service secondary teachers who engaged in reciprocal peer coaching supported by video use with the aim of expanding and strengthening their teaching competence. These efforts took place in a PLC, i.e. a group of professionals collaborating in their daily work situation in order to reflect on and actively develop their knowledge and work (Vescio, Ross, & Adams, 2008, p. 81). The PLC studied is also characterised well by the definition provided in the review by Stoll, Bolam, McMahon, Wallace and Thomas (2006, p. 223): "a group of people sharing and critically interrogating their practice in an ongoing, reflective, collaborative, inclusive, learning-oriented, growth-promoting way, operating as a collective enterprise".

The aim of this case study was to find out what impact peer coaching with video had on the teachers' instruction, how this was experienced by their pupils and which features of this form of PD the teachers found helpful for enacting changes in their teaching, both during the PLC and several years afterwards. With the findings, we hope to contribute to the knowledge about the effectiveness of teacher PD in general and of visual teacher learning (VTL) in particular.

DOI: 10.4324/9780429331091-6

Introduction

In this chapter, we first reflect on theory and research about the features of effective PD and the contribution of video use to teacher learning. The research questions are stated and the case studied is described. Then, after elaborating on how the study was conducted, we present the findings. In conclusion, we answer the research questions and discuss implications for theory, practice and research.

Features of effective professional development

During the last decades, educational research has pursued the question to what extent and in which ways PD interventions contribute to in-service teachers' work and professional learning. This research and the reviews of it have produced a canon of features of effective PD interventions. Such interventions are coherent with teachers' current knowledge, beliefs and daily practice as well as with school, district and state policies. They are focussed on subject-matter content and pedagogy and not only on generic aspects of teaching. Participating teachers are engaged in active learning and do so in collegial collaboration. Effective PD extends over sustained periods, is supported by school management and enables teachers to examine existing theories and policies critically (see the section *Professional development* in Chapter 1).

Despite the above consensus in the literature, a number of gaps remain in the knowledge about the effectiveness of teacher PD. Relatively little is known about the nature of changes in teachers' instructional action and their influence on pupils' learning. An unresolved issue is also which changes in instruction teachers sustain after their PD participation ends. Finally, evidence is only scarcely available about the question in which ways and under what influences teachers actually change their instruction (see the sections *What we need to know more* in Chapter 2 and *Conclusions* in Chapter 3). Below, we elaborate on each of these knowledge gaps.

An important assumption underlying the research into the effectiveness of PD is that teaching practices should benefit learners' achievement. After all, "what students learn as a result of changed teaching practices … is the ultimate measure" of the value of reform efforts (Fishman, Marx, Best & Tal, 2003, p. 643). This criterion implies that teacher PD is effective when it promotes changes in teaching practices that, in turn, help pupils attain learning objectives. Some evidence indeed indicates such a positive impact of PD. Analysis of large-scale databases has shown that PD produces small, but consistent effects on pupil achievement (Wallace, 2009) and that teacher collaboration and its quality are related to pupil achievement and the rate at which teachers improve their instruction (Ronfeldt, Farmer, McQueen, & Grissom, 2015).

From research about VTL, we know more about its impact on teachers' thoughts about instruction than on their actual teaching behaviour. How teachers' thoughts and actions relate remains virtually a blank spot (see the section *Studying teaching and learning* in Chapter 2). Evidence does exist showing that after participating in VTL, teachers succeed in raising pupils' cognitive achievement and social–emotional engagement in learning (see the section *Impact on pupil learning* in Chapter 3).

Evidence about the sustainability of PD effects on changes in teachers' instruction is only scarcely available (cf. Kennedy, 2016, p. 951 and 973–974). A recent meta-analysis (Kraft, Blazar, & Hogan, 2018) confirms that teacher coaching can produce clear effects on instruction and learning. However, "[a]mong the 60 studies we reviewed, only five reported outcomes from a follow-up year after coaching had ended. ... These studies present very mixed evidence about the degree to which effects are enhanced, sustained, or fade out over time" (Kraft et al., 2018, p. 575). One longitudinal study sheds some light on conditions fostering long-term instructional improvement. Coburn, Russell, Kaufman, & Stein (2012) found that during the year after a collaborative PD initiative in mathematics instruction had ended, the participating teachers were better able to sustain changes in their instruction to the extent that strong ties and high-depth interaction occurred among colleagues as well as having access to high-quality expertise.

With regard to the effects of video-supported PD, only nine out of the 79 studies reviewed in Chapter 3 included follow-up data. The findings from these studies do suggest, however, that after PD participation, teachers retain at least part of the changes they made in their instruction (see the section *Sustainability of teacher outcomes* in Chapter 3).

The issue in which ways and under what influences changes in teachers' instruction and pupil learning precisely come about is not widely addressed by research, even though such knowledge is indispensable for designing and implementing VTL effectively. Kennedy (1998, p. 17) and Vescio et al. (2008, p. 89) conclude in their reviews that pupil learning is enhanced, when during PD, teachers collaborate with a focus on understanding how pupils learn the contents of specific school subjects. Still, changing classroom instruction is not easy for teachers. As Opfer and Pedder (2011, p. 386) note: "teachers may change their beliefs but not their practices, may change their practices but not their beliefs, and ultimately may change their practice but not the learning outcomes of their students."

An influential conceptualisation of this issue is the process model introduced by Guskey (1986), in which he posited a chain of events leading from teachers' PD participation through changes in their classroom practices and subsequent pupil learning outcomes to changes in their beliefs and attitudes. Whether and how teachers will translate thoughts about instruction into actions appears strongly predicated on their assessment of "what works" or more precisely of what their actions contribute to pupils' learning.

Teachers take this perspective because they know that their actions directly influence pupils' learning experiences and thus the production of learning outcomes. When teaching practices change, pupils' learning experiences change. At the same time, pupils' actions and reactions influence teachers' experience. In particular, teachers evaluate the impact of their actions on the basis of their pupils' reactions. As Fishman and colleagues point out:

> As they teach, teachers intuitively look to their students for feedback about the instruction. Sometimes this feedback is affective in nature (e.g., "My

students seemed to enjoy the activity", or "My students were all engaged in the activity"). Sometimes this feedback is cognitive in nature (e.g., "My students' answers were evidence that they understood the concepts being taught"). In either case, this information forms a key component of the feedback loop that shapes teachers' beliefs about their students and about their own teaching.

(Fishman et al., 2003, p. 646)

Teachers' classroom practice, then, unfolds in a reciprocal relationship with pupil behaviour. Accordingly, we assume in this study that teachers' experiences during classroom teaching influence to a considerable extent whether and how they will change their instructional practices. This assumption explains why changes in teachers' beliefs probably follow rather than precede changes in their actions, as argued by Guskey (1986 and 2002, p. 386–388) and Clarke and Hollingsworth (2002, p. 958–962). Collaborating with colleagues during PD can foster teacher learning by complementing and counterbalancing their daily interaction with pupils. Collaborative PD provides teachers with an additional sphere of interaction which can help them examine and change their work (cf. the section *Visual Teacher Learning, a model* in Chapter 2).

The knowledge gaps described above led us to pinpoint issues needing clarification. These issues are which changes VTL can bring about in teachers' instruction and pupils' learning, what kinds of processes teachers move through during as well as after PD participation and how PD efforts influence these processes. Understanding these issues can contribute to designing effective PD approaches. We considered peer coaching with video a valuable context to study these issues, because it took place in the midst of everyday teaching and learning. The complexity of the conditions and processes inherent in teachers' work could thus be addressed.

Research questions

Given what we know about the features and outcomes of effective PD, the relevance of this case study is that it explores not only to what extent and how teachers enacted in their daily teaching what they learned from peer coaching with video, but also which changes in their instruction pupils experienced as contributing to their learning. Furthermore, we wanted to know how teachers' instructional behaviour developed after their PLC participation ended. It was on these issues that our research questions were focussed:

I. What impact did peer coaching with video have on the teachers' instruction during PLC participation?

II. Which of the teaching behaviours targeted in the PLC did pupils perceive and regard as contributing to their learning?

III. How did the teachers' instructional behaviour develop after PLC participation?

IV. Which peer coaching activities and which features of the learning environment did the participating teachers find helpful for enacting changes in their teaching?

We consider these research questions to be equally relevant from a scholarly and a practical point of view. The answers sought in this case study are meant at the same time to inform schools' management and teachers about the outcomes and functioning of peer coaching with video and to contribute to knowledge growth in educational science.

Peer coaching and Visual Teacher Learning

In the PLC studied, teachers' collaboration took the form of reciprocal peer coaching. They used lesson observation and DV recordings to study their interaction with learners. The decision to design PD as a combination of these two elements is supported by what is known about the influence of peer coaching and video use on teacher learning.

Among the research findings on which the canon of features of effective PD is based, teacher collaboration figures prominently. However, not all initiatives undertaken under the flag of "collaboration" lead to changes in instruction. As Little (1990) cautions, it probably depends on the nature of teachers' collaboration whether such changes occur. Both Little and Kennedy (2016) emphasise that collegial collaboration can help teachers change their classroom behaviour in particular when collaboration focusses on the exigencies and concerns arising from daily instruction. This is possible in the context of instructional coaching – an important reason why this PD approach fulfils the canon of features of effective PD (Desimone & Pak, 2017).

Improving instruction is encouraged when teachers receive feedback and support while implementing new instructional approaches (Guskey, 2002) and cooperate while proceeding through repeated cycles of planning, performing and evaluating their teaching, as in Lesson Study (Dudley, 2015). This presupposes, as Cordingley, Bell, Thomason and Firth (2005) point out, that teachers are allowed ownership over their professional learning. Such ownership means being able to take daily experiences and personal needs as starting points and foci for learning and to engage regularly in collegial observation, feedback and dialogue.

Teacher peer coaching creates a collegial learning environment which encourages horizontal working relationships and enhances relevance to concrete, local practice (Acheson & Gall, 2003, p. 95-111; Allen & LeBlanc, 2005; Nolan & Hoover, 2011, p. 123-143; Zwart, Wubbels, Bergen, & Bolhuis, 2009). In a review of 29 peer coaching projects, Ackland (1991, p. 23–24) points out characteristics distinguishing peer coaching from coaching by experts. "Peer coaching is distinct from evaluation" in the sense of teacher appraisal. It "includes observation followed by feedback [and] . . . focuses on improving instructional techniques."

Research has shown that when coaching involves specific and repeated feedback on teachers' classroom behaviour, this can raise the extent to which their behaviour promotes pupils' achievement. This is apparent from large-scale studies about coaching both without the use of video (Matsumura, Garnier, & Spybrook, 2013 and Neuman & Cunningham, 2009 about literacy instruction) and with video

(Kersting, Givvin, Thompson, Santagata, & Stigler, 2012 and Roth et al., 2011 about science instruction).

Using DV holds promise for developing teachers' understanding of how their classroom behaviour helps or hinders pupils' learning. As detailed in the section *The special affordances of digital video* in Chapter 2, using DV helps teachers focus their attention on the "pedagogical triangle", i.e. the interaction between their own and their learners' activity and the content of learning. Secondly, because of its concreteness, video use entails that lesson observation and discussion of lessons are specific to the school subjects involved. Thirdly, it invokes vicarious experience and emotional engagement. Last but not least, video use enables repeated analysis of teaching from different perspectives without the need for immediate action.

The reviews reported in Chapters 2 and 3 of this book show that teachers can advance their professional competence considerably by engaging in collaborative VTL. They take a more activating role in the classroom. They talk less themselves, instead eliciting learners to engage with and talk more about the lesson content, which results in increased on-task learner behaviour. Teachers use more open and probing questioning, thus stimulating higher-order thinking. They give more and more focussed feedback and (re)act more adaptively to learners. Finally, teachers increasingly try out effective teaching behaviours (see the sections *Outcomes: What do teachers learn when using digitial video?* in Chapter 2 and *Teacher and pupil outcomes* in Chapter 3).

Together, the research findings referenced above support our choice for peer coaching with video as a strategy for improving instruction.

Case description

In this section, we describe how the PLC studied was created, what were its goals, how its activities were organised and which principles were followed in carrying them out.

The PLC was organised by a "gymnasium", i.e. a secondary school preparing for university entry, in the Netherlands serving about 1,000 pupils. During the four years of its existence, about half the teaching staff participated. The PLC began as a result of a quality assurance initiative in which 36 teachers serving as class mentors attended and observed during one school day all the lessons of their "mentor class". At the end of this day, both the pupils and their mentor teachers filled out questionnaires about how varied and motivating they found the instruction in the lessons.

The main findings were that the school's pupils experienced the lessons as rather monotonous and that their role in learning was rather passive. Analysis and discussion of these findings led the school's teaching staff and management to the shared conclusion that they needed to develop instruction in three respects: increasing variety in learning activities in order to activate pupils, offering them more opportunities for differentiation and increasing pupils' autonomy as learners (Scheepens, 2004). These became the goals for a PLC in which both parties joined forces and embarked on peer coaching with video.

The teachers felt that the best way to improve their instruction was by observing each other at work and deriving ideas from this for their own lessons. They expected that video would help them see in which ways their colleagues' teaching made their pupils learn. The school's management went along with their wishes. The idea of learning from each other was embodied in the name given to the PLC: "Didactisch Afkijken", an untranslatable pun. "Didactisch", from classical Greek, means "instructional". The Dutch word "afkijken", which literally translates as "looking off", has the general meaning of observing others' behaviour with the intent to emulate it, but in the context of the classroom, it also has the specific meaning of cribbing.

Goals

The school chose the above three goals on the basis of its own local problem diagnosis. These goals embody what the school considered necessary changes in teaching practice and guided the PLC. What is known from research on effective teaching informed the work of the PLC in the context of this diagnosis. Together, the PLC goals represent the ideal to make teaching more effective in activating learners cognitively, socially and motivationally (Mayer, 2008; Reusser 2019).

Table 6.1 shows how these goals were operationalised. For each goal, key teaching behaviours were selected and formulated by a steering group consisting of the deputy school leader, one other member of the management team, two participating teachers and the first author. The resulting three lists in Table 6.1 were used by the participating teachers to select personal learning goals that they wanted to focus on.

The first goal of increasing variety in learning activities reflects established knowledge about the effectiveness of direct instruction (Brophy & Good, 1986; Good & Brophy, 2008; Rosenshine, 2010), mastery learning (Guskey, 2007) (see in Table 6.1 items 1 through 5) and of collaborative learning (Cohen, 1994; Hattie, 2009, p. 212–214; Johnson & Johnson, 1991; Topping & Ehly, 1998) (see in Table 6.1 items 6 through 11). The second goal of increasing opportunities for differentiation reflects the school's wish to encourage pupils to pursue personal learning needs and interests (Lawrence Brown, 2004; Tomlinson, 2014) (see in Table 6.1 items 12 through 17). The third goal of promoting self-directed learning reflects the idea that learners' achievement will benefit from increased learner autonomy (cf. Ryan & Deci, 2000; Simons, Van der Linden, & Duffy, 2000) and teaching approaches to promote this (Alderman, 1999) (see in Table 6.1 items 18 through 21).

Learning environment and peer coaching activities

To enable the teachers to work on these goals, the school created a learning environment as follows.

Firstly, working time was made available for peer coaching. Each participating teacher agreed to spend one hour per week on peer coaching out of the PD time allocated on the basis of the collective labour contract in Dutch secondary education, while the school invested one additional hour of release time per week. An

TABLE 6.1 PLC goals

No.	Content	Criterion variables
	I. INCREASING VARIETY IN LEARNING ACTIVITIES	
1.	EXPLAINING	explain subject matter stepwise
2.	PRECISE INSTRUCTIONS	give precise instructions for exercises and assignments
3.	HOMEWORK	coordinate classroom activity and homework
4.	INSTRUCTIONAL DIALOGUE	use instructional dialogue to engage pupils
5.	SEAT WORK	have pupils work by themselves
6.	GROUP WORK	have pupils cooperate in groups
7.	PEER COMMENT	have pupils comment on each other's work
8.	PEER ASSESSMENT	have pupils assess each other's work
9.	PUPIL PRESENTATION	have pupils present to the group
10.	DEBATE SUBJECT MATTER	have pupils debate subject matter together
11.	GAMES	engage pupils with subject matter in the form of games
	II. INCREASING OPPORTUNITIES FOR DIFFERENTIATION	
12.	WORK OUTSIDE CLASSROOM	have pupils work also outside the classroom
13.	ADDITIONAL MATERIAL	have pupils study additional material
14.	ADDITIONAL ASSIGNMENTS	have pupils work on additional assignments
15.	OWN PACE	have pupils work at their own pace
16.	OWN TOPICS	have pupils work on topics of their own choice
17.	COMPUTER WORK	have pupils work with the computer
	III. PROMOTING SELF-DIRECTED LEARNING	
18.	PUPIL PLANNING	have pupils plan their own work
19.	PUPIL AS CO-TEACHER	have pupils present part of the lesson
20.	INTEREST IN SUBJECT	have pupils develop an interest in the school subject
21.	REFLECT ON FUTURE SUBJECT	have pupils reflect on what they want to do with the school subject in the future

important condition for enabling professional learning (Stoll et al., 2006;Vescio et al., 2008) was thus fulfilled. However, when after four years the school reallocated the latter resource to other purposes, the PLC ceased to exist.

Secondly, the teachers grouped themselves in pairs of colleagues, which stayed together for one school year in order to visit, observe, film and discuss each other's lessons. The use of video by the teachers steadily increased over time. The members of the peer coaching pairs filmed each other during teaching, selected personally significant fragments from the recordings and viewed, analysed and discussed those fragments together.

Thirdly, all participating teachers attended plenary meetings, which took place at about six-week intervals during the school year and usually lasted three afternoon hours. During these meetings, skills for carrying out peer coaching and filming lessons were trained, teaching experiences were shared and instructional issues discussed. About half the time available was used for viewing and discussing video clips of each other's lessons. From time to time, also role-plays were performed, in which one teacher taught a lesson and the others took the roles of pupils, so that they could vicariously experience what it is like to receive instruction and engage in learning activities about subject matter that is new to you.

An important element of the PLC activities was that the teachers drew consequences from their lesson analyses by collaborating on lesson planning, both during their pair work and the plenary meetings. Figure 6.1 shows the typical sequence of activities carried out during one school year by each cohort of participating teachers.

The PLC was coordinated by two of the participating teachers and the first author, who programmed and evaluated all activities in regular consultation with the other members of the steering group. The first author supported the PLC in his role as teacher educator and provided practice-oriented materials about instructional approaches and evaluation support. The materials were made accessible in a reader and an electronic learning environment. Technical support was given by the school's audiovisual department and the first author. The school's management informed all parents in writing that lessons would be filmed strictly confidentially and for the sole purpose of teacher peer coaching. Parents were offered the opportunity to exclude their children from being filmed, but no parents used this.

Principles of collaboration

Throughout the existence of the PLC, the teachers' collaboration was guided by three principles: volunteering, ownership and egalitarianism.

Firstly, teachers participated voluntarily and could choose freely with which colleague they wanted to be partners in a peer coaching pair.

Secondly, all participants were free to choose their personal learning goals. Although in the beginning, the school's management was sometimes concerned that this might allow for serious departures from the PLC goals, this "risk" never materialised.

Thirdly, everyone was respected and recognised for participating, regardless of employment status, teaching experience or any other consideration. This principle implied that any problem, challenge, question or perspective that a participant would deem important was valued in its own right. In the same spirit, peer coaching was organised in reciprocal form, i.e. the teachers regularly switched roles from observing colleagues to being observed by them.

The intent behind these principles of collaboration was to create and uphold a climate of collegial trust. The school felt that this was indispensable in order to encourage the teachers to open up their classrooms for observation, feedback and making changes in instruction.

PLENARY MEETINGS	1 AUGUST SEPTEMBER	2 OCTOBER	3 NOVEMBER	4 JANUARY	5 FEBRUARY MARCH	6 APRIL	7 JUNE
Themes	Observation and feedback	Principles of direct instruction. Activating learners	Cooperative learning	Homework, Self-directed learning	Educative ICT uses	Differentiation	Programme evaluation
Training and learning	Peer coaching	Electronic learning environment. Video use	Role play and feedback / discussion	Viewing and discussing video recordings of each other's teaching	Viewing and discussing video recordings of each other's teaching. Sharing views and discussing practices concerning topics of own choice	Viewing and discussing video recordings of each other's teaching. Sharing views and discussing practices concerning topics of own choice.	Poster presentations about each other's work and learning
Pair work	Formulating personal learning needs and goals. Planning activities in pairs	Focussing personal learning goals	Filming lessons Lesson planning	Filming lessons Lesson planning	Filming lessons		
Monitoring	Entry questionnaire			Group discussion of progress			Pupil consultation Exit questionnaire

Pair work: observing and filming lessons / peer coaching / preparing and trying out instructional approaches together

FIGURE 6.1 Sequence of PLC activities

Research model

To guide this study, we developed the research model shown in Figure 6.2. This model assumes that experienced teachers' learning evolves during a chain of events in which the interaction between teaching and learning activities is the driving force. To conceptualise this chain of events, independent, mediating and dependent variables are distinguished. We expect features of the PLC as a learning environment, the baseline from which teachers began their participation and their background characteristics to function as independent variables. The peer coaching activities undertaken, the teachers' experiences with lesson observation and video viewing, the feedback they gave each other, their experiences during classroom enactment on the one hand and pupils' learning experiences on the other are considered mediating variables. The outcomes of teachers' learning constitute the dependent variables.

The arrows in Figure 6.2 represent the relationships addressed in the research questions. Question I focusses on the development of teachers' instruction. Question II focusses on how pupils perceived and rated their teachers' classroom behaviour. Question III focusses on the sustainability of changes in teaching behaviour in the longer term. Question IV focusses on how the features of the learning environment and the activities they enabled influenced the teachers' enactment of changes in classroom practice.

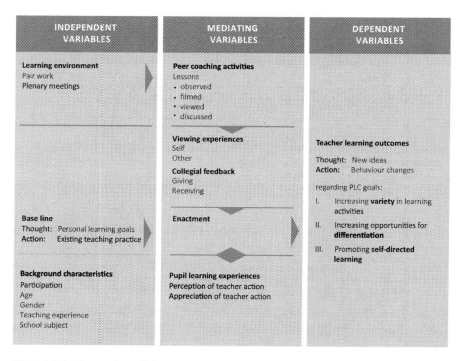

FIGURE 6.2 Research model

Method

In the following sections, we account for the research design employed, the sampling and response, the instruments for data collection and their operationalisation and the techniques used for data analysis.

Research design

When one wishes to understand what works in PD, how it works and how it can be improved, the relationships need to be made explicit between PD activities, teacher behaviour change, pupils' experience of its contribution to their learning and eventually their achievement (Desimone, 2009, p. 188). This is how we conceptualised "impact" of PD in this study. The methodological challenge, then, was to cover the chain of events extending from the design and implementation of peer coaching with video through changes in teachers' thoughts and actions on to a possible impact on pupil learning. To meet this challenge, we sought a research design that would make it possible to reconstruct not only what, but also in which ways and under what conditions teachers learned over time under the influence of PLC participation. This intent to reconstruct how teachers' learning developed is based on a causal-genetic approach to research, which rests on three paradigmatic assumptions or epistemological perspectives concerning the object of research: the ecological, the genetic and the activity perspective.

The ecological perspective assumes that the research object in the social sciences always consists of a social system, which is at the same time internally structured and embedded within a wider, often institutional context. The genetic perspective recognises all learning as a set of processes, whose unfolding influences learning. This perspective assumes that understanding learning outcomes requires understanding the processes which produce them. The activity perspective entails a focus on the actions of people as these express the continual tension between their personal motives on the one hand and contextual constraints on the other. From these perspectives, we derive the requirement that valid evidence should rest not only on a quantification of input and output factors, but also on an understanding of how learning unfolds in social contexts. Such an approach requires combining measurement of phenomena on the level of groups with in-depth description on the level of individuals (Brouwer, 2010, p. 507; Brouwer & Korthagen, 2005, p. 167–168).

At the same time, considerations of feasibility had to be taken into account. The PLC and our study of it developed in continual interaction with the school. Consequently, the research design took shape and data collection began after the PLC had started. In addition, although the participating teachers were willing to share their experiences, they were also slightly apprehensive about exposing what could be seen as individual weaknesses, especially in the beginning of each school year. Finally, both their workload and earlier experiences with research made them sceptical about formal data collection. For these reasons, we restricted ourselves to forms of data collection that were minimally intrusive and required as little work from the teachers as possible.

The research design for this study was thus determined by considerations of validity as well as feasibility. To answer the first research question, we traced the development of teachers' thoughts and actions by administering criterion measures based on the PLC goals (see Table 6.1) in entry and exit questionnaires at the beginning and at the end of a school year, respectively. In addition, information about the teachers' learning was derived from posters which they presented as part of the evaluative last plenary meeting of each school year. To answer the second research question about how pupils experienced teachers' actions, analogous criterion measures were administered in pupil questionnaires. To answer the third research question about long-term outcomes, in-depth follow-up interviews were conducted with a subsample of teachers years after the PLC ended. To answer the fourth research question about how the teachers evaluated the features of the learning environment and the peer coaching activities, questions were included in the teachers' exit questionnaires as well as the follow-up interviews. Also, the first author wrote field notes and the teachers wrote brief evaluations about the plenary meetings. The operationalisation of these instruments and their use for data collection are detailed below.

To clarify what we did and did not address in this study, it is useful to distinguish between "impact" and "effect". We define "impact" in terms of learning process, i.e. as the extent to which and the ways in which learning activities change a person's cognitions, actions and/or attitudes during or shortly after those learning activities. We define "effect" in terms of learning outcomes, i.e. as the extent to which and the respects in which changes resulting from learning activities are integrated in the longer term in a person's knowledge, skills and/or attitudes. In this study, we had the opportunity to measure and explore through qualitative means the impact of PD on teachers. In addition, we could explore qualitatively PD effects on teachers in the longer term. Indications of whether and how behaviour change in teachers affected pupils' learning experiences could be gained through quantitative means. No evidence could be gathered about pupils' learning achievement.

Given the research design, this study can be characterised as a site-based, mixed-methods case study, in which multiple data sources were used to assess the influence of a PD effort on teacher and pupil learning. Quantitative methods were used to survey all participants to determine to which extent specific outcomes and experiences occurred. Qualitative methods were used among subsamples of participants to clarify which learning experiences contributed to these outcomes.

Respondents

The data collected through teacher and pupil questionnaires, posters, evaluations and field notes about plenary meetings and follow-up interviews stem from different subsamples of respondents. In this section, we first describe how these subsamples are composed and related. Then, the response rates are given.

Sampling

During each of the four school years that the PLC existed, one cohort of teachers participated. Background and questionnaire data were collected from all teachers in the four consecutive cohorts. Together, they taught seventeen different subjects. The total number of participating teachers was 45, eighteen women and 27 men. Their average age was 41, with a minimum of 26, a maximum of 61 and a standard deviation (SD) of 9.5. The participants had an average of 14.05 years of teaching experience, with a minimum of 1, a maximum of 31 and an SD of 8.52.

Two women and eleven men participated twice. These teachers came to be known as "veterans". Six veterans participated in the first and second cohorts. The other seven veterans participated in the fourth cohort, three of whom began their participation in the first, one in the second and three in the third cohort. This composition of cohorts is shown in Table 6.2. From the numbers in this table, it can be seen that in all, 45 participants are responsible for 58 participations.

Follow-up interviews were conducted with ten teachers three years after the last PLC cohort completed its activities. In selecting the interviewees we sought to create a subsample as representative as possible for the total group of 45 PLC participants. The following selection variables were used in particular. The means for these selection variables are given between brackets for the interviewees and the non-interviewees, respectively:

- total number of teaching behaviours for which teachers reported changes in end-of-year measurements (M = 8.7 vs. 8.4),
- years of teaching experience (M = 14.6 vs. 14),
- proportions of teachers who participated once or twice (M = 36.4% vs. 26.5%) and
- gender defined as the percentage of women (M = 70% vs. 46.7%).

Data from pupils could be collected in classes of teachers in the second and third cohorts. These teachers taught the following subjects: physics and chemistry; Dutch,

TABLE 6.2 Composition of teacher cohorts

School years/cohorts	1	2	3	4	Total
Participations	20	18	10	10	58
Women	7	7	5	2	18
Men	13	11	5	8	27
New participants	20	12	10	3	45
Veterans	0	6	0	7	13

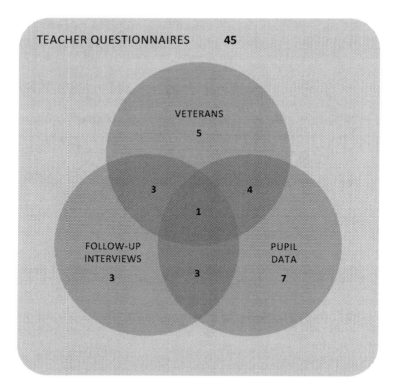

FIGURE 6.3 Data sources and subsamples

English, German, French, classical Latin and Greek; history, social studies, economics and philosophy; art and art history; and physical education. 93% of the pupil data are about subjects mandatory in the secondary school curriculum.

Figure 6.3 shows which subsamples of respondents provided the various data sources. The shaded areas and the numbers within them indicate how these data sources are distributed over the subsamples.

For nineteen out of the 45 participating teachers, i.e. 42%, questionnaires were the only data source. Additional data were collected among 26 teachers, i.e. 58%.

To find out how representative the subsamples were for the whole group of PLC participants, comparisons were carried out between teachers who did or did not belong to the respective subsamples, using as the test statistics chi-square for binomial dependent variables and t for independent groups for dependent interval variables.

These analyses showed that the veteran teachers did not differ significantly in gender and teaching experience from the one-time participants ($p < .05$). Similarly, the teachers who gave follow-up interviews did not differ significantly from those who did not, neither in the selection variables listed above nor in other variables in the teacher questionnaires (p < .05), with one exception: there were relatively more women in the interview subsample. Finally, gender, teaching experience and age did not differ significantly between teachers in whose classes pupil data were or were not collected (p < .05). Given these findings, we assume that the subsamples are reasonably representative of the total group of PLC participants.

Response

Table 6.3 shows the response to the teacher questionnaires. In the first cohort, only an exit questionnaire was administered, because the measures used were developed during the first year. The overall response is satisfactory, although it was slightly lowered by the last cohort because some teachers could not access the school's computer network.

The pupil data were collected from ten out of the eighteen, i.e. 56% teachers in the second cohort, and five out of the ten, i.e. 50% teachers in the third cohort. These fifteen teachers are one third of the total of 45 PLC participants. 254 pupils from eleven classes were surveyed in the second cohort and 118 pupils from five classes in the third cohort. Of one teacher in the second cohort, two classes were surveyed. Thus, data became available from a total of 372 pupils in sixteen classes. Within the classes surveyed, the pupil response was 80% on average.

The response rates for the qualitative data are reported below.

Instrumentation and data collection

The topics distinguished in the research model (see Figure 6.2) served as the basis for operationalisation. In this section, the contents of the data collection instruments and their modes of operationalisation are described.

Teacher background data

The teachers' background characteristics age, gender, school subject and years of teaching experience were retrieved from the personnel administration. During the plenary meetings, their attendance was recorded.

TABLE 6.3 Response to teacher questionnaires

| School year | 1 | 2 | | 3 | | 4 | |
	exit	entry	exit	entry	exit	entry	exit
Response	14	17	17	9	9	5	5
% response	70.0%	94.4%	94.4%	90.0%	90.0%	50.0%	50.0%

Teacher questionnaires

The teacher questionnaires contained criterion measures derived from the PLC goals in Table 6.1 and a number of descriptive and evaluative questions.

Criterion measures

To measure the teachers' thoughts and actions, the PLC goals formulated by the steering group were used as criterion variables (CVs). This operationalisation was chosen in order to maximise ecological validity.

The wordings of the teaching behaviours in Table 6.1 were used both at the beginning and at the end of the school years. They were preceded by the following stems. For teacher thought in the entry questionnaires: "Through peer coaching with video I want to get to know (more) ways to … in my teaching." For teacher thought in the exit questionnaires: "Peer coaching with video has helped me get to know (more) ways to … in my teaching." For teacher action in the entry questionnaires: "In my teaching, I usually …" For teacher action in the exit questionnaires: "Peer coaching with video has helped me … (more often) in my teaching."

The teachers responded to these items by ticking a yes or no box. This forced-choice format was used instead of a Likert-type scale to encourage them at the beginning of the school year to make clear choices as to which personal learning goals they did or did not want to work on. Likewise, at the end of the school year, we wanted to ascertain which instructional behaviours the teachers felt peer coaching had or had not helped them change.

An important consequence of these operationalisations is that the criterion measures in this study cannot be interpreted as repeated measures. If for instance 60% of teachers gave the answer "yes" at the beginning of the school year for "coordinating classroom activity and homework" (CV 3 in Table 6.1) and 40% did so at the end, this does not mean that fewer teachers came to practice this behaviour. What this does mean is that before peer coaching, a majority already practised this behaviour and that afterwards, a sizeable minority felt supported by peer coaching in introducing or strengthening this behaviour. If, to give another example, 30% of teachers reported at the beginning of the school year having pupils comment each other's work (CV 7) and 70% did so at the end, this means that relatively few teachers practised this behaviour before peer coaching and that afterwards, quite a few felt supported by peer coaching in introducing or strengthening this behaviour.

As mentioned above, the criterion measures were again administered in questionnaires at the beginning of the follow-up interview. This time, the wordings in Table 6.1 were preceded by the statement "Since peer coaching, this [behaviour] has become a regular part of my teaching" and the instruction "Please choose one of the following options: yes, no or temporarily". This operationalisation made it possible to ascertain if the criterion behaviours targeted had become part of the interviewees' teaching and whether this was the case durably or only temporarily. These response categories served to trace the impact of peer coaching after the PLC had ended. Only if teachers reported having changed teaching behaviours durably, do we speak of sustainable behaviour change.

Descriptive and evaluative items

In addition to the criterion measures, the teacher exit questionnaires also contained descriptive and evaluative questions. These are shown in Box 6.1.

The descriptive items measured how many lessons the teachers observed, filmed, viewed on video and discussed. With the evaluative items, the teachers

---

BOX 6.1 DESCRIPTIVE AND EVALUATIVE TEACHER QUESTIONNAIRE ITEMS

During school weeks I observed on average ... of my colleague's lessons per month.
[Please state an average number of lessons per month.]

During school weeks I discussed on average ... lessons per month with my colleague.
[Please state an average number of lessons per month.]

For my own learning, I found it very unhelpful <> helpful that...	very unhelpful				very helpful
I received feedback from the colleague in my pair	O	O	O	O	O
I had to give feedback to the colleague in my pair	O	O	O	O	O

This school year ... of my lessons have been recorded on video.
[Please state the total number.]

I viewed the video recordings of my lesson(s) ... times.	O once	O 2 times
	O 3 times	O 4 or more times

How unhelpful < > helpful did you find the following activities for your own learning?

Viewing my OWN lesson(s) on video was ... for REFLECTING on my way of teaching.	very unhelpful				very helpful
	O	O	O	O	O

Viewing my OWN lesson(s) on video was ... for CHANGING my way of teaching.	very unhelpful O O O O O	very helpful
The feedback from the colleague in my pair and/or from other colleagues on the video recordings of my OWN lesson(s) was ... for REFLECTING on my way of teaching.	very unhelpful O O O O O	very helpful
The feedback from the colleague in my pair and/or from other colleagues on the video recordings of my OWN lesson(s) was ... for CHANGING my way of teaching.	very unhelpful O O O O O	very helpful
Viewing video recordings of OTHERS' lesson(s) was ... for REFLECTING on my way of teaching.	very unhelpful O O O O O	very helpful
Viewing video recordings of OTHERS' lesson(s) was ... for CHANGING my way of teaching.	very unhelpful O O O O O	very helpful

were asked to judge on five-point Likert scales how helpful they found self-viewing and other-viewing and giving and receiving feedback for achieving the learning goals they had selected in their entry questionnaires. Both types of items were formulated in behavioural and descriptive terms, as advocated by Desimone (2009, p. 191). This mode of operationalisation was similarly employed in the early German research into practice shock (cf. the section *The influence of occupational socialisation on teacher learning* in Chapter 1 and the validity argument put forward by Dann, Cloetta, Müller-Fohrbrodt, & Helmreich, 1978, p. 128–141).

Pupil questionnaires

In order to find out which teacher behaviours were perceived by pupils and to explore which behaviours they felt contributed to their learning, the criterion behaviours formulated in Table 6.1 were again used. This was done in order to produce measures that allowed direct comparison with those among the teachers.

For each teaching behaviour in Table 6.1, the pupils indicated on an ordinal scale how often per month their teacher had displayed it: never, once, twice or three or more times. In addition, the pupils rated on a four-point interval scale how useful for their own learning they found each behaviour: not useful at all; not very useful; useful; or very useful.

These criterion measures were collected among pupils at the end of the school year in classes selected by teachers in which they felt they had attempted most intensely to apply what they learned during peer coaching. This procedure was followed in order to allow the impact of any behaviour changes in teachers to manifest itself.

The operationalisation described above is in accordance with requirements formulated by De Jong and Westerhof (2001) and Kunter and Baumert (2006). These authors conclude from large-scale validity studies that pupil ratings of the instructional quality of secondary teachers can be used as valid indicators when the items used address specific descriptions of teaching behaviour and when these ratings are aggregated on the level of classes. Both these conditions were fulfilled in this study.

Plenary meeting field notes and evaluation forms

What was said and done during the plenary meetings was recorded by the first author in field notes about twenty out of the total of 26 meetings.

At the end of nine meetings, the teachers wrote comments in an evaluation form containing four rubrics. In the first rubric, they summarised what progress they had made during the past period during their work with the partner in their pair. In the second rubric, they assessed how the pair work was organised. In the third rubric, they commented on how the plenary meetings were conducted and in the fourth, they voiced needs and suggestions. The response rates to these evaluation forms were on average 68%.

Poster presentations

At the end of each school year, each pair of teachers presented posters to each other using the following prompts.

- The most important pupil reactions were …
- What did I begin doing differently this school year?
- What was for me/us the most important outcome of peer coaching with video?
- (In which respects) did I change in my work as a teacher because of peer coaching?
- For improving peer coaching next year I/we suggest …

Records of these poster presentations are available for 40 out of the total of 58 participations. This amounts to a response rate of 69%.

Follow-up interviews

The follow-up interviews with a representative subsample of ten teachers (cf. the section *Sampling* above) took place between three and six years after their PLC participation. For one teacher from the first cohort, participation was six years ago. For three teachers from the second cohort including one veteran, it was five years ago. For one teacher from the third cohort, it was four years ago and for five teachers including three veterans, it was three years ago. To our knowledge, no other study has followed up VTL participants after such a long period.

The interviewers were Prof. Dr. Fred Korthagen and Dr. Fokelien Robijns, senior teacher educators and researchers, and Mr. Jan Vermeij, a senior teacher educator. The interviews lasted on average 62.4 minutes with a minimum of 46 and a maximum of 79 minutes. All interviews were recorded on video, except with one teacher, who preferred hand-written notes to be taken. The interviewees were rewarded for their time and effort with a €50 book gift voucher.

The purpose of the interviews was twofold: firstly to find out which effects participation in peer coaching with video had had in the longer term on the development of the respondents' teaching repertoires and secondly to reconstruct how these effects had come about. To cover these issues, most interview questions were divided into sub-questions. The interviewer instructions and the wording of the questions and sub-questions are found in Box 6.2.

BOX 6.2 FOLLOW-UP INTERVIEW QUESTIONS

Note:
- signs denote follow-up and/or probing questions about topics already addressed.

Issue 1:

Which *effects* does participation in peer coaching with digital video have *in the longer run* on the development of teaching repertoires?

Interview questions 1 through 5 are meant to determine WHAT, if any, ARE effects of participation in peer coaching with digital video.

---

1. You *participated* in peer coaching with digital video in the *school year...– ...* (and ...– ...). I'd like to know what you learned then. Please tell me.

2. It is now ... *years since* you participated in in peer coaching with digital video. What has remained in your teaching at this moment of what you learned at that time?

3. (If available, show video fragment and/or poster presentation of respondent for stimulated recall. Also, probe responses to follow-up questionnaire about the development of teaching behaviours).

    To revive the times when you participated in peer coaching with digital video I want to show you a *video fragment.*

    - Now that you see this, do you think you changed in your work, since this was recorded?

    - (encourage to tell freely about oneself)

    - I also want to show you the poster that you presented in the last plenary session of the school year ... together with ... [partner in work pair].

      Now that you see this, do you think you changed in your work since you presented this poster?

4. (Underlying this question are the three LPC goals.)

    Let's have a look at the questionnaire [follow-up measures analogous to pre- and post-questionnaires completed during participation] that you filled out. I'm especially interested in the items where you marked "temporarily".

    (Check for each item:) Why did you mark "temporarily" here?

    (Say where applicable: "under the influence of (your participation in) peer coaching with video".)

    - *4.1* (about *Diversifying* teaching repertoire/qualitative development of existing skills:)

      - Which skills that you already possessed/used before you participated in peer coaching with digital video have you used *more/ less* since then? Please explain with examples.

      - Did you begin to use existing skills/approaches *differently*? If so, how and in what situations?

      - For instance, did you *"polish"* certain skills in direct instruction or did you do other "instructional maintenance work"?

    - *4.2* (about *Expanding* teaching repertoire in the classroom / adding new skills:)

      - Which new instructional skills/approaches did you begin to use routinely in your lessons?

- Did you develop new routines in your classroom? If so, which ones?
- *4.3* (about *Cognitive activation* of pupils/learning with deeper understanding:)
  - *What kind of learning* do you try to achieve in pupils?
  - Which instructional skills/approaches do you find (most) suited to bring pupils to learn with understanding?
  - After participating in peer coaching with digital video, do you feel you succeed better in making pupils learn *with (more) understanding*?
  - If so, what makes you think so?
  - If not, why is that?
- *4.4* (about *Social activation* of pupils/better cooperation of pupils with each other and with the teacher:)
  - What kind of *cooperation with pupils* do you like best?
  - Which kinds of behaviours do you think are (most) suitable to achieve that kind of cooperation?
  - After participating in peer coaching with digital video, do you feel you succeed better in achieving productive cooperation with pupils?
  - If so, what makes you think so?
  - If not, why is that?
- *4.5* (about *Increasing autonomy*/encouraging pupils to take (more) responsibility for learning:)
  - Which sorts of *opportunities* do you give pupils to determine their learning activities by themselves?
  - Can you bring pupils to *take responsibility* for their own learning?
  - If so, in which way(s)? How do you work on that?
  - Do you have pupils work with *computers* in order to make (more) *differentiation* possible?
  - If so, could you give an example?

5. (about *Well-being* during work as a teacher, in particular managing own energy and motivation at work and for continuing one's teaching career:)

    Did you acquire certain skills/approaches under the influence of peer coaching which have made your *work as a teacher more pleasant*?

    - If so, which skills/approaches especially? Could you give examples?

- Has your work become less *taxing* because of what you learned through peer coaching?
- Do you feel your work has become *nicer* because of what you learned through peer coaching?
- Has peer coaching helped you *continue in teaching*? Could you please explain?

Issue 2:

How do effects of participation in peer coaching with digital video *come about*?

Interview questions 6 through 9 are meant to determine IN WHICH WAY(S) and UNDER THE INFLUENCE OF WHICH FACTORS any effects of participation in peer coaching with digital video, especially on professional action, DEVELOP.

---

6. So far, we discussed if and in which respects your *action* as a teacher has *changed* under the influence of peer coaching with digital video.
    - *6.1* If such changes occur, how do they come about in your experience? Does your *thinking change first and then your action*? Or does it work the *other way round*?
        - Participants in peer coaching sometimes said: When I get new ideas for my teaching, I first consider them and only after that will I try them out. Others said: I first try them out and then I'll find out why they work. How does that work for you? Please explain.

      (Insofar as applicable:)
        - *In which situations* do you first try out a new idea and then find out why it works?
        - And in which situations do you first consider a new idea and try it out later?
        - Do you *prefer* one approach over the other? (If so) why do you have that preference?
        - Where does that preference come from?
    - *6.2* Over what *period* of time and at what *pace* do you change your action?
        - *How long* does it take you to make a new skill/approach your own?

- *What helps you* make such a new skill/approach a standard part of your daily action?
- Do you sometimes have the feeling that you *fall back upon old habits*?
- (If so:) Why is that?
- And what might you do about that?

7. (About (development of) own PERSON as professional:)

   Which *factors within yourself* promote or hinder your learning through peer coaching with digital video?

   - *What helps* you personally learn during peer coaching? Please explain.
   - And what *hinders* you in learning during peer coaching? (Insofar as not mentioned by the respondent him-/herself:)
   - Are there any *routines* that help or hinder you? If so, which ones and how do they work?
   - Do you have a certain *work style* that helps or hinders you? If so, which one and how does that work?
   - Are there any *other factors* that help or hinder you in learning through peer coaching? Please explain.

8. (About the INTERVENTION):

   - *8.1* (about *effective features* of peer coaching with digital video:)

     Looking back on your own work during the last few years, has your participation in peer coaching with digital video paid off for you?

     - What, in your opinion, were "effective features" of peer coaching with digital video?
     - What did you find useful in *cooperating in pairs*?
     - To *which activities* did you pay most attention with your workmate: observing each other's lessons; discussing each other's lessons; preparing lessons together; other activities…?
     - Why did you pay much attention to just that/those activity/-ies?
     - What did you find useful in the plenary meetings?

   - *8.2* (about impact of *video* use:)

     - How did you feel about being recorded on video?
     - How did you feel about it in the beginning? Was that different later on? (If so) how?
     - What did you learn from reviewing your own lessons?
     - Did you view the recordings of your own lessons on a *surface* level or also *repeatedly* and using specific *viewing questions* and

viewing points? Did that make a difference to you? (If so,) what kind of difference?

- What was it like for you to be able to *see* (instead of only talk about) lessons during peer coaching?
- Participants in peer coaching mentioned *"having a look into each other's kitchen"*. Was that of any use to you? (If so,) what use?
- Did you ever adopt approaches from colleagues that you saw on video and *tried out* in your own lessons? (If so,) what impact did that have on you in the longer run?
- Did you begin to look differently at your own work because of using video? (If so,) what kind of *different look* did you develop: on pupils, on what they had to do with the subject matter, on your own role in this?

- 8.3 (about *counterproductive features* of peer coaching with digital video:)
  Were there also features in peer coaching that hindered your learning?
  - (If so:) Which features?
  - Please explain.
  - During peer coaching, did you cooperate with a partner with less *work experience*?
  - (If so:) What impact did that have on your own learning?
  - Did you cooperate with a partner from a (completely) different *school subject*?
  - (If so:) What impact did that have on your own learning?

9. (About CONTEXT):
   - 9.1 (about factors in the school context which *promote* learning effects):
     Which factors in your work situation *promote* your learning during peer coaching?
     - In which way(s) does this help you?
   - 9.2 (about factors in the school context which hinder learning effects):
     Which factors in your work situation hinder your learning during peer coaching?
     - In which way(s) does this hinder you?

- During peer coaching, did you run into any *scheduling prob-lems* that prevented you from observing your partner as intended?
- (If so:) What impact did that have on your own learning?
10. (Final question:)
    Would you like to raise any more issues that are important to you in con-nection to peer coaching with digital video?

The first issue addressed in the interview – effects of participation – was cov-ered by questions about whether or not the teaching behaviours targeted in the PLC (cf. Table 6.1) had become part of the interviewees' teaching repertoires and to what extent they attributed such effects to their participation. In order to focus the conversation, the teachers were asked, before the interview began, to fill in a questionnaire similar to the ones they had completed at the beginning and the end of the school year(s) in which they had participated. This time, they indicated whether since their PLC participation, each criterion behaviour had become part of their teaching durably or only temporarily (see the section *Criterion measures* above). This questionnaire was completed by nine out of the ten interviewees. It should be noted that this follow-up measurement addressed only which changes in teaching behaviour had occurred since the PLC had ended. Accordingly, instruc-tional behaviours that the interviewees already practised at the end of the PLC were scored as unchanged.

In addition, as PLC participation was years ago, the interview started off with two open questions inviting the respondents to describe in their own words what in hindsight, they regarded as the net outcome for them personally of participating in peer coaching with video. To elaborate on their answers, the third question was based on cues meant to arouse the interviewees' memories. Of three interviewees from the first cohort, a video fragment was available in which they gave their col-leagues in the plenary group a mid-term account of the personal learning goals they had pursued and which peer coaching activities they had carried out with the partner in their pair. For the other seven interviewees, no such video fragment was available. Instead, the interviewer showed them the poster(s) about their peer coach-ing activities, which they had presented at the end of the school year(s) in which they had participated. Against this background, the interviewees' scores on the CV at the beginning of the interview were probed in the fourth interview question. The issue what video use had contributed to the interviewees' learning was covered by the fifth question.

The second issue addressed in the interview – how PLC effects had come about – was covered by questions about processes and conditions involved in the teachers' learning. With the sixth question, the interviewers probed how teachers' thoughts and actions regarding their instruction influenced each other. The seventh question addressed the influence of personal factors. Aspects of peer coaching were probed in

TABLE 6.4 Response to follow-up interview questions

Question	Topic	Response frequency
1	What teachers felt they learned	9
2	Durable effects of PLC participation	9
3	Cued recall	8
4	Development of teaching behaviour in the longer term	6.6
5	Well-being at work	4.40
6	How teachers changed their instructional behaviour	6.45
7	Personal factors	5.40
8	Factors in the intervention	6.48
9	School-context factors	6.17
10	Additional remarks	5

the eighth question, particularly how the interviewees had experienced working in pairs, observing and viewing recordings of their own and colleagues' lessons, giving and receiving feedback, and the collegial exchange during the plenary meetings. The ninth question addressed the influence of factors in the school context. The tenth and last question was meant to check for any topics teachers felt they needed to complement.

Table 6.4 contains the response frequencies achieved for each interview question. The frequencies for questions 4 through 9 are averages, as these questions were subdivided. In all, seven out of the ten questions were answered by a majority of at least six out of the ten interviewees. The response frequencies for the sub-questions are further detailed in the *Findings* section.

Data analysis

To answer the first and second research questions, the quantitative teacher and pupil data were analysed by means of descriptive statistics, group comparisons and correlations. As thirteen teachers participated in two cohorts, the unit of analysis differed where applicable between participation ($N = 58$) and participant ($N = 45$) (cf. the section *Sampling* above). The analyses were conducted and the results below are reported in sequences moving from larger to smaller subsamples, from descriptive statistics to significance testing and from quantitative to qualitative data.

To answer the third and fourth questions, descriptive statistics and correlations were generated from the teacher questionnaires and combined with cross-case content analyses on the qualitative data. The findings are structured according to themes, underlying which are the relevant field notes, evaluations of plenary meetings, poster presentations and/or follow-up interviews.

Below, we specify how the teacher and pupil data were analysed as well as how the cross-case content analyses were conducted.

Teacher data

In order to trace if and how the teachers' thoughts and actions changed during the school years, the entry and exit criterion measures (see the section *Criterion measures* and Table 6.1 above) were analysed as follows. First, frequencies were calculated for the entry and exit criterion measures in all cohorts. Then, in order to find out in which ways teachers developed their instruction over the school years, the entry and exit measures were compared. This was done in two ways. The numbers of teaching behaviours which the teachers reported having changed during the school year were calculated. In addition, we distinguished four possible "change sequences" as defined by the score combinations that a teacher could move through, as shown in Table 6.5.

If a teacher scored "no" both at the beginning and at the end of the school year, we interpreted this as standstill, i.e. where teacher thought is concerned, no new ideas were sought or discovered and where teacher action is concerned, no changes in classroom behaviour were sought or made (cell A). If a teacher scored "yes" at the beginning of the school year and "no" at the end, we interpreted this as adversity, i.e. new ideas were sought but not discovered, and changes in teaching actions were not achieved (cell B). If a teacher scored "no" at the beginning of the school year and "yes" at the end, we interpreted this as a sequence of serendipitous learning, i.e. although unintended, new ideas were discovered and new teaching actions were developed (cell C). If a teacher scored "yes" both at the beginning and at the end of the school year, we interpreted this as success, i.e. new ideas were sought and discovered and existing teaching actions were changed (cell D).

The change sequences defined according to Table 6.5 were established by means of crosstabulation, so that the frequencies appearing in the crosstabulation cells showed how often the different change sequences occurred for each CV. When we performed these crosstabulations, the numbers of valid score pairs appearing in the cells did not allow chi-square values to be calculated. However, by

TABLE 6.5 Teacher change sequences

		Entry *questionnaire*	
		No	Yes
Exit question-naire	No	*A Standstill* No personal learning goal set, No outcome achieved	*B Adversity* Personal learning goal set, No outcome achieved
	Yes	*C Serendipity* No personal learning goal set, Outcome achieved	*D Success* Personal learning goal set, Outcome achieved

averaging the relative frequencies in the cells for each PLC goal it was possible to discern on a descriptive level how many instances of standstill, adversity, serendipity and success occurred for each of the project goals.

Descriptive statistics were also calculated for the teachers' background data as well as their descriptions and judgements of the pair composition and the peer coaching activities with video. To explore if and what relations existed between the quantitative data, correlations were calculated using Pearson's r. To counter the risk of spurious correlations, we report in the *Findings* section only correlations based on at least 25, i.e. 43% of the 58 PLC participations and surpassing .30 on the .05 significance level.

Pupil data

Also from the pupil data, descriptive statistics were generated. The analogy between the criterion measures among teachers and pupils has made it possible to compare the frequencies of classroom behaviours as reported by the teachers and as perceived and rated by the pupils at the end of the school years. For this purpose, these pupil measures were first averaged at the class level (De Jong & Westerhof, 2001, p. 53 and 79).

In addition, possible associations between pupil and teacher data were explored by means of parametric and non-parametric correlations. One-way analysis of variance (ANOVA) was used to test if classes' ratings of their teachers' behaviours differed between individual teachers.

Content analyses

Cross-case content analyses (Miles & Huberman, 1994) were conducted on all qualitative data, i.e. on the teachers' written evaluations of the plenary meetings, the field notes about the plenary meetings, the posters presented by the teachers in the last plenary session of each school year and the follow-up interviews. For each qualitative data source a database was created in the form of tables listing the respondents' answers to the prompts used (cf. the sections *Plenary meeting field notes and evaluation forms*, *Poster presentations* and *Follow-up interviews* above).

Where the data about the plenary meetings and posters were concerned, the above procedure was first carried out separately for each cohort. Findings pertaining to all cohorts together were then derived from the summaries for each cohort.

The teachers' answers to the follow-up interview questions were partly transcribed and partly summarised from the video recordings. These answers were then indexed and listed for each sub-question (cf. the section *Follow-up interviews* and Box 6.2). Where respondents made links to other sub-questions, these were cross-referenced. All transcriptions and summaries were checked for correctness by experts not involved in data collection. Seven were checked by Mrs. Coby Bos, a senior teacher educator, and two by the second author. These checks resulted in minor corrections.

The resulting database was analysed in a three-step procedure. First, all responses were categorised under headings denoting similar topics derived deductively from the instruments. Then, these topics were subdivided and specified as they emerged from the data, i.e. inductively. For all topics, response frequencies were established. 75% of the interview questions were answered by a majority of at least six of the ten interviewees. Finally, cross-case summaries of the responses about each topic were written by the first author. 42% of these summaries were verified by the second author. This final check resulted in minor corrections and elaborations.

The fourth interview question illustrates well how the content analyses were conducted. This question opened with: "Which skills that you already possessed/used before you participated in peer coaching with video have you used more/less since then? Please explain with examples." Nine out of the ten interviewees responded to this question. From the responses, the following topics emerged (frequencies are given between brackets): Lesson planning (2); Changes introduced in instruction: activating learning activities (3), content-focussed dialogue with pupils (7) and forms of cooperative learning (8); Seeking to strengthen contact with pupils (3); Increased use of information and communication technology (ICT) (2). The cross-case summaries of topics such as these formed the basis for the narrative presentation of the findings, illustrated with quotes, in the following section.

In the *Findings* section, we generally prioritise interview findings with response frequencies exceeding 50%. However, findings with lower frequencies are also reported, when these are illuminating from a qualitative point of view.

Findings

This section is structured on the basis of the four research questions. The findings about the PLC's impact on teachers and pupils are presented in the following two sections. Then, we recount how the teachers' instructional behaviour developed during the years after the PLC ended. Finally, we present the findings about how the teachers experienced their PD activities and the learning environment provided by the school.

Teacher learning during participation

We begin our examination of the impact of teachers' PLC participation on their instruction – the first research question – by describing and comparing the criterion measures at the beginning and the end of the four school years on the aggregate level of all PLC participations. Then, the change sequences found in individual teachers are explored. In both accounts, the focus is on the teachers' classroom behaviour.

Changes in teachers' thoughts and actions

Criterion measures of teachers' thoughts at the end of the school year are available for 36 out of the total of 58 participations, i.e. 62.1%. After 29 of these 36 participations, i.e. 80.6 %, teachers felt that participation had helped them develop one or more new ideas for their teaching.

Criterion measures of teachers' actions at the end of the school year are available for 31 participations, i.e. 53.4%. After 30 of these 31 participations, i.e. 96.8%, they felt they had developed one or more new teaching behaviours. One to five behaviour changes were reported after 22.2% of participations, six to ten after 36.1%, 11 to 15 after 19.4% and 16 to 17 after 5.6% of participations. On average, the teachers reported having changed 8.32 of the 21 criterion behaviours constituting the three PLC goals, i.e. 39.6% (cf. Table 6.1).

Individual teachers differed considerably in how many criterion behaviours they changed during peer coaching. Figure 6.4 ranks the 31 participations for which exit criterion measures are available according to the number of criterion behaviours changed. The vertical axis denotes the number of criterion behaviours changed. Each bar represents one participation.

Figure 6.4 shows that only one participation occurred during which the teacher did not change any instructional behaviour. After all the other 30 participations, the teachers felt that peer coaching had helped them develop their teaching behaviours. The minimum of zero, the maximum of 17 and the SD of 4.59 show that large individual differences occurred among the participants.

On the level of PLC goals separately, clearly more behaviour changes were reported for the first than for the second and the third PLC goals. The teachers changed on average 5.35, i.e. 48.6% of the eleven criterion behaviours constituting the first goal of increasing variety in learning activities. They changed on average 1.74 or 29% of the six behaviours constituting the second goal of increasing opportunities for differentiation and 1.23 or 30.7% of the four behaviours constituting the third goal of promoting self-directed learning.

Significant correlations exist between the numbers of behaviour changes reported for the different PLC goals (Pearson's r ranging between .36 and .49; p < .01). The numbers of behaviour changes for each goal are also strongly related to the

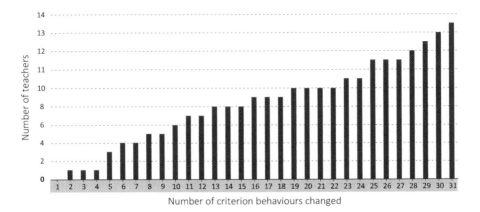

FIGURE 6.4 Distribution of behaviour change during participation

total numbers of behaviour changes reported (Pearson's r = .92 for the first, .75 for the second and .66 for the third goal; p < .01).

There was a significant correlation between the total number of behaviour changes reported and teaching experience (r = .39; p = .031). Teaching experience was similarly related to the numbers of behaviour changes reported for the second and third goals of increasing opportunities for differentiation and promoting self-directed learning (r = .48 and .52; p = .006 and .003, respectively), but not with those for the first goal of increasing variety in learning activities. Also, the higher the teachers' age, the more often they reported having promoted self-directed learning (r = .41; p = .023). A t-test showed that the 13 veterans reported more behaviour changes after their second year of participation than the one-time participants, both in total and for each PLC goal separately. However, this difference was not significant (p > .05).

Table 6.6 shows which teacher thoughts and actions are involved here. For each CV, the columns specify from left to right how often teachers chose it as a personal learning goal at the beginning of the school year and felt afterwards that participation had helped them achieve their personal learning goals. The second and third columns show the percentages of participations for which the teachers confirmed that they sought and had developed new ideas about teaching (entry and exit measurements of thought, respectively). The fourth and fifth columns show the percentages of participations for which the teachers confirmed that the pertinent criterion behaviours were already part of their existing practice and that their PLC participation had helped them change these behaviours (entry and exit measurements of action, respectively). The bottom of Table 6.6 contains a summary of the response percentages found.

Increasing variety in learning activities

Before their PLC participation, most teachers found themselves proficient at giving direct instruction (CVs 1 through 5). Afterwards, a majority felt that participation had given them new ideas about this and had helped them develop the precision of instructions, coordinating classroom activity and homework, explaining, instructional dialogue and seat work. Where fostering cooperation between pupils is concerned (CVs 6 through 11), far fewer teachers already practised this at the beginning of the school year. Afterwards, almost half of them felt that participation had helped them practice cooperative learning to a greater extent. Overall, more behaviour changes were reported for cooperative learning than for direct instruction.

The discussions during the plenary meetings and the poster presentations at the end of the school years show that the teachers faced two dilemmas while changing their practice. Usually in the first half of the school year, teachers "polished" or "did maintenance work" on their direct instruction, as they called it. As this reminded them of the important influence of giving precise instructions on pupils' learning activity, they sought for more ways to activate pupils, notably through forms of collaborative learning. While they experienced that collaborative learning activities can generate elaboration and deeper learning, they also found that these require more time than transmission-oriented instruction. When the mandatory curriculum did

TABLE 6.6 Teacher criterion measures during participation

Criterion variables		Thought		Action	
		entry	exit	entry	exit
I. Increasing variety in classroom activity formats					
1.	EXPLAINING	52	49	96	50
2.	PRECISE INSTRUCTIONS	52	63	74	22
3.	HOMEWORK	32	22	82	24
4.	INSTRUCTIONAL DIALOGUE	73	59	79	53
5.	SEAT WORK	70	82	86	71
6.	GROUP WORK	89	79	38	80
7.	PEER COMMENT	81	51	27	49
8.	PEER ASSESSMENT	84	40	23	44
9.	PUPIL PRESENTATION	63	40	52	39
10.	DEBATE SUBJECT MATTER	67	23	32	27
11.	GAMES	82	61	30	60
II. Increasing opportunities for differentiation					
12.	WORK OUTSIDE CLASSROOM	63	23	23	33
13.	ADDITIONAL MATERIAL	85	30	14	33
14.	ADDITIONAL ASSIGNMENTS	59	26	35	33
15.	OWN PACE	81	44	48	39
16.	OWN TOPICS	73	35	67	29
17.	COMPUTER WORK	67	29	24	32
III. Promoting self-directed learning					
18.	PUPIL PLANNING	63	26	33	25
19.	PUPIL AS CO-TEACHER	81	32	16	29
20.	INTEREST IN SUBJECT	58	56	79	64
21.	REFLECT ON FUTURE SUBJECT	58	16	50	9
Response					
Lowest		33	53	52	52
Average		42	72	50	72
Highest		48	76	50	78

not allow for freeing such time, they reverted to direct instruction more than they wanted to. Another dilemma was that when the teachers did use collaborative learning activities, they repeatedly observed that pupils' learning activity was less effective than they thought desirable. From this experience, they concluded that they had to structure pupils' learning activity to a greater extent, but this then conflicted with the goal of promoting self-directed learning.

Increasing opportunities for differentiation

At the beginning of the school years, the teachers reported considerable differences in their use of differentiation. Having pupils work at their own pace on topics of their own choice (CVs 15 and 16) was most prevalent. Afterwards, slightly more than one third of the teachers felt that participation had helped them enlarge the opportunities for their pupils to work by themselves on different assignments and materials.

The plenary discussions showed, however, that they found one issue particularly hard to solve: for differentiated forms of learning, more diverse contents, materials and assignments are needed than are usually available in the context of transmission-oriented teaching based mainly on direct instruction. They recognised the opportunities offered by multimedia and blended learning to tackle this problem, but they often lacked the working time needed to search, produce and make available materials and assignments suitable for differentiation.

Promoting self-directed learning

Before participation, self-directed learning by pupils did not occur habitually in the teachers' practice. Afterwards, about one third of them felt participation had helped them develop new ideas about self-directed learning. About a quarter had allowed pupils more influence on how lessons were carried out and to act as co-teachers (CVs 15 and 16). Almost two thirds felt they had acquired new ideas about and had succeeded in rousing interest in their school subjects (CV 20).

Change sequences in teachers' development

The poster presentations clearly showed individual differences in the personal learning goals on which the teachers focussed their peer coaching activities. They valued the cooperation between colleagues positively and noted that they became more aware of how they functioned in the classroom. As a result, they began to put more effort into lesson planning, but they also pointed out that this did not always pay off in the form of recognisable changes in their lessons.

During each school year, indications surfaced that the teachers were learning more and/or different things than they had initially chosen as learning goals for themselves. This phenomenon is clarified by the frequencies of the four types of change sequences that we distinguished (cf. Table 6.5). Figure 6.5 shows how often standstill, adversity, serendipity and success occurred on average in the behaviour changes that the teachers reported for each PLC goal. The quantitative findings visualised here should be considered tentative, as the numbers of valid score pairs in the underlying crosstabulations are relatively low, i.e. about 25 or 43% of the 58 participations.

The vertical axis in Figure 6.5 denotes percentages. The distribution of change sequences over the behaviour changes is also shown for all project goals together.

The vertical bars in Figure 6.5 show that the four change sequences occurred to different extents. Standstill predominated, except for the first goal of increasing variety in learning activities. As regards the latter, the PLC mostly promoted a success experience for the teachers. For their attempts at increasing opportunities for differentiation and promoting self-directed learning, however, we found that standstill predominated. Still, for these two goals, serendipity and success together occurred more frequently than adversity. The same is true for all behaviour changes together.

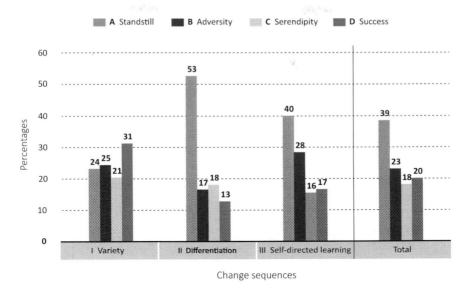

FIGURE 6.5   Change sequences in teacher action

It is interesting to note that in almost one fifth of the participations, serendipity played a role, i.e. the teachers felt supported in developing classroom behaviours that were not yet part of their usual teaching repertoires. Taken together, the two change sequences indicating behaviour change, serendipity and success, accounted for 38% of all the sequences for which data are available.

Pupil learning

Throughout the PLC's existence, the participating teachers wondered if and what benefits their pupils experienced from their peer coaching efforts. In their posters, they presented mixed observations about this issue. They noted that on the one hand, pupils appreciated being actively engaged during lessons and enjoyed the variation this introduced. On the other hand, the teachers felt that the added value of activating lesson plans sometimes appeared unclear to pupils.

This section about the second research question begins with an overview of how pupils perceived their teachers' classroom behaviour in comparison with the teachers' self-reports of their actions. Then, an examination follows of how the pupils felt their learning was affected.

Pupils' experience of teaching

In Table 6.7, the frequencies in the Perceptions column show how often per month the pupils in the classes of the teachers surveyed (cf. the sections *Sampling* and *Pupil questionnaires* above) actually perceived the teaching behaviours targeted in the PLC.

TABLE 6.7 Pupil perceptions and ratings

Criterion variables		Perceptions			Ratings		Differences between classes	
		0x pm	1-3x pm	≥4x pm	Mean	SD	F	p
I. Increasing variety in learning activities								
1.	EXPLAINING	3	54	43	3.20	.60	2.783	.001 ★★
2.	PRECISE INSTRUCTIONS	6	64	30	3.02	.64	3.448	.000 ★★
3.	HOMEWORK	8	54	38	2.93	.73	5.608	.000 ★★
4.	INSTRUCTIONAL DIALOGUE	9	59	33	2.87	.75	3.417	.000 ★★
5.	SEAT WORK	1	34	65	3.18	.67	2.422	.003 ★★
6.	GROUP WORK	15	73	12	2.89	.76	1.699	n.s.
7.	PEER COMMENT	41	55	4	2.65	.75	2.723	.001 ★★
8.	PEER ASSESSMENT	47	52	1	2.54	.74	2.195	.01 ★
9.	PUPIL PRESENTATION	55	37	7	2.75	.80	2.731	.002 ★★
10.	DEBATE SUBJECT MATTER	69	27	4	2.93	.82	2.147	.018 ★
11.	GAMES	43	52	4	2.79	.79	1.690	n.s.
II. Increasing opportunities for differentiation								
12.	WORK OUTSIDE CLASSROOM	53	36	11	2.84	1.07	1.369	n.s.
13.	ADDITIONAL MATERIAL	37	59	5	2.57	.77	1.699	n.s.
14.	ADDITIONAL ASSIGNMENTS	36	59	5	2.58	.82	1.611	n.s.
15.	OWN PACE	20	55	25	3.22	.68	1.817	.041 ★
16.	OWN TOPICS	62	34	4	3.03	.75	1.894	.037 ★
17.	COMPUTER WORK	58	33	9	2.92	.84	1.670	n.s.
III. Promoting self-directed learning								
18.	PUPIL PLANNING	50	37	13	2.92	.74	1.610	n.s.
19.	PUPIL AS CO-TEACHER	68	29	4	2.72	.70	1.952	.03 ★
20.	INTEREST IN SUBJECT	20	66	15	2.99	.83	.807	n.s.
21.	REFLECT ON FUTURE SUBJECT	62	36	2	2.89	.79	.942	n.s.

The means and standard deviations in the Ratings column show how much they felt this contributed to their learning – based on the four-point interval scale used. The F and p values in the Ratings column show for which teaching behaviours these classes' ratings differed significantly between individual teachers – based on the one-way ANOVA performed (cf. the section *Pupil data* above). One asterisk indicates a significance p < .05. Two asterisks indicate a significance p < .01. Non-significant differences are marked "n.s.".

Comparing the teachers' self-reports of their classroom behaviour (see the entry and exit measures in the Action column in Table 6.6) with the pupils' perceptions of it (see the Perceptions column in Table 6.7) yields the following findings. The pupils perceived all of the teachers' criterion behaviours. The percentages indicate that not only the teachers, but also the pupils felt that the teachers displayed the most behaviours grouped under the first PLC goal and fewer behaviours grouped under the second and third goals.

On the level of the PLC goals, the pupil perceptions correspond quite closely to the teacher self-reports. Averaged per goal, the percentages found among teachers and pupils diverged by 26 points for variety in learning activities, 23 points for differentiation and eighteen points for self-directed learning. At the same time, the pupils mostly reported higher frequencies than the teachers. Also, the pupil perceptions exceeded the teachers' self-reports at the end of the school years more markedly than at the beginning.

Instructional behaviours appreciated by pupils

The pupils' average ratings of their teachers' classroom behaviours (see the Ratings column in Table 6.7) were all above the scale midpoint. They felt most positive about three direct-instruction behaviours – explaining subject matter stepwise, giving precise instructions and having pupils work by themselves – and two behaviours enabling differentiation – having pupils work at their own pace and on topics of their own choice.

It should be noted that significant variation existed in how the pupils rated different teachers' classroom behaviour. This was the case for twelve out of the 21, i.e. 57% of the criterion behaviours.

Below, we examine how the pupils' perceptions and ratings of their teachers' behaviours were related to each other. The account focusses on those correlations between perceptions and ratings ≥.30 with a significance < .01 (Spearman's rho among perceptions and between perceptions and ratings; Pearson's r among ratings). These correlations indicate by which (combinations of) teaching behaviours in particular the pupils felt that their learning experiences were affected.

Variety in learning activities

Teachers who explained subject matter stepwise and gave precise instructions for exercises and assignments also coordinated classroom activity with homework (CVs 1 through 3; rho = .36). The pupils found the combination between stepwise explanations and precise instructions useful for their learning (CVs 1 and 2; r = .3). Pupils who found instructional dialogue with their teachers useful felt the same way about debating subject matter together (CVs 4 and 10; r = .31).

When pupils cooperated in groups, they worked with computers, commented upon and assessed each other's work and gave presentations in class (CVs 6 through

9 and 17; rho ranging between .30 and .32). They felt that giving presentations contributed to their learning (CVs 6 and 9; rho = .31) and they similarly found combinations of commenting upon and assessing each other's work useful (CVs 7 and 8; r = .64). When their teachers used games to engage them with the subject matter, pupils also found this useful (CV 11; rho = .32).

The above associations indicate that when teachers structured learning activity through direct instruction and collaborative learning, this was recognised and valued positively by their pupils.

Differentiation

The differentiation practices of working with computers at your own pace, working outside the classroom on topics of your own choice and debating subject matter together were experienced in connection to each other (CVs 10, 12 and 16 through 18; rho ranging between .32 and .50). The pupils also perceived and rated studying additional materials and working on additional assignments in connection to each other (CVs 13 and 14; rho = .48; r = .55).

Working with computers contributed to pupils' learning, when it was combined with instructional dialogue with their teachers, group work and debating subject matter together (CVs 4, 6, 10 and 17; r ranging between .37 and .44). The pupils similarly rated the combination of working with computers with giving presentations (CVs 9 and 12; r = .35). When working with computers, the pupils liked doing so outside the classroom and at their own pace. Under these conditions, they felt this contributed to their learning (CVs 12, 15 and 17; rho ranging between .32 and .38).

The above associations indicate that when teachers created opportunities and gave instructions for differentiated group work connected with plenary presentations and debates, pupils felt that this contributed to their learning. However, we also found that the more actions teachers reported for organising differentiation, the less their classes felt that stepwise explanations of the subject matter encouraged their learning (r = -.69).

Self-directed learning

Planning your own work and presenting parts of lessons were experiences connected to working with computers on topics of your own choice and at your own pace (CVs 9 and 15 through 19; rho ranging between .31 and .36). The pupils' ratings of working with computers and presenting parts of lessons were related to cooperating in groups (CVs 6, 17 and 19; r ranging between .34 and .44).

Four fifths of the pupils perceived that their teachers tried to interest them in their school subjects, but slightly more than one third felt encouraged to reflect on what they wanted to do with them in the future. On average, these teacher actions were rated positively (CVs 20 and 21). When pupils felt that their teachers tried to make them reflect on what they wanted to do with the school subject in their futures, this also helped them develop their interest in it (CVs 20 and 21; rho = .31; r = .43). The above associations indicate that pupils experienced and positively rated forms of self-directed learning when they were related to cooperative activities in classroom settings.

Development of teaching after participation

The third research question was how the participating teachers' instructional behaviour developed in the years after the PLC ended. The findings about this question are presented below. We begin by describing what the teachers who gave follow-up interviews regarded as the net outcome of their participation in peer coaching with video. Then, we elaborate in which respects they felt they strengthened and expanded their instructional repertoires in interaction with pupils and what kinds of processes were involved in this development. Finally, consequences of PLC participation for the interviewees' workload and motivation for teaching are described. In this as well as the next section, frequencies of interview responses are included where necessary for readers to judge their representativeness.

Net outcomes of peer coaching with video

As reported earlier, the interviewees can be regarded as representative for the whole group of teachers in this study (see the section *Sampling* above). Below, we first present the total numbers of criterion behaviour the teachers reported having changed since the end of the PLC, followed by an examination of these changes for each PLC goal. These findings are then illustrated with responses to the first three interview questions (see Box 6.2).

The criterion measures administered among the interviewees indicate that in the years after peer coaching with video, they had changed on average 5.22, i.e. 25% of the 21 criterion behaviours in Table 6.1. The interviewees changed on average 3.33, i.e. 30% of the eleven criterion behaviours constituting the first goal of increasing variety in learning activities. They changed on average 1.11, i.e. 20% of the six behaviours constituting the second goal of increasing opportunities for differentiation and .78, i.e. 25% of the four behaviours constituting the third goal of promoting self-directed learning. These figures are lower than those found at the end of participation (see Table 6.6). Nonetheless, the interviewees' responses showed that during the years after peer coaching had ended, all of them continued changing their instruction.

Figure 6.6 shows for each PLC goal how many instructional behaviours the interviewees changed before and after peer coaching ended. The vertical axis represents the numbers of criterion behaviours changed. For each goal, a pair of bars is presented. The left bar in each pair shows the number of behaviour changes reported at the end of peer coaching. The right bar shows the number of behaviour changes the interviewees reported having made since that time.

The bars in Figure 6.6 show that also during the years after peer coaching had ended, more instructional behaviours were changed for the first than for the second and third PLC goals, just as was the case at the end of participation. Three criterion

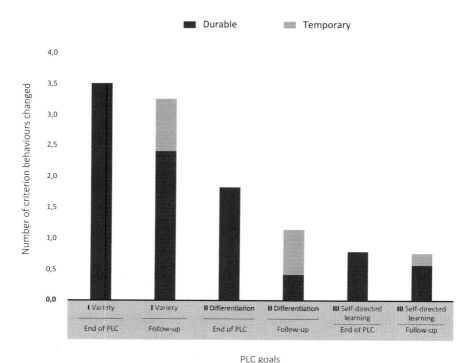

FIGURE 6.6   Behaviour changes per PLC goal in interviewees

behaviours were sustained by at least one third of the interviewees. Three of them had continued using instructional dialogue to engage pupils, while four had continued having pupils assess each other's work and engage them with subject matter through games (see in Table 6.1 CVs 4, 8 and 11, respectively).

As we asked the interviewees to distinguish between durable and temporary behaviour changes, we could determine for each PLC goal how many behaviour changes they eventually sustained. The right bar within each pair is stacked, distinguishing how many of the instructional changes made were durable and how many were temporary. Durable changes prevailed for the first goal of increasing variety in learning activities and the third goal of promoting self-directed learning. Temporary changes prevailed for the second goal of increasing opportunities for differentiation.

On the individual level, the interviewees differed considerably in how many durable and temporary changes they made in their teaching after the end of the PLC. This is shown in Figure 6.7 for each of the nine interviewees who provided criterion measures after the end of the PLC. One interviewee reported having changed a maximum of 14 criterion behaviours, while the minimum was 1 and the SD 4.1. Three interviewees had made only durable changes and one only temporary changes. The remaining five interviewees had made both durable and temporary changes.

When the interviewees described in their own words what they regarded as the net outcome of participating in peer coaching with video, two topics stood out: the

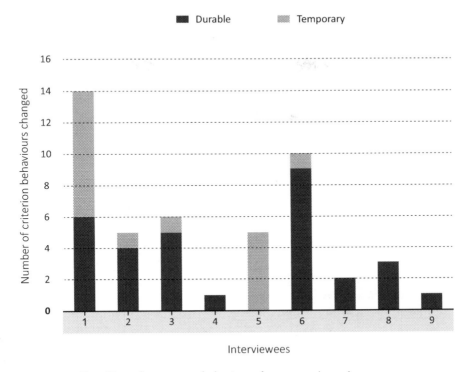

FIGURE 6.7   Durable and temporary behaviour changes per interviewee

types of activating instruction that participation had fostered and how peer coaching had raised the teachers' awareness of their work in the classroom, encouraging them to engage in redesigning and experimenting with their lessons.

Five interviewees pointed out that they had improved their use of direct instruction and had enlarged the variety of learning activities in their lessons, including group tasks and games. They felt that these changes had become permanent and had helped them raise their pupils' activity levels. Notably, they gave their pupils more complete and concise instructions, engaged more in content-focussed dialogue and shifted their interaction with them towards inductive sequences, i.e. using examples and experiences to build understanding rather than proceeding from general rules and abstract statements.

> Peer coaching has worked as a catalyst for me to pass on questions to [other] pupils instead of answering them myself as the expert.

> I try to have more discussions with pupils. I learned that from [my partner]. It is a pleasure to activate pupils.

Four teachers stated that peer coaching had encouraged them more generally to invest in lesson planning, to clarify lesson goals and to engage in instructional experimentation.

I began to plan my lessons not only six weeks ahead (including tests), but also on the level of single lessons and to ask myself what should be achieved in that lesson. I began to handle this more consciously and this has remained.

Three teachers mentioned that differentiation had remained a complex issue. However, the school had made this a goal for development.

How can I make sure that all pupils stay at work on their own level? I still find that difficult. This lingers in the back of my mind. It has become an item in school, though: how to use ICT in order to differentiate better.

Peer collaboration with colleagues, three interviewees said, had worked as a stimulus to become more aware of the strong and weak points in your teaching and to start changing it.

I cannot concretely pinpoint what I learned [from peer coaching], but afterwards, I did engage more in experimenting. That includes accepting that things go wrong once in a while and then, you just try something new. In connection with peer coaching, I did develop a sort of experimenting attitude.

What you become aware of during peer coaching, you can apply that in your lessons. It's hard to pinpoint what follows from what, but because of peer coaching, your development just goes faster. ... It did me a lot of good, even though beforehand I had my reservations.

Teaching behaviour after participation

After the opening questions of the follow-up interview, the teachers were asked to elaborate on their responses to the follow-up questionnaire about whether and how they had changed their teaching behaviour during the years since the PLC had ended (see question 4 in Box 6.2). In the following subsections, we relate in which respects they strengthened and expanded their instructional repertoires and how they experienced their classroom interaction with pupils while doing so.

In response to the interviewers' attempts to trace the specific influence of peer coaching on behaviour change, nine remarks from the interviewees indicated that this influence could be hard to isolate from other factors.

It's quite a while ago. You also develop by yourself and meanwhile we did other PD activities ... so then you don't know anymore what resulted from what.

It's been so long since [the PLC] that I wonder if I can indicate what the consequences for my teaching practice might have been. ... The outcome for me was small.

I increasingly use all sorts of groupings, bigger and smaller ones within classes. I strongly developed this *since* peer coaching, but I don't know if it's *because* of that [italics added].

Even so, the following types of behaviour change emerged as characteristic from the interviewees' statements.

Strengthening and expanding instructional repertoires

When asked which current teaching skills they had come to use more or less or differently since peer coaching, the teachers confirmed that their direct instruction had become more precise (cf. the above section *Net outcomes of peer coaching with video*). At the same time, whole-group instruction had become less dominant in their lessons, while their use of cooperative learning had increased. Seven teachers used whole-group settings more for content-focussed dialogue. Eight teachers used small-group settings to have pupils work on assignments and prepare presentations about the outcomes to the whole group.

> I already had pupils assess each other's work – for instance when they write texts and give oral presentations, I use the whole group as an audience and for mutual feedback – so that wasn't new, but since peer coaching, I do use that form more broadly. Peer coaching gave me new input for this. For instance, … when I teach literature, instead of doing all sorts of repetitive and reproduction tasks after my instruction, I now ask them to write a poem in Romantic style and incorporate as many Romantic characteristics as they remember. That is a more creative and activating task and then I have them read those poems aloud or I recite them. We fling those poems back into the group and then I ask: Do you really find this a successful Romantic poem and why do you think so or why not?

As four teachers recounted, it was the observation and discussion of each other's lessons during peer coaching that made them aware of the impact of their instructional behaviour on pupils' learning and led them to use teaching approaches with more emphasis and direction. Two teachers also pointed out that exchanging assignments with colleagues helped them practise activating approaches differently.

> I did learn to use my loose style more consciously. A common format [in science teaching] is: you do an experiment, give them a protocol and let them work. … The discussions were more vehement than I had in mind they should. I let it go and this yielded more cognitive outcomes and I got a better contact with them.

When asked which new teaching routines they had introduced in their lessons since the PLC had ended, six teachers answered that they now used more different and more activating learning activities and that because of this, their lessons were characterised by increased interaction with pupils.

> I did develop more ease in classroom discourse. And I am no longer afraid to introduce a lot of different transitions in a lesson.

Also, five teachers explained that while applying cooperative learning more frequently, they took care to introduce group work by giving clear instructions and structuring the learning activities to be carried out and to conclude it with a focussed debriefing discussion.

> Group work with a written assignment including clear instructions was quite new to me. I didn't get that in my preservice training. ... What was new was that I began premeditating precisely how I was going to debrief and to whom I gave which task. I wasn't used to doing that.

At the same time, developing new teaching practices into routines required an effort in itself.

> I still find it difficult to have pupils work at their own pace. I do try, but I easily fall back on my old pattern. That happens because of having to complete things and then again, I make one big standard recipe out of it.

During the latter half of the PLC's existence, the school began upgrading its ICT infrastructure and launched an experiment with "laptop classes" in order to promote differentiation. Nine teachers described how they introduced opportunities for pupils to use computers for work on assignments. In doing so, they encountered opportunities as well as challenges. The Internet offers a wealth of sources, they said, but it may also distract pupils.

> Differentiating our teaching is something we still do too little, really. We cannot yet find adequate forms for that.

As two interviewees pointed out, they considered it a necessary condition for productive ICT use to have available a selection of relevant subject-specific sources and assignments.

> They make a test online and get an outcome and tips what to study further. I also use it to get pupils to learn to do certain [chemical] analyses. On the Internet there are modules for that. I can demonstrate it with the beamer, but they learn more when they do it all themselves. Yes, they're very busy with that. When you say clearly which assignment they are to do with which web site, then a clear majority of the class works on that. When they're done, I allow them a little more freedom. Then they can find out something extra or make assignments without a laptop. I also find it an advantage that they know where to find [the material], so they can continue working on it at home. We place a lot of our material such as PowerPoints in the electronic learning environment, so they can watch it at home. Usually, those PowerPoints are made by colleagues, but I add to them and use them. I like that a lot, also for when pupils have missed a lesson.

> I find a nice assignment for example: search the Internet about what it is like to be young in Athens. About such a theme, you can gather 25 facts in ten minutes. As an

introduction to a lesson I think that's great, but for note-taking I find [laptops] a disaster, because you see very little of those faces behind the screens. I very much dislike that. And you can't imagine how many screens I see being clicked away when I walk around: Facebook, email, Minecraft, you name it. That's far more important to them and I understand, because I would have the same inclination. But I don't want it for my subject. When they work on a Greek or Latin text, they need that text, the notes about it and in fact, they should also be able to watch their grammar overviews and their word lists. That means they need four screens at the same time and that doesn't work on such a screen [demonstrates].

Classroom interaction

All three LPC goals involve teacher behaviours with implications for the social interaction in the classroom. Below, we describe how the interviewees sought to influence pupils' cognitive and social activation, their understanding of subject matter and their attitudes towards learning.

Eight teachers replied to the question what kind of learning they tried to achieve in pupils. The common denominator in their statements was that they wanted their pupils to learn actively and to analyse and understand subject matter, in contrast to memorisation and reproduction.

> I guess my main goal is to get them to think critically. I sometimes feel they should listen to things passively and understand them. I also feel that they should be able to learn actively and apply subject matter to new situations and new problems.

> I find thorough, "boring" declarative knowledge important in the sense of "This is what you should know". Because I like that myself. I like to know things, so I bring that across. And I love to make them learn from each other. I tend more and more to see myself as someone who only directs, helps, guides and less as someone who says: "This is the knowledge that you should be able to demonstrate at the end." Sometimes, unfortunately, that is unavoidable. ... What I try to achieve [through learning activities] is that they learn from each other what they are able to do and that they learn to make the best out of their personal potential. I very much like them to ask questions with hypotheses in them, like "Is this a ..." instead of "What is this?". I mean, they should think first before they ask the question. And that also holds between each other, so they learn to work out solutions by themselves.

To achieve such learning, nine teachers said they preferred to alternate learning activities by pupils with explanations by themselves as well as alternating more with less structured learning activities.

> [During science practica,] I ask questions like: What is it you're doing, What do you expect to happen or How are you going to write these results down, How do you want to represent this in a table? So while they're active doing something practical, I want to see the cogs in their minds turn around as well. Or by having them explain things to each other. I don't want to explain everything myself.

A question that teachers apparently found difficult to answer was whether since peer coaching, they were better able to promote learning with understanding among their pupils. Out of seven teachers, four couldn't say and one thought not.

> I find it hard to gauge if understanding is really achieved in pupils. Sometimes you see a pupil who can answer all grammatical questions correctly and then is not able to translate a text, so then he apparently understands everything I told him, but he cannot apply it at all. There are also pupils who can make a superb translation without being able to explain two cases, but then they have that very strong feeling for the text as a whole. You also have pupils who can do it all or not at all. Well, this … [shakes head, makes wondering gestures].

Five out of seven interviewees made explicit what kind of cooperation with pupils they preferred and how they thought this could be achieved. They liked best to offer opportunities for motivating experiments and games during 1½-hour lessons and to organise group work structured through questioning and Socratic dialogue, distributing turns evenly, observing wait time and putting little stress on grades. In these ways they hoped to achieve that pupils work together actively towards an understanding of subject matter before asking the teacher questions.

> I do think that peer coaching helped me achieve better cooperation with pupils. … we have focussed on this issue, so also in that respect, it has worked a little as a catalyst … perhaps because the focus was not only on the what, but also on the how.

About the issue how to encourage pupils to take responsibility for their own learning, all ten interviewees shared their experiences and opinions. Seven of them felt they did not allow pupils a great deal of autonomy to determine their own learning activities. The teachers kept control of planning over periods of weeks, but within the span of one or two lessons, they did allow pupils more freedom to decide about where and how to work on assignments, whether in small groups or individually. More autonomy was generally allowed to higher age groups, especially those preparing for final examinations. Three interviewees stated that they would like to allow pupils more autonomy. However, they felt curriculum overload and examination requirements prevented them from doing so.

Eight teachers described that pupils reacted quite differently to their attempts to promote their responsibility and autonomy during learning. Their impression was that older pupils could handle this better than younger ones.

> I always set up a framework within which pupils get a measure of freedom, but I'm surprised that they do not use that space, that they rather go along with the rest and do not want to excel, even in a gymnasium.

Not all pupils reacted positively to extra assignments with which teachers tried to enable differentiation. Still, the teachers saw a need for themselves to actively pursue, guide and coach pupils' taking responsibility.

It is becoming more of an issue among colleagues. We want a school in which making homework is normal. I find personal responsibility for learning very important, but in this age bracket it also is quite a lofty ideal. We will not be able to get pupils to take responsibility for their own learning to a high degree.

How teachers changed their instructional action

The quantitative evidence presented earlier showed that different sequences were involved in how the PLC participants changed their teaching behaviours and that some changes were durable and others temporary (see the above sections *Change sequences in teachers' development* and *Net outcomes of peer coaching with video*, respectively). The findings from the follow-up interviews in this section reveal in which ways changes came about and what factors influenced whether the behaviours involved became a regular part of the teachers' instructional repertoires (see question 6 in Box 6.2).

Translating thought into action

Exchanges with colleagues during peer coaching led five of the interviewees to develop current teaching behaviours further and to introduce new ones. In some situations, their thinking changed first and then their actions. In other situations, it was the other way round. Which of these scenarios happened when, depended on how wide-ranging the consequences were: if an instructional approach required only minor changes, teachers tried it out quickly without much deliberation. However, if a whole lesson had to change, teachers took time first to rethink its design and to modify the lesson plan.

> Whether I change my action or my thinking first depends on how big the issue is. With small things – for instance I see someone else note down the homework in the left-hand corner of the blackboard and I find that a good idea – I would try out right away if it's effective and then after a few weeks, I'd consult pupils about it. But if it's something with bigger consequences for my work or sequence of working, I would first consider by myself how I would exactly go about it. Something like that I won't do one day later. Then I need a pause to think. … Before I translate others' ideas into action, I do a number of things: I make a lesson plan in order to think through how I will handle it; I look what it brings myself; I discuss with pupils if it brings them something (questionnaires and the like I'd do only in case of drastic changes) and I discuss it in my team.

> I'm in the first category [changing thinking first and then action]. I first ask myself: Can I get something out of that in my lessons? I'm not going to introduce that in my lesson in a brainless rush and then find out: Oh, this doesn't work out at all in this part of the lesson. I do have to think that through carefully in advance … I will write that out point for point: first I let them do this and that's how I'll tell them that. I put that on paper completely and then I'll try it out, preferably in a parallel class, so that I can see … finetune an instruction midway for example.

The effect of instructional changes on pupils was foremost in teachers' minds when deciding whether or not to maintain them. For the interviewees, a key consideration was if and what benefits for pupils' learning they could observe. If they could, they would embark on finetuning their lesson planning.

> Pupils hold up a mirror to you. If you are not completely convinced of [a new approach] yourself and you don't know how to present it, then you get chaos and they ask you: "But why? How should we do this?" If I can present this in advance on the basis of my conviction that it is a good method for this lesson, then they will do it the way I think they should. So that's the reason [for my preference].

> When I think: this adds something, this makes the pupils more active, then I will do it. It may not work or it may work less well, but then you adapt it. I do try that.

Routines in teaching

According to six teachers, the time needed to change their instructional behaviour and the pace at which this happened varied. Simple changes could happen fast, they said, but to make a complex approach such as group work your own might take months or even longer.

> I think I learn reasonably fast. I don't need to do a series of lessons five times before it becomes automatic. Trying out a new approach and making it part of my repertoire is a matter of a few weeks and at the end of the year that has become more your way of doing things.

> Using instructional approaches and making them your own on a deeper level, that will ultimately work only by doing it. … It won't stay with you until after having done it for a year or even longer. It becomes your own thing by doing. Then you can further adjust and finetune it on a micro level, so the next time you won't have to discover the wheel.

Four teachers explained that as peer coaching provided the impetus for exchanges with colleagues, it helped them turn new instructional approaches into a standard part of their teaching.

> What helps you is to talk about it with someone. Peer coaching has an added value in that it forces you to think about it, because you must explain it to someone and that person will also say something about it. … It really helps when you have to explain why you have done something. Then you're inclined to think about it seriously and more or less investigate: "Does this work?" Then you're also inclined to adapt it more quickly and keep using it. … It already helps to just tell: what is this [instructional] format like and get some questions and feedback about it. I find it valuable that you will then start to wonder: How does a pupil experience this?

> Discussion and feedback during peer coaching changes your action quite fast. You're forced to do it quickly. You almost make an appointment out of it. If you don't do peer coaching, an idea will sooner land in the dustbin or a drawer. Perhaps it will come back later, but that will be a slower process. So peer coaching helps you keep up the pace.

Changing routines could also become a habit in itself:

> I relapse less and less because of new habits which meanwhile have aged themselves. When I have to put brakes on myself and think: "Now I should do something differently", then I already have quite a few different learning activities [at my disposal] that I can implement. So what I did ten years ago – explain subject matter for 20 minutes and then making homework for 30 minutes – never happens anymore. There's always something extra, an extended assignment or some variation or other.

At the same time, countervailing forces were at work. All interviewees responded to the question if they sometimes relapsed into old habits. Nine out of ten teachers said they did. Behaviours they tended to relinquish after a while were keeping instructions brief, reducing their own speaking time, engaging in discourse and interaction with pupils, organising learning activity less in whole-group and more in small-group settings, having pupils work on assignments and paying attention to pupils' solution methods.

Nine interviewees explained why they relapsed. The main reason, mentioned by five teachers, was their high workload. This led them to pay less attention to interaction with pupils and developing their instruction. As a result, they resorted to more teacher-centred practices. Preparing and organising group work, notably, could in their experience be time-consuming, while its outcomes were uncertain.

> For example, in a pre-exam literature class, I had put them together to work on a text with questions I had prepared myself. I had invested quite a lot of time in those questions and then this text turns out to be far too difficult, they get bored, don't understand the text and then this class tends to behave in the way of: "Well, I don't get it" and begins to chat. … If you have underestimated the difficulty of the text and that's why they give up after the first obstacle they meet, well, then I think: had I kept more control, then A. I had got a better outcome and B. they had learned more, because by asking questions I could have made them work and be active anyway – without giving everything away – in contrast to group work that stagnates at a certain moment. Then I would have said "OK, everybody, sit back in rows" and I would have taken them back unto me. In a case like that I just observe: this doesn't work. It is often true that things go slow. You really must have good assignments where you know for certain that they fit to pupils' level, if it is to be workable. Well, that's hard sometimes. When the content is difficult, it is often easier to keep a little more control of the lesson yourself.

Other reasons for returning to teacher-centred practices, mentioned less frequently, included personal inclinations such as being content-focussed, easy-going or forgetful, examination requirements, passivity in pupils and early socialisation by pre-service teacher education at a time when activating instruction was not yet taught.

As a remedy against relapsing into old habits two interviewees suggested discussing your work with colleagues, so that you are reminded what your instruction is like and will get new insights and ideas for developing it.

Well-being at work

Half of the interviewees responded to the question if developing or acquiring any skills through peer coaching had promoted their well-being at work (see question 5 in Box 6.2).

One teacher was not sure about this issue and one did not think peer coaching had contributed to his well-being at work, but no one felt that PLC participation had detracted from their work satisfaction. Four interviewees did feel that collaborating with colleagues during peer coaching had increased their work satisfaction.

> [What peer coaching contributed to my skills] I can't say, but my attitude [has changed]: it is good to observe each other. I am more and more convinced of that and I keep saying that we should do this more. I have always wanted to be a teacher and I love being one, so well-being in the profession is there anyway.

> I think [peer coaching has increased] a certain relaxedness [in me]. That's because of the partner I worked with. While biking to school I think about this. I am someone who tends to worry at times: How will I manage, because then you have a day of eight hours ahead of you and I think that's quite a lot. Then I feel slightly tense and think about content that may be hard for pupils or whatever … it can be anything. After all, this is a profession where you don't have everything under control. I am now a little more relaxed in how I handle this.

Nine interviewees clarified if they felt their work had become more pleasant because of what they had learned through peer coaching. One of them thought not and one could not say. Five teachers felt that peer collaboration had promoted their creativity and therefore their pleasure at work. Two others felt that PLC participation had increased their flexibility in designing and structuring their lessons.

> I'm getting more fun out of it. I never was a moody type, but I have become a little more playful. Yes, peer coaching has made my work nicer. It has become more pleasant because I let pupils do more by themselves. That is nice for me, because I look around and see lots and lots of things happening. I hear them talk and that gives me inspiration, because I think: "Oh yes, that's something I might pick up and use sometime".

Five teachers answered the question if peer coaching had helped them continue in the teaching profession. Although all of them felt positive about how peer coaching had contributed to their work satisfaction, no one said it had directly helped them continue in teaching. Their motivation for teaching was already present for other reasons such as a diversity of tasks or a "genetic predisposition".

> It's in the family and it's genetic. The older I get, the more I see that this was a good choice, except financially, but OK, that's how it is. I just like it too much, I keep on learning, absolutely. I feel good here. I was a gymnasium kid myself and I know how frustrated I felt that I wasn't allowed to learn in my own way, so that's why I find it important that these kids do get that chance from me.

Influence of the learning environment

In this section, the findings about the fourth research question are presented, i.e. which peer coaching activities and which features of the learning environment the teachers found helpful for enacting changes in their teaching. Results from the questionnaires and the qualitative data collected during the PLC are here combined with the interviewees' retrospective statements. We first describe how the PLC participants experienced the peer coaching activities undertaken. Then, the teachers' evaluations of the learning environment as provided by the school are described.

Peer coaching activities in the learning environment

For teachers, the PLC provided two settings in which they could work on their PD. The pair work with a colleague enabled them to engage in lesson observation, video viewing of each other's lessons and mutual feedback. The plenary meetings enabled them to exchange ideas and practices as a team. Our account of the teachers' experiences with these activities begins with the interviewees' opinions about the overall effectiveness of peer coaching (see question 8 in Box 6.2).

What teachers experienced as effective

Nine out of the ten interviewees responded to the question whether they felt peer coaching with video had paid off for them. Five of them explicitly stated that in their experience, they had benefitted from peer coaching.

> [Improving my] direct instruction I might have learned from a book, cooperating with [my partner] I might have organised myself and we're also proficient in post-lesson conferencing, but without the PLC I think I wouldn't have done it.

The interviewees also clarified the main reason why they had benefitted: connecting the observation of teaching action and speaking about it with colleagues had provided them with concrete feedback which had enabled them to change their own teaching. This effect occurred especially, they said, when the partner in your pair taught the same or a related subject.

> What really made me learn is observing each other's lessons ... and speaking about it. Getting ideas and hearing comments, that's what made the most sense to me. ... Then you wonder why [such cooperation] doesn't happen more often. When that stops, it's a pity. Then you land in the treadmill again or in some format. That's worrying. I think [peer coaching] should be a standard part of your work. If you want to develop education, I feel you should focus not on all sorts of higher structures, but on cooperation between teachers and on your love for the subject. All of that is included in [peer coaching].

> Observing each other is fun. What is useful about it is that you always have the link between thinking and doing. You observe the doing – a lesson, practice – and you link

it during pre- and post-conferences with considerations about "Why do you do it this way?" and outcomes. As I said earlier, you need to act if you are to develop a command [of new teaching practices]. In my idea, this has far more concrete effects than just talking about things during a team conference or meeting.

Two other features of peer coaching considered effective had to do with external inputs and were each mentioned once: video fragments coupled with conceptual information about teaching and the reader that was handed out to the PLC participants.

What I like about a reader is that you can look at it when it suits you. For me, that makes the threshold to inquire into something a lot lower than when I have to go to the library myself. A "pile to start with" is fine. Then there's a good chance that I'll read it eventually, not immediately, but later.

Seven interviewees answered the question if any features of peer coaching had hindered their learning. Four of them valued peer coaching with video only positively, because it had offered opportunities for experimenting in their teaching and receiving feedback about it. At the same time, four teachers pointed out conditions that should be fulfilled for peer coaching to be productive. They felt in particular that working time should be available for and scheduling should facilitate visiting and discussing each other's lessons. One teacher added that participation should be voluntary, because unmotivated participants would inhibit others in the group. One teacher felt that more resources should be available for collecting learning materials enabling differentiation.

Pair composition

Both in the questionnaires and the interviews, we asked the PLC participants if and how their pair work was influenced by the way in which the pairs were composed. During the PLC, the teachers found it quite helpful for their own learning if they could decide freely with whom they were going to work together (M = 4.19 on a five-point scale). In practice, this was not always possible. With respect to school subject, three interviewees noted that they were coupled with a colleague in a different subject than they had requested.

Within the whole group of PLC participants, working with a partner in the same school subject was preferred most (M = 4 on a five-point scale) and working with a partner in a related subject to an almost equal degree (M = 3.86). Cooperating with a partner in a different subject was appreciated to a lesser extent (M = 2.77). A similar pattern was found among the teachers in the interview sample. Out of the eight interviewees who stated their preference, four preferred working with a partner in the same subject and three with one in a related subject, while no one preferred pairing with a partner in a different subject.

The interviewees clearly considered it an important topic whether pairs were composed of teachers in the same, a related or a different subject. Among all PLC participants this made no significant difference in the numbers of criterion behaviours changed ($p > .05$), but the interviewees explained that when both colleagues in a pair taught the same subject, this was helpful to achieve the most and the most concrete outcomes.

> With a partner in the same subject you can work far more concretely. Otherwise it remains restricted to instructional variation, pace and that sort of thing.

> I did peer coaching with someone from history and with someone from economics. I teach French. A colleague of mine did peer coaching with someone from Spanish and that person had lots of instructional benefits from it or at least could exchange a lot of things. With such different subjects, that's quite a bit harder.

> For us, it was important that we had the same subject, because we only wanted to participate if it has direct practical use. For us, that's when we could see how a colleague in our subject teaches. But I do have an interest in how other subjects are taught. In that respect, I found the plenary meetings interesting.

However, pair work with a colleague in a different subject also helped teachers cross boundaries:

> I partnered with someone from English and from maths and I found it fun and fascinating to have the chance and watch a maths lesson from within. It was very interesting to me to see how pupils react to someone with a completely different style.

Concerning pairing with a colleague with the same, more or less teaching experience, the questionnaires indicated a preference for working with a partner with the same or more teaching experience (M = 3.45 and 3.32 on five-point scales, respectively) over pairing with a partner with less experience (M = 2.75). Out of the seven interviewees who stated their preferences in this respect, two had partners with less and two partners with more experience, but they felt these differences did not have a specific impact.

> [My partner had] more experience, but that didn't matter. I have now worked here for 20 years and she for 25, so that isn't much of a difference.

However, three interviewees noted that for beginning teachers, a larger difference in experience might be influential in the area of classroom management. A veteran said:

> … neither of us had classroom management problems. When you are a beginning teacher, that's where all your energy goes, but with [two partners] our intention was

rather, when you're past that, [to discuss] how you can then begin to make it even more worthwhile.

Observing, filming, viewing and giving feedback on each other's lessons

Below, we describe how the teachers cooperated in pairs, i.e. which activities they carried out; how they experienced observing each other's lessons and viewing and analysing the recordings together; and what outcomes these activities produced for their personal learning.

The teachers in the PLC succeeded almost twice per month in observing colleagues' lessons (M = 1.78) and discussing them within their pair (M = 1.78). Lessons observed were mostly also discussed by them (r = .82; p = .00). The frequency of peer observations was slightly correlated with the number of behaviour changes reported for the first PLC goal of increasing variety in learning activities (r = .37; p = .04).

In their comments written during the PLC, the teachers pointed out aspects which influenced productive cooperation during pair work. They felt that making progress was promoted by an open work atmosphere between colleagues characterised by mutual trust. As one teacher reported about her pair:

> We're enjoying it. We see things in each other's lessons that we emulate. I like thinking about my lessons and making them more worthwhile for the kids.

Nine interviewees described the peer coaching activities they had carried out in their pair. Eight of them had observed and discussed their lessons with their partner. Preparing lessons together had occurred less frequently. In this activity, three interviewees had engaged incidentally or not at all, because they felt that observing and discussing lessons yielded the most concrete and practical ideas for classroom teaching. Four teachers especially valued filming and discussing lessons with a focus on using variations of learning activities in the same school subject. For two interviewees, working in their pair had the advantage over the exchanges during the plenary meetings that in their pair, they found it easier to pursue specific, personal goals.

> I certainly learned how to carry out a group work assignment in chemistry. In chemistry, we don't use group work a lot, so I wanted to do something with group assignments outside the practica. I produced an assignment about proteins with [my partner]. … I learned a lot, because I now know a little better how you can debrief assignments and ensure that every pupil makes their own contribution to the work.

During the school year, 1.65 lessons per teacher were filmed on average. The teachers viewed the video recordings of their lessons 1.48 times on average. The following correlations indicate that both other-viewing and self-viewing were related to teachers' reflecting on and changing their classroom teaching. The relationships involved are visualised in Figure 6.8.

The more helpful the teachers found other-viewing for changing their own teaching, the more behaviour changes they reported (r = .43; p = .02). This was

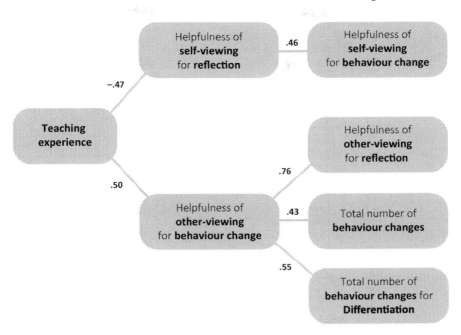

FIGURE 6.8 Correlations involving other-viewing and self-viewing

especially the case for the second PLC goal of increasing opportunities for differentiation (r = .55; p = .00). Viewing colleagues' lessons appeared about equally influential on reflecting on one's own teaching as on changing it (M = 3.65 and 3.92, respectively). These judgements were strongly correlated (r = .76; p = .00).

The teachers experienced self-viewing as quite helpful, but more so for reflecting on their own teaching than for changing it (M = 4.30 and 3.55, respectively). These judgements were moderately correlated (r = .46; p=.02). Interestingly, the more years of teaching experience the PLC participants had, the less helpful they found self-viewing for changing their own teaching (r = −.47; p = .02) and the more helpful they found other-viewing (r = .50; p = .00).

Out of nine interviewees, two had not been filmed during teaching. Four interviewees found being filmed quite valuable, although two of them also felt a little uncomfortable. One teacher felt neutral, and one felt negative about it.

> [I found it] awful, I mean: extremely useful and quite horrible. It stays that way, I can't say why.

Two interviewees noted that compared to just observing lessons, filming them required an additional effort which did not necessarily pay off.

> I always find filming lessons rather a hassle. I felt the time investment was not always outweighed by what it brought you, but I always appreciate having someone observe your lessons and discussing their remarks and suggestions.

Three interviewees answered the question if being filmed felt differently in the beginning rather than later on during peer coaching. Two of them felt there was no difference. One teacher said about pupils' reactions:

> In the beginning, the class reacts a bit silly and after that it quickly becomes normal. If you participate in something like this, it's part of the game. It would be a great drawback if you didn't do it.

Six interviewees recounted what they had learned from reviewing their lessons on video. Most conclusions from lesson viewing concerned behaviours that teachers felt they should improve, but they also made positive discoveries about behaviours they wanted to maintain. The behaviours involved had to do with the clarity and pace of teaching as well as aspects of speech and expression.

> Seeing a clip of myself leads me to discover that I can be more expressive: especially when I'm tired, I should do more to magnify everything. Then I become more aware that my thinking is "Yes, but I explained everything, didn't I?" But that is only verbal, I should also magnify it through my expression.

> From [reviewing lesson clips] I learned for instance that I talk a lot and fast. I also hear that from pupils, so I already knew about this. Also that I cannot use the blackboard in an orderly way, but then that becomes very visible. At the same time [I see] that my interaction with pupils is quite nice and productive. It's great to see that confirmed.

> I wasn't aware of the speed I'm making. [My partner] said: "Wow, you put a lot of pressure." I wasn't going to change that, though. For me, it's a way to keep the kids' minds alert.

Six out of seven interviewees felt that being able to see colleagues' lessons on video was an added value compared to only talking about lessons. They found that watching lesson videos was mostly stimulating and could lead to new discoveries. However, two interviewees felt that observing classrooms live was an even better experience,

> … because then you can also look around, for instance to what a pupil to the left of you is doing. You see the interaction between pupils very well. When you're in front, you miss a lot of things, whereas from your colleague in the back, you hear many things that you didn't see yourself. I find that enormously informative.

In their written comments, the teachers stated that post-lesson discussions were more productive when they were guided by clear observation points:

> Looking in each other's kitchen gives you a taste of what teaching competence means. I admired watching how patience in [my partner] has a beneficial impact when there are "bothersome" pupils in a class.

When asked if they had viewed lesson recordings on a surface level or also repeatedly and using specific viewing questions or points, five interviewees' answers indicated that they had most often watched lesson recordings once, noted conspicuous points and discussed them, while viewing points had been used in about half of the post-lesson conferences. Two teachers gave examples showing that repeated viewing can make you aware of more and more specific aspects of lessons.

> [When I watched a video twice,] I focussed on a pupil who engaged with the subject matter in a very funny way and on another who rested his head on the table. Then you see differences between pupils.

After observing and filming each other's lessons within their pairs, the teachers experienced receiving as well as giving feedback as very helpful for their own learning (M = 4.48 and 4.30, respectively). Of all the evaluative questionnaire items, these were the most highly rated. They were also highly correlated (r = .88; p = .00). Moreover, the more lessons were filmed, the more helpful the teachers found peer feedback for reflecting on their own teaching (r = .43; p = .03). Also other correlations indicate that receiving and giving feedback were related to teachers' reflecting on and changing their classroom teaching, as visualised in Figure 6.9.

These outspoken evaluations went hand in hand with how positively the teachers judged the contribution of giving each other feedback to reflecting on their own teaching (r = .62; p = .00 and .62; p = .00, respectively). The feedback received influenced the teachers' reflection on their own teaching slightly more than their changing it (M = 4.16 and 3.84, respectively). These judgements were slightly correlated (r = .39; p = .047).

Together, the above findings show that observing and discussing each other's lessons were clearly associated with how helpful the teachers found these activities for reflecting

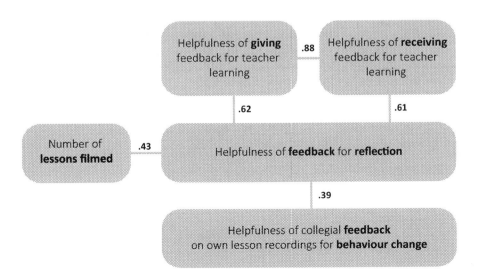

FIGURE 6.9 Correlations involving feedback

on and changing their instruction. The statements from the interviewees clarify what the teachers found helpful about these experiences.

Seven interviewees answered the question if and how using video had led them to look differently at their own work. Two of them couldn't remember this, but the other five said that video use had led them to change their views of themselves more than of their pupils:

> Video does add something: you can change your view of yourself by observing carefully from a distance what you are doing. You're slightly less involved yourself.

> By watching those clips I didn't learn so much about my interaction with pupils as about how I saw myself and what impact the pace [of my teaching] had. [Learning and teaching] is a slow process, far slower than you think. You know, lots of things cross your mind. I think it's valuable to notice that: all sorts of things whirl around in my mind, but that needn't be visible to everybody else.

Six interviewees answered the question if and what use "having a look into each other's kitchen" through peer coaching with video had for them. All of them explicitly appreciated this. Three interviewees gave examples of teaching behaviours they had emulated after seeing them used by the colleague in their pair.

> The good thing about having a look into each other's kitchen was how recognisable things were. but it was also in the differences. It was really funny to look in [my partner's] lesson. He teaches exactly the same subject matter, but he does that in such completely different ways.

> With [my partner] we focussed on variation. That was helpful. Those smaller units of instruction [in her lesson planning] were something effective. I began shortening my instruction to a maximum of ten minutes.

The above examples illustrate how viewing experiences influenced the PLC participants during their pair work. However, "looking into each other's kitchen" played a role also during the plenary meetings.

Plenary meetings

The teachers' average attendance during plenary meetings ranged between 76% and 83% per school year. The content analyses of the qualitative data collected during the PLC and the follow-up interviews yielded findings about three themes: how the activities during the plenary meetings and the issues discussed there typically developed over a school year; what the teachers felt were productive ways of conducting these meetings; and what benefits they derived from the plenary exchanges among colleagues.

On the basis of the field notes and the poster presentations, it was possible to summarise for each school year which activities were undertaken and which issues were discussed during the consecutive plenary meetings. These summaries were then compared over the four cohorts of participants. The resulting reconstruction showed that the teachers' collaboration typically developed in three stages.

During the first two to three months, the teachers agreed on the peer coaching procedure to follow and viewed and discussed video fragments about the use of direct instruction – first in others', then in their own lessons. These activities, as well as role-play, made them aware of their own routines in giving instructions, explaining subject matter, checking on homework and interacting with pupils. On this basis, they selected and formulated personal learning goals, which mostly regarded becoming more precise in their instructions, clarifying to pupils what learning activities they expected from them and activating them through group work.

During the second and longest stage, lasting from approximately the third into the sixth or seventh month, peer coaching in pairs took place in repeated cycles of observing, filming and discussing each other's lessons. Video fragments of this pair work were viewed and discussed during the plenary meetings. The central concern during this core stage was how to encourage pupils to cooperate and give each other feedback while learning. With respect to this issue the teachers discussed what impact different types of instructions had on their pupils' learning activities in terms of both process and outcomes. Questions often debated were: "How active do the pupils become?", "What especially encourages their activity?" and "What do they learn from it?"

The process of activating pupils – particularly through group work – repeatedly raised dilemmas. Group work required more lesson time than the existing curriculum provided. Teachers tried to free this time by reordering or shifting contents in their year planning, but felt rather constrained in doing so. This then forced them to switch back to traditional transmissive teaching methods which worked faster, but made themselves more active and their pupils less active. Also without time pressure, however, the teachers experienced it as a challenge to find ways of teaching that would lead pupils to exert themselves more. While shifting responsibility for active learning to pupils, the teachers did want to control the quality of pupils' activities. They felt this quality was at times compromised either because the type of learning activity they had chosen turned out less suitable or because pupils resisted activation or both.

During the second stage, part of the plenary meeting time was also devoted to collaborative lesson planning. This activity functioned as a bridge towards deliberations about how to incorporate the use of instructional approaches discovered as valuable in routine teaching practice.

Incorporating such approaches usually became the main theme during the third stage, which lasted during the final quarter of the school year. In the poster presentations and discussions concluding each school year two challenges surfaced, which considerably influenced the teachers' personal competence development, i.e. how to proceed from thought to action and – once they deemed changes in their teaching worth sustaining – how to consolidate these in daily practice. The posters showed that how teachers met these challenges was a gradual process which differed between individuals, as manifested in the goals they set themselves, the pace of their progress and the extent and nature of behaviour changes they achieved in the classroom.

In their written comments, the teachers voiced the following experiences, needs and suggestions indicating how they felt the plenary meetings should be conducted in order to be productive. Some of these indications also surfaced in the posters and follow-up interviews. Below, illustrative quotes from the written comments are given between brackets.

First, the teachers noted that it was helpful for their learning when the plenary meetings took place with a certain regularity, i.e. about once per month. They also felt that the plenary meetings did and should provide a context which favoured commitment and cooperation among the PLC participants. The latter point was also noted by two interviewees.

> I think the group context created by the plenary meetings was useful and necessary. … Exchanging in a group and engaging with topics you may not have thought about yourself but which may rouse you, do have an added value. It also gives you a stimulus to go on [with peer coaching], to stick to appointments. And [it helps you] see that several other people are working on it.

Secondly, the written comments showed that for every plenary meeting it should be clear from the beginning what outcomes are pursued. ("We should prepare our homework better. Better instruction is advisable about the output we expect from ourselves.")

Comments were made, thirdly, about the design of meetings and the use of time. The teachers preferred having alternating opportunities for being active, for listening and for viewing and discussing each other's lesson recordings ("Retain the alternation between theory and practice"). They also felt that when they wished, part of the time should be spent on working within the pairs ("Very nice to have some time for discussion in pairs!"). Furthermore, the meeting's pace should be neither too slow nor too hurried ("Good that the agenda was adapted. Better do two things well than three things half").

The written comments showed, fourthly, that the teachers clearly appreciated that the meetings had a good atmosphere and that there was mutual trust in the group ("I think we need the long term for an atmosphere of trust to grow. This process seems to be happening now.")

Finally, connecting practice and theory figured prominently, both in the written comments and in the interviews. The teachers felt that the background materials about instructional theory – in the reader and the electronic learning environment – should remain succinct ("Apply theoretical input directly on the spot. Prevent paper and electronic tigers"). In addition, the video cases and the observation points guiding their discussion should be recognisably relevant to the meeting's agenda ("Such a video is very much alive for me. I love a video as a vehicle for thinking about all sorts of aspects." "Viewing assignments were a little vague this time. We could get more out of this.")

The issue of connecting practical examples and experience with conceptual information was again brought up by four interviewees when asked about features of peer coaching that hindered their learning. They felt that in the plenary meetings this connection should always be recognisable, otherwise they experienced them as far less useful:

It's the same as in the subject of Philosophy that I teach: I feel it's the most ideal in a lesson – but that is very difficult – when you have something from pupils' concrete practice that you can couple the theory with, that you can look at and can think about. In fact, that also holds for this PLC, I mean: considering practice from the angle of theory.

I felt quite irritated by the plenary meetings. Some of those, in my eyes, were prepared quite weakly. Those preparations were done by different people [members of the steering group]. Then I found it a waste of time and I wondered: What topic are we talking about? What do we want to achieve together? In my view, the plenary meetings were too unconnected from the lesson observations in the work pairs. For a while, it looked like we had a theme for each period, but this was soon dropped. I found that frustrating and a hindrance.

About the benefits the plenary meetings brought, all interviewees made statements. Three of them said they found watching and discussing each other's video clips a useful activity. Five teachers appreciated getting to know practices, experiences and ideas from other school subjects. This, they said, provided them with ideas that otherwise they would not have become acquainted with.

In the plenary meetings … I hadn't expected this … teachers gave presentations and showed new ways of teaching. They also showed that they ran up against themselves or their limitations. That was something of an eye opener for me. It was a protected environment. That was very good about it. … That makes it easier to join in and just speak out how things go in a lesson and that not everything is fine, while you want every lesson to be a success.

Both the posters and the follow-up interviews contained indications that the plenary meetings could be a starting point for changing classroom teaching. As five interviewees said, they had adopted and tried out instructional approaches they had seen in colleagues' lessons. Two of them explained that this had also entailed adaptations. Interestingly, out of the eight examples the interviewees gave, they had seen six in video clips shown during the plenary meetings by colleagues from a different subject.

I remember that we saw a clip from a colleague teaching history, who had deposited a host of [written] questions in groups of pupils, but also about group work in mathematics. So you can find forms of instruction in other subjects and see that they work there, for instance having pupils present [geometry proofs on] posters. We have the idea that in such a subject you cannot do things like that, but that is then shown not to be the case.

All those things I told you about, I adopted those, but not literally. One colleague had done something funny in a German lesson while explaining [differences between the third and fourth] cases [by means of gesturing]. I guess because I was inspired by that, I began explaining different sorts of angles [in geometry] by means of arm gestures [demonstrates]. And I let some lithe first-year pupils demonstrate "overstretching angles" through a gymnastic exercise. I really learned from my colleagues to work concretely and with my own expression.

Interactions between person and school context

Besides the peer coaching activities in which the teachers engaged, we also asked them which factors within themselves and in the school context promoted or hindered their personal learning (see questions 7 and 9 in Box 6.2). The interviewees' answers mostly addressed interactions between themselves and the conditions created by the school for the activities in the PLC.

When asked what helped or hindered them learn during peer coaching, seven out of eight interviewees stressed that cooperation and discussion with colleagues had helped them experiment with new forms of instruction during their classroom teaching. This also entailed adapting and changing lesson plans.

> My main stimulus is my colleagues. Yes, you follow good examples.

> What helps me is my contact with the other. That in itself makes me less conservative [and makes] that I develop faster, that I'm more progressive. It's very stimulating. It doesn't look like that. Peer coaching is threatening, but if you engage with it, then it has a tremendous added value. You must cross a threshold.

What teachers felt hindered them had to do with personal tendencies on the one hand and with work conditions on the other.

> Like many teachers, I am quite opinionated, so I'm not easily convinced. I am seriously willing — more and more, I'd say — to listen and try something out when someone else says it's a good idea while I myself am not convinced. This laptop class is a good example: I was quite skeptical about that, but this and last year, I tried it out really seriously. I must have reasons now to say that I don't find it practical. It does help that I can correct my tendency to be obstinate. Willingness to try something out just because it's different also helps. Then you're inclined more quickly to adopt something.

> It takes a lot of time. Those enormous quantities of subject matter that we must press through. Additional material, role playing and the like require relatively much time, so that perishes immediately when lessons are cancelled. Then the nice things are skipped, because you move through content faster. That's a pity. What we have to cover for exams is quite a lot.

> External factors, the fact that I have quite a lot of duties and find little time for what it's all about here in school. This year I had intended to first make sure that my lessons are in order, that the pupils get what they have a right to. Where personal contact and homework correction are concerned, that does work out, but not yet where pedagogy is concerned.

Six interviewees' statements indicated what kinds of influence personal tendencies and work conditions had on their routines and work style.

> When I relapse [into old habits], I'm quite frustrated. When that happens, I think it's because ultimately I'm a contents person and then I don't have as much attention for pupils' creative ways, having contact with them and making the subject interesting.

I do have moments when I love to focus only on content. ... And yes, when I'm in that mood sometimes, then there's a risk of losing them. When [my attention for interaction is lowered], that's very frustrating. That just has to do with being tired, the daily ... [buzzer sounds].

Hmm. Well, I think I want to keep control a little too much. Yes, I think so. I think I'm rather directive. You can have a good lesson sometimes by handing things over a little more. [Being more directive] surely is a method to engage large numbers of pupils. Yes, my feeling is: when you keep a little more control, you also see better where things go astray.

For me, it makes quite a difference who among the colleagues tells you [about changes in teaching]. With some colleagues, I'm not inclined to follow their example, because I think: "I have no confidence in that" or "That doesn't fit with who I am". Whereas, when another colleague tells me, I think a lot sooner: "Hey, I'll do that too." I am prejudiced to a certain degree. I cannot judge such a story on its merits 100% objectively. Sometimes I don't believe it and I think that someone makes it sound better than it is.

Teaching is a very hectic profession, so you have to improvise often, solve things on the spot. Fortunately, I'm good at that, but it causes you to engage in reflective thinking not very often.

All ten interviewees answered the question which factors in the school context promoted their learning and in which ways. They greatly appreciated that the school's management had made working time available for visiting and observing each other's lessons.

It was a luxury that you got release time for it, because you may agree on watching each other's lessons, but here you have a framework, you were forced to it. And that's when it becomes productive, I think. It was great that the school offered this opportunity.

Five teachers felt that the culture of openness existing in the school had promoted their learning. This, they said, also helped new teachers become team members and made peer coaching with video worth incorporating into personnel policy.

Already after one week in this school I had the feeling of being at home here. That helps me see things in proportion. When I am criticised, I can shut down, but in this school, that is no issue at all. That helps to have a positive attitude. That's why you get an upwards spiral.

Just like colleagues of mine I have felt good about the PLC even though nothing measurable came out of it. In a sense, it's regrettable to look at it that way. What was valuable about it was reflecting together about education. That disrupted working in isolation, which is so characteristic of teaching. That was valuable. It did not strengthen my relations with colleagues. I feel it's important to know from each other what you're working on, but despite the attempts that were made, this has not improved here in school.

A few years after [the end of the PLC, my partner] and I applied again because we wanted to delve into differentiation, but in the end this didn't work out, because we could work on it, but we had to do it in our own time. ... It would be good to organise peer coaching every few years – also to keep it affordable – so that every few years you can appeal to a new group of colleagues, because the team composition changes over the years. Because of the cuts there is no money for it now, but it would be a good moment to pick it up again. It would be a good element of the school's personnel policy.

When asked which factors in the school context hindered their learning and in which ways, nine interviewees again pointed out facilitation of peer coaching and school culture as influential factors. Four of them noted that the discontinuation of the PLC had made it difficult or impossible to observe and comment on each other's lessons regularly. Six responses indicated that workload and curriculum requirements made it hard to find the time needed to incorporate new instructional approaches in preparing and giving lessons.

It's a great hindrance that [the PLC] has stopped.

I feel that in this school, we still exchange far too little, especially by observing each other's lessons and exchanging materials, ideas and good practices. This hardly happens. I found that a great plus in peer coaching.

It's the old tune: busy busy, lots of things to do. Yes, that's school stress.

The school's culture is one of remoteness, after all. Peer coaching breaks through that a little, perhaps even quite a lot. I'd almost say: this should happen far more often. ... I also think there are many colleagues who think: "Peer coaching, no, I don't participate, that's nothing for me" and they preserve the school's culture, while ... it's exactly those colleagues who should first of all engage in peer coaching.

In their written comments about the organisation of the pair work and the progress this brought, the PLC participants pointed out that such cooperation was encouraged when the school's timetable offered opportunities not only for visiting, observing and filming each other's lessons, but also allowed for discussing them immediately or shortly afterwards. This organisational issue surfaced again in the follow-up interviews. Five out of the ten interviewees had experienced that their lesson schedules enabled them to observe each other's lessons as intended. The five others had experienced that this had at times been difficult to organise. They all pointed out that for peer coaching to be productive, it is a necessary condition to have working time available for observing as well as discussing each other's lessons. In addition, they felt it would be ideal to have time also for preparing lessons together.

We didn't have big scheduling problems. That was quite a feat. I would have liked to observe and be observed even more.

We usually succeeded [in observing lessons], but then discussing them also takes time. And talking together about lesson preparation was altogether out of the question.

In our team, we tried [after the end of the PLC] more or less to observe each other's lessons one more year. I succeeded once or twice, but it did not work out any further because it wasn't doable in terms of scheduling. We asked the school management to facilitate it, but when this didn't happen, it quickly faded away.

The timetable is always an obstruction when you can't find shared hours. … For me, being busy was more of a problem than scheduling problems.

The timetable is an obstruction and perhaps even the whole organisational principle of 50-minute lessons and classes. That's a classical piece of school culture which hinders you to cooperate on the classroom level, for instance through team teaching. We do that just once in a while, but if the timetable weren't such a determining factor, then you could cooperate on these things a lot more creatively.

Conclusions and discussion

In this case study, we sought to understand what impact teachers' participation in peer coaching with video had on their instruction and on their pupils' learning. To this end, we reconstructed how their teaching competence developed, both while and after they participated in the PLC. In this final section, we first answer the research questions on the basis of the evidence produced. We then discuss what this study contributes to the knowledge about teacher PD and formulate recommendations for designing and implementing peer coaching with video. We conclude with an outlook on future developments.

Conclusions

Below, we formulate our conclusions in separate sections about each of the research questions. This account focusses on the changes occurring in the teachers' interaction with their pupils and colleagues and on the conditions and processes which promoted or hindered the teachers' professional learning. To keep a grasp on the multitude of underlying findings, we first summarise, then synthesise the evidence in each section.

Shifts in instruction during participation

Our first research question was: What impact did peer coaching with video have on the teachers' instruction during PLC participation?

During the PLC, participation helped almost all teachers, regardless of teaching experience, develop new ideas for and introduce changes in their teaching. Those teachers who participated during two school years – the "veterans" – reported more behaviour changes than the one-time participants, but this difference was not statistically significant.

The teachers attained most changes in instruction for the first PLC goal of increasing variety in learning activities by making their direct instruction more effective and introducing and structuring forms of cooperative learning. Classroom teaching changed to a lesser extent where the second goal of increasing opportunities for differentiation and the third goal of promoting self-directed learning were concerned. The teachers enlarged the opportunities for their pupils to work by themselves, but in doing so, they felt hampered by a lack of time needed for developing materials and assignments suitable for differentiated learning activities. They recognised the opportunities offered by multimedia and blended learning, but did not find enough time to search, produce and make available materials and assignments in blended learning environments.

On the individual level, the teachers developed their teaching competence in quite different ways. The four change sequences distinguished – standstill, adversity, serendipity and success – occurred to different extents. Success predominated for the first and standstill for the second and third PLC goals. Insofar as behaviour change did occur, serendipity and success played about equal parts. Also, where increasing opportunities for differentiated learning and promoting self-directed learning were concerned, teachers with more years of experience benefitted more from participation. In addition, the higher teachers' age, the more they felt they succeeded in encouraging self-directed learning.

In sum, the participating teachers succeeded in activating their pupils through forms of teaching and learning that were more characterised by responsiveness and dialogue than those they practised before participation. What we see here are shifts away from transmission-oriented teaching and towards cognitive activation. Such shifts contribute to raising the quality of instruction.

Pupils' learning experience

Our second research question was: Which of the teaching behaviours targeted in the PLC did pupils perceive and regard as contributing to their learning?

Not only teaching, but also learning was affected by the teachers' activity in the PLC, as the classroom behaviours of teachers who reported having changed them were perceived and positively rated by their pupils. The pupils' perceptions of their teachers' classroom behaviours were more outspoken than the teachers' self-reports, not only at the beginning of the school years, but even more markedly at the end. At the same time, the pupils clearly experienced differences between the classroom behaviours of different teachers.

Just as the teachers, the pupils reported that the teachers enacted a variety of learning activities during their teaching. What they felt contributed most to their learning was when their teachers gave stepwise explanations and precise instructions and allowed them to work by themselves, at their own pace and on topics of their own choice. Such forms of direct instruction and collaborative learning were recognised and valued positively by pupils. However, pupils felt to a lesser extent that their teachers enabled differentiated learning or promoted self-directed learning, thus mirroring the teachers' self-reports. When teachers created opportunities and gave instructions for differentiated group work, pupils felt that this contributed to their learning in particular when it was connected with plenary presentations and debates. Pupils similarly appreciated forms of self-directed learning when they were related to cooperative activities in classroom settings.

In sum, most pupils valued being actively engaged in lessons as their teachers used an increased variety of learning activities. They valued the freedom to work outside the classroom and decide for themselves how to go about this, as long as their teachers gave them clear instructions about presenting and exchanging their work in the plenary class setting.

Sustainability of changes in instruction

Our third research question was: How did the teachers' instruction develop after PLC participation?

During the years after the PLC ended, the teachers who had participated felt supported in strengthening and expanding existing instructional practices, in introducing new ones and in sustaining these practices. The teacher learning outcomes reported from this period show a similar pattern as those at the end of the PLC. The teachers reported having continued practising a greater variety of learning activities. However, they felt they succeeded less in providing opportunities for differentiation and promoting self-directed learning.

Most of the changes in instruction after the end of the PLC proved durable, while some were only temporary. Again, considerable individual differences became apparent, both in the number of criterion behaviours changed and in how many behaviour changes were durable or temporary. These changes were mostly durable where the variety in learning activities was concerned. Most teachers wanted their pupils to learn actively and to analyse and understand subject matter, in contrast to memorisation and reproduction, but they found it hard to say whether since peer coaching, they had become better able to promote learning with understanding. To achieve this, they had increased their use of cooperative learning and alternated less with more structured learning activities. Through these changes, the teachers felt that their classroom interaction with pupils had become less dominated by their own instruction and had come to consist more of content-focussed dialogue. In this way, they felt they succeeded better in increasing pupils' learning activity. However, changes in instruction aimed at differentiated learning remained largely temporary. When teachers did promote self-directed learning, these efforts were more often durable than temporary.

Changing teaching in these ways created tensions for the teachers themselves. They were concerned that the effectiveness of their instruction might diminish if they loosened control of pupils' learning activity. Most teachers felt they did not allow pupils a great deal of autonomy to determine their own learning activities.

When they did so, it was more often within shorter than longer time spans and more often in older than in younger age groups. The teachers did introduce opportunities for pupils to use computers during school hours for work on assignments. However, just as during PLC participation, they felt they still lacked sufficient working time to develop appropriate collections of subject-specific materials needed for such assignments. In their attempts to increase opportunities for differentiated learning, they felt constrained by curriculum overload and examination requirements.

Both pupils and teachers considered the social context of the classroom group to be of essential importance for learning, both cognitively as it provided the forum for content-focussed learning activities and motivationally by eliciting cooperation and commitment. In the teachers' experience, self-directed learning can only be a long-term goal, the achievement of which presupposes their taking initiative and upholding the effort needed to structure and guide pupils' learning.

When teachers began to change their classroom behaviour, it depended on the magnitude of the change how they operated. When small changes were involved, most teachers "first acted, then thought". When changes were bigger, i.e. when they involved restructuring the design of lessons, the teachers first spent more time than usual on planning and collegial consultation. The prevailing criterion for assessing whether a new or modified teaching approach "worked" was its perceived efficacy in eliciting desired learning activities in the majority of pupils. If they judged a new instructional practice capable of achieving this, the teachers would engage in repeated trials of it, finetune it and consolidate it into a new routine. Adopting a complex approach such as group work along these lines could take months or even years.

Almost all teachers relapsed from time to time into teacher-centred habits, i.e. they reduced their initiatives to activate pupils without wanting to. The main factors they pointed out as triggering such relapse were excessive workload and the discontinuation of release time and scheduling facilities for peer coaching.

The teachers rated the influence of PLC participation on their work satisfaction as moderately positive. About half of them felt that their collaboration with colleagues had contributed to their work satisfaction, while none felt it had detracted from it. Whether or not the teachers wanted to stay in the profession was apparently not influenced by PLC participation.

In sum, our reconstruction of teachers' development from the beginning of peer coaching with video till three to six years later shows that this form of PD can have a positive impact on sustainable changes in instruction. All but one of the teachers in this study reported that participation helped them strengthen and expand their repertoires of instructional behaviours during the PLC. In the years following it, all the interviewees continued changing their instruction in ways that increased their pupils' cognitive activation.

The main evidence about the shifts that peer coaching with video encouraged in the participants' teaching and in their pupils' learning are summarised in Box 6.3.

BOX 6.3   OUTCOMES IN TEACHERS AND PUPILS

Shifts in instruction during peer coaching with video

Teacher outcomes

- During participation, almost all teachers, regardless of teaching experience, developed new ideas for and practices in their teaching.
- The teachers mostly increased the variety of learning activities in their lessons. They made their direct instruction more effective and introduced and structured forms of cooperative learning. Their instruction changed less where opportunities for differentiation and self-directed learning were concerned.
- In all, the teachers' instruction shifted from transmission-oriented teaching towards cognitive activation of pupils.

Change sequences

- The four change sequences distinguished in teachers' development – standstill, adversity, serendipity and success – occurred to different extents. Success predominated for increasing the variety in learning activities and standstill for increasing opportunities for differentiation and promoting self-directed learning.
- Insofar as changes in instruction occurred, success and serendipity played about an equal part.

Pupils' learning experience

- The instructional behaviours of teachers who reported having changed them were perceived by their pupils. They recognised and appreciated the changes their teachers made in direct instruction and cooperative learning.
- When teachers created opportunities and gave instructions for differentiated group work, pupils felt that this contributed to their learning in particular when it was connected with plenary presentations and debates. They similarly appreciated forms of self-directed learning when they were related to cooperative activities in classroom settings.

Sustainability of changes in instruction after peer coaching with video

- Between three to six years after peer coaching with video, the participants felt supported in strengthening and expanding existing instructional practices, in introducing new ones and in sustaining these practices.

- They reported having continued changing their instruction in ways that increased their pupils' cognitive activation, but felt they succeeded less in providing opportunities for differentiation and promoting self-directed learning.
- Teachers as well as pupils considered the social context of the classroom group to be of essential importance for learning, both cognitively as it provided the forum for content-focussed learning activities and motivationally by eliciting cooperation and commitment.
- Most of the changes in instruction made after peer coaching with video ended, proved durable. Teachers mostly assessed whether a new or modified teaching approach "worked" by its efficacy in eliciting desired learning activities in the majority of pupils.
- When teachers judged a new instructional practice efficacious, they engaged in repeated trials of it, finetuned it and consolidated it into a new routine. Adopting a complex approach such as group work along these lines could take months or even years.
- Almost all teachers relapsed from time to time into teacher-centred habits. The main factors triggering such relapse were excessive workload and the discontinuation of peer coaching.
- The teachers rated the influence of peer coaching with video on their work satisfaction as moderately positive.

Working mechanisms in teachers' learning environment

Our fourth research question was: Which peer coaching activities and which features of the learning environment did the participating teachers find helpful for enacting changes in their teaching?

How the teachers' professional learning unfolded during peer coaching with video was shaped by the learning environment within which it took place. The working mechanisms operating in their learning depended on the relationship between the processes and conditions involved in peer coaching with video. Observing, filming, viewing and giving feedback on each other's lessons in the two settings of pair work and plenary meetings were the peer coaching activities that encouraged developing new ideas and changing instruction. In both settings, the teachers experienced an open work atmosphere and mutual trust. They regarded this as vital for their professional learning.

Observing each other's lessons usually took place without the use of video. The teachers liked live observation best because they felt this made it easier for them to focus on events of their choice than in a video recording. Live observation also provided more of the context information they needed. However, using video was also highly valued by the teachers, as this made teaching action visible and accessible for feedback and reflection. They mostly watched lesson recordings once, noted conspicuous points and discussed them. Most teachers appreciated "looking into each other's kitchen" either live or through video viewing because its concreteness allowed them to understand exactly how colleagues operated in the classroom.

The teachers experienced both self-viewing and other-viewing as helpful for reflecting on and changing their instruction, but their impact differed. Self-viewing mostly helped teachers discover what teaching behaviours they wanted to change or maintain, while other-viewing functioned more as a stimulus for changing instruction. Other-viewing led most teachers to adopt and adapt in their own lessons approaches they had seen colleagues using. Such emulation was prompted not only during pair work. It also resulted from other-viewing during plenary meetings, whether teachers saw video recordings from colleagues' lessons in the same, related or different school subjects. The teachers experienced repeated viewing of lesson recordings as more useful than one-time viewing. In addition, they found viewing and discussing lessons structured by explicit viewing points as more useful than doing so without viewing points.

The impact of the teachers' video use was closely bound to receiving and giving feedback to each other. Within their pairs, they experienced both processes as very helpful for reflecting on and changing their instruction. Using video in the context of peer coaching raised the teachers' awareness of strong and weak points in their instruction and encouraged them to clarify lesson goals, to engage in instructional experimentation and to invest in lesson planning. Seeing each other teach, whether live or on video, enabled them to step in each other's shoes and suggested alternatives for instructional action to them. Especially when observing and viewing lessons were coupled to discussing them with colleagues, the teachers felt enabled to change their teaching practices.

The processes of teacher learning summarised above were influenced by factors in the learning environment as follows.

Whether pairs were composed of teachers in the same, related or different school subjects made no significant difference to the numbers of criterion behaviours changed, but the PLC participants clearly preferred cooperating with a colleague in the same or at least a related subject. In this setting, they felt that peer feedback and discussion could generate the most and the most concrete ideas to make planning and implementation of a changed lesson realisable. The teachers also preferred cooperating in a pair with a partner with the same or more years of teaching experience. In general, they preferred being able to decide freely with whom they were going to work together.

During a school year, the plenary meetings typically developed in three stages. During the first two to three months, the teachers agreed on the peer coaching procedures to be followed and formulated their personal learning goals. During the second stage, lasting from approximately the third into the sixth or seventh month, peer coaching in pairs took place in repeated cycles of observing, filming and discussing each other's lessons. During this stage, part of the plenary meeting time was also devoted to collaborative lesson planning. This activity functioned as a bridge towards the third stage, lasting during the final quarter of the school year, in which the central concern was consolidating changed teaching practices.

The teachers felt the plenary meetings were most productive when they took place regularly, i.e. about once per month. Meeting periodically provided a context which favoured commitment and cooperation. What also made the meetings productive in the teachers' experience was when the outcomes pursued in each meeting were clear from the beginning and when practice and theory were connected in recognisable ways. They criticised isolated presentations of instructional theories. Instead, their preference was to keep background materials succinct and to ensure that the video cases and the observation points guiding their discussion were relevant to the meeting's agenda. Their appreciation of the plenary meetings was enhanced further, when they had alternating opportunities for being active, for listening, for viewing and discussing each other's lesson recordings and for working together in the pairs.

The teachers unanimously praised the school's management for having made working time available for peer coaching. They felt that discontinuing the PLC had made it difficult or impossible to observe and give feedback on each other's lessons regularly. For peer coaching to be productive, they considered it a necessary condition to have working time available for observing as well as discussing each other's lessons. Likewise, the school's timetable should make these activities possible. Time was a pervasive issue in the teachers' experience. They felt that workload and curriculum requirements made it hard for them to find the time needed to incorporate new instructional approaches in preparing and giving lessons.

In sum, for the teachers in the PLC studied, video use embedded in reciprocal peer coaching functioned as a useful tool for introducing and sustaining changes in instruction. These outcomes were achieved because the video-supported activities facilitated in the learning environment made the teachers' daily instruction amenable to collegial dialogue and change.

The main evidence about the processes and conditions involved in peer coaching with video are summarised in Box 6.4.

BOX 6.4   THE INFLUENCE OF PROCESSES AND CONDITIONS

Peer coaching activities

- Observing, filming, viewing and giving feedback on each other's lessons in the two settings of pair work and plenary meetings were the peer coaching activities that encouraged teachers to develop new ideas for and change their instruction.
- In both settings, the teachers experienced an open work atmosphere and mutual trust. They regarded this as vital for their professional learning.

Using video

- The teachers highly valued using video, as this made teaching action visible and accessible for feedback and reflection. They appreciated "looking into each others' kitchen" either live or through video viewing because its concreteness allowed them to understand exactly how colleagues operated in the classroom.
- Self-viewing mostly helped teachers discover what teaching behaviours they wanted to change or maintain, while other-viewing functioned more as a stimulus for changing instruction. Other-viewing led most teachers to adopt and adapt in their own lessons approaches they had seen colleagues using.
- The teachers experienced repeated viewing of lesson recordings as more useful than one-time viewing.
- They found viewing and discussing lessons structured by explicit viewing points more useful than doing so without viewing points.

Receiving and giving feedback

- The impact of the teachers' video use was closely bound to receiving and giving feedback to each other.
- Especially when observing and viewing lessons were coupled to discussing them with colleagues, the teachers felt enabled to change their teaching practices.

Pair composition

The teachers preferred:

- being able to decide freely with whom they were going to work together,
- cooperating with a colleague in the same or at least a related subject and
- cooperating with a partner with the same or more years of teaching experience.

Plenary meetings

- During a school year, the plenary meetings typically developed in three stages.
  - During the first stage, the teachers agreed on the peer coaching procedures to be followed and formulated their personal learning goals.
  - During the second stage, peer coaching in pairs took place in repeated cycles of observing, filming and discussing each other's lessons.
  - During the third stage, the central concern was consolidating changed teaching practices.

- The teachers felt the plenary meetings were most productive when they took place about once per month.
- What also made the meetings productive in the teachers' experience was when:
  - the outcomes pursued in each meeting were clear from the beginning and
  - practice and theory were connected in recognisable ways.

Working time

- For peer coaching to be productive, the teachers considered it a necessary condition to have working time available for observing as well as discussing each other's lessons.

Discussion

Below, we discuss what the evidence from this study adds to the knowledge about teacher PD. In doing so, our focus will first be on the issue what kinds of outcomes peer coaching with video can foster in teachers and the working mechanisms involved in this form of VTL. Then, we consider what these working mechanisms imply for the design and practice of teachers' PD. Finally, we note the limitations of the study and formulate suggestions for future research and development.

The potential of teacher peer coaching with video

This case study has clarified in which respects and in which ways peer coaching with video can support teachers in introducing and sustaining changes in their instruction during as well as after participating in it. In this section, we interpret the evidence presented above in relation to the state of the art in the VTL literature. We do so by comparing it to the conclusions from the systematic review in Chapter 3 (see Box 3.2). This comparison allows us to determine what this study confirms in or adds to our current knowledge. We thus seek to specify what potential peer coaching with video has for raising the quality of instruction.

A strategy for achieving sustainable increases in the quality of instruction

None of the conclusions from our review of the VTL literature has been disproved by this study. Its significance is, rather, that it shows the potential of peer coaching with video for helping teachers achieve sustainable increases in the quality of their instruction. In the PLC studied, this approach to PD was capable of fostering shifts in teachers' classroom instruction which promoted the cognitive activation of pupils. This result confirms our conclusion from the VTL literature that quality of instruction – being a key mediator influencing learners' achievement – can be raised by video-supported PD efforts. We therefore feel justified in designating peer coaching with video as a suitable strategy for encouraging higher-order teaching and learning. If peer coaching with video has the potential to promote such alterations in teachers' instructional action as were found in this study, this is a promising perspective for developing the teacher workforce.

In addition, the significance of this study is that it suggests explanations of the ways in which peer coaching with video can lead to changes in instruction. In the following sections, we discuss a number of issues that are evidently involved.

The cyclical and gradual nature of teachers' competence development

The findings from this study show that teacher behaviour change is not a quick, linear or uniform process. Rather, it is gradual and cyclical in nature. Durable changes in instruction developed over a period of years extending beyond the end of the PLC. Apparently, a period of years had to elapse, before they became a sustainable result (cf. Cordingley et al., 2005, p. 4). These findings confirm the need to recognise that developing professional competence and improving instruction are challenging processes for teachers, as pointed out by Guskey (2002, p. 386). Several findings help explain why this is the case.

In the first place, instructional behaviours do not develop in isolation, but in relation to each other. As the studies by Šeďová (2017a, 2017b) and Damhuis, De Blauw, Tammes and Sytema (2009) illustrate, shifting instruction in the direction of dialogic teaching involves changing several behaviours together, notably questioning, responding and time management. This makes establishing new teaching routines a complex endeavour (see the section *Engaging in repeated activity cycles* in Chapter 3).

Secondly, this study shows that the more advanced goals of organising differentiation and encouraging self-directed learning were attained to a lesser extent. Insofar as teachers did so, they were helped by the personal background factors of teaching experience and age. This evidence – together with the finding that teachers who participated twice achieved significantly more changes in instruction – suggests that teachers' professional competence develops quite gradually and cumulatively over the whole career span. This pattern resembles the developmental stages of teaching skills found in the large-scale survey research conducted by Kyriakides, Creemers and Antoniou (2009).

Finally, the cycles of activities involved in introducing and sustaining changes in teaching routines require targeted and sustained efforts. For the teachers in this study, translating thoughts into actions meant moving through repeated cycles, each involving a number of steps: becoming aware of and examining consequences of their instructional behaviour for pupils' learning; developing new instructional ideas and lesson plans; trying out new behaviours and discussing their impact on pupils with colleagues; redesigning or finetuning, re-enacting and re-evaluating lessons; and finally deciding whether or not and how to make temporary changes in instruction durable, i.e. consolidating them into readily usable practices. This sequence of activities corresponds to the ALACT model of reflection developed by Korthagen, in which teacher learning is represented as a cycle consisting of five phases: Action; Looking back at the action; Awareness of essential aspects; Creating alternative methods of action (Korthagen, Kessels, Koster, Lagerwerf, & Wubbels, 2001, p. 44).

Teachers' personal development in the profession

Individual differences played a considerable role in the types and pace of changes in teachers' instruction found in this study. Different change sequences occurred to different degrees for different teaching behaviours. Also, the pupil ratings of teachers' classroom behaviours showed a considerable number of significant differences between individual teachers. Together, these findings confirm that teacher behaviour change is characterised by considerable individual differences (see the review findings in the section *Individual differences* in Chapter 3).

Our findings about the role of change sequences in teachers' development suggest that teacher learning is highly personal in nature. The occurrence of standstill, adversity, serendipity and success varied considerably between criterion behaviours as well as individuals. This underscores the importance of encouraging teachers engaging in peer coaching with video to specify personal learning goals. An illuminating case study of one teacher's development by Tharp and Gallimore suggests that the probability of achieving changes in instruction increases when the learning goals chosen remain within her or his zone of proximal development. To develop higher-order teaching skills, teachers need the opportunity to move through those successive learning activities that fit their personal situation (Tharp & Gallimore, 1988, p. 217–266). In the PLC we studied, this was also our experience.

Besides the development of teachers' professional competence, there is also their professional motivation to consider as an area of PLC impact. Engaging in peer coaching with video appears to fit well with teachers' professional well-being. Also in this respect, it appears to be a suitable PD strategy.

The catalysing function of video use

This study has clarified the added value of using video in the context of reciprocal peer coaching. By visualising the interplay between teaching and learning video makes teachers' work accessible for peer feedback, dialogue, reflection and change. This affordance makes DV an eminently suitable medium for learning from experience. We know from practice as well as theory and research that teachers learn foremost through practical experience (see the section *Quality standards for teacher learning* in Chapter 1).

Our findings confirm the conclusion from the VTL literature that video use adds objectification and explication to teachers' professional learning (see the section *Processes* in Chapter 3). The findings also go beyond this conclusion, because they reveal on the basis of empirical evidence how video use fulfils a catalysing function for teachers' learning. It works in two ways. When embedded in collegial collaboration, self-viewing helps teachers become aware of how their instructional action promotes or hinders pupils' learning. Other-viewing in a setting of collaboration helps teachers discover alternatives for instruction and introduce them in their work. Stepping in each other's shoes with the help of classroom video provides them with starting points for raising the effectiveness of their teaching.

Analysing video records of their own and colleagues' lessons can help teachers open up routine instructional behaviour for intentional change. Much of experienced teachers' daily instructional behaviour is "unconscious" or routinised. They rely on automated patterns of cognition and response in order to be able to function in their inherently complex and dynamic work environment (Miller, 2011). When planning lessons, they visualise the teaching and learning activities they will be orchestrating and anticipate learners' responses in the form of mental pictures (Clark & Peterson, 1986, pp. 262 and 265). What moving images do during lesson analysis is to slow down teachers' perception and judgement and thus help them examine and reinterpret their teaching with more detachment than they normally muster. This, in turn, encourages judgement and decision-making about possible changes in instruction, followed by redesigning, trialling and consolidating these. These kinds of change processes have been well characterised by Kurt Lewin in his three-phase model of "unfreezing, moving and refreezing" (Lewin, 1951, p. 228–229).

The above interpretation leads us to suggest that observation and visualisation of teaching deserve to become additional features of effective PD. Whether through live observation or vicariously through self- and other-viewing, visual experience affords access to the full reality of the interplay between teaching and learning. When this experience is focussed, it lends the necessary concreteness to teachers' collaboration (cf. Little, 1990; Vescio et al., 2008) and can contribute to selective attention and knowledge-based reasoning (cf. Sherin, Jacobs, & Philipp, 2011). When these cognitive processes are embedded in social meaning-making and are combined with redesigning lessons, changes in instruction can ensue.

Interdependence of teachers' interaction with pupils and colleagues

This study shows that peer coaching with video has the potential to alter the interplay between teaching and learning by eliciting and driving changes in teachers' instruction. When we consider how the above outcomes came about, the evidence gathered makes quite clear that they resulted from activities and experiences in the two spheres of interaction represented in the VTL model.

For example, it was the pupils' actions and reactions which made the teachers experience tensions regarding the right degree of control over their pupils' learning activity and which challenged them to decide whether or not to retain activating instructional practices they had introduced. Then, when discussion with colleagues about repeated trials of these practices confirmed that they increased pupils' engagement with the subject matter, the teachers decided to develop and consolidate their new practices into routines (see the section *Sustainability of changes in instruction* above).

Two factors, then, crucially influenced whether and how durably teachers changed their teaching: learners' reactions on the one hand and exchange and dialogue with colleagues on the other. Both kinds of interaction were characterised by a close interdependence. As the teachers' professional learning unfolded, peer coaching provided a counterweight to their daily interaction with pupils. Classroom interaction demands high-speed decision-making and immediate action from teachers, inviting them to preserve existing practices, while peer coaching slows them down and encourages them to reflect on and change those same practices.

The above account of teacher learning confirms the argument put forward by Fishman et al. (2003), Guskey (2002) and Clarke and Hollingsworth (2002) that teachers' decision-making about how to teach and how to change their teaching depends foremost on its perceived effect on learners (cf. the section *Features of effective professional development*). Our study has clarified in which way peer coaching with video may intervene in these processes.

How the learning environment affected peer coaching with video

The evidence from this study confirms the canon of features of effective PD current in the literature (see the section *Features of effective professional development* in Chapter 1). What greatly supported the functioning of the PLC studied is that it arose from a dialogue between the teaching staff and the school's management. This alignment produced a common ground between both parties and a shared commitment to improving instruction (cf. Supovitz, 2002), which was made concrete in the form of release time and scheduling facilities, enabling teachers to engage in peer coaching. Collective participation over a sustained period – a necessary condition for achieving the outcomes sought – was thus fulfilled. Also, teachers' learning processes were characterised by goal-directed collaborative activity and a focus on subject content and pedagogy. Observation and visualisation ensured concrete and focussed examination of instructional practices. Last but not least, teachers cooperated in an atmosphere of community and trust, which gave them the confidence needed to open their classrooms for mutual lesson observation and analysis, to engage in experimentation and to enact step-by-step changes in their teaching.

What happened here, from an organisational point of view, is that on the meso-level of school policy, decisions were made to invest in creating opportunities for raising the quality of instruction. This made the teachers' PD efforts possible, even in the face of workloads as high as they are for Dutch secondary teachers (OECD, 2017, p. 388–389). Workload is a "frame factor" originating from the macro-level of national education policy (Dahllöf & Lundgren, 1970; Lundgren, 1973) which can place severe constraints on teachers' opportunities for making their teaching more effective (cf. Buczynski & Hansen, 2010). By causing relapse, workload can obstruct introducing and consolidating new routines in teaching, as was found also by Bakkenes, Vermunt, & Wubbels (2010, p. 540).

The school's investment in the PLC as a learning environment was a unidirectional influence operating from the top down, while the cooperation between teachers and school management during the PLC's existence involved reciprocal influences between the micro- and meso-levels. Also the interplay between teaching and learning and the teachers' collegial interaction in the PLC are instances of reciprocity. We agree therefore with Opfer and Pedder (2011, p. 390–396), where they emphasise that teacher learning should in large part be explained in terms of reciprocal influences. However, whether or not learning environments for teachers are created is a condition operating in just one direction, which either fosters or constrains teacher learning. This constellation of influences is an instance of how schooling operates as represented in the Dynamic model of educational effectiveness proposed by Kyriakides, Creemers, Antoniou, and Demetriou (2010).

The above account implies that the effects of the PLC studied probably depended on a specific combination of features in its design – a conclusion which already followed from my systematic review of the VTL literature (see the section *Conditions* in Chapter 3). Such combinations will have to be different in the unique situation of each school engaging in PD. In the world of special education, this need for situational adjustment has been pointed out by Gersten and Dimino (2001). These authors argue on the basis of research and experience that effective PD involves setting up collegial networks, building understanding of how pupils learn on the work floor and linking changes in instruction to pupils' performance (cf. also Joyce & Showers, 2002).

Creating opportunities for teacher learning through peer coaching with video

Peer coaching with video has potential for raising the quality of instruction not only because it can foster higher-order teaching and learning, but also because it is a form of teacher collaboration that is feasible for schools to organise on the work floor. To this end, we derive from this study the following recommendations. We present these from the perspective of school leaders who wish to create PD opportunities that will make teacher learning effective.

Facilitating sustainable competence development

Using video as a medium for PD should be firmly embedded in a learning environment whose design conforms to the canon of features of effective PD. To achieve this, providing teachers with working time is of essential importance. Time is the currency of education. However, it is not enough to just provide time. Teachers need "dedicated and protected times where [they] meet on a regular basis to get important work done" (Ermeling, 2010, p. 387), i.e. to observe each other's lessons, give feedback on instructional practices and use it for redesigning lessons.

These conditions can be fulfilled, when management and teachers agree on how to schedule working time not only for observing and filming each other's lessons during pair work, but also for following up these activities as soon as possible with peer feedback and discussion. Likewise, it is advisable to plan plenary meetings for collegial exchange across subject boundaries regularly, i.e. once every five or six weeks, in order to maintain momentum and commitment in the group.

In the long run, a necessary condition for these settings to function effectively is that they are sustained over time. Otherwise, teachers' advice networks may wither (cf. Coburn et al., 2012).

Combining VTL design features

To meet the challenges of guarding and raising the quality of instruction, a school's management and teachers should ideally define and embark on joint efforts. Once school management has invested in teacher collaboration and alignment with teachers on the work floor is in place, the question becomes which combination of features will promote the desired outcomes. This combination will probably vary across specific local contexts.

The findings of this case study suggest that in deciding about this combination, the relation between the two settings of pair work and plenary meetings is an important one. The basis of individual teachers' learning lay in their pair work, but the plenary meetings were necessary as a framework encouraging commitment and interpreting individual experiences in a broader perspective. To achieve this, the relevance of the plenary meetings for teachers' daily work should always be recognisable, while at the same time offering them opportunities for widening their views beyond their own school subjects and the specific pedagogies involved.

Voluntary or mandatory participation

A recurrent issue in the discussion about PD design for teachers is whether participation should be voluntary or not. Timperley, Wilson, Barrar and Fung (2007, p. 194) conclude from their literature review of the that engagement in active learning influences effectiveness more than whether participation is voluntary or mandatory (cf. the section *Collegial collaboration* in Chapter 1). Our experience with this issue is as follows.

On the one hand, openness to feedback and new information and a willingness to experiment clearly appear to be favourable antecedents for achieving outcomes. This is an argument for making participation voluntary. On the other hand, volunteering carries the risk that those teachers in a school team who need it most would refrain from efforts to improve instruction. As some participants in this study became gradually convinced of the benefits of peer coaching, we would recommend school leaders to opt for forms of nudging teachers to participate.

Allowing and respecting teacher control

In this study, translating thoughts about instruction into action was shown to be a highly personal process (see the section *Teachers' personal development in the profession* above). This points towards the importance of allowing teachers participating in peer coaching sufficient autonomy to engage in personalised learning, i.e. to set their own specific goals and agenda (see Brouwer & Yusko, 2009).

Similarly, teachers should be allowed to choose freely with whom to cooperate during pair work. Given the benefits experienced by the majority of teachers in this study, it does appear preferable to compose peer coaching pairs of colleagues in the same or related school subjects.

Principles guiding collegial collaboration

In this study, the value of the three principles guiding collaboration – volunteering, egalitarianism and ownership and voice – were clearly borne out. School leaders and teachers should therefore observe principles of collaboration which allow teachers to be confident that opening up their classrooms and instruction for collegial observation and discussion will serve exclusively to further their personal learning. The chances of promoting teachers' learning are raised when they work together locally in an atmosphere of trust and collegiality (cf. Borko, Jacobs, Eiteljorg, & Pittman, 2008). Then, frank examination of existing practices and experimentation with new ones can produce improvements in instruction (cf. Ronfeldt et al., 2015). The two settings of pair work and plenary meetings can foster these outcomes in different ways. During pair work, teachers can set personal learning goals and work on analysing and redesigning lessons, while periodic plenary meetings provide the forum for exchange on the team level.

Using the knowledge base about teaching

As noted in the beginning of this chapter, guidelines for the design and implementation of learning environments for teachers should be based on knowledge about the effects of teaching on learners (see the section *Features of effective professional development* above). Also, these guidelines should have a clear content focus (see the section *Focus on subject-matter content and pedagogy* in Chapter 1). An important issue in the design of learning environments for teachers is therefore if and how subject-specific expert input is ensured.

In the PLC studied, this input could have been stronger, but organisational disarray on the part of our university prevented us from recruiting subject experts from the staff of teacher educators. As it was, the participating teachers drew on their own subject-specific expertise and that of other PD providers. From our side, input was provided in the form of brief presentations and a reader containing a selection of practice-oriented articles on a generic level. This was appreciated only by part of the participants and/or after a period of delay. A better approach than providing oral and/or written information is to provide video records of other teachers' instruction for teachers to analyse, preferably as part of a package of web-mediated resources (see the sections *Conditions: In what kinds of learning environments do teachers learn when using digital video?* in Chapter 2 and *Conditions* in Chapter 3).

When such video records are combined with structured viewing guides pinpointing subject-specific effective teaching behaviours, this helps teachers notice and interpret those behaviours as well as judge and decide for themselves whether and how to use them in their own teaching. When teachers use viewing guides for self-viewing, this can help them target and develop effective instructional behaviours and focus peer feedback and dialogue (see Chapter 4).

Finally, rules for giving constructive feedback should be upheld during collegial discussions. Facilitators of peer coaching groups therefore have an important role. They can use specific conversational moves to encourage teachers to make the rationales underlying their work explicit (Andrews-Larson, Wilson & Larbi-Cherif, 2017; Horn & Little, 2010; Mumme & Seago, 2003; Van Es, Tunney, Goldsmith & Seago, 2014). Ensuring such input during peer coaching can increase its quality and thus contribute to its outcomes (for guidelines and exercises for facilitating peer coaching, the section *Analysing and discussing video clips* in Chapter 9 and Allen & LeBlanc, 2005; Humpert & Dann, 2001 and Martin-Kniep, 2004).

Limitations

Given the possibilities in the school where this study was carried out and given the resources available, we feel that it has contributed to reducing the knowledge gaps noted in the introduction to this chapter. The mixed-methods research design used on the basis of a causal-genetic approach has made it possible to explore not only the outcomes of teacher learning, but also how collaborative processes and contextual conditions influenced teachers' competence development and its impact on pupils' learning. In particular, the extended time span of this study has allowed exploring the impact of peer coaching with video years after it ended and thus producing scarce evidence about the sustainability of PD outcomes. As we assumed, a chain of events, i.e. a sequential and mediated type of causation, was involved (cf. the section *Research design*). At the same time, this study has the following limitations.

Firstly, it is a case analysis based in one site, in which the instruments used were developed locally. While their ecological validity benefitted from this approach, the conduct of similar case studies with an extended time span is desirable. To advance our knowledge of what constitutes effective PD – including the additional feature of observation and visualisation as suggested in the section *The catalysing function of video use* above – comparisons of case studies such as provided by Gaudin and Chaliès (2015) and in Chapters 2 and 3 are needed.

Secondly, this study relies wholly on self-report data. Including classroom observations would have been desirable to verify and deepen findings.

Thirdly, the pupil data are limited to their learning experiences. While we think it is productive to consult learners about what they experience as educative teacher behaviour (Lewis & Lovegrove, 1984; Lovegrove, Lewis, Fall, & Lovegrove, 1985), the resulting findings only concern their learning processes. Research into PD effectiveness should ideally also encompass data about pupils' achievement. As the MTP impact studies show, this makes it possible to trace to what extent and in which ways changes that teachers introduce in their instruction can improve pupils' cognitive learning and social-emotional engagement in school (see the section *MyTeachingPartner* in Chapter 2). Researching this causal chain is challenging, but evidence about how it functions makes a formidable contribution to designing effective PD environments for teachers.

Suggestions for research and development

Peer coaching with video has a potential which merits investment in researching and developing it as a strategy for teachers to make their daily interaction with learners more responsive and educative. To this end, we make the following suggestions for research and development.

To begin with, more evidence is needed about what constitutes effective teaching, not only on a generic level, but particularly in specific school subjects. As the pioneering TIMSS studies (Hiebert et al., 2005) have shown, video studies of classroom interaction can clarify what teaching a subject effectively looks like. In our view, such classroom research and investigations into VTL could and should inform each other, also in fields other than mathematics, science and literacy (cf. Riegel & Macha, 2013).

Secondly, longitudinal studies are needed to clarify further how teachers can develop subject-specific teaching competence with the help of VTL. The follow-up data in our study were collected years after the end of the PLC, so that it was sometimes hard for interviewees to remember and disentangle what were the dominant influences on their learning outcomes, activities in the PLC, other PD experiences and/or personal background characteristics. Such limitations can be avoided in longitudinal studies designed to include sufficient data points at regular intervals as well as classroom observations. This would allow for reconstructing teacher development not only on a group level, but also on an individual level.

Thirdly, this study has yielded several indications that individual differences play an important role in how teachers develop. Some teachers introduced more changes in their teaching than others and pupils noticed differences between individual teachers. Also, teaching experience and age influenced teachers' behaviour change. These findings suggest devoting more research to competence development over the career span than is now available. In such research, attention should preferably be paid to subgroup as well as individual differences depending on career phase (see the pertinent sections in Chapter 3).

Fourthly, this study confirms that teacher collaboration plays an indispensable role in peer coaching with video as a form of PD. Practice-oriented research should further clarify how teachers can collaborate in ways that contribute to improvements in instruction. The following topics appear to us especially worthy of investigation.

Different types of viewing – self- and other-viewing – of different types of video – model and action videos – in different situations – pair work and plenary meetings – probably have a different impact on teachers. It would benefit both teachers and facilitators to know more about how combinations of these parameters influence teachers' redesigning and changing their instruction. Research in this area could include how teachers adapt and adopt or emulate models they see in colleagues' teaching. Future research should also address how different degrees and ways of structuring teachers' lesson viewing may influence their becoming aware of the impact of their instruction on pupil learning (cf. Borko, Koellner, Jacobs, & Seago, 2011). Research in this area should include the use of viewing guides and other tools for lesson analysis (cf. Chapters 4 and 5).

As this study indicates, collegial dialogue plays an important role in how teachers translate thoughts about instruction into action. Research in this area could address how such dialogue influences teachers' judgement, decision-making and planning (cf. Yinger, 1979) as well as their practical arguments about introducing and sustaining changes in instruction (cf. Fenstermacher & Richardson, 1993).

Finally, it would be a valuable contribution to PD design to study how teacher teams benefit from support systems that systematically make collective and expert knowledge accessible (Fishman, 2004; Hiebert, Gallimore, & Stigler, 2002; Morris & Hiebert, 2009). The development of such support systems could be enhanced in particular by empirical knowledge about how and why teachers use evidence-based and web-mediated resources to develop their work (cf. Downer, Locasale-Crouch, Hamre, & Pianta, 2009).

Outlook

We began this chapter by noting the multiplier role of teacher education and PD for education and society. The argument that ensuring quality of instruction in schools can help raise pupil achievement applies not only to industrialised, but also to industrialising countries (cf. Bruns & Luque, 2014; Hanushek, 2005; OECD, 2005). This argument only gains weight as technological developments place increasing demands on the qualifications of teachers and the populations they serve.

Almost half a century ago, Dan Lortie (1975) argued that teaching is a semi-profession lacking an explicit knowledge base and that teachers, carrying with them "apprenticeships of observation", reproduce the kinds of teaching they themselves have experienced as pupils. Moreover, the expectations from pupils, parents, colleagues, school leaders and public opinion would discourage them from questioning and changing habitual behaviour and routines. We believe that this diagnosis need no longer apply. It is true that the conditions under which many teachers work foster a certain conservatism, especially the fact that most teaching takes place in fixed groups, at fixed times and in fixed places. However, teacher collaboration of the type taking place in the PLC studied can alleviate teachers' isolation in the traditional "cellular" school organisation. In such PLCs, teachers' instructional repertoires are amenable to purposeful change. Teachers can discover which of their actions help or hinder pupils' learning and change their instruction accordingly.

If quality of instruction is a key mediator influencing pupil achievement, then peer coaching with video may serve as a PD strategy that teachers anywhere in the world can engage in to improve their work. In this day and digital age, teacher teams with access to cameras, smart phones, laptops and the Internet can help each other improve their instruction, if properly resourced and facilitated.

In order to bring about significant increases in the quality of instruction, it will be indispensable for schools and governments to make structural investments in curriculum development and teacher collaboration and embed PD efforts in institutional policies that take teachers' needs and motives into account. It will be necessary to make these efforts an integral part of school life, so that teachers' professional learning can be sustained during their whole career span. The task of the education sciences in this endeavour is to engage deeply with and to support teachers in enabling their pupils to understand the world in which they grow up. Ideally, teachers' practical wisdom and scientific knowledge about the effectiveness of teaching go hand in hand. When this happens, pupils and teachers alike will be active learners.

7

THE PRODUCTION OF CLASSROOM VIDEO

Niels Brouwer

Since the digitisation of video, the use of video clips showing teaching and learning – for other-viewing as well as self-viewing – has been booming, offline as well as online. In the field of teacher development, as elsewhere, technological development has caused the production of video to be democratised. While in the analog era, video production was the reserve of professionals, now anyone can produce and distribute video worldwide. Video is no longer exclusively provider-generated, but has become user-generated as well.

These developments will no doubt proceed, but what is it exactly in classroom video that helps teachers examine the effectiveness of instruction? To seek answers to this question, I examine in this chapter how the nature of video material influences teachers' viewing experience.

Introduction

The development of video technology continues to generate new capabilities, such as 360° video (Kosko, Ferdig, & Zolfaghari, 2021; Roche & Gal-Petitfaux, 2017; Walshe & Driver, 2019); HV (Sauli, Cattaneo, & Van der Meij, 2018); mobile video uses (Baran, 2014) and applications of virtual reality (VR) and augmented reality (AR) (The Economist, 2020). In teacher development, these uses and applications are still in the stage of exploration. The possibilities and effects of DV use with more accessible and affordable hardware are better known, as the literature reviews in Chapters 2 and 3 show. However, even with regard to these applications, only a few large-scale survey findings are available indicating how widespread specific DV uses are and which characteristics of the video clips involved make them most useful to teachers.

In one study, Christ, Arya, and Chiu (2017) surveyed 208 teacher educators, mostly from universities in the US, about how they used DV in 977 courses. These

DOI: 10.4324/9780429331091-7

were mostly undergraduate courses in literacy and science. The respondents predominantly used ready-made video clips from the Internet to illustrate to their students what "good teaching" looks like. Most of them did so on their own initiative and with little infrastructural support from their institutions. Another survey focussed on the uses that 37,000 teachers made of one video platform, also in the US. These teachers preferred viewing videos about immediately practical issues, notably classroom management and parts of lessons or games. They attended foremost to the pedagogy shown and applauded the clips they viewed. What most attracted their interest was how pupils engaged in learning activities. Apparently, watching pupils in action especially spurred them to think about how different ways of teaching might promote learning (Bates, Phalen, & Moran, 2016, p. 24–25).

Survey research is also emerging about the utility of teacher-generated video, although still with smaller numbers of respondents than in the surveys about provider-generated video referenced above. Dobie, Leatherwood and Sherin (2021) found among 84 primary teachers participating in an online PD module about mathematics teaching that they were well able to capture classroom interaction in their own lessons with enough technical quality to make lesson analysis possible (see also the preceding study by Richards, Altshuler, Sherin, Sherin, & Leatherwood, 2021). This study also indicated that editing self-captured footage can encourage teachers to study the interplay between teaching and learning, in particular when this activity is guided by prompts (cf. Calandra, 2015).

What these findings suggest is that teachers appreciate video clips of teaching and learning in particular when they display pupils' learning activity and how their instruction influences it. This confirms the conclusions about VTL processes drawn from the literature reviews in Chapters 2 and 3. Showing the interaction within the instructional triangle, then, is one requirement that producers of video clips for teacher development should fulfil.

The impact of video production on teachers' viewing experience is an underestimated issue. There is an urgent need for more comprehensive guidelines for the production of classroom video, because the qualities of this kind of video predetermine what teachers can learn from it. What is shown in video clips of teaching and learning and how it is shown influence what teachers will perceive, how they will interpret and judge what they perceive and – last but not least – what practical consequences they will draw from their viewing experience. This is why I present in this chapter a checklist that teacher educators, PD providers and teachers may use when designing and producing classroom video. It is based on the insights described in the previous chapters and my own experience. With this checklist, I attempt to systematise which features of video clips may help teachers decide if and how they will change their instruction.

Before presenting and discussing the checklist, I provide some background on what is known from cognitive and social psychology about the human tendency towards bias in perception and interpretation. Also, because of the increasing role of visual imagery in contemporary society, I refer to a number of insights from semiotics.

The social nature of perception and interpretation

When teachers use video to understand the interplay between teaching and learning, this medium – just like other forms of representation – involves a mix of subjectivity and objectivity. It is instructive to address this issue by using the metaphor of sender and receiver, as it stresses that perception and interpretation are fundamentally social in nature. Video producers are the senders of messages and viewers – in this case teachers – are the receivers.

On the part of the sender, the realism and concreteness of video images make it possible to approach the reality of the classroom more directly than any verbal representation. In this sense, video use may enhance objectivity. However, at the same time, subjectivity is unavoidably introduced by the video producer's selection of images and by how these images guide viewers' attention. On the part of the receiver, willingness to perceive the outside world is at least a precondition for understanding it. At the same time, however, viewers' interests, needs and prior knowledge direct their attention and colour their interpretations, thus introducing a substantial amount of subjectivity.

The viewer as receiver

To start with the receiver part of the issue, we know from cognitive psychology that human attention is always selective. For teachers, this means that, like other people, they spontaneously attend to the sort of sensory input that affords them to react immediately to the events surrounding them. Such immediate, "in-the-moment" reactions probably flow from less conscious, value-laden "Gestalts", i.e. beliefs shaped by a person's biography (Dolk, 1997; Korthagen & Lagerwerf, 2001). Such beliefs influence people's "situation awareness" and differ depending on their cultural backgrounds (Miller & Zhou, 2007; cf. the section *Perception and cognition* in Chapter 2). In his bestselling book *Thinking, fast and slow*, Daniel Kahneman (2011) contrasts such spontaneous, intuitive modes of perception to more deliberate and analytic modes of perception, which require more time and effort.

These two modes of perception appear to relate in different ways to teachers' decision-making and action (cf. Kersting, Smith, & Vezino, 2021). While "thinking fast" enables teachers to react immediately to the flow of a lesson, "thinking slow" helps them look back on and reason about their instructional action in more conscious and rational, reflective ways. Applied to teachers' viewing of classroom video, this distinction means that, when video images engender a vicarious experience, this may make them think either fast or slow. When their thinking is fast, social psychology informs us that it may suffer from all sorts of bias. Then, especially, perception and thinking are intertwined and teachers risk falling prey to what is called the "fundamental attribution error" or the tendency to attribute events to personal characteristics rather than social circumstances (Ross & Nisbett, 2011). Another type of bias is "self-serving bias", people's tendency to attend to what they know and like while ignoring what they do not know and dislike.

Erickson (2007, p. 148–153) describes his experiences with having teachers view video clips without or with the help of viewing points. When viewing clips without such points, spontaneously, student teachers tended to overlook relevant pedagogical clues, while experienced teachers tended to search for a pedagogical narrative, thereby often confirming their practical experience and the beliefs shaped by it. It was only when instructions elicited more analytic viewing that the teachers began to see different things in the visual records presented to them. My own experience with using video with teachers is similar, as the example in Box 7.1 illustrates.

The conclusion is that spontaneous viewing is good to begin with, but for teachers to learn about and develop their teaching, analytic viewing is also necessary. The latter is not what they are usually inclined to do. Instead, it needs to be trained. Routinised, "automatic" perception of the work situation is characteristic of experts (Miller, 2011, p. 52 and 59–61). Therefore, it is valuable to focus such perception on aspects relevant to high-quality performance. Using explicit and research-based viewing points during teacher collaboration is an effective way of doing so.

Pitfalls to avoid in viewing and interpreting classroom video can be derived from the review of observation as a research method by Evertson and Green (1986, p. 183). The following are among the most salient. One should be aware of how "theoretical, experiential or commitment-based assumptions" and values influence one's judgement, for example "the assumption that because a teacher shows warmth to a class, she/he is also instructionally effective". Instructional behaviour observed may be unrepresentative of a teacher's usual behaviour. Also, an observer's "initial impressions [can] have a distorting effect on later judgments". One should therefore carefully consider what is the valid scope of an observation. When interpreting specific instances of teachers' behaviour, one should take into account the speed and simultaneity of the action in classrooms as well as the goal-directed nature of instruction. It is therefore always necessary to "consider the perspective of [the] observed".

The producer as sender

In 1972, the art historian and artist John Berger and colleagues released their now famous BBC series *Ways of Seeing*. In this series, they showed how persuasive images have been in human history. "Seeing comes before words", they say (Berger, 1972, p. 7) and exemplify this with images reflecting the history of the oil painting, the male gaze in photography, the display of worldly status and the public role of advertising. Their analysis is a seminal exercise in semiotics.

Semiotics is the branch of science that studies how people convey meanings to each other. These meanings are carried by signs, which are mostly verbal and/or visual. Applied to education, semiotics is useful for understanding how learners interpret messages (Tochon, 2013). In the interplay between teaching and learning, learners can be not only pupils, but also teachers, such as when they engage in peer coaching with video.

BOX 7.1 SPONTANEOUS VERSUS ANALYTIC VIEWING OF CLASSROOM VIDEO

For the peer coaching project described in Chapter 6, I produced an action video entitled *Geometrical proof* about a mathematics lesson based on cooperative learning. The goal was for pupils – approximately seventeen years old and preparing for university entry – to understand the criteria by which a geometrical proof is judged valid. At the start of the lesson, the teacher composed groups of four according to a random procedure and instructed them to prepare a plenary presentation in which the steps needed to prove a geometrical formula were listed in a logical order. After they completed their group work, all groups presented a poster with the proof they developed to the rest of the class and had a discussion about it. The teacher concluded this learning activity with comments synthesising all presentations and comments. Usually, one and a half or two 50-minute periods were needed to complete this lesson plan.

In a viewing exercise with this clip, I asked different groups of teachers to view it as a whole and comment on how they felt the teacher instructed his pupils for the learning activity intended. At this stage, I only asked this global question and did not provide any viewing points. Most teachers reacted negatively. They felt the teacher's instruction was unclear, he took a static position in front of the class, talked monotonously etcetera.

Then, during a second viewing round, I asked teachers to note if and when they saw the teacher in the video provide his pupils with answers to the four questions that define a good instruction for learning activity according to the Dutch psychologist Van Parreren (1988, p. 60; see the section *The relation between teaching and learning* in Chapter 1):

- What should I do exactly?
- Why should I do it?
- How should I do it?
- Why should I do it in this way?

In some cases, all teachers present during viewing would observe the teacher's instructional behaviour while attending to all four points. In other cases, different subgroups would each attend to just one of the four points.

Using their notes during the discussion following the second viewing round, most teachers discovered that the teacher actually gave answers to all four questions. Another conclusion they drew more than once went beyond the clip shown, namely that pupils often do not get answers to the two why questions, whereas this could greatly help engage and motivate them.

When one considers video use from the vantage point of semiotics, it quickly becomes clear that video production and video viewing are not neutral activities. As semiotic practices, they create value-laden meanings. This happens not only through the content that video clips convey, but also through their form features. The aesthetics employed in visual media shape viewers' expectations and interpretations. For instance, Erickson (2007, p. 145–146) compares the ways in which three different visual genres represent reality. Fictional film and video are highly scripted and edited and thus seek to immerse the viewer in a story. Documentary or ethnographic film usually stays closer to real events, but it still guides viewers' interpretation. "Minimally edited video", in contrast, renders the events filmed in almost raw form, thus challenging viewers to make sense of what they see. However, in all these genres, form features such as the length of takes and scenes and the amount and pace of zooming and panning do influence viewers' interpretations. Visual imagery is subject to conventions in which viewers are socialised. These conventions underlie their "visual literacy" (Dondis, 1973).

It is important to be aware what kind of role the content and form of video messages play in the interaction between sender and receiver. This has recently become even more important as artificial intelligence has raised the possibilities for image manipulation to new levels. These days, "deep fakes" can be produced, i.e. videos in which real persons or synthetic personae tell you things that never happened or report "facts" that do not exist. Although it is hard to imagine how deep fakes could compromise classroom video, this new technique does put the credibility of video images up for grabs (Schick, 2020).

Given the above considerations, producers of classroom video would do well to ask themselves what impact their work will have on their audiences' viewing experience. This is a tried and tested principle in the arts, especially the visual and the performing arts. The checklist presented in the following section is meant to apply this principle to the production of classroom video.

Guidelines for the production of classroom video

Teacher judgement is a missing link in VTL research. Still, it is an important – perhaps the most important – turning point in how teachers translate thought into action (see Chapter 6). Therefore, when one produces video with the aim of supporting teachers in improving their instruction, a suitable question to proceed from is this: Which features of video clips of teaching and learning help teachers judge and decide if and how they want to adopt or adapt the instructional behaviour shown?

The clip features promoting VTL, as I call them for short, are presented in Box 7.2 under four headings. The first category, "What is portrayed as good teaching", is about purposes and contents of the messages one conveys through video and their underlying assumptions. The second category, "Video type, capture and

BOX 7.2 VIDEO PRODUCTION CHECKLIST

I. WHAT IS PORTRAYED AS GOOD TEACHING

Explicit and implicit messages about evaluation criteria:

- learning processes and/or outcomes
- theory and/or empirical evidence about effective teaching
- practical experience
- ideological assumptions

II. VIDEO TYPE, CAPTURE AND EDITING

VIDEO TYPE

- trigger
- modelling
- action

CAPTURE

- image selection I:
  - whole lesson
  - parts of lesson
  - board
  - pupil work
  - related images
- participants:
  - teacher
  - learners
  - colleagues
  - school leaders
  - parents
- lesson structure:
  - learning goals, explanation and instruction
  - content and learning activities
  - whole-class, subgroup and/or dyadic interaction
  - transitions between lesson phases
- camera use:
  - number: one or more
  - position: stationary, hand-held or wearable
  - shots: long, medium and/or close-up

- movement:
  - zooming and panning
  - variation in frequency and speed
- microphone use:
  - one or more
  - fixed or movable

EDITING

- image selection II:
  - scenes
  - episodes
- linear vs. non-linear sequence
- transitions
- verbal information:
  - voiceovers
  - (sub)titles and captions
- music
- user control:
  - navigation
  - hyperlinks and hotspots

III. FRAMING

CONTEXT INFORMATION

- curriculum and grade level
- lesson plans
- teaching materials
- pupils' work
- background of learners and teachers
- interviews with learners and teachers

PERSPECTIVES

- generic and/or subject-specific
- resources
  - practice reports
  - research reports
  - viewing guides
- teachers' concerns and learning needs

- comparisons and discrepancies
- expert and/or craft language

IV. PRIVACY

- consent from:
  - school management
  - teachers
  - learners
  - parents
- duties of:
  - producers
  - viewers

editing", deals with choosing the type of video and with the clip features that come into being during capture and editing. The third category, "Framing", addresses how video clips can be contextualised and prepared for use during collegial collaboration. The last category, "Privacy", points out what to consider in order to guarantee the rights of all persons involved.

In the following discussion of the points in Box 7.2, my emphasis is on video uses that are feasible for teachers and teacher educators to implement under average work conditions. Where possible and useful, I add suggestions and recommendations.

What is portrayed as good teaching

Video clips of teaching and learning carry meanings about what constitutes good teaching. Whether explicitly or implicitly, they elicit notions and suggest norms about the kinds of instruction that teachers ought to pursue or avoid.

Please consider the example in Box 7.3. It contains an example of how normative issues in the production and reception of video are disregarded. Such disregard can lead to unwarranted suggestions about pedagogy.

BOX 7.3 "SNOEZELEN", NEGATIVE EXAMPLE

One of the videos appearing on an early version of the platform Leraar24 for Dutch teachers (see the eponymous section in Chapter 2) was about *Snoezelen*. This word is a contraction of the Dutch verbs for "browsing" and "drowsing". It refers to a treatment method originally developed for patients with advanced dementia and people with multiple handicaps. The seven-minute video clip – now removed – shows the application of this method in a school for special primary education.

Children are brought into a room equipped with relaxation seats and diverse objects to touch and play with. Lighting in different colours, soothing music and a scent dispenser create an environment providing multisensory stimulation. According to a voiceover at the beginning of the clip, this room is meant to activate children or to calm them down, "so that in the classroom, they are better concentrated and participate longer in group activities". In addition to visual, auditive and olfactory stimulation, also tactile stimulation takes place through interchangeable plates on an "active wall ... depending on pupils' needs." Here, children "become active" and "enter into communication with each other". In a question-answer sequence, one child says: "I liked it a lot." Teacher: "What did you like best?" Child: "The tub with balls." Teacher: "And how do you feel now after the snoezel room?" Child: "Fine and also a little active."

The teacher also explains that one problem of the children in this school is that they receive either too many or too few stimuli and that they have low awareness of their own bodies. Therefore, "sensory integration" is necessary. By lying under a "weight blanket", children "become aware of what they feel and where they are". This "works" during and after snoezelen. The snoezel activities are monitored in a log and observation lists are used to register to what stimuli a child reacts "in a nice way". This helps teachers to "take into account" children's feelings, also during a lesson. While a teacher strokes a child's back, the voiceover explains that snoezelen makes the children feel "recognised and safe" and that they develop a "close bond" with the teacher.

The video concludes with the recommendation that also other schools should begin with snoezelen.

In this clip, teachers are giving verbal explanations most of the time. The viewer does see children, but just one child is speaking for one second in a heavily teacher-led question-answer sequence.

One teacher uses quasi-professional jargon and speaks in rapturous tones, while she praises the impact of snoezelen, not only on pupils' experience, but also on their behaviour in the classroom. However, this impact is not visible to the viewer. What also remains unclear is which behaviours or reactions shown in the clip make the rationale underlying snoezelen plausible. How does one determine whether a child should be activated or rather calmed down? Are the desirable classroom behaviours of concentration and participation (also) a consequence of snoezelen? How do we know? What is the use of lying under a weight blanket? What benefits for learning can ensue from playing and lounging in a room whose atmosphere is dominated by soothing music and all colours of the rainbow?

A few minutes browsing on Google Scholar suffice to conclude that the research evidence about the effects of snoezelen on special education pupils is inconclusive (e.g. Lotan & Gold, 2009). No references to any scientific evidence accompanied this video clip. Nevertheless, other schools were recommended to introduce snoezelen.

When viewing classroom video spontaneously, teachers are easily led to judge the quality of the instruction shown by whether learners appear to enjoy the lesson. However, learning is not always fun. It can also be hard, but that may be necessary for the eventual outcome. Learners' momentary well-being is usually a necessary condition for learning, but it is not a sufficient condition for achievement. There is the paradox that learning requires effort and at times involves delay of gratification (Mischel, Shoda, & Rodriguez, 1989).

Another reason why during video viewing, aspects of process tend to override aspects of outcome, is that the immediacy of the medium makes it easier to show the processes than the outcomes of a lesson. Still, it is the outcomes that inform teachers best about the value of the processes. Ideally, therefore, video clips about teaching and learning should make both processes and outcomes accessible, so that viewers are enabled to reconstruct and understand how effective the teacher's instruction was.

The example in Box 7.3 illustrates the importance of being aware of the explicit and implicit messages one sends about the quality of instruction. What is portrayed as good teaching and how is this justified? Do video clips suggest that teachers should direct the course of a lesson to a high or a low degree? Or that pupils should work most of the time alone, in pairs or in groups? Or what messages could viewers pick up from video about who should do most of the talking in a lesson, the teacher or the pupils? Such criteria for evaluation deserve to be taken seriously in the design and production of classroom video.

To decide the issues addressed above, there are basically two sources of knowledge available. On the one hand, there is the propositional knowledge based on educational theory, research and evidence. On the other hand, there is the experiential knowledge that teachers derive from their daily practice, concerns and needs. Obviously, considerable tension exists between both. However, I see no inherent or necessary contradiction between them nor do I see reasons to glorify either. What we need, rather, are ways to strike a sensible balance.

Video clips of teaching and learning should not remain in the realm of pedagogical beliefs, but also refer to what is known from theory and research about the pedagogy of the subjects involved. They should, in other words, offer access to the pedagogical content knowledge (PCK) that is relevant to the lesson shown. At the same time, video clips need to address the issues faced by individual teachers working in unique local situations. After all, they have to judge and decide which instructional practices are valuable and feasible to pursue.

Finally, video clips may convey ideological assumptions. I define "ideology" not so much in the sense of worldview as in the Marxian sense of half-truths requiring scrutiny and critique or refutation (Behrens et al., 1979). When producing classroom video, it is therefore desirable to avoid confirming or encouraging bias and prejudice. In terms of the four classic categories of class, race, gender and handicap, it would be good custom to ask oneself: "What misunderstandings might I raise and how can I prevent them?"

The above considerations are foundational, but also rather broad. In the following sections, they are made more concrete.

The making of moving images about teaching and learning

Video production proceeds in three stages: planning, capture and editing. The considerations presented in the following sections deal specifically with video production for and by teachers. They are based on my own work as well as the work of colleagues. Useful publications to consult are in particular O'Dell (in Dowrick, 1991), a book chapter from analog times, but still very applicable; Van Es, Stockero, Sherin, Van Zoest and Dyer (2015), a report co-authored by LTN researchers (see the section *Learning to notice in video clubs* in Chapter 2); and Brunvand (2010). Comprehensive information about DV production in general can be found in Ascher and Pincus (2007).

Planning

What to capture in a lesson and how to show it depends foremost on the goal of the video production. This goal can be operationalised first of all by choosing the type of video – model, action or trigger video (see about these distinctions Table 2.1 Video functions and features in the section *Concepts and terminology* in Chapter 2).

When the goal is to present and explain effective instructional behaviours, making a model video is a logical choice. Where norms for the quality of instruction are involved, model videos are explicit, as they advocate certain kinds of pedagogy. Action videos are meant to support analysis of classroom events and therefore represent them as they unfold. This may make this type of video appear neutral, but also in this case, as argued above, normative implications are present. Trigger videos, in contrast, have a more controversial character, as they are intended to raise questions and promote discussion.

Regardless of which video type is chosen, the question presents itself whether to film a whole lesson or parts of it. For model videos, it may suffice to film only those events which clarify the specific instructional behaviours to be shown. Similarly, for trigger videos, it may suffice to film only those events which clarify the dilemmas to be pointed out. For action videos, capturing the whole lesson is preferable, because then, it remains possible to reconstruct the lesson as a whole and select relevant parts for analysis.

Choosing to film a whole lesson or parts of it is important because it is during capture that video producers determine what viewers may see in the final product. This is the first step in image selection. Later, during editing, they make further decisions about what viewers will see (see in Box 7.2 the entries Image selection I and II, respectively). In both phases of image selection, it is advisable to take into account if and which viewing points should guide viewers' attention and analysis.

The decisions to be made about image selection can be a part of scriptwriting. This approach was followed in the project Classroom Management Competencies (see the eponymous section in Chapter 2). Piwowar, Barth, Ophardt and Thiel (2018) describe the three-step procedure employed. The video authors first selected the teaching practice they wanted to present on the basis of the research literature about effective classroom management. The second step was to develop scripts for vignettes illustrating best practice versus problematic teacher behaviour. The final step was the video production itself.

For purposes of VTL, however, recording teaching and learning as they happen in full will be the prevalent case. Such "authentic" video requires relatively little preparation, at least less than scripted video.

Capture

As argued above, video clips of teaching and learning will only be effective in supporting VTL insofar as their features enable teachers to understand and examine the instruction shown. The key decision to take during the first step in image selection is therefore which images will make relevant events visible to viewers. Answering this question helps one determine whom, what and how to film. The following discussion of these topics is based to an important extent on the guidelines for filming followed by the videographers collecting data for the TIMSS-R video study (Stigler & Rankin, 1998; document kindly made available by LessonLab).

Whom to film

The first point to consider when preparing for capturing lessons is whom to film. The teachers and learners will naturally be recorded, but other participants, such as colleagues and school leaders, can also provide relevant information, for example in interviews. In some cases, it can also be useful to include parents.

What to film

Throughout this book, a variety of research findings demonstrates the need to make the content-focussed interaction between teacher and learners visible and understandable. Video clips should therefore reproduce the basic structure of the lesson involved. This can be achieved in many ways, but to bring across how a lesson unfolds, it is minimally necessary to show how the teacher orchestrates opportunities for learning activity by her or his learners.

Such orchestration can be made concrete by showing how the teacher clarifies the learning goals, explains the lesson's contents and instructs pupils how to go about exercises, tasks and assignments. In addition, it should be visible which learning activities the pupils actually perform, which interactions between them and the teacher take place and in which groupings these interactions happen – in the plenary setting, in subgroups or in dyads. An essential element to pay attention to is furthermore which kinds of feedback pupils receive and how (cf. Table 1.1 Feedback on mounting levels). To make the course of a lesson understandable, it is often illuminating to show how the transitions between lesson phases take place – including how pupils enter and leave the classroom. Finally, viewers will benefit when they can see what is written on the blackboard or whiteboard as well as samples of pupil work.

How to film

An ideal set-up to achieve a comprehensive record of a lesson is to use two cameras, one to capture the teacher's activity and another to capture the learners' activity. This is clearly the option of choice for research purposes (Ulewicz & Beatty, 2001). However, for teachers in everyday work situations, this will often not be feasible and one camera will be used (see Musburger & Ogden, 2014). In that case, it is best to have another person do the filming. This can be a colleague, a student teacher or even a pupil. Otherwise, the teacher herself or himself may place the camera in a fixed spot and use it as a "fly on the wall".

Regardless of whether one or more cameras are used and who does the filming, it is essential from which position or positions the lesson is captured. The best position is with your back to the daylight and somewhere in between the teacher and the pupils, as shown in the frequent situations depicted in Figures 7.1 and 7.2.

How viewers experience a video clip depends crucially on how the camera person handles the camera. To decide about this, the videographers in the TIMSS-R study followed two general principles. They firstly pointed the camera to where one would expect an ideal pupil to turn her or his attention. Secondly, they kept track of the teacher at all times (Stigler & Rankin, 1998, p. 15). How these principles play out depends on the types of shots taken and by the camera movements.

There are basically three types of shots. A "long" or "master" shot is wide, taken from the largest possible distance and encompasses the surroundings in which the action takes place. A "medium" shot is closer to the action and directs attention to specific events. A "close-up" shot is very near the action and focusses on meaningful details. Examples of these three types of shots in the classroom situation can be seen in Figures 7.3 through 7.5.

Viewers' experience is equally influenced by how the camera person switches between these types of shots. A general principle to guide camera movement is that the camera should not draw attention to itself, but to the events recorded. A camera person can achieve this by zooming in and out only when necessary and only gradually (Stigler & Rankin, 1998, p. 29–30). The same is true for "panning" or horizontal camera movement. Using a tripod helps stabilise the footage, but filming with a hand-held or wearable camera allows more flexibility. A useful compromise between these two options is to use a lightweight tripod and move it around while the camera remains mounted on it. To keep track of classroom interaction, one functional camera movement is to zoom in or out while keeping the teacher in the left- or right-hand upper corner of the screen. Another type of movement, suitable in particular for recording group work, is to circulate slowly among pupil groups.

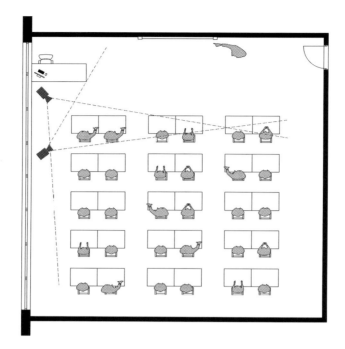

FIGURE 7.1 Camera positions with pupils in rows

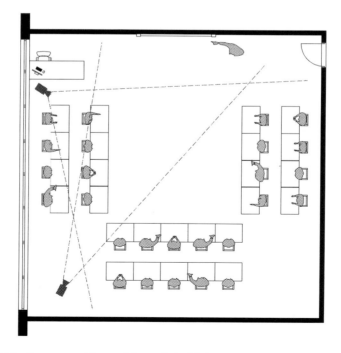

FIGURE 7.2 Camera positions with pupils in U shape

FIGURE 7.3   Classroom long shot

FIGURE 7.4   Classroom medium shot

Observing the above principles and practices conforms to visual conventions. As television viewers and consumers of film we have been socialised into these conventions. For instance, zooming in entails a request for attention, emphasis or suspense, while zooming out broadens one's scope and directs attention towards the environment. In panning, it is customary to follow the gaze of persons filmed rather than moving against it. When people are interviewed, placing them slightly asymmetrically in the image often makes for more interesting viewing than placing them in the middle (Stigler & Rankin, 1998, p. 25–29).

The above considerations assume that the teacher is filmed from what is called a third-person perspective, i.e. as seen by someone else. Another interesting option is a first-person perspective. In this case, teachers film their own lessons with cameras worn on a headset or pinned to their clothing (Miller & Correa, 2009). An

FIGURE 7.5 Classroom close-up shot

innovative variation to this approach is using a camera that offers the possibility to store during capture only those minutes of footage that teachers judge in the moment as interesting for further analysis (Sherin, Russ, Sherin, & Colestock, 2008).

Recording sound

An essential part of the production of classroom video, finally, is the use of microphones. For film-making, classrooms are a difficult environment, because they are full of ambient noise. Still, not only teachers, but especially pupils need to be well audible (Stigler & Rankin, 1998, p. 15). Whether one or more cameras are used, the best option is to use external microphones, as these usually produce better audio than built-in microphones. The teacher should preferably wear a wireless lapel microphone.

Using one camera with a built-in microphone is the simplest setup, so this will occur frequently. However, it is not ideal. When the camera person moves around the classroom and zooms in on groups of pupils or individual pupils, this setup can, but will not always produce sufficient sound quality. One alternative is to place an external microphone on pupils' desks or suspend it above them to prevent knocks and bumps in the footage.

Information specifically about video sound is available in Lyver (2005) and Thomas (2001).

Editing

In the beginning days of fictional film, scholars have highlighted the far-reaching influence of editing on how viewers experience moving images. In an essay from 1927, Boris Ejchenbaum (2003) reasons that the individual viewer's perception is bound to an inner monologue in which she or he continually seeks to make sense of what is shown on screen. The viewer, he argues, wants to discover the story. This idea equally applies to teachers' video viewing.

Classroom video needs to provide teachers with the minimum of information they need to be able to understand the lesson shown. In this section, I suggest a number of editing practices that may help achieve this minimum. More information about video editing can be found in Bowen and Thompson (2018).

Scenes and episodes

How teachers interpret classroom video highly depends on how scenes and episodes – i.e. sequences of related scenes – are selected and sequenced. When video producers make decisions about this issue, the total duration of a clip is an obvious concern. It is said that the longer clips are, the fewer viewers will persist till the end. Although this must not always apply, a useful rule of thumb is to make clips no longer than five minutes. Another reason to stick to this rule is that video is so rich that one minute of it can rouse ten or more minutes of discussion.

Retaining lesson sequence

How to achieve a comprehensive story about a lesson within five minutes? A well-known design principle is the minimalist maxim "Less is more", meaning that generally, providing less quantity of something leads to more quality. Consequently, when conveying information, one should present only core ideas and events in concise forms. To achieve this in classroom video, my main recommendation is linear editing, i.e. to retain in a clip the chronological sequence of the lesson and to inform viewers about the basic activities by teacher and learners.

As detailed in the previous sections, an important element in the structure and flow of a lesson is how transitions between lesson phases take place. These can be edited into a clip by using cuts and transitions between scenes. When deciding where to place cuts on the timeline of a video, it is a good idea to listen to the words spoken, as these often determine the flow of a lesson.

Still, condensing a lesson into a five-minute clip brings in the risk of undue simplification. Erickson warns that "rather than to simplify the visual image of the classroom by using close-ups, or by shortening clips, or by using clips in which everything seems to be happening smoothly and ideally", "new means of scaffolding for viewer attention and interpretation" are needed (Erickson, 2007, p. 154). Two of such means are addressed in the following section.

Including spoken and written words

While images can be captivating, it should not be underestimated how much guidance spoken and written words can give to viewers.

Spoken words in voiceovers can be a very direct and effective clip feature. To paraphrase John Berger, the spoken word comes before the written word. Narration can begin simultaneously with the images they belong to, but they can also begin briefly before the visual scene to which it refers.

Written words can be included in the form of (sub)titles and captions summarising during which lesson phases events are happening. Each of these forms can be used at the beginning, anytime during a clip and at the end of it.

User control

An important point to consider in video editing is which opportunities for user control to include. When viewing a video clip, teachers can always take notes of important moments on the timeline and move backwards and forwards along it while they analyse and communicate about a clip. Annotation software can support these activities. In any case, it is advisable to include markers of the structure of a video clip in the clip itself. These can take the form of captions, transitions and/or a hyperlinked overview of contents. User control can be further increased when video clips come with hyperlinks and hotspots enabling access to supporting resources (cf. Figure 2.1 Basic and additional features of hypervideo in the section *The special affordances of digital video* in Chapter 2).

Music

A feature that occurs repeatedly in commercial productions of classroom video is music. In video meant for entertainment, music is often used to influence viewers' moods. For purposes of VTL, it can be redundant or even irritating.

Framing

How teachers interpret and analyse video clips of teaching and learning depends not only on the nature of the video, but also on the viewing situation. Viewing situations can be placed along a continuum ranging from local to global.

When teachers within one school engage in peer coaching – in pairs, other subgroups and/or plenary team settings – the viewing situation is strictly local. When teachers view video clips from partner schools in the same town, region or nation, they are a little less familiar with each other's work context. When they work in different schools, sectors or cultures than the teachers shown, this lack of familiarity increases. When VTL goes online in electronic learning environments and worldwide through web platforms, the context becomes truly global and the teaching and learning shown can appear altogether foreign.

Now, the further teachers engaging in VTL find themselves towards the global end of the continuum described, the more information they will need to be able to understand the teaching situation shown. In other words, there is a risk that decontextualisation produces misunderstandings. This risk raises important questions about how video production and video viewing for VTL purposes interact. How can we reduce the risks of decontextualisation when producing and presenting video clips of teaching and learning? Which constellations of the viewing situation are most effective in encouraging teachers to examine, reconsider and possibly change their instruction? Minimally necessary conditions for productive video viewing are when teachers have working time available and find themselves in a culture of collaboration. However, even when these conditions exist, the influences operating in the viewing situation appear hard to disentangle.

Attempts to do this were made in two studies, which yielded findings that are interesting, but hard to generalise. In a study of 63 preservice teachers, Hatch, Shuttleworth, Jaffee and Marri (2016) attempted to assess the separate influences of clip features such as content, length and technical quality, the situations and activities involved in clip viewing and teachers' prior knowledge of and experience with video viewing. These researchers conclude that designers of VTL interventions should consider how all these factors interact in specific situations. One element, however, appeared common to the different conditions studied. When videos provided opportunities "to see [instructional] course concepts in practice, but where there is also enough ambiguity in the videos and enough time and support to allow for the development of different perspectives", it appeared a promising approach "to promote 'productive disagreements'" (Hatch et al., 2016, p. 283).

Beisiegel, Mitchell and Hill (2018) used a factorial design to study among 146 experienced teachers the influence of self-viewing vs. other-viewing, using video from familiar versus unfamiliar contexts and facilitator-led or peer-led video analysis (Beisiegel et al., 2018, p. 74). Only slight differences were found in the teachers' reflections on the videos viewed, but the "teacher-led, own-video condition [appeared] slightly superior to all other conditions", at least when constructive norms for collegial dialogue were upheld (Beisiegel et al., 2018, p. 86).

My conclusion is that the more widely videos of teaching and learning are distributed, the more it will be necessary to frame them. The word "framing" may carry the negative connotation of manipulating information for political purposes. However, this is not what I mean here. I use the word to refer to context information for supporting video viewing and to perspectives for guiding video analysis. I recommend to video producers firstly to provide the context information that teachers need to be able to understand and judge the lessons and lesson fragments they view. Secondly, I recommend providing different perspectives that teachers can use to analyse the clips they view. These are the topics of the following sections. Some of the following suggestions and recommendations may require more resources than are available to teachers and teacher educators under average conditions.

Context information

In viewing situations where decontextualisation can occur, there are choices to be made by video producers about how to select and present the information that teachers need in order to understand the teaching and learning shown. Providing such context information is possible by embedding video in hypermedia, i.e. a network of different types of media connected by hyperlinks in a virtual environment (for an overview of issues in media production for open and distance learning, see Lockwood, 1998). In its simplest form, this can be an offline folder with different files accessible from an index file and/or linked to each other. When placed online, hypermedia can be part of an electronic learning environment with access limited to teachers and teacher educators affiliated to a particular institution or of a web platform requiring registration or open to anybody. An example of an environment with limited access is MTP in the US. An example of an open environment is Leraar24 in the Netherlands (see the eponymous sections in Chapter 2). Both environments offer a variety of online resources supporting video analysis and enabling further study of specific instructional issues.

The types of information one can make available alongside video are no longer only traditional written documents. Podcasts, graphics and animations (cf. Herbst, Aaron, & Erickson, 2013) are also attractive forms. Whatever the choice, teachers accessing web platforms will make better use of the information offered when it is well structured and easily accessible and navigable (see the section *Video platforms for teachers* in Chapter 2). Users' professional learning will be served in particular by context information about the following topics.

Teachers viewing colleagues' lessons will want to know into which curriculum they fit and what grade levels the pupils are in. Secondly, knowing about the lesson goals, the lesson plan and the teachers' intentions in implementing it will help them understand and assess the instruction shown. Teaching materials and examples of pupils' work, thirdly, can provide teachers with further resources to study the PCK aspects in lessons (Seago, Jacobs, Heck, Nelson, & Malzahn, 2014). Finally, teachers viewing lesson clips can benefit from background information about the learners and teachers involved. One way to provide such information is to include interviews about what, why and how they are teaching and learning, as in the Didiclass project (see the eponymous section in Chapter 2).

Perspectives

To support teachers viewing classroom video, I argued above, it is advisable to provide them not only with context information about the teaching and learning shown, but also with perspectives that they can choose to use during collaborative analysis. To advance professional understanding and judgement, I advocated that such perspectives should strike a balance between evidence-based and experiential knowledge. Below, I specify a number of perspectives that may help achieve such a balance. This is especially important when videos are embedded in online platforms, because in that case, the teaching and learning shown are loosened from their original context. The risks of decontextualisation are real. Petko, Prasse and Reusser (2014), pp. 251–252) note that such platforms "are in most cases not aimed at differentiated annotation and discussion" of video content. Tochon (2007, p. 64) warns that

> [t]he potential of video cases is to bring a rich source of content for a community to use and change. Nonetheless, it seems to currently benefit the industry more than learning, and to propel neoliberal consuming in knowledge factories rather than community feel and shared experiences … the risk is that video cases transform knowledge into products whereas it should remain a process.

The issues video producers face in framing classroom video are illustrated in Box 7.4 with an example from the Dutch video platform Leraar24 (see the eponymous section in Chapter 2).

The example in Box 7.4 illustrates one way in which teachers' practical knowledge can be combined with relevant expert knowledge.

Teachers can benefit from such combinations especially when generic and subject-specific perspectives are related (for an example from mathematics teaching, see West & Staub, 2003). However, also other types of perspectives can be chosen, among others sector-specific ones or those dedicated to specific topics such as urban or rural education, special needs or technology integration.

When teachers analyse lesson recordings, they can deepen their understandings, when they get references or access to practice and research reports focussed on classroom teaching and learning. Video producers and/or teachers themselves can make the insights contained in such reports applicable in the form of viewing guides – on paper or in digital form. Viewing guides become especially useful when they contain observation points that are structured, evidence-based, domain-specific, focussed on classroom interaction and personally relevant to teachers (see the section *Intervention design* in Chapter 4).

VTL is further enhanced when video clips and supporting resources explicitly relate to the concerns involved in teachers' daily decision-making. Teachers' judgement and decision-making can be supported by contrasting and comparing multiple perspectives. When video clips and supporting resources highlight different experiences and interpretations of teaching, it becomes easier to focus collegial discourse on the rationales underlying teaching practices. For example, the practice of self-confrontation interviews developed in the Collaborative Video Learning Lab and Néopass@ction projects encourages teachers to view their personal experiences in a new light and discover alternatives for instructional action (see the eponymous sections in Chapter 2).

Such an approach recognises that discrepancies are inherent in the work of teaching. Prospective and beginning teachers, notably, face discrepancies between their expectations and the realities of work in the classroom (cf. the section *The influence*

BOX 7.4 INFLATION GAME, POSITIVE EXAMPLE

In the eight-minute video clip *Misunderstanding inflation*, a frequently occurring problem in secondary economics lessons is addressed. The clip begins with a fragment of a class discussion and the teacher's introduction from a lesson in which the card game *Horse trading* is played. In this game, pupils use red and green cards to simulate how bidding during an auction drives up the prices for the animals traded. The teacher and a PCK expert explain what current misconceptions about inflation – in this case demand inflation – entail. Then, we see how pupils in groups play the game. They take turns being the auctioneer, who displays green cards symbolising the animals traded. Red cards serve to hand out €90 entry fees to pupils, while each open green card brings in extra money. Following this fragment, the author of the assignment in the game explains that "integrating" the concept of inflation in this way helps pupils experience inflation for themselves. In the following fragment, the teacher discusses with the pupils how they experienced the game. While doing so, he asks a number of pupils to give definitions of (demand) *inflation* and provides them with feedback. One of the pupils gives a definition that is almost correct. The author of the assignment then states that teachers can motivate pupils with this game. Finally, looking back on the lesson, the teacher states that the pupils have indeed participated in a motivated way and have "almost spontaneously" given meaning to the concept of demand inflation.

What I find positive in this clip is that it shows how a lesson proceeds and that during almost a quarter of the clip, pupils are speaking. Also, subject-specific instructional considerations underlying the lesson are explained by the teacher, the colleague who developed the assignment and a PCK expert. This helps interested economics teachers develop ideas about how they may prepare and implement similar lessons themselves. The clip does not completely clarify which features of the game exactly assist pupils in acquiring the intended insight in (demand) inflation. The explanations about the game are rather fast-paced, so that interested economics teachers will be left with questions, also after repeated viewing. However, the clip is accompanied by (links to) resources about misconceptions in the teaching and learning of economics as well as suggestions about how to prevent and counter them. One of these resources is a publication including ideas for economics teachers intending to change their lessons.

of occupational socialisation on teacher learning in Chapter 1 about "practice shock"). They can therefore benefit from examining explicitly how the course of their lessons diverges from their lesson planning. Several VTL applications illustrate how such examination can help them improve their teaching, notably the Web-based cognitive apprenticeship model for instructional planning and Video for Interactive Lesson preparation by Mentor and Student (see the eponymous sections in Chapter 2; cf. also the section *Visibility* in Chapter 3).

By focussing on dilemmas inherent in teaching (cf. Berlak & Berlak, 1981) such VTL approaches help recognise that translating thought into action is a complex process for teachers and that consequently, competence development is a gradual process. VTL may thus contribute to countering obstacles to changing teaching, such as the "culture of privacy", i.e. the tendency to ward off any comments that might threaten one's existing beliefs and practices (Little, 1990) and the "culture of niceness", the tendency to withhold comments for fear of offending colleagues (Tochon, 2007, p. 57; MacDonald, 2011). These tendencies hinder teachers in considering and introducing improvements in their work. Instead, capitalising on difference, as I would like to call it, appears a valuable strategy to develop teaching through VTL.

A final point to keep in mind when producing and presenting video clips and related resources is to avoid unnecessary jargon, whether of the managerial or of the scholarly kind. Most teachers are willing to familiarise themselves with new insights, but they dislike terminology or verbosity whose relevance to their daily work appears unclear.

Privacy

When teachers and learners are filmed during their interaction, they expose themselves. This may make them vulnerable. Filming classroom interaction and viewing the recordings are therefore only allowed when all the parties involved have given their consent. Privacy has to be respected and confidentiality guaranteed. For video producers, this has consequences for how they capture, edit, store and distribute the images they make. In what follows, I discuss these consequences in terms of guidelines for fair use and good habits to adopt, rather than from a strictly legal vantage point (for overviews of digital rights management issues for teacher educators, see Ludlow & Duff, 2007 and Sonnleitner, Manthey, & Prock, 2020).

When a camera person films teachers and learners, they have "portrait rights". This means that the resulting footage, when they are recognisable in it, may only be published with their consent. The copyright to the images remains with the camera person, but her or his liberty to publish them is limited by the portrait rights of the persons portrayed.

In the case of teachers and learners, there are specific reasons to respect their portrait rights in the strictest fashion. It is not only that exposure on video may make them vulnerable. Already the interplay between teaching and learning itself makes them vulnerable. During learning, learners find themselves by definition in a situation where they have an incomplete understanding of the content and an incomplete mastery of the skills they are meant to acquire. Learners make mistakes and must be able to do so.

Teachers, similarly, work in conditions over which they have incomplete control. They may lack part of the means necessary to achieve the outcomes intended. Also, it is a fact of classroom life that unexpected events regularly occur. This inherent characteristic of the teaching profession is one among three dimensions of teachers' vulnerability distinguished by Kelchtermans (2009, p. 265–267). The second is that teachers can never be sure whether the learning outcomes intended are achieved, when and how this becomes apparent and what is their specific contribution to these outcomes. Thirdly, teachers must make manifold instructional judgements and decisions on uncertain grounds. If and how teacher decision-making promotes learning is never wholly predictable.

For all these reasons, teachers and learners are vulnerable to being viewed in a negative light, especially when the video in which they appear is presented in a decontextualised way. Now, in an age where populism rages virtually unchecked on the Internet, web sites even exist where people can "denounce" teachers anonymously. Such risks of teacher bashing underscore the need to guarantee the confidentiality of classroom video.

During capture, the camera person should adhere to the practice to place persons who do not want to be filmed behind the camera. It is also strongly advisable to avoid filming people in ways that they themselves might find uncomfortable.

During editing, it is wise to keep in mind a rule of thumb for when people are considered recognisable, i.e. when they are less than five metres away from the camera. If necessary, faces can be blurred during editing.

Where storage is concerned, video data are best secured when they are saved onto removable disks which are then kept in safe places physically separated from computers. It is a good habit to hand over files of classroom video exclusively to the teacher filmed, so that she or he can determine what will be done with it or not. The safest option is to save classroom video only locally and offline and never upload it to a cloud. Otherwise, the risk of privacy problems will exceed zero. Myself, I never upload classroom video anywhere. This, of course, is a very strict policy, so how about using video in blended learning environments and on web platforms?

Whether classroom video is distributed locally or more widely, it is always necessary to consider who is portrayed and who will be able to view it and in which setting. In principle, the wider the distribution, the stricter the rules for securing consent will have to be. In all cases, filming in classrooms must have the prior permission of a school's management and the teachers and parents or guardians involved. When video clips are used only for purposes of teacher development within the school and the teacher education institution with which it cooperates, it can be a sufficient policy to notify parents or guardians of this type of use. Such notification should take place in writing and in advance of filming. It should also include an opportunity for parents or guardians to decline filming their child or children. An example of a release form including such an opt-out is found in the section *Film and discuss your lesson* in Chapter 9 (for other examples, see Derry, 2007, p. 81–85).

When classroom video is distributed more widely than locally, other forms of consent are necessary. Especially when video clips are produced with the intent to include them in electronic learning environments and web platforms, video producers should inform school management, teachers, learners and parents in advance of this intent and seek their written consent by means of release forms which state explicitly how the images involved are to be published. When necessary, parties involved need to be given opportunities to define restrictions. When such images are published, viewers should commit themselves in writing to respect the portrait rights of the persons portrayed. This includes not distributing or using the video clips concerned otherwise than is necessary for purposes of teacher development.

8
USING VIDEO FOR ACTIVATING INSTRUCTION

Niels Brouwer

When videos are used for developing teaching competence, their content is classroom interaction and their context of use is teachers' collegial cooperation. When videos are used for instruction, their content is subject matter and their context of use is classrooms, physical and/or virtual. This chapter explores how the latter of these two kinds of video use impacts teachers' professional roles and how it may converge with the first.

Introduction

The developments in educational technology have profound consequences for teachers' work. The introduction of multimedia and electronic learning environments, in particular, expand teachers' opportunities to foster learning.

Since learning was institutionalised in schools, the predominant modality of information transmission has been text. Now, images and sound are rapidly catching up. Smart boards, laptops, smart phones and other devices enable teachers to present information through combinations of verbal, visual and auditory channels and learners to process this information hands-on. In science teaching, for example, Java applets were among the early digital applications that helped visualise complex relationships through animated graphics. They also enabled learners to manipulate input variables in models of physical phenomena and track what changes this generated in output variables. Another such application are computerised math games (cf. Roschelle, Pea, Hoadley, Gordin, & Means, 2000).

The potential of using multimedia in education is that they make it easier to represent and explain knowledge in ways that are more accessible and learnable than text alone. This can empower teachers and learners alike in generating understandings of abstract and transferable concepts. In other words, multimedia use may

DOI: 10.4324/9780429331091-8

help achieve higher-order teaching and learning (cf. the section *Quality learning and quality teaching* in Chapter 1).

Multimedia can be used in offline as well as online learning environments. In the classroom situation, teachers can connect the information presented in the diverse modalities of text, images and sound orally, but in electronic learning environments, these connections depend on hyperlinks serving to help learners navigate these environments effectively. Multimedia then become hypermedia. For teachers, the expansion of the traditional physical learning environment with online environments brings the challenge of blending offline and online learning activity. One strategy for such blending is "flipping the classroom", i.e. presenting lesson content and homework assignments through online video and other media, having pupils use these resources to prepare themselves for classroom learning activity and using class time predominantly for practice and feedback. When this strategy works as intended, it activates pupils and can thus raise achievement.

Blended learning with the help of hypermedia is causing a shift in teachers' instructional roles. Teachers' monopoly on information transmission has disappeared, so in the classroom, they can and probably will spend less time on this function in favour of supporting pupils during learning activities (cf. the section *Electronic learning environments* in Chapter 1). Teacher education and PD are similarly expanding from offline towards online contexts. This development has been accelerated by the Covid-19 pandemic.

The above perspectives for the future of schooling will not automatically materialise or raise the quality of instruction. To achieve this, certain design features will have to be built into multimedia and hypermedia, while teachers will need to put these to good use. These topics are addressed in the following two sections. Against this background, I describe two examples of teaching and learning in which video use for instruction and video use for teacher learning converge to strengthen the cooperation between teachers and learners.

Video as a medium for instruction

What makes video such a strong medium is its inherent combination of images and sounds. This combination is probably one of the features responsible for the effectiveness of instructional video (IV). The use of IV appears to be effective both in higher education (Noetel, Griffith, Delaney, Sanders, Parker et al., 2021) and in the upper grades of primary education and in secondary education (Lo & Hew, 2017). The combination of images and sounds has been shown to advance knowledge acquisition in a variety of situations. Richard Mayer, the founder of the Cognitive Theory of Multimedia Learning (CTML), has termed this finding the "multimedia principle" (Mayer, 2001). Below, I summarise what is known from research about the impact of multimedia and specifically IV on learning.

The central issue in this body of research is which design features of multimedia promote the acquisition of knowledge and skills and in which combinations these features are effective. Many such combinations are possible, because verbal information can consist of written and/or spoken words, while visual information can consist of static and/or dynamic images. Mayer's CTML is based on a model of human information processing which assumes that people's working or short-term memory has a limited capacity to process incoming information before it is transferred to long-term memory. The second assumption behind CTML is that for this transfer to occur, the learner has to perform focussed cognitive activity. The third assumption is that working memory can process verbal and visual information simultaneously, because such processing takes place through separate channels for words and images (Mayer, 2001, p. 41–53).

These assumptions have helped design experimental research into the impact of multimedia and explain its findings. Many of these findings are reported in the form of effects and principles that designers of multimedia may take into account. Mayer has formulated seven basic principles of multimedia learning (Mayer, 2001, p. 183–195), from which the following commonalities can be derived.

The coherence principle means that learners retain more information when non-essential words, pictures and sounds are omitted from its presentation. The redundancy principle means that when information is presented through animation and narration, more of it is retained when additional on-screen text is omitted. Together, these principles confirm the wisdom of seeking parsimony in multimedia messages, reminding us of the design maxim "Less is more" (cf. the section *Retaining lesson sequence* in Chapter 7). The spatial contiguity principle means that when corresponding words and pictures are presented near to each other, more of the information in them will be retained. When they are presented at the same time instead of following each other, the same can be expected – as formulated in the temporal contiguity principle. The coherence, redundancy and contiguity principles confirm the assumption behind CTML that human working memory can easily be overloaded. Multimedia messages should therefore be presented in ways that can be processed with the least possible cognitive load (Sweller, 2005).

The multimedia principle indicates that it is good practice to combine words and images, but this raises the issue how to do so. The modality principle states that combinations of animation and narration are more effective than combinations of animation and on-screen text, suggesting a preference for narration. This is confirmed in a research review by Kalyuga (2012, p. 156), who recommends using "spoken instead of written words when information is complex AND text is limited in duration AND referred parts of the pictures are cued or signalled AND learners are novices". Finally, the individual differences principle means that multimedia design principles are usually more influential among learners with low rather than high prior knowledge and spatial ability. Together, the multimedia, modality and individual differences principles suggest that the effectiveness of multimedia messages depends on how different influences interact in specific learning situations.

Research has yielded three further basic principles which are specially relevant to video use. The segmenting, personalisation and voice principles mean that "people learn better when a multimedia message is presented in learner-paced segments rather than as a continuous unit" and "when the words [in it] are in conversational style rather than in formal style and when the words are spoken in a standard-accented human voice" (Mayer, 2005, p. 6).

A good example of how these basic principles can enhance learning is given in an experimental study by Ibrahim (2012). This researcher assessed the learning outcomes of 226 students aged about twenty after viewing different versions of a BBC documentary about insect life. 116 students in a control group viewed the original, uninterrupted 34-minute documentary, while 110 students in an experimental group viewed the same documentary in a version edited by means of "segmenting", "signalling" and "weeding" (SSW). Segmenting meant that the video was split into "five conceptual segments … each about six minutes long". Signalling meant that "a one-screen introduction and summary" and "text-based cues for the main concepts" were added to each segment. Weeding meant that fragments non-essential for understanding core content were removed. After viewing, the experimental group performed significantly better on three knowledge tests (Ibrahim, 2012, p. 94–96).

Another characteristic of IV that may influence the outcomes of learning is whether users can control how they view it (cf. the section *The special affordances of digital video* in Chapter 2 about interactive video). Zhang, Zhou, Briggs and Nunamaker (2006) compared post-test and satisfaction scores of four groups of undergraduate students who studied the same content – the operation of Internet search engines – in different learning environments. One group (n = 35) studied this content using an interactive IV presented through an e-learning environment, i.e. they could access any portion of the video at will, in non-linear ways, by clicking control buttons. The second group (n = 35) studied the same content in the same e-learning environment, but using a non-interactive video allowing only stop, pause, fast-forward and rewind functions, i.e. in a predominantly linear way. The third group (n = 34) studied only PowerPoint slides in the e-learning environment. The fourth group (n = 34) was offered a traditional classroom lecture. The first interactive IV group significantly outperformed the other groups and indications were found that this was due to their using the interactive control buttons provided. Interestingly, the performance levels of the e-learning groups with non-interactive video and without video did not differ significantly. This suggests that just offering video does not necessarily produce differences in post-test performance. It appears to be learners' interaction with the content that makes the difference.

Further research into the specifics of IV use confirms the assumption behind CTML that learner activity is a necessary ingredient of multimedia learning. In two research syntheses, Fiorella and Mayer (2018) and Mayer, Fiorella and Stull (2020) conclude that learners benefit more when IV is segmented and when they can control how they view it by pausing and winding, particularly when the material is complex. Furthermore, adding subtitles to video narration when this narration is in learners' second language and adding prompts to engage in summarising or explaining material can promote learning. Learners' benefits also increase when practice activities with the material are accompanied by feedback. Finally, mixing third-person and first-person camera perspectives enhances learners' engagement. They benefit more when they can see the instructor's hand while drawing graphics and when the instructor shifts her or his eye gaze between the audience and the board. When the instructor's face is visible on the screen, this does not necessarily promote learning. This indicates that the phenomenon of "talking heads" may be a weak feature in IV.

In addition to the basic principles of multimedia learning described above, Mayer describes a number of advanced principles for multimedia design that are in agreement with the findings about online VTL applications summarised in the section *Video platforms for teachers* in Chapter 2. The advanced principles of "guided discovery", "site map" and "navigation" mean that multimedia presentations are better understood when they provide the user with guidance, navigation aids and "a map showing where the learner is". The advanced principle of "collaboration" means that participants in online learning environments benefit more when they are provided with tasks and assignments around which they can interact in order to understand and elaborate on the multimedia content presented (Mayer, 2005, p. 7). Such forms of CSCL were also found to be a strong stimulus to VTL (see the section *Computer-supported collaborative learning around video* and for an example the section *My TeachingPartner* in Chapter 2).

The teacher as multimedia user and producer

Since about 2010, teachers have used IV for their work at an increasing rate. One might even speak of a surge in IV use, beginning with video provided by publishers and educational institutions and downloaded or streamed from the Internet. Then, teachers as well as members of the public began producing and distributing video themselves, as a host of YouTube channels with instructional content testifies. This growth in provider-generated and user-generated IV, respectively, continues to be facilitated by the increasing affordability of hardware and user-friendliness of software (see for practical information about DV production for instruction Koumi, 2006 and Koumi, 2015). From a pedagogical point of view, this development further drives the shift in teachers' roles from "sage on the stage to guide on the side" (King, 1993).

Teachers find themselves operating more and more in blended learning environments, where facilities such as massive open online courses (MOOCs) are available and practices such as "flipping the classroom" become normal phenomena. Cheng, Ritzhaupt and Antonenko (2019, p. 795) "operationally define the flipped classroom instructional strategy as students learning with IVs and supporting materials before class and then engaging in interactive and collaborative learning activities that facilitate them to understand, apply, analyze, evaluate, and create during class." When implemented as intended, the flipped classroom strategy frees time for pupils to spend more in-class time on learning activities and for teachers to assist them with more contingent instruction and feedback (cf. the section *Contingent teaching* in Chapter 1). Teachers can now shift the presentation of content to pre-class time and concentrate in-class time on what is cumbersome to do outside lessons, namely cooperate with pupils in person.

Research reviews indicate that flipping the classroom leads to significant increases in learning outcomes (Cheng et al., 2019, p. 805–810) or has a neutral or positive impact on achievement (Lo & Hew, 2017, p. 8–9). Pupils and teachers mostly confirm that the advantage mentioned above of freeing in-class time for learning activity is indeed materialising (Lo & Hew, 2017, p. 9–10). Santos-Espino and colleagues surveyed in a sample of secondary and university teachers that appears reasonably representative for the European situation which video uses and styles teachers practised. They found that regarding frequency of use, the secondary teachers were the forerunners. Most teachers reported using provider-generated IV, while a small minority engaged in IV production themselves. Obstacles to implementation were experienced to a moderate degree. A lack of working time was the most prominent (Santos Espino, Afonso Suárez, & González-Henríquez, 2020, p. 153–156).

Overall, the respondents preferred the following video styles, in descending order of frequency: hands-on demonstration; whiteboard presentation; PowerPoint presentation; screencast; and chalk-and-talk lecture (Santos Espino et al., 2020, p. 156–158). In an earlier survey of IV styles in MOOCs, Santos-Espino and colleagues found that these styles were predominantly "speaker-centric" or "board-centric", meaning that IV presentations were either still based on the traditional lecture format or prioritised the visualisation of content (Santos-Espino, Afonso-Suárez, & Guerra-Artal, 2016). IV styles appear to develop constantly. They probably do so faster than research can keep up with (Lukeš, 2000).

Several authors referenced above touch upon the cost–benefit analysis of multimedia and IV use in schools. The production of educational media and video has always been a costly and time-consuming endeavour. Even though technological advances are making this less of a problem, it will remain a challenge for teachers and schools that searching, selecting, producing and making available IV resources require an initial investment, especially in infrastructure and in working time. This was also the experience of the teachers in the case study reported in Chapter 6. However, the long-term benefits of developing these resources appear to be considerable.

On the basis of their research review, Lo and Hew (2017, p. 13–18) present a useful set of guidelines for developing IV use. For teachers, important challenges emerge from these guidelines. Firstly, when flipping classrooms, they should carefully control and monitor the time pupils need to view, understand and process IV content before coming to class. Secondly, teachers should provide sufficient orientation and instruction to pupils for this new type of homework activity. Thirdly, they should seek to base production and use of IV on the principles developed in multimedia research (see the previous section).

What do the above developments and findings mean for the qualifications that teachers and teacher educators should bring to their work? In short, they need to become multimedia users and producers. It appears sensible and realistic to differentiate the qualifications involved. It would seem necessary for all teachers and teacher educators to be able to prepare and plan IV use while controlling pre-class, in-class and after-class learning time and to conform their IV use to CTML-based guidelines. Designing and producing multimedia and IV resources, on the other hand, can well be the work of an enthusiastic minority willing to make this their specialism (for an example, see Hathaway & Norton, 2012).

Technology integration in schools and institutions for teacher development probably has the best chances for success, when it is undertaken as teamwork. Personnel policy should therefore include investment in infrastructure and support for developing multimedia and IV resources and in working time for searching, selecting, producing and distributing these resources. A promising strategy for this work is design-based research, i.e. assessing user experiences with successive trials over the course of an iterative development process (cf. Pieters, Voogt, & Pareja Roblin, 2019; Madariaga, Nussbaum, Gutiérrez, Barahona, & Meneses, 2021).

Hypervideo for teacher–learner cooperation

Hypervideo (HV) is an IV tool which offers teachers and learners highly flexible options for active learning (see Figure 2.1 Basic and additional features of hypervideo introduced by Sauli, Cattaneo, and Van der Meij (2018) in the section *The special affordances of digital video* in Chapter 2).

In a project called IV4VET, Alberto Cattaneo and colleagues from the Swiss Federal Institute for Vocational Education and Training (SFIVET) have developed and tested a HV application called ivideo for use in vocational education and training (VET) and PD (http://ivideo.education/ivideo/login.jsp). This application consists of software for playing and editing HV. The player software integrates features enabling users to navigate through a video, to access related resources through hyperlinks, to annotate contents and to collaborate with others, all from one and the same screen. These features make HV a suitable medium for use in online and blended learning environments (Cattaneo, Evi-Colombo, Ruberto, & Stanley, 2019). The editing software enables users to produce HVs with these features by themselves. Teachers, PD providers, mentors and students in VET can apply at the Internet platform ivideo.education for registration as users and download the software they need for their operating systems.

The idea behind ivideo is that both teachers and learners get basic IT tools at their disposal which they can use as they see fit in order to cooperate independently from time and place with the goal of acquiring and developing knowledge and skills specific to their vocational field. ivideo is being used in training programmes for cooking, auto repair and fashion design and other fields of work. As the web site summarises, it allows users

> to customise and structure didactic material for his/her own teaching or training activity, using existing footage and linking it to all sorts of different resources (text documents, images, audio files, …). It also enables individual learners or groups of learners to insert notes directly onto the video.

Teachers and learners use ivideo during preparation, production and use (Cattaneo, Van der Meij, Aprea, Sauli, & Zahn, 2018, p. 10), the three phases characteristic for all video production (cf. the section *The making of moving images about teaching and learning* in Chapter 7). The purposes of generating and studying HVs with ivideo can differ. In initial VET training, for instance, ivideo can be used in collaboration with schools offering internships in order to "foster the connection between theoretical concepts and work practices" (Perini, Cattaneo, & Tacconi, 2019). Another example is the use of ivideo for expository instruction in a training programme for fashion design (Cattaneo, Van der Meij, & Sauli, 2018).

Depending on the purposes chosen, different instructional scenarios are possible, in which teachers and learners use ivideo in different groupings and settings. They can do so individually and in small or plenary groups and in online or blended environments. In all these situations, their roles may vary along a continuum ranging from teacher-controlled to learner-controlled. To illustrate this continuum, Cattaneo et al. (2018, p. 13–16) describe five scenarios, which I summarised in Box 8.1.

BOX 8.1   FIVE SCENARIOS OF IVIDEO USE

1. A mechatronics teacher writes a storyboard and records a simulated interaction with a client in the garage where he works. He edits the resulting footage in a video clip in order to illustrate how to serve customers in connection with electrotechnical problems. The teacher edits hyperlinks to additional pictures, schemes and documents into this clip and uses it in a lesson for second-year students. During playback, he uses these hyperlinks to involve the students in a discussion about the underlying technical and professional concepts regarding electrotechnics and client interaction, respectively.

2. An IT teacher, who also works as a software developer in his own company, downloads an existing video illustrating a practical case from the Internet. Into this video, he edits definitions of technical terms and quizzes. During a lesson in a computer lab, his students study the resulting HV clip and answer the quizz questions individually at their own pace, while the teacher is available to answer questions. Afterwards, the students work on a task asking them to connect their own experiences to the video content and argue their statements.

3. A former chef, who now teaches cooking, asks his students to film cooking practices in their workplaces while wearing head-mounted cameras. He uses this first-person perspective in order to procure authentic video material that his students can easily relate to. He edits fragments of the footage into a HV clip to illustrate different uses of the cooking practices involved and inserts cues and short reflective questions to highlight specific aspects. In a discussion with first-year students, he uses the HV clip as a basis for further elaboration on its contents.

4. A teacher in the field of commercial consulting instructs student groups to roleplay and record conversations with commercial customers. Then, after listening to a lecture and viewing a demonstration video, each student analyses the clips from two groups by annotating them. To conclude, the resulting notes are used in a plenary discussion.

5. A teacher of surgery room technicians gives his students a lecture on technical vocabulary and provides them with documents containing guidelines for how to perform a surgical procedure. Four subgroups of four students each then study different parts of the procedure, consult with the teacher about a storyboard for a video clip about it, which some group members record in a surgical lab, while others take notes on additional topics to include. Using these notes, the whole group discusses all the videos, both in class and online through the annotation function. On this basis, the teacher finally produces two HV clips.

By using ivideo to produce HV clips teachers, mentors and teacher educators can build collections of locally relevant, subject-specific VET materials. By uploading them on the ivideo platform, they can make these materials accessible anytime anywhere to colleagues in their own and other training programmes. By using them in scenarios as illustrated in Box 8.1 they can use the HV affordances operationalised in ivideo to activate learners towards higher-order learning. As these scenarios show, teaching and learning with the help of HV clips may also involve shifts in teachers' and learners' roles. From a vertical relationship with learners, in which the teacher has a predominantly transmissive role, she or he may move towards a horizontal relationship characterised more by cooperation. The potential of HV use is to make information transmission more efficient and to transform teaching and learning into active co-production between teachers and learners.

Video for pupil consultation

One way for teachers to seek productive working relationships with pupils is to consult them periodically about their learning experiences. In this section, I illustrate how video can be used for this purpose.

Pupils generally come to school with the expectation that they will learn and they experience teaching day in day out. For these reasons, pupils can be a valuable source of feedback for teachers. Consulting them about what helps or hinders their learning is a sensible strategy for improving the quality of schooling (Flutter & Rudduck, 2004; Rudduck & McIntyre, 2007).

Two teachers, one of whom participated in the peer coaching project reported in Chapter 6, developed a series of lessons entitled tEchna about the theme of Electricity. Below, I describe this lesson series and how video was used as one of the instruments to evaluate it in dialogue with pupils.

tEchna, a project about Electricity

The goal of tEchna was to acquaint pupils with the societal challenge of sustainable energy production in the 21st century. 27 pupils aged about thirteen participated during six weeks in four coordinated 50-minute lessons as scheduled for the subjects of technology and science. Each week, the technology teacher carried out a 100-minute practicum in a laboratory room and the science teacher two 50-minute theory lessons. In the science lessons, the pupils studied physical and social topics involved in energy production – such as magnetism and the transition from fossil to renewable energy sources, respectively – while in the technology lessons, they experienced the same topics by building models of electromotors and wind turbines. A study guide included content materials, study and practice assignments, an activity log and a report card. All pupils worked on the study assignments in dyads (cf. Topping & Ehly, 1998; O'Donnell & King, 1999) and on the practice assignments in subgroups of four (cf. Cohen, 1994). They concluded their work with subgroup presentations during the last week about the questions "Which mix of energy sources do you expect in the Netherlands twenty years from now?" and "What are the pros and cons of these sources?"

The above materials and assignments were meant to guide the pupils during self-directed learning activity in ways that would allow them optimal autonomy, i.e. encouraging them on the one hand towards active discovery without having to lose their sense of direction or to waste time and energy on the other. While developing and implementing tEchna, the teachers saw it as their instructional challenge to find a productive middle road between these opposites.

Evaluating tEchna

To evaluate tEchna, I filmed all technology lessons and part of the science lessons, as well as mid-term interviews with the technology teacher and one subgroup of pupils. The interview questions were derived in part from the project Learners' Perspective Study undertaken by David Clarke and colleagues (Clarke et al., n.d.; see Box 8.2). In addition, I developed and administered in cooperation with the teachers a written survey for the pupils containing four-point Likert scales and open questions about the study guide, their cooperation in subgroups and their help-seeking behaviour during their learning activities (Karabenick, 1998). Nineteen of the 27 pupils, i.e. 70%, completed this survey at the end of the lesson series.

To inform other teachers in the school, I edited fragments from the lessons and mid-term interviews into an action video along the lines suggested in the section *The making of moving images about teaching and learning* in Chapter 7. This video was presented during the annual conference of the Dutch Association of Teacher Educators. In the last lesson of tEchna, it served as an introduction to a presentation of the survey findings to the pupils and the teachers. This presentation and the

BOX 8.2 QUESTIONS FOR VIDEO INTERVIEWS WITH TEACHERS AND PUPILS

Instructions for the camera person/interviewer
To start with, speak into the microphone:

- which lesson this interview is about
- who is the teacher
- when and where the interview took place
- your own name

Not all of the below questions are necessary. Please select and vary. Use your observations to elaborate.

1. How do you feel about this lesson?
2. Was it different than usual?
3. If so, what was different?
4. Which pupil actions or reactions did you find special or important? Please explain.
5. Which part(s) of the lesson was particularly important to you? Please elaborate.
6. How did the group work go?
7. How did the pupils react to your
   - instructions,
   - assistance,
   - feedback?
   Please explain.
8. How did the pupils cooperate in
   - dividing work,
   - managing time,
   - presenting work?
9. Could you allow more freedom to some groups than others?
10. If so, why did this work out well or less well?
11. Did you compose the groups or was this done differently? Please explain how and why.
12. Did any pupils "lean on" others?
13. Did you try to prevent or correct this?
14. How did this influence the lesson?
15. How much did the pupils learn from this lesson?
16. What was the goal of this lesson?
17. Do you feel this goal was reached?
18. Which part(s) of the lesson was/were most instructive? Please explain.
19. Which part(s) of the lesson was/were least instructive? Please explain.

Instructions for the camera person/interviewer
To start with, speak into the microphone:

- which lesson this interview is about
- which pupils are present
- when and where the interview took place
- your own name

Not all of the below questions are necessary. Please select and vary. Use your observations to elaborate.

1. How do you feel about this lesson?
2. Was it different than usual?
3. If so, what was different?
4. Which of the teachers'
   - explanations,
   - instructions,
   - help
   were the most useful to you? Please explain.
5. Which of the teacher's
   - explanations,
   - instructions,
   - help
   were the least useful to you? Please explain.
6. How did the group work go?
7. Within your group, how did you
   - divide who did what,
   - decide when work should be ready?
8. How did you like presenting your work to others?
9. How did you like the assignments?
   - too many/too few?
   - difficult/easy?
10. Did you have enough time for the assignments? Please explain.
11. Do you like learning in groups? Please explain.
12. How much did you learn in this lesson?
13. What did you learn/discover in this lesson?
14. From which part(s) of the lesson did you learn most? Please explain.
15. From which part(s) of the lesson did you learn least? Please explain.

discussion I had about it with the pupils were filmed by the science teacher, while the technology teacher circulated through the group with a hand-held microphone.

The survey findings show that almost all pupils appreciated and enjoyed the group work they engaged in. They felt it made learning easier and more effective. Almost three quarters found the explanations in the study guide clear. In particular, the figures provided in this guide were experienced as helpful, but the pupils stressed that it should always be clear how figures relate to the text. They also suggested providing more preselected Internet resources to help them answer the theory questions in the study guide.

The assignments and activity log had helped the pupils keep their cooperation on track. Clear majorities felt that they succeeded in dividing the work assigned and discussing it together. If any group member was late doing homework, the others would order them to catch up and sometimes even give them extra work. During the discussion of the findings, pupils estimated that they voluntarily spent on average one and a half to two hours' extra time outside lessons per week on tEchna work in the laboratory room.

Most of the discussion with the pupils was devoted to the issue what was helpful for the subgroups to proceed with their work by themselves. The activities reported as most helpful for this purpose were explaining content and assignments to each other and discussing together how to interpret figures. Vigorous discussion arose about when and why to consult the teacher. The pupils agreed that it would be a good rule to first try and find out things within your subgroup, but they did want to be able to decide for themselves when they would approach the teacher. Understandably, they found queues at the teacher's table inefficient, but they expected this issue to solve itself, because nobody would want to wait too long anyway. In his mid-term interview, the technology teacher remarked about this issue that his science colleague and he chose not to circulate too often through the classroom. "In that way," he said, "you get rid of most unnecessary questions".

Conclusion

Filming the lessons, the mid-term interviews and the evaluative discussion with pupils has generated a concrete visual record of the tEchna lesson series. Such a record can provide teachers with feedback about pupils' learning experiences and serve as input for curriculum development, making teaching and learning accessible in concrete detail to colleagues within and outside a school. Further digitising and packaging the contents, study guide and evaluation of lesson series such as tEchna in the form of hypermedia or HV would be an approach in which VTL and IV converge and contribute towards developing learning as well as teaching.

9

RESOURCES FOR PRACTITIONERS

Niels Brouwer

In the preceding chapters of this book, I have described a range of DV applications and their uses for purposes of teacher development. In addition, I reviewed the available evidence base (Chapters 1 through 3). I then reported my own research (Chapters 4 through 6), proposed guidelines for the production of classroom video (Chapter 7) and explored developments in instructional video (Chapter 8). Together, these chapters provide the basis for the practical lessons drawn in this final chapter. These lessons take the form of resources for practitioners.

To begin with, an overview is given of publicly accessible video platforms for teachers. Then follow resources that schools, teacher education programmes and PD providers can use to implement VTL. Issues to consider when organising peer coaching with video are summarised as well as issues regarding data protection and how to produce viewing guides. Building on these resources, I present a manual for filming and analysing lessons. In conclusion, I summarise guidelines for producing classroom video, using instructional video and consulting learners.

The resources in this chapter are presented in a loosely chronological order, i.e. beginning with the task of creating conditions conducive to teacher learning and moving from there to practices for optimising VTL processes. All resources, except the first, are formulated as short recommendations in the second person and the imperative voice. I choose this form only for brevity's sake, so they are not to be understood as commands, but rather as "can do" statements. I invite readers to judge for themselves to what extent and in which ways these recommendations are sensible and feasible to follow in their own unique, local situations. Most resources are placed in Boxes 9.1 through 9.9, including references to underlying chapters and sections. All resources can also be found on the companion web site to this book, www.teacheredsupport.net.

DOI: 10.4324/9780429331091-9

Video platforms listed

Table 9.1 contains a list of video platforms for teachers which are publicly accessible at no cost. This list is not exhaustive, if only because Internet resources are dynamic. Only such platforms were included in which videos of classroom teaching and learning are the central resource. Another criterion for inclusion was that – at the time of writing – platforms were well maintained and navigable. Platforms providing video for instructional purposes were excluded.

The first column in Table 9.1 states each platform's name and Internet address. The second column gives information about registration. In most cases, registration is necessary to log in and enjoy full functionality (see the legend below the table). The third column specifies in which language(s) the videos and/or any additional resources on a platform – such as transcriptions, lesson plans, teaching materials and suggestions for further reading – are. The fourth and fifth columns show in which school types the videos were recorded (see legend) and which school subjects are shown, respectively. The last column characterises which type(s) of videos a platform mostly includes (see legend). The platforms Leraar24 and Néopass@ction are described in the section *Video platforms for teachers* in Chapter 2. More information about ivideo is given in the section *Hypervideo for teacher–learner cooperation* in Chapter 8.

Most video platforms in Table 9.1 were created in the US. However, the one platform from Germany, Unterrichtsvideos.net, is a portal to eight separate platforms developed by higher education institutions. The remaining platforms are from France, Switzerland, the Netherlands and Chile. The TIMSS project (referenced in the section *Science Teachers Learning from Lesson Analysis* in Chapter 2) was the basis for the development of the three platforms Timssvideo, Unterrichtsvideos. ch and Teknoclips. In all, lessons in eight different languages can be viewed. More videos are from primary and secondary than from vocational schools. Besides the subject of mathematics, which is clearly predominant, at least eight other subjects are represented.

Organising and facilitating peer coaching with video

Box 9.1 provides school leaders and teacher leaders with guidelines for organising and facilitating peer coaching with video as a form of workplace learning for teachers. It summarises how schools can create the organisational conditions needed to make teacher peer coaching with video effective.

Data protection

Box 9.2 summarises which points producers of classroom video should attend to during the various production stages in order to guard the privacy of all persons involved. Box 9.2 has no legal status. Its contents are recommendations for fair use.

TABLE 9.1 Publicly accessible video platforms

Platform	Log-in	Language(s)	School type(s)	School subject(s)	Video type(s)
Everyday Mathematics Virtual Learning Community **https://vlc.uchicago.edu/**	+ -	English	P	Mathematics	A
Inside Mathematics **https://www.insidemathematics.org/** **classroom-videos/public-lessons**	-	English	P S	Mathematics	A
ivideo **http://ivideo.education/ivideo/login.jsp**	+	English French German Italian	V	vocational	A
Leraar24 **www.leraar24.nl**	-	Dutch	P S V	all	M A
Néopass@ction **http://neo-ens.lyon.fr**	+	French	P S	all	A T
Réseau Canopé **https://www.reseau-canope.fr/BSD/index.aspx**	+ -	French	P S	all	M A
Timssvideo **http://timssvideo.com/**	-	Chinese Czech English German Japanese	S	Mathematics Science	A

(Continued)

TABLE 9.1 (Continued)

Platform	Log-in	Language(s)	School type(s)	School subject(s)	Video type(s)
Unterrichtsvideos.ch **http://www.unterrichtsvideos.ch/**	+ -	German	P S	Drawing English German History Informatics Mathematics Human geography	A
Unterrichtsvideos.net **www.unterrichtsvideos.net**	+ -	German	P S	all	M A
Videomosaic **https://videomosaic.org/**	+ -	English	P S	Mathematics	M A
Videotecadocente **http://videotecadocente.cl**	+	Spanish	P S	Mathematics Spanish	M
Teknoclips **www.teknoclips.org**	+	English	P S	Mathematics	A

Legend:
Log-in: – not necessary; + necessary; + – necessary for full functionality
School type(s): P primary; S secondary; V vocational
Video type(s): M model; A action; T trigger (cf. Table 2.1)

BOX 9.1 ORGANISATIONAL CONDITIONS FAVOURING PEER COACHING WITH VIDEO

- Let school management and teacher team agree about goals, organisation and procedures.
- Make participation voluntary, but do not shy away from gentle nudging.
- Facilitate participating teachers with release time.
- Make different groupings (dyads, subgroups, plenary group) and settings (offline, online, blended) possible.
- Compose teacher pairs from the same or related school subjects.
- Schedule time for teacher pairs not only to observe, but also to discuss each other's lessons.
- Organise plenary meetings for teacher teams about every six weeks.
- Make both practice-oriented and evidence-based resources accessible online.
- Provide technical support.

Underlying chapters and sections:

2. Imaging teacher learning. From analog to digital
   Conditions: In what kinds of learning environments do teachers learn when using digital video?
3. Changing instruction through Visual Teacher Learning
   Conditions
6. Activating learners. The impact of peer coaching with video on teaching and learning
   Case description
   Discussion

Producing viewing guides

The research reported in Chapters 4 and 5 shows that the use of SVGs to support video analysis increases the effectiveness of VTL. SVGs can focus teachers' attention on relevant aspects of teaching and learning while reducing bias in interpretation. To achieve this, it is helpful when SVGs possess certain features. These features are summarised in Box 9.3. They specify which content and form SVGs should have in order to maximise the probability that teachers will learn from using them.

BOX 9.2 GUARDING PRIVACY

- Before filming in classrooms and schools, inform and obtain consent from school management, teachers, pupils and their parents/guardians.
- Use written consent forms specifying copyrights and portrait rights involved during capture, editing, storage and distribution of all images.
- During capture,
  - place persons who do not want to be filmed behind the camera and
  - avoid filming people in ways they might find uncomfortable.
- Save video files on separate removable disks.
- Never upload video files, unless written consent was obtained from the school leaders, teachers, pupils and/or parents/guardians involved specifying for which purposes and in which situations the images concerned may be used.
- Use and distribute classroom video only for purposes of teacher development.

Underlying chapters and sections:

7. The production of classroom video
   Privacy

When teachers and teacher educators produce SVGs, it is advisable to use different types of sources. Findings from local quality assurance efforts will help target SVGs on the learning needs of teachers in the specific situation at hand, as in the peer coaching project described in Chapter 6 (see the section *Case description*). Consulting practice-oriented publications as well as research articles will help ground practical work for teacher development in evidence-based knowledge. Examples of sources aiming at such a combination are MTP (see the section *MyTeachingPartner* in Chapter 2) and *"Teaching diagnostics"*, a book (Helmke, 2009) and web site (www.unterrichtsdiagnostik.de) produced in Germany.

Film and discuss your lesson

The following manual is a do-it-yourself guide for teachers who want to engage in peer coaching with video. It specifies step by step what you need to do to prepare for filming lessons, to conduct the filming itself and edit the resulting footage, to share video clips, to analyse and discuss them with colleagues and to use the conclusions for planning new lessons.

BOX 9.3   FEATURES OF STRUCTURED VIEWING GUIDES

Formulate viewing points so that they:

- describe effective teacher behaviours
- on generic and/or domain-specific levels,
- are observable in the interaction between teacher and pupils,
- link expert and craft language,
- are structured in categories and
- allow teachers to select and/or add viewing points based on personal learning goals.

Underlying chapters and sections:

1. Introduction
   Quality learning and quality teaching
2. Imaging teacher learning. From analog to digital
   Perception and cognition
4. The power of video feedback with structured viewing guides
   Intervention design
   Conclusions and implications
7. The production of classroom video
   The social nature of perception and interpretation

Preparing for peer coaching with video

A1. Consult with school management to determine which privacy policy the school has regarding filming in classrooms and follow this policy at all times.

A2. For filming in classrooms, seek consent from parents and guardians.

When lessons are filmed, the portrait rights of all people involved – first of all pupils and teachers – must be respected, as detailed in the section *Privacy* in Chapter 7. This can only be ensured when the school informs parents and guardians in advance of filming. A feasible policy is for the school to include a general statement in the school guide informing parents and guardians that lessons can be filmed and that this will serve purposes of teacher development only. However, when filming is actually undertaken, it is still necessary to inform parents and guardians in advance of each specific instance and to offer them the possibility of an opt-out. For this purpose, Box 9.4 contains a template letter including an opt-out form.

BOX 9.4   TEMPLATE LETTER AND OPT-OUT FORM FOR FILMING IN CLASSROOMS

To: parents/guardians of pupils in class [...]
Re: video recording of lesson(s) [...]
[place; date]

Dear parent/guardian,

Our school [name] cooperates with [teacher education institution] in order to contribute to teacher education and professional development. To achieve these goals, video recordings will be made in the following lesson(s) to your child's class: [specify]. The purpose of these recordings is to help teachers study how they can make their work as effective as possible. [If applicable:] Also, short interviews with pupils will be recorded immediately after the lesson(s).

The recordings will be used exclusively for teacher education and professional development. This means that they will be studied only by the teachers and teacher educators involved.

We hope that you will consent to video recording for this purpose. Should this not be the case – for any reason – we request you to notify us before [date] using the response slip below. Then we will ensure that no video recordings of your child are made. If you wish to receive more information about the use of video for teacher education and professional development, please contact me/us.

Yours sincerely,

[name, function and email address of school leader(s) responsible]

Response slip regarding video recordings in [class] (please hand in to [...])

I object against video recordings being made of pupil ....
in the lesson(s) [...] in [class] of [school].

Date: ....

Name parent/guardian: ....

Signature: ....

A3. Choose the class and the lesson(s) in which you want to film. Inform your pupils in advance what is the purpose of filming – you want to make teaching more effective in collaboration with colleagues.

A4. Determine which aspect(s) of teaching you want to examine. Use structured viewing guides for this purpose (see Box 9.3).

A5. If you have not filmed in classrooms before, practice this in advance (see the section *Capture* in Chapter 7).

A6. Find a colleague or a student teacher who will film the lesson(s) chosen. Plan with the cameraperson in which classroom(s) she or he will do the filming.

A7. On the day of filming, make sure that the necessary equipment is ready on time.

Filming in classrooms

B1. If possible, record the whole lesson, i.e. from when the pupils enter the classroom until they have left, so that the complete course of the lesson can be reconstructed.

B2. To obtain usable video recordings, record the main events in the instructional triangle. These events include:
- the teacher's instruction, so that the intent behind the lesson becomes clear,
- the main learning activities, to make clear what pupils do and practice, and
- feedback activities such as debriefing after making assignments, to make clear what pupils are learning.

(see the section *What to film* in Chapter 7)

B3. Ask the camera person – before filming – to focus on the viewing points you selected.

B4. Ensure the best possible camera position(s).
- If no camera person is available, place the camera in a corner of the room providing the widest possible angle – as a "fly on the wall".
- If any pupil(s) cannot be filmed, place the camera before them.
- Avoid moving outside the camera range.
- Avoid filming the teacher and pupils in ways they might find uncomfortable, especially when they are within five metres from the camera.

(see the section *How to film* in Chapter 7)

B5. To achieve sufficient video and audio quality,
- film with your back to the daylight,
- make sure that the teacher's and pupils' faces are visible,
- use a lightweight, movable tripod and
- keep camera movements calm, so zoom and pan gradually.

(see the section *How to film* in Chapter 7)

B6. If pupils have not been filmed during lessons before, let them get used to it. Often, they will first wave and grimace to the camera. Allow them this opportunity, but make clear – if necessary – that once is enough. Being filmed usually becomes a routine quickly, but should any pupils object seriously, place them behind the camera.

B7. Once pupils are used to a camera in the lesson, it becomes easier to choose situations to film close-up. For example, in case of group work, it is very informative during viewing to be able to see which learning activities pupils carry out and to hear what they say and ask, what they find unclear or difficult etcetera. To capture such events, the camera person needs to move closer to pupils and stay there for a while. If necessary, agree with pupils beforehand that this may or will happen.

Sharing classroom video with colleagues

C1. When saving and storing video files, act responsibly (see the section *Data protection* above).

C2. When a clip is longer than five minutes, use time markers and/or captions to make it navigable for viewers (cf. the sections *Editing* in Chapter 7 and *Video as a medium for instruction* in Chapter 8).

C3. Depending on how familiar or unfamiliar your audience is with the context of the lesson, provide necessary context information and relevant perspectives for viewing (see the section *Framing* in Chapter 7).

Analysing and discussing video clips

Analysing and changing instruction is most effective when it is undertaken in dialogue with colleagues. Such dialogue can take place in personal meetings, in blended learning environments and/or online consultation. See the section *Collegial collaboration* below for more detail.

To make collegial consultation constructive and productive, I developed in an earlier project the sequencing shown in Figure 9.1 (Brouwer, 2002, p. 120).

When a group of teachers discusses video recordings of each other's lessons, it is advisable to appoint a chairperson who moderates the conversation. The middle column in Figure 9.1, derived from the ALACT reflection model (Korthagen & Wubbels, 2001, p. 43), shows the four phases through which collegial dialogue should move. The right-hand column shows questions the moderator can use to introduce each phase. The left-hand column gives suggestions for written notes that participants may prepare. The following suggestions are meant to shape the collegial dialogue about lesson recordings more concretely.

D1. Prepare the conversation by viewing each other's video clips, preferably using selected viewing points.

D2. First describe as objectively as possible the events in the lesson.

D3. Then, analyse how and why the events took place as they did, by developing interpretations and searching for causes and explanations.

D4. Finally, formulate together possible alternatives for instructional action.

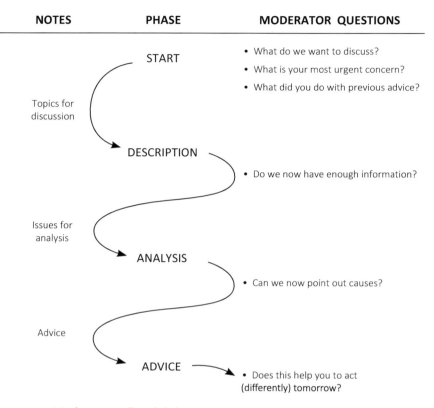

NOTES	PHASE	MODERATOR QUESTIONS
	START	• What do we want to discuss? • What is your most urgent concern? • What did you do with previous advice?
Topics for discussion		
	DESCRIPTION	• Do we now have enough information?
Issues for analysis		
	ANALYSIS	• Can we now point out causes?
Advice		
	ADVICE	• Does this help you to act (differently) tomorrow?

FIGURE 9.1   Moderating collegial dialogue.

In each phase, different opening and probing questions can guide the conversation. Both the participants and the moderator can use these questions. Suggestions for how to formulate them are given in Box 9.5 (Brouwer, 2002, p. 125; Korthagen & Wubbels, 2001, p. 214–216).

Planning new lessons

Once you have analysed your video clips together with colleagues and have received their advice, it is time to judge and decide if and how to change your instruction.

E1. When planning new lessons, you can use the following questions.
   • Which comments did my colleagues make about the video fragments discussed?
   • Which alternatives for instructional action did they suggest?
   • How do I assess those suggestions?
   • Which alternatives shall I try out?
   • Which new knowledge, skills and/or attitudes do I need to develop?

BOX 9.5   OPENING AND PROBING QUESTIONS DURING COLLEGIAL DIALOGUE

Description

Opening questions	*Probing questions*
What happened?	What preceded it?
Who was involved?	Who was not involved?
What did you do? What did you intend?	What did you think? How did you feel?
How did pupils react?	What did pupils react to?
How did you react?	What did you react to?

Analysis

Opening questions	*Probing questions*
What is your concern?	What do you mean by…?
What did you find the most important?	In which respect(s) is this important?
What did pupils learn?	Which activities made pupils learn?
What did you discover now?	What does this discovery tell you about your instruction?

Advice

Opening questions	*Probing questions*
Do you see things you could change in your instruction?	Which alternatives do you see for instruction?
What could you achieve by acting differently?	What are the pros and cons?
Will you change your lesson plan?	Which changes will you make?
How might pupils react next time?	What will you do then?

Producing classroom video

Box 9.6 summarises features that video clips of teaching and learning should possess so as to enable teachers viewing them to understand, analyse, interpret and discuss what happened during the lessons shown. These features specify visual content, form features and ways of framing classroom video which have been shown by research to promote VTL.

For more detail, see the section *Guidelines for the production of classroom video* in Chapter 7 including Box 7.2 Video production checklist.

BOX 9.6 CLIP FEATURES PROMOTING VISUAL TEACHER LEARNING

When producing classroom video clips, make sure that they:

Visual content
- retain the lesson's original sequence
- show the instruction by the teacher
- show the interaction between teacher, pupils and content
- show different actors' perspectives
- prevent misunderstandings regarding class, race, gender or handicap
- confront teachers with ambiguity, discrepancies, dilemmas inviting critical collaborative analysis, interpretation and discussion

Form features
- are clearly structured
- are no longer than five minutes or include segments no longer than five minutes
- include captions, subtitles and/or voiceovers
- are easily navigable
- take into account conventions in visual language

Framing
- offer access to context information, pedagogical content knowledge and other supporting resources
- help teachers judge and decide if and how they want to adopt or adapt the instructional approach shown

Underlying chapters and sections:
1. Introduction
   Quality learning and quality teaching
2. Imaging teacher learning. From analog to digital
   Video platforms for teachers
   Conditions: In what kinds of learning environments do teachers learn when using digital video?
7. The production of classroom video
   Guidelines for the production of classroom video
8. Using video for activating instruction
   Video as a medium for instruction

Collegial collaboration

Box 9.7 summarises how teacher leaders can encourage participants in peer coaching with video to achieve constructive forms of collaboration that can promote changes in teachers' instruction and increases in pupils' learning outcomes.

BOX 9.7   COLLABORATING TO ANALYSE LESSONS AND CHANGE INSTRUCTION

- Make participants' concerns about their daily teaching the starting point for collaboration.
- Build an atmosphere of trust.
- Encourage participants to formulate goals for personal learning in relation to challenges and questions shared by colleagues.
- Engage in repeated cycles of lesson planning, classroom experimentation and collegial dialogue.
- Encourage participants to distinguish between describing, interpreting, judging and deciding.
- Focus lesson observation and video analysis on the interplay between teaching and learning.
- Use structured viewing guides to explicate viewing points.
- Engage in both other-viewing and self-viewing.
- Engage in repeated viewing, moving from exploratory to analytic.
- Focus on what teachers' actions add to or detract from pupils' learning.
- Link collegial dialogue to relevant lesson observations.
- Keep collegial dialogue focussed on a central issue, but also allow it to wander along related topics.

Underlying chapters and sections:

2. Imaging teacher learning. From analog to digital
   Processes: How do teachers learn when using digital video?
3. Changing instruction through Visual Teacher Learning
   Processes
6. Activating learners. The impact of peer coaching with video on teaching and learning
   Peer coaching and visual teacher learning
   Influence of the learning environment

Using instructional video

Teachers may use IV in offline, blended or online settings. Whether you operate in the role of user or maker of IV clips or both, following research-based guidelines will increase the effectiveness of teachers' work. These guidelines are summarised in Box 9.8.

BOX 9.8 EFFECTIVE INSTRUCTIONAL VIDEO

When selecting, producing and using instructional video clips,

- seek parsimony, so follow the maxim "Less is more"
- avoid overlap between spoken and written words
- segment, signal and weed clip contents
- provide learners with control options allowing non-linear study
- provide learners with a site map, guidance and navigation aids
- provide learners with tasks and assignments encouraging elaboration and computer-supported collaboration
- control and monitor the time learners need to view, understand and process clip contents

Underlying chapters and sections:

8. Using video for activating instruction
   Video as a medium for instruction
   The teacher as multimedia user and producer

Consulting learners

Box 9.9 summarises how teachers can use surveys, interviews and video to consult learners about how they experience teaching and learning. It specifies steps to take while collecting data, reporting findings and drawing consequences for curriculum development.

BOX 9.9   VIDEO AS A RESOURCE FOR PUPIL CONSULTATION

- When collecting survey data among pupils, ask them to rate observable teacher behaviours.
- When interviewing teachers on video, ask them to describe their inter-action with pupils and to explain how it relates to pupils' learning outcomes.
- When interviewing pupils on video, ask them to describe which teacher actions helped or hindered their learning and why.
- Produce an action video of the lessons under evaluation and show it to the teacher and pupils.
- Discuss the findings from surveys and interviews with the teacher and pupils and record their reactions on video.
- Report and utilise conclusions and recommendations for curriculum development.

Underlying chapters and sections:

6. Activating learners. The impact of peer coaching with video on teaching and learning
   Pupil questionnaires
8. Using video for activating instruction
   Video for pupil consultation

REFERENCES

Acheson, K.A., & Gall, M.D. (2003). *Clinical supervision and teacher development. Preservice and inservice applications.* Hoboken, NJ: John Wiley & Sons.

Ackland, R. (1991). A review of the peer coaching literature. *Journal of Staff Development, 12*(1), 22–27.

Ainsworth, M.D.S., Blehar, M.C., Waters, E., & Wall, S. (1978). *Patterns of attachment. A psychological study of the strange situation.* Hillsdale, NJ: Lawrence Erlbaum.

Alderman, K. (1999). *Motivation for achievement. Possibilities for teaching and learning.* Mahwah, NJ: Lawrence Erlbaum Associates.

Allen, D.W., & LeBlanc, A.C. (2005). *Collaborative peer coaching that improves instruction. The 1+2 performance appraisal model.* Thousand Oaks, CA: Corwin Press.

Allen, D.W., & Ryan, K. (1969). *Microteaching.* Reading, MA: Addison-Wesley.

Allen, J.P., Gregory, A., Mikami, A., Lun, J., Hamre, B., & Pianta, R.C. (2013). Observations of effective teacher–student interactions in secondary school classrooms: Predicting student achievement with the classroom assessment scoring system—secondary. *School Psychology Review, 42*(1), 76–98.

Allen, J.P., Hafen, C.A., Gregory, A.C., Mikami, A.Y., & Pianta, R.C. (2015). Enhancing secondary school instruction and student achievement: Replication and extension of the My Teaching Partner-Secondary intervention. *Journal of Research on Educational Effectiveness, 8*(4), 475–489. doi:10.1080/19345747.2015.1017680.

Allen, J.P., Pianta, R.C., Gregory, A., Mikami, A.Y., & Lun, J. (2011). An interaction-based approach to enhancing secondary school instruction and student achievement. *Science, 333,* 1034–1037. doi:10.1126/science.1207998.

Anderson, L.W., & Krathwohl, D.R. (Eds.). (2014). *A taxonomy for learning, teaching, and assessing. A revision of Bloom's taxonomy of educational objectives.* Boston, MA: Allyn & Bacon.

Andrews, T.E., & Barnes, S. (1990). Assessment of teaching. In W.R. Houston & M. Haberman (Eds.), *Handbook of research on teacher education* (pp. 569–598). New York: Macmillan.

Andrews-Larson, C., Wilson, J., & Larbi-Cherif, A. (2017). Instructional improvement and teachers' collaborative conversations: The role of focus and facilitation. *Teachers College Record, 119*(2), 1–37.

Arnett, J. (1989). Caregivers in day-care centers: Does training matter? *Journal of Applied Developmental Psychology, 10,* 541–552.

Ascher, S., & Pincus, E. (2007). *The filmmaker's handbook. A comprehensive guide for the digital age.* New York: Plume/Penguin Group.

Bacevich, A.E. (2010). *Building curriculum for teacher education. A study of video records of practice.* Ann Arbor, MI: University of Michigan.

Bakkenes, I., Vermunt, J.D., & Wubbels, T. (2010). Teacher learning in the context of educational innovation: Learning activities and learning outcomes of experienced teachers. *Learning and Instruction, 20,* 533–548. doi:10.1016/j.learninstruc.2009.09.001.

Bandura, A. (1997). *Self-efficacy. The exercise of control.* New York: Freeman.

Baran, E. (2014). A review of research on mobile learning in teacher education. *Educational Technology & Society, 17*(4), 17–32. doi:10.2307/jeductechsoci.17.4.17.

Barnhart, T., & Van Es, E.A. (2015). Studying teacher noticing: Examining the relationship among pre-service science teachers' ability to attend, analyze and respond to student thinking. *Teaching and Teacher Education, 45,* 83–93. doi:10.1016/j.tate.2014.09.005.

Barnhart, T., & van Es, E.A. (2018). Leveraging analysis of students' disciplinary thinking in a video club to promote student-centered science instruction. *Contemporary Issues in Technology and Teacher Education, 18*(1), 50–80.

Barth, V.L., Piwowar, V., Kumschick, I.R., Ophardt, D., & Thiel, F. (2019). The impact of direct instruction in a problem-based learning setting. Effects of a video-based training program to foster preservice teachers' professional vision of critical incidents in the classroom. *International Journal of Educational Research, 95,* 1–12. doi:10.1016/j.ijer.2019.03.002.

Bast, J., & Reitsma, P. (1998). Analyzing the development of individual differences in terms of Matthew effects in reading: Results from a Dutch longitudinal Study. *Developmental Psychology, 34*(6), 1373–1399.

Bates, M.S., Phalen, L., & Moran, C.G. (2016). If you build it, will they reflect? Examining techers' use of an online video-based learning website. *Teaching and Teacher Education, 58,* 17–27. doi:10.1016/j.tate.2016.04.004.

Baumgartner, M. (2018). Performanzfortschritt in der Lehrerausbildung durch die Arbeit an eigenen video-und textbasierten Unterrichtsfällen? Eine Interventionsstudie zur Verbesserung des Feedbacks bei angehenden Sportlehrkräften [Performance progress in teacher education through video-based and text-based work on cases of own classroom teaching? An intervention study for improvement of feedback in preservice sports teachers]. *Zeitschrift für Erziehungswissenschaft, 21*(6), 1135–1155. doi:10.1007/s11618-018-0829-8.

Beardsley, L., Cogan-Drew, D., & Olivero, F. (2007). VideoPaper: Bridging research and practice for preservice and experienced teachers. In R. Goldman, R. Pea, B. Barron, & S.J. Derry (Eds.), *Video research in the learning sciences* (pp. 479–495). Mahwah, NJ: Lawrence Erlbaum Associates.

Beck, I.L., & McKeown, M.B. (2006). *Improving comprehension with Questioning the Author. A fresh and expanded view of a powerful approach.* New York, NY: Scholastic.

Behrens, M., Bosch, H., Elfferding, W., Haug, W.F., Laugstien, T., Nemitz, R. et al. (1979). *Theorien über Ideologie* [Theories about ideology]. Berlin: Argument-Verlag (AS 40).

Beisiegel, M., Mitchell, R., & Hill, H.C. (2018). The design of video-based professional development: An exploratory experiment intended to identify effective features. *Journal of Teacher Education, 69*(1), 69–89. doi:10.1177/0022487117705096.

Bellack, A.A., Kliebard, H.M., Hyman, R.T., & Smith Jr., F.L. (1966). *The language of the classroom.* New York: Teachers College Press.

Berger, H. (1974). *Untersuchungsmethode und soziale Wirklichkeit* [Research method and social reality]. Frankfurt a/M: Suhrkamp.

Berger, J. (1972). *Ways of seeing.* London: Penguin Books. Accessed 3 June 2021 at https://www.youtube.com/watch?v=utEoRdSL1jo

Berlak, A., & Berlak, H. (1981). *Dilemmas of schooling. Teaching and social change*. London: Methuen.

Berliner, D.C. (2001). Learning about and learning from expert teachers. *International Journal of Educational Research, 35*, 463–482.

Berliner, D.C. (2004). Describing the behavior and documenting the accomplishments of expert teachers. *Bulletin of Science, Technology & Society, 24*(3), 200–212. doi:10.1177/0270467604265535.

Biancarosa, G., Bryk, A.S., & Dexter, E.R. (2010). Assessing the value-added effects of literacy collaborative professional development on student learning. *The Elementary School Journal, 111*(1), 7–34.

Blanton, W.E., Moorman, G., & Trathen, W. (1998). Chapter 7: Telecommunications and teacher education: A social constructivist review. *Review of Research in Education, 23*(1), 235–275.

Blijleven, P.J. (2005). *Multimedia-cases. Naar een brug tussen theorie en praktijk* [Multimedia cases. Towards bridging theory and practice]. Enschede: Universiteit Twente.

Bliss, T., & Reynolds, A. (2004). Quality visions and focused imagination. In J. Brophy (Ed.), *Using video in teacher education. Advances in research on teaching* (Vol. 10, pp. 29–53). Amsterdam: Elsevier.

Blomberg, G., Renkl, A., Sherin, M.G., Borko, H., & Seidel, T. (2013). Five research-based heuristics for using video in pre-service teacher education. *Journal for Educational Research Online, 5*(1), 90–114.

Blomberg, G., Stürmer, K., & Seidel, T. (2011). How pre-service teachers observe teaching on video: Effects of viewers' teaching subjects and the subject of the video. *Teaching and Teacher Education, 27*, 1131–1140. doi:10.1016/j.tate.2011.04.008.

Bloom, B.S. (1968). Learning for Mastery. Instruction and curriculum. Regional Education Laboratory for the Carolinas and Virginia, Topical Papers and Reprints, Number 1. *Evaluation comment, 1*(2). Accessed 3 June 2021 at https://files.eric.ed.gov/fulltext/ED053419.pdf

Bonset, H., Hoogeveen, M. (2009). *Een inventarisatie van empirisch onderzoek naar begrijpend lezen, leesbevordering en fictie* [A review of empirical research into reading comprehension, reading promotion and fiction]. Enschede: SLO.

Bonset, H., Hoogeveen, M. (2015). *Schrijven in het basisonderwijs opnieuw onderzocht. Een inventarisatie van empirisch onderzoek van 2004 tot 2014* [Writing in primary education revisited. A review of empirical research from 2004 till 2014]. Enschede: SLO.

Borg, W.R. (1968). *The Minicourse rationale and uses in Inservice Education of Teachers*. Berkeley, CA: Far West Laboratory for Educational Research and Development (ED 024647).

Borko, H., Jacobs, J., Eiteljorg, E., & Pittman, M.E. (2008). Video as a tool for fostering productive discussions in mathematics professional development. *Teaching and Teacher Education, 24*(2), 417–436. doi:10.1016/j.tate.2006.11.012.

Borko, H., Jacobs, J., & Koellner, K. (2010). Contemporary approaches to teacher professional development. *International Encyclopedia of Education, 7*, 548–556.

Borko, H., Koellner, K., Jacobs, J., & Seago, N. (2011). Using video representations of teaching in practice-based professional development programs. *ZDM, 43*(1), 175–187. doi:10.1007/s11858-010-0302-5.

Bourdillon, H. (2007). *Case studies on using Teachers' TV in school-focused CPD. Summary, conclusions and recommendations*. London: London Centre for Leadership in Learning, The Institute of Education, University of London.

Bowen, C.J., & Thompson, R. (2018). *Grammar of the edit*. Abingdon, UK: Routledge.

Bowlby, J. (1997). *Attachment and loss: Attachment* (Vol. 1). New York: Random House.

Boyd, D.J., Grossman, P.L., Lankford, H., Loeb, S., & Wyckoff, J. (2009). Teacher preparation and student achievement. *Educational Evaluation and Policy Analysis*, *31*(4), 416–440. doi:10.3102/0162373709353129.

Brainbox Research (2010). *Teachers TV Annual Review 2009* (Research Report DCSF-RR188). Leeds: Brainbox Research.

Brantlinger, A., Sherin, M.G., & Linsenmeier, K.A. (2011). Discussing discussion: A video club in the service of math teachers' National Board preparation. *Teachers and Teaching: Theory and Practice*, *17*(1), 5–33. doi:10.1080/13540602.2011.538494.

Brock, M.E., & Carter, E.W. (2015). Effects of a professional development package to prepare special education paraprofessionals to implement evidence-based practice. *The Journal of Special Education*, *49*(1), 39–51. doi:10.1177/0014402915585564.

Bronfenbrenner, U. (1979). *The ecology of human development*. Cambridge, MA: Harvard University Press.

Brophy, J. (1986). Teacher influences on student achievement. *American Psychologist*, *41*(10), 1069–1077.

Brophy, J. (2004). Introduction. In J. Brophy (Ed.), *Using video in teacher education. Advances in research on teaching* (Vol. 10, pp. ix–xxiv). Amsterdam: Elsevier.

Brophy, J., & Good, T.L. (1986). Teacher behavior and student achievement. In M.C. Wittrock (Ed.), *Handbook of research on teaching* (pp. 328–375). New York: Macmillan.

Brouwer, C.N. (1989). *Geïntegreerde lerarenopleiding, principes en effekten. Een longitudinaal onderzoek naar organisatie, didactiek en leereffekten van de Utrechtse universitaire lerarenopleiding (Stageonderzoek PDI-RUU 1982–1986)* [Integrative teacher education, principles and effects. A longitudinal study of the organisation, curriculum-in-use and learning effects of preservice teacher education programmes in Utrecht State University (1982–1986)]. Amsterdam: Brouwer (ISBN 90-9003172-3).

Brouwer, C.N. (2002). Intervisie. Leraren leren van elkaar [Collegial consultation. Teachers learning from each other]. In C.N. Brouwer, T. Brouwers, N. Kienstra, J. Leisink, R. Liebrand, S. Van Maanen, et al. *Voor de klas. Voorbereidingen op de praktijk* [Learn and let learn. A handbook of teacher education methods] (pp. 109–131). Bussum: Coutinho.

Brouwer, C.N. (2007). Evaluating alternative teacher education in the Netherlands. A standards-based synthesis. *European Journal of Teacher Education*, *30*(1), 21–40. doi:10.1080/02619760601119934.

Brouwer, C.N. (2010). Determining long-term effects of teacher education. In P. Peterson, E. Baker, & B. McGaw (Eds.), *International encyclopedia of education* (Vol. 7, pp. 503–510). Oxford: Elsevier (ISBN 9780080449005).

Brouwer, C.N. (2011). *Imaging teacher learning. A literature review on the use of digital video for preservice teacher education and professional development. Paper presented at the Annual Meeting of the American Educational Research Association*. Nijmegen: Radboud Graduate School of Education.

Brouwer, C.N. (2014). Was lernen Lehrpersonen durch die Arbeit mit Videos? Ergebnisse eines Dezenniums empirischer Forschung [Visual Teacher Learning: Review of a decade of research]. *Beiträge zur Lehrerinnen- und Lehrerbildung*, *32*(2), 176–196.

Brouwer, C.N., Brouwers, T., Kienstra, N., Leisink, J., Liebrand, R., & Van Maanen, S. et al. (2002). *Voor de klas. Voorbereidingen op de praktijk* [Learn and let learn. A handbook of teacher education methods]. Bussum: Coutinho. Accessed 3 June 2021 at https://portal.coutinho.nl/9789062833016/studiemateriaal/.

Brouwer, C.N., & Kerssies, C. (1983). Over spraakkunst gesproken [Speaking about grammar]. *Nieuwsbrief BNVU*, *6*(2), 14–19

Brouwer, C.N., & Korthagen, F.A.J. (2005). Can teacher education make a difference? *American Educational Research Journal*, *42*(1), 153–224.

Brouwer, C.N., & Kreijns, K. (2014). *Framing online teacher video: How to conceptualise it. Presentation at the symposium "Understanding Teachers' Professional Competencies" of the Special Interest Group 11 Research in Teaching and Teacher Education of the European Association for Research on Learning and Instruction* (Chiemsee, Germany, 16 June 2014).

Brouwer, C.N., & Yusko, B. (2009). *Teacher Autonomy in Using Digital Video for Fostering Reflection among Practicing Teachers. Symposium at the Annual Meeting of the American Educational Research Association.* San Diego: April, 14, 2007. Accessed 3 June 2021 at http://academic.csuohio.edu/yuskob/aera2009.htm

Brown, J.S., Collins, A., & Duguid, P. (1989). Situated cognition and the culture of learning. *Educational Researcher, 18*(1), 32–42

Brown, K., & Kennedy, H. (2011). Learning through conversation: Exploring and extending teacher and children's involvement in classroom talk. *School Psychology International, 32*(4), 377–396. doi:10.1177/0143034311406813.

Browning, B., & Porter, A. (2007). The effect of computer-assisted self-observation on the eye contact behaviors of preservice music teachers. *Journal of Music Teacher Education, 17*(1), 62–76.

Bruns, B., & Luque, J. (2014). *Great teachers: How to raise student learning in Latin America and the Caribbean.* Washington, DC: Worldbank.

Brunvand, S. (2010). Best practices for producing video content for teacher education. *Contemporary Issues in Technology and Teacher Education, 10*(2), 247–256.

Buczynski, S., & Hansen, C.B. (2010). Impact of professional development on teacher practice: Uncovering connections. *Teaching and Teacher Education, 26*(3), 599–607. doi:10.1016/j.tate.2009.09.006.

Cain, D.W., Rudd, L.C., & Saxon, T.F. (2007). Effects of professional development training on joint attention engagement in low-quality childcare centers. *Early Child Development and Care, 177*(2), 159–185. doi:10.1080/03004430500375927.

Calandra, B. (2015). A process of guided, video-based reflection. In B. Calandra, & P.J. Rich (Eds.), *Digital video for teacher education: Research and practice* (pp. 36–54). London/New York: Routledge.

Capizzi, A.M., Wehby, J.H., & Sandmel, K.N. (2010). Enhancing mentoring of teacher candidates through consultative feedback and self-evaluation of instructional delivery. *Teacher Education and Special Education, 33*(3), 191–212. doi:10.1177/0888406409360012.

Carpenter, S. (2012). Psychology's bold initiative. *Science, 335*, 1558–1561.

Carpenter, T.P., Fennema, E., Franke, M.L., Levi, L., & Empson, S.B. (1999). *Children's mathematics. Cognitively Guided Instruction.* Portsmouth, NH: Heinemann.

Carpenter, T.P., Franke, M.L., & Levi, L. (2003). *Thinking mathematically. Integrating arithmetic and algebra in elementary school.* Portsmouth, NH: Heinemann.

Carter, K., Cushing, K., Sabers, D., Stein, P., & Berliner, D.C. (1988). Expert-novice differences in perceiving and processing visual classroom information. *Journal of Teacher Education, 39*(3), 25–31.

Cattaneo, A.A., Evi-Colombo, A., Ruberto, M., & Stanley, J. (2019). *Video pedagogy for vocational education. An overview of video-based teaching and learning.* Turin: European Training Foundation.

Cattaneo, A.A., Van der Meij, H., Aprea, C., Sauli, F., & Zahn, C. (2018). A model for designing hypervideo-based instructional scenarios. *Interactive Learning Environments, 27*(4), 508–529. doi:10.1080/10494820.2018.1486860.

Cattaneo, A.A., Van der Meij, H., & Sauli, F. (2018). An empirical test of three instructional scenarios for hypervideo use in a vocational education lesson. *Computers in the Schools, 35*(4), 249–267. doi:10.1080/07380569.2018.1531597.

Chan, P.Y. (2003). *A qualitative study of teachers' cognitive activities when interacting with video ethnography.* Provo, Utah: Brigham Young University.

Chan, P.Y., & Harris, R.C. (2005). Video ethnography and teachers' cognitive activities. In J. Brophy, & S. Pinegar (Eds.), *Advances in research on teaching* (Vol. 11, pp. 337–375). Amsterdam: Elsevier JAI.

Charalambous, C.Y., Philippou, S., & Olympiou, G. (2018). Reconsidering the use of video clubs for student-teachers' learning during field placement: Lessons drawn from a longitudinal multiple case study. *Teaching and Teacher Education, 74*, 49–61. doi:10.1016/j.tate.2018.04.002.

Cheng, L., Ritzhaupt, A.D., & Antonenko, P. (2019). Effects of the flipped classroom instructional strategy on students' learning outcomes: A meta-analysis. *Educational Technology Research and Development, 67*(4), 793–824.

Chi, M.T.H., & Menekse, M. (2015). Dialogue patterns in peer collaboration that promote learning. In L.B. Resnick, C.S.C. Asterhan, & S.N. Clarke (Eds.), *Socializing intelligence through academic talk and dialogue* (pp. 263–275). Washington, DC: American Educational Research Association.

Christ, T., Arya, P., & Chiu, M.M. (2014). Teachers' reports of learning and application to pedagogy based on engagement in collaborative peer video analysis. *Teaching Education, 25*(4), 349–374. doi:10.1080/10476210.2014.920001.

Christ, T., Arya, P., & Chiu, M.M. (2017). Video use in teacher education: An international survey of practices. *Teaching and Teacher Education, 63*, 22–35. doi:10.1016/j.tate.2016.12.005

Clark, C.M., & Peterson, P.L. (1986). Teachers' thought processes. In M.C. Wittrock (Ed.), *Handbook of research on teaching.* (3rd ed. pp. 255–297). New York: MacMillan.

Clarke, D. (n.d.). *"The Learners' Perspective Study".* Research design. Melbourne, VIC: University of Melbourne.

Clarke, D., & Hollingsworth, H. (2002). Elaborating a model of teacher professional growth. *Teaching and Teacher Education, 18*(8), 947–967. doi:10.1016/S0742-051X(02)00053-7.

Coburn, C.E., Russell, J.L., Kaufman, J.H., & Stein, M.K. (2012). Supporting sustainability: Teachers' advice networks and ambitious instructional reform. *American Journal of Education, 119*(1), 137–182.

Cochran-Smith, M., & Zeichner, K.M. (2005). *Studying teacher education. The report of the AERA panel on research and teacher education.* Mahwah, NJ: Lawrence Erlbaum.

Cohen, E.G. (1994). *Designing groupwork. Strategies for the heterogeneous classroom.* New York: Teachers College Press.

Colestock, A., & Sherin, M.G. (2009). Teachers' sense-making strategies while watching video of mathematics instruction. *Journal of Technology and Teacher Education, 17*(1), 7–29.

Collins, A., Brown, J.S., & Newman, S.E. (1989). Cognitive apprenticeship: Teaching the crafts of reading, writing, and mathematics. In L.B. Resnick (Ed.), *Knowing, learning, and instruction. Essays in honor of Robert Glaser* (pp. 453–495). Hillsdale, NJ: Lawrence Erlbaum.

Cooper, J.M., & Allen, D.W. (1970). *Microteaching: History and present status.* Washington, DC: Office of Education (ED 036471).

Corcoran, E. (1981). Transition shock: The beginning teacher's paradox. *Journal of Teacher Education, 32*(3), 19–23.

Cordingley, P., Bell, M., Thomason, S., & Firth, A. (2005). *The impact of collaborative continuing professional development (CPD) on classroom teaching and learning.* Accessed 7 February 2019 at http://wsassets.s3.amazonaws.com/ws/nso/pdf/09598003e49523abff794962e27 52c81.pdf

Cordingley, P., Higgins, S., Greany, T., Buckler, N., Coles-Jordan, D., Crisp, B. et al. (2015). *Developing great teaching. Lessons from the international reviews into effective professional development.* London: Teacher Development Trust

Counterpoint Research (2006). *Teachers' TV impact study. Report on a qualitative research study.* London: Counterpoint Ltd.

Crasborn, F.J.A.J., & Hennissen, P.P.M. (2010). *The skilled mentor. Mentor teachers' use and acquisition of supervisory skills.* Eindhoven: Eindhoven School of Education, Eindhoven University of Technology. Accessed 3 June 2021 at http://alexandria.tue.nl/extra2/675808.pdf

Dahllöf, U.S., & Lundgren, U.P. (1970). *Macro and micro approaches combined for curriculum process analysis: A Swedish educational field project. Paper presented at the annual meeting of the American Educational Research Association.* Gothenburg: Institute of Education, Gothenburg University.

Damhuis, R., & De Blauw, A. (2008). High quality interaction in classrooms. a focus for professional learning. *L1 Educational Studies in Language and Literature, 8*(4), 107–126.

Damhuis, R., De Blauw, A., Tammes, A.-C., & Sytema, S. (2009). *En wat denken júllie? Over de leerbaarheid van interactievaardigheden bij (aanstaande) leerkrachten* [And what do you think? About the learnability of interaction skills by (preservice) teachers] *Paper presented at the 13th biennial conference of the European Association for Research on Learning and Instruction (Amsterdam).* Amsterdam: University of Amsterdam.

Dangel, J.R., & Guyton, E.M. (2005). *Research on alternative and non-traditional education. Teacher education yearbook XIII.* Lanham, MD: The Association of Teacher Educators/Scarecrow Education.

Danielowich, R.M. (2014). Shifting the reflective focus: Encouraging student teacher learning in video-framed and peer-sharing contexts. *Teachers and Teaching: Theory and Practice, 20*(3), 264–288. doi:10.1080/13540602.2013.848522.

Daniels, H., Cole, M., & Wertsch, J.V. (2007). *The Cambridge companion to Vygotsky.* New York: Cambridge University Press.

Danielson, C. (2007). *Enhancing professional practice. A framework for teaching.* Alexandria, VA: Association for Supervision and Curriculum Development (ISBN 978-1-4166-0517-1).

Dann, H.-D., Cloetta, B., Müller-Fohrbrodt, G., & Helmreich, R. (1978). *Umweltbedingungen innovativer Kompetenz. Eine Längsschnittuntersuchung zur Sozialisation von Lehrern in Ausbildung und Beruf* [Contextual conditions of innovative competence. A longitudinal study of teacher socialization during preservice training and beginning teaching]. Stuttgart: Klett-Cotta.

Dann, H.-D., Müller-Fohrbrodt, G., & Cloetta, B. (1981). Sozialisation junger Lehrer im Beruf. Praxisschock drei Jahre später [Occupational socialization in young teachers. Practice shock three years later]. *Zeitschrift für Entwicklungspsychologie und Pädagogische Psychologie, 13*(3), 251–262.

Darling-Hammond, L. (2000). How teacher education matters. *Journal of Teacher Education, 51*(3), 166–173.

Davies, P., Perry, T., & Kirkman, J. (2017). *IRIS Connect: Developing classroom dialogue and formative feedback through collective video reflection. Evaluation report and executive summary.* London: Educational Endowment Foundation.

Davydov, V. (1977). *Arten der Verallgemeinerung im Unterricht* [Types of Generalization in Education]. Berlin: Volk und Wissen.

De Jong, R., & Westerhof, K.J. (2001). The quality of student ratings of teacher behaviour. *Learning Environments Research, 4*(1), 51–85. doi:10.1023/A:1011402608575.

Derry, S. (Ed.). (2007). *Guidelines for video research in education. Recommendations from an expert panel.* Chicago. IL: Data Research and Development Center, University of Chicago.

Desimone, L.M. (2009). Improving impact studies of teachers' professional development: Toward better conceptualizations and measures. *Educational Researcher, 38*(3), 181–199. doi:10.3102/0013189X08331140.

Desimone, L.M., & Pak, K. (2017). Instructional coaching as high-quality professional development. *Theory Into Practice, 56*(1), 3–12. doi:10.1080/00405841.2016.1241947.

Dobie, T.E., Leatherwood, C., & Sherin, M.G. (2021). A look inside teacher-captured video. *Journal of Technology and Teacher Education, 29*(1), 45–66.

Dolk, M.L.A.M. (1997). *Onmiddellijk onderwijsgedrag. Over denken en handelen van leraren in onmiddellijke onderwijssituaties* [Immediate teaching behavior: On teacher knowledge and behavior in immediate teaching situations]. Utrecht: Utrecht University.

Donaldson, J.F., & Graham, S.W. (2001). *Accelerated Degree programs: Policy implications and critique: What we know about adult learners and its implications for policy. Paper presented at the American Educational Research Association national conference, Seattle Washington,* April 12, 2001 (ED EJ646656).

Dondis, D.A. (1973). *A Primer of visual literacy.* Cambridge, MA/London: The MIT Press.

Downer, J.T., Locasale-Crouch, J., Hamre, B.K., & Pianta, R.C. (2009). Teacher characteristics associated with responsiveness and exposure to consultation and online professional development resources. *Early Education and Development, 20*(3), 431–455. doi:10.1080/10409280802688626.

Downer, J.T., Pianta, R.C., Fan, X., Hamre, B.K., Mashburn, A., & Justice, L. (2011). Effects of web-mediated teacher professional development on the language and literacy skills of children enrolled in prekindergarten programs. *NHSA Dialog, 14*(4), 189–212. doi:10.10 80/15240754.2011.613129.

Dowrick, P.W. (1991). *Practical guide to using video in the behavioural sciences.* New York: John Wiley & Sons.

Doyle, W. (1986). Classroom organization and management. In M.C. Wittrock (Ed.), *Handbook of research on teaching. Third edition* (pp. 392–431). New York: MacMillan.

Doyle, W. (2006). Ecological approaches to classroom management. In C.M. Evertson, & C.S. Weinstein (Eds.), *Handbook of classroom management. Research, practice and contemporary issues* (pp. 97–125). Mahwah, NJ: Lawrence Erlbaum Associates.

Dudley, P. (Ed.). (2015). *Lesson study: Professional learning for our time.* London: Routledge.

Duke, N.K., & Pearson, P.D. (2002). Effective practices for developing reading comprehension. In A.E. Farstrup & S.J. Samuels (Eds.), *What research has to say about reading instruction* (pp. 205–243). Newark, DE: International Reading Association.

Dunkin, M.J., & Biddle, B.J. (1974). *The study of teaching.* New York: Holt, Rinehart & Winston.

Durand, M. (2013). Human activity, social practices and lifelong education: An introduction. *International Journal of Lifelong Education, 32*(1), 1–13. doi:10.1080/02601370.2012.7344 95.

Early, D.M., Maxwell, K.L., Ponder, B.D., & Pan, Y. (2017). Improving teacher-child interactions: A randomized controlled trial of making the most of classroom interactions and my teaching partner professional development models. *Early Childhood Research Quarterly, 38,* 57–70. doi:10.1016/j.ecresq.2016.08.005.

Ejchenbaum, B. (2003). Probleme der Filmstilistik [Problems of film style]. In F.-J. Albersmaier(Ed.), *Texte zur Theorie des Films* [Texts on film theory]. Stuttgart: Philipp Reclam.

Ely, E., Kennedy, M., Pullen, P.C., Williams, M.C., & Hirsch, S.E. (2014). Improving instruction of future teachers: A multimedia approach that supports implementation of evidence-based vocabulary practices. *Teaching and Teacher Education, 44,* 35–43. doi:10.1016/j. tate.2014.07.012.

Engeström, Y., Miettinen, R., & Punamäki, R.L. (1999). *Perspectives on activity theory.* Cambridge, UK: Cambridge University Press.

Eraut, M. (1994). *Developing professional knowledge and competence.* London: Routledge/Falmer.

Erickson, F. (2007). Ways of seeing video: Toward a phenomenology of viewing minimally edited video. In R. Goldman, R. Pea, B. Barron, & S.J. Derry (Eds.), *Video research in the learning sciences* (pp. 145–155). Mahwah, NJ: Lawrence Erlbaum Associates.

Erickson, F. (2011). On noticing teacher noticing. In M.G. Sherin, V. Jacobs, & R. Philipp (Eds.), Deciding how to respond on the basis of children's understandings. *Mathematics teacher noticing. Seeing through teachers' eyes* (pp. 17–35). New York: Routledge.

Ermeling, B.A. (2010). Tracing the effects of teacher inquiry on classroom practice. *Teaching and Teacher Education, 26*(3), 377–388. doi:10.1016/j.tate.2009.02.019.

Evertson, C.M., & Green, J.L. (1986). Observation as inquiry and method. In M.C. Wittrock (Ed.), *Handbook of research on teaching. Third edition* (pp. 162–214). New York: Macmillan.

Evi-Colombo, A., Cattaneo, A.A., & Bétrancourt, M. (2020). Technical and pedagogical affordances of video annotation: A literature review. *Journal of Educational Multimedia and Hypermedia, 29*(3), 193–226.

Fabiola, A., & Chavez, A.F.R. (2007). Classroom videos in professional development. *School Science and Mathematics, 107*(7), 269–271. doi:10.1111/j.1949-8594.2007.tb17787.x.

Feiman-Nemser, S., Schwille, S., Carver, C., & Yusko, B. (1999). *A conceptual review of literature on new teacher induction.* East Lansing, MI: Michigan State University (ED449147).

Fend, H. (1974). *Gesellschaftliche Bedingungen schulischer Sozialisation* [Social conditions of socialisation in school]. Weinheim: Beltz.

Fenstermacher, G.D., & Richardson, V. (1993). The elicitation and reconstruction of practical arguments in teaching. *Journal of Curriculum Studies, 25*(2), 101–114. doi:10.1080/0022027930250201.

Filliettaz, L., & Billett, S. (2015). *Francophone perspectives of learning through work.* Basel, Switzerland: Springer International.

Finn, J.D., Pannozzo, G.M., & Achilles, C.M. (2003). The "why's" of class size: Student behavior in small classes. *Review of Educational Research, 73*(3), 321–368.

Fiorella, L., & Mayer, R.E. (2018). What works and doesn't work with instructional video. *Computers in Human Behavior, 89*, 465–470. doi:10.1016/j.chb.2018.07.015.

Fishman, B.J. (2004). Linking on-line video and curriculum to leverage community knowledge. In J. Brophy (Ed.), *Using video in teacher education. Advances in research on teaching* (Vol. 10, pp. 201–235). Amsterdam: Elsevier.

Fishman, B.J., Marx, R.W., Best, S., & Tal, R.T. (2003). Linking teacher and student learning to improve professional development in systemic reform. *Teaching and Teacher Education, 19*(6), 643–658. doi:10.1016/S0742-051X(03)00059-3.

Flandin, S. (2015). *Analyse de l'activité d'enseignants stagiaires du second degré en situation de vidéo-formation autonome. Contribution à un programme de recherche technologique en formation* (Thèse de Doctorat en Sciences de l'Éducation) [Analysis of secondary student teachers' activity in an individual video training setting. Contribution towards a technological research programme in education. Doctoral dissertation in educational science]. Clermont-Ferrand: Laboratoire Activité, Connaissance, Transmission, Éducation, Université Blaise Pascal Clermont-Ferrand.

Flandin, S., & Gaudin, C. (2014). *The effects of video viewing on preservice teachers' classroom activity: Normative versus developmental approaches. Presentation at conference of the Special Interest Group 11 Research in Teaching and Teacher Education of the European Association for Research on Learning and Instruction* (Chiemsee, Germany).

Flandin, S., & Ria, L. (2015). *What do trainee teachers seek, see and learn with video? Understanding the activity of trainee teachers using a video-enhanced teacher-learning environment autonomously.* Presentation for the CIDREE-IFÉ seminar Professional vision and video-enhanced teacher development (17 March, 2015, Lyon). Lyon: École Normale Supérieur de Lyon.

Flutter, J., & Rudduck, J. (2004). *Consulting pupils: What's in it for schools?* London: Routledge Falmer.

Fortkamp, J. (2002). *'Leren reflecteren in beeld'. Literatuuronderzoek naar de rol van video en reflectie in de opleiding tot leraar basisonderwijs* ["Learning to reflect in view". Literature study of the role of video and reflection in primary teacher education]. Enschede: Universiteit Twente.

Franks, I.M., & Maile, L.J. (1991). The use of video in sport skill acquisition. In P.W. Dowrick (Ed.), *Practical guide to using video in the behavioural sciences* (pp. 231–244). New York: John Wiley & Sons.

Frederiksen, J.R., Sipusic, M., Sherin, M.G., & Wolfe, E.W. (1998). Video portfolio assessment: Creating a framework for viewing the functions of teaching. *Educational Assessment, 5*(4), 225–297.

Fukkink, R.G., & Tavecchio, L.W. (2010). Effects of video interaction guidance on early childhood teachers. *Teaching and Teacher Education, 26*(8), 1652–1659. doi:10.1016/j.tate.2010.06.016.

Fukkink, R.G., Trienekens, N., & Kramer, L.J. (2011). Video feedback in education and training: Putting learning in the picture. *Educational Psychology Review, 23*(1), 45–63. doi:10.1007/s10648-010-9144-5.

Fuller, F.F. (1969). Concerns of teachers: A developmental conceptualization. *American Educational Research Journal, 6*(2), 207–226.

Fuller, F.F. (1974). A conceptual framework for a personalized teacher education program. *Theory into Practice, 13*(2), 112–122.

Fuller, F.F., & Bown, O.H. (1975). Becoming a teacher. In K. Ryan, *Teacher Education. The 74th Yearbook of the NSSE* (pp. 52–55). Chicago, IL: University of Chicago Press.

Fuller, F.F., & Manning, B.A. (1973). Self-confrontation reviewed: A conceptualization for video playback in teacher education. *Review of Educational Research, 43*(4), 469–528.

Fulton, K. (Ed.). (2000). *Teacher Preparation StaR Chart: A self-assessment tool for colleges of teacher education.* Washington, DC: CEO Forum on Education & Technology. Accessed 3 June 2021 at http://www2.ed.gov/programs/teachtech/resources.html

Gallimore, R., Ermeling, B.A., Saunders, W.M., & Goldenberg, C. (2009). Moving the learning of teaching closer to practice: Teacher education implications of school-based inquiry teams. *The Elementary School Journal, 109*(5), 537–553.

Garet, M.S., Porter, A.C., Desimone, L.M., Birman, B.F., & Yoon, K.S. (2001). What makes professional development effective? Results from a national sample of teachers. *American Educational Research Journal, 38*(4), 915–945.

Gaudin, C., & Chaliès, S. (2015). Video viewing in teacher education and professional development: A literature review. *Educational Research Review, 16*, 41–67. doi:10.1016/j.edurev.2015.06.001.

Gaudin, C., Chaliès, S., & Amathieu, J. (2018). The impact of preservice teachers' experiences in a video-enhanced training program on their teaching: A case study in physical education. *Contemporary Issues in Technology and Teacher Education, 18*(1), 168–196.

Gaudin, C., Flandin, S., Ria, L., & Chaliès, S. (2014). An exploratory study of the influence of video viewing on preservice teachers' teaching activity: Normative versus developmental approaches. *Form@re 14*(2), 21–50. doi:10.13128/formare-15126.

Geerts, W. (2018). *The curious case of cases. An inquiry into the effects of video upon teachers in training.* Leeuwarden: NHL Hogeschool.

Geerts, W., Van Laeken, M., & Mitzschke, M. (2009). *Wat zou jij doen? Leren van dilemma's in de onderwijspraktijk* [What would you do? Learning from dilemmas in teaching practice]. Bussum: Coutinho.

Gersten, R., & Dimino, J. (2001). The realities of translating research into classroom practice. *Learning Disabilities Research & Practice, 16*(2), 120–130. doi:10.1111/0938-8982.0013.

Gibson, J.J. (1979). *The ecological approach to visual perception*. Boston, MA: Houghton Mifflin.

Gillies, R.M. (2015). Teacher dialogue that supports collaborative learning in the classroom. In L.B. Resnick, C.S.C. Asterhan, & S.N. Clarke (Eds.), *Socializing intelligence through academic talk and dialogue* (pp. 335–347). Washington, DC: American Educational Research Association.

Ginsburg, H.P. (1997). *Entering the child's mind. The clinical interview in psychological research and practice*. Cambridge, MA: Cambridge University Press.

Ginsburg, H.P., Jacobs, S.F., & Lopez, L.S. (1998). *The teacher's guide to flexible interviewing in the classroom. Learning what children know about math*. Boston, MA: Allyn & Bacon.

Gobeil-Proulx, J. (2015). Les dispositifs collaboratifs de confrontation et le rôle des interactions dans le contexte de l'analyse de pratique avec la vidéo [Collaborative settings for confrontation and the role of interaction during video analysis of practice]. *Canadian Journal for New Scholars in Education/Revue canadienne des jeunes chercheures et chercheurs en éducation, 999*(999), 46–56.

Goldman, R., Pea, R., Barron, B., & Derry, S.J. (2007). *Video research in the learning sciences*. Mahwah, NJ: Lawrence Erlbaum Associates.

Good, T.L., & Brophy, J.E. (2008). *Looking in classrooms*. Boston, MA: Pearson.

Goodwin, C. (1994). Professional vision. *American Anthropologist, 96*(3), 606–633.

Gregory, A., Allen, J.P., Mikami, A.Y., Hafen, C.A., & Pianta, R.C. (2014). Effects of a professional development program on behavioral engagement of students in middle and high school. *Psychology in the Schools, 51*(2), 143–163. doi:10.1002/pits.21741.

Gregory, A., Hafen, C.A., Ruzek, E., Mikami, A.Y., Allen, J.P., & Pianta, R.C. (2016). Closing the racial discipline gap in classrooms by changing teacher practice. *School Psychology Review, 45*(2), 171–191. doi:10.17105/SPR45-2.171-191.

Grissom, R.J., & Kim, J.J. (2005). *Effect sizes for research. A broad practical approach*. New York: Lawrence Erlbaum Associates.

Gröschner, A., Seidel, T., Pehmer, A.-K., & Kiemer, K. (2014). Facilitating collaborative teacher learning: The role of "mindfulness" in video-based teacher professional development programs. *Gruppendynamik und Organisationsberatung, 45*(3), 273–290. doi:10.1007/s11612-014-0248-0.

Grossman, P., & Loeb, S. (2008). *Alternative routes to teaching. Mapping the new landscape of teacher education*. Cambridge, MA: Harvard Education Press.

Guskey, T.R. (1986). Staff development and the process of teacher change. *Educational Researcher, 15*(5), 5–12. doi:10.3102/0013189X015005005.

Guskey, T.R. (2000). *Evaluating professional development*. Thousand Oaks, CA: Corwin Press.

Guskey, T.R. (2002). Professional development and teacher change. *Teachers and Teaching: Theory and Practice, 8*(3), 381–391. doi:10.1080/135406002100000512.

Guskey, T.R. (2005). *Formative classroom assessment and Benjamin S. Bloom: Theory, Research, and Implications. Paper presented at the Annual Meeting of the American Educational Research Association*. Lexington, KY: College of Education, University of Kentucky.

Guskey, T.R. (2007). Closing achievement gaps: Revisiting Benjamin S. Bloom's "Learning for Mastery". *Journal of Advanced Academics, 19*(1), 8–31.

Haanstra, F. (2008). Research into goals and effects of arts education. In J. Zeelen, C. van Beilen, & M. Slagter (Eds.), *Max van der Kamp remembered. Contributions to arts education, lifelong learning and international development co-operation* (pp. 23–31). Amsterdam: Max Goote Kenniscentrum voor beroepsonderwijs en volwasseneneducatie.

Haenen, J. (2001). Outlining the teaching–learning process: Piotr Gal'perin's contribution. *Learning and Instruction, 11*(2), 157–170. doi:10.1016/S0959-4752(00)00020-7.

Hafen, C.A., Hamre, B.K., Allen, J.P., Bell, C.A., Gitomer, D.H., & Pianta, R.C. (2015). Teaching through interactions in secondary school classrooms: Revisiting the factor structure and practical application of the Classroom Assessment Scoring System–Secondary. *The Journal of Early Adolescence, 35*(5–6), 651–680. doi:10.1177/0272431614537117.

Hall, I., & Wright, D. (2007). *Literature review of the use of video as a resource for professional development of mathematics teachers.* Newcastle upon Tyne: The Research Centre for Learning and Teaching (RCfLaT), School of Education, Communication and Language Sciences, Newcastle University.

Hamre, B.K., Pianta, R.C., Burchinal, M., Field, S., LoCasale-Crouch, J., Downer, J.T. et al. (2012). A course on effective teacher-child interactions: Effects on teacher beliefs, knowledge, and observed practice. *American Educational Research Journal, 49*(1), 88–123. doi:10.3102/0002831211434596.

Hamre, B.K., Pianta, R.C., Downer, J.T., DeCoster, J., Mashburn, A.J., Jones, S.M. et al. (2013). Teaching through interactions: Testing a developmental framework of teacher effectiveness in over 4,000 classrooms. *The Elementary School Journal, 113*(4), 461–487.

Hamre, B.K., Pianta, R.C., Mashburn, A.J., & Downer, J.T. (2012). Promoting young children's social competence through the preschool PATHS curriculum and MyTeachingPartner professional development resources. *Early Education & Development, 23*(6), 809–832. doi:10.1080//10409289.2011.607360.

Hanushek, E.A. (2005). *Economic outcomes and school quality.* Brussels: International Academy of Education. Accessed 3 June 2021 at http://www.iaoed.org/downloads/Edpol4.pdf

Hare, P., Mohn, B.E., Vogelpohl, A., & Wiesemann, J. (2019). *Face to face - Face to screen. Early childhood and media. 24 camera ethnographic miniatures.* Berlin: LIT Verlag Dr. W. Hopf.

Harlin, E.M. (2014). Watching oneself teach–long-term effects of teachers' reflections on their video-recorded teaching. *Technology, Pedagogy and Education, 23*(4), 507–521. doi:10.1080/1475939X.2013.822413.

Harris, R.C., Pinnegar, S., & Teemant, A. (2005). The case for hypermedia video ethnographies: Designing a new class of case studies that challenge teaching practice. *Journal of Technology and Teacher Education, 13*(1), 141–161.

Harris, R.C., Turner, J., Livingstone, N., Turner, J., Hoy, M.A.A., Sauser, A. et al. (2001). *The Jean Turner case: A video ethnography of fourth grade balanced literacy classroom.* Provo, UT: Harris Video Cases.

Haskell, R.E. (2001). *Transfer of learning. Cognition, instruction, and reasoning.* San Diego, CA: Academic Press.

Hatch, T., Shuttleworth, J., Jaffee, A.T., & Marri, A. (2016). Videos, pairs, and peers: What connects theory and practice in teacher education? *Teaching and Teacher Education, 59,* 274–284. doi:10.1016/j.tate.2016.04.011.

Hathaway, D., & Norton, P. (2012). Video production: Bridging teacher education and classroom practice. *Journal of Technology and Teacher Education, 20*(2), 127–149.

Hattie, J.A.C. (2009). *Visible learning. A synthesis of over 800 meta-analyses relating to achievement.* London: Routledge.

Hawkins, S.M., & Heflin, L.J. (2011). Increasing secondary teachers' behavior-specific praise using a video self-modeling and visual performance feedback intervention. *Journal of Positive Behavior Interventions, 13*(2), 97–108. doi:10.1177/1098300709358110.

Helmerhorst, K.O.W., Riksen-Walraven, J.M.A., Fukkink, R.G., Tavecchio, L.W.C., & Gevers Deynoot-Schaub, M.J.J.M. (2017). Effects of the caregiver interaction profile training on caregiver-child interactions in Dutch child care centers: A randomized controlled trial. *Child and Youth Care Forum, 46*(3), 413–436. doi:10.1007/s10566-016-9383-9.

Helmke, A. (1988). *Das Münchener Aufmerksamkeitsinventar (MAI): Manual für die Beobachtung des Aufmerksamkeitsverhaltens von Grundschülern während des Unterrichts* [The Munich Observation of Attention Inventory (MAI): Manual for the observation of primary pupils' attention behaviour during teaching and learning]. München: Max-Planck-Institut für psychologische Forschung.

Helmke, A. (2009). *Unterrichtsqualität und Lehrerprofessionalität. Diagnose, Evaluation und Verbesserung des Unterrichts* [Quality of instruction and teacher professionalism. Diagnosis, evaluation and improvement of instruction]. Stuttgart: Klett.

Helms-Lorenz, M., Van de Grift, W., & Maulana, R. (2016). Longitudinal effects of induction on teaching skills and attrition rates of beginning teachers. *School Effectiveness and School Improvement, 27*(2), 178–204. doi:10.1080/09243453.2015.1035731.

Hemmeter, M.L., Snyder, P., Kinder, K., & Artman, K. (2011). Impact of performance feedback delivered via electronic mail on preschool teachers' use of descriptive praise. *Early Childhood Research Quarterly, 26*(1), 96–109. doi:10.1016/j.ecresq.2010.05.004.

Henning, J., Massler, U., Ploetzner, R., & Huppertz, P. (2007). Collaborative lesson analysis in virtual groups: The impact of video on student teachers' analysis and reflection processes. In C.A. Chinn, G. Erkens, S. Puntambekar (Eds.), *CSCL'07: Proceedings of the 8th International Conference On Computer Supported Collaborative Learning* (pp. 286–288). London: International Society of the Learning Sciences.

Herbst, P., Aaron, W., & Erickson, A. (2013). How preservice teachers respond to representations of practice: A comparison of animations and video. *Paper presented at the annual meeting of the American Educational Research Association.* Ann Arbor: University of Michigan.

Hiebert, J., Gallimore, R., & Stigler, J.W. (2002). A knowledge base for the teaching profession: What would it look like and how can we get one?. *Educational Researcher, 31*(5), 3–15.

Hiebert, J., Stigler, J.W., Jacobs, J.K., Givvin, K.B., Garnier, H., Smith, M. et al. (2005). Mathematics teaching in the United States today (and tomorrow): Results from the TIMSS 1999 video study. *Educational Evaluation and Policy Analysis, 27*(2), 111–132.

Hinsch, R. (1979). *Einstellungswandel und Praxisschock bei jungen Lehrern, eine empirische Längsschnittuntersuchung* [Attitude change and practice shock in beginning teachers, an empirical longitudinal study]. Weinheim: Beltz.

Hixon, E., & So, H.J. (2009). Technology's role in field experiences for preservice teacher training. *Educational Technology & Society, 12*(4), 294–304. doi:jeductechsoci.12.3.294.

Hoetker, J., & Ahlbrand Jr., W.P. (1969). The persistence of the recitation. *American Educational Research Journal, 6*(2), 145–167.

Holzkamp, K. (1972). *Kritische Psychologie. Vorbereitende Arbeiten* [Critical psychology: Preliminary essays]. Frankfurt am Main: Suhrkamp.

Hoogeveen, M. (2012). *Writing with peer response using genre knowledge.* Enschede: University of Twente.

Hoogeveen, M., & van Gelderen, M. (2015). Effects of peer response using genre knowledge on writing quality. A randomized control trial. *The Elementary School Journal, 116*(2), 265–290. doi:10.1086/684129.

Horn, I.S., & Little, J.W. (2010). Attending to problems of practice: Routines and resources for professional learning in teachers' workplace interactions. *American Educational Research Journal, 47*(1), 181–217. doi:10.3102/0002831209345158.

Humpert, W., & Dann, H.-D. (2001). *KTM Kompakt. Basistraining zur Störungsreduktion und Gewaltprävention* [Basic Training for Reducing Disruption and Preventing Aggression]. Bern: Verlag Hans Huber.

Huppertz, P., Massler, U., & Ploetzner, R. (2005). In T. Koschmann, D.D. Suthers & T.W. Chan (Eds.), *Proceedings of the international conference on computer support for collaborative learning* (pp. 232–236). Mahwah, NJ: Lawrence Erlbaum Associates.

Huppertz, P., Ploetzner, R., & Massler, U. (2007). Usability in the computer-based analysis of video in distributed groups. In C. Montgomerie, & J. Seale (Eds.), *Proceedings of ED-MEDIA 2007--World Conference on Educational Multimedia, Hypermedia & Telecommunications* (pp. 3343–3352). Waynesville, NC: Association for the Advancement of Computing in Education (AACE).

Hylton, I.E. (2000). *Classroom management skills: Can video-modeling make a difference?* New York: New York University.

Ibrahim, M. (2012). Implications of designing instructional video using cognitive theory of multimedia learning. *Critical Questions in Education, 3*(2), 83–104.

IEA (2011). *Progress in international reading literacy study 2011* Accessed 3 June 2021 at http://www.iea.nl/six_subject_reading.html

Ingersoll, R.M. (2001). Teacher turnover and teacher shortages: An organizational analysis. *American Educational Research Journal, 38*(3), 499–534.

Ingersoll, R.M., & Strong, M. (2011). The impact of induction and mentoring programs for beginning teachers: A critical review of the research. *Review of Educational Research, 81*(2), 201–233. doi:10.3102/0034654311403323.

Interstate New Teacher Assessment and Support Consortium [INTASC] (1992). *Model standards for beginning teacher licensing and development: A resource for state dialogue.* Washington, DC: Council of Chief State School Officers.

Jacobs, V.R., & Empson, S.B. (2016). Responding to children's mathematical thinking in the moment: An emerging framework of teaching moves. *ZDM, 48*(1–2), 185–197. doi:10.1007/s11858-015-0717-0.

Jacobs, V.R., Lamb, L.L.C., Philipp, R.A., & Schappelle, B.P. (2011). Deciding how to respond on the basis of children's understandings. In M.G. Sherin, V. Jacobs, & R. Philipp (Eds.), *Mathematics teacher noticing: Seeing through teachers' eyes* (pp. 97–117). New York: Routledge.

Jilink, L., Fukkink, R., & Huijbregts, S. (2018). Effects of early childhood education training and video interaction guidance on teachers' interactive skills. *Journal of Early Childhood Teacher Education, 39*(4), 278–292. doi:10.1080/10901027.2017.1408042.

Johnson, W.D., & Johnson, R.T. (1991). *Cooperation in the classroom.* Edina, MN: Interaction Book Company.

Johnson, W.D., & Johnson, R.T. (1999). *Learning together and alone* (5th ed.). Boston, MA: Allyn and Bacon.

Jonassen, D.H., & Rohrer-Murphy, L. (1999). Activity theory as a framework for designing constructivist learning environments. *Educational Technology Research and Development, 47*(1), 61–79.

Joyce, B.R., & Showers, B. (2002). *Student achievement through staff development.* Alexandria, VA: Association for Supervision and Curriculum Development (ISBN 0-87120-674-9).

Juffer, F., Bakermans-Kranenburg, M.J., & Van IJzendoorn, M.H. (2014). Attachment-based interventions: Sensitive parenting is the key to positive parent-child relationships. In P. Holmes, & S. Farnfield (Eds.), *The Routledge handbook of attachment. Implications and interventions* (pp. 83–103). London: Routledge.

Kahneman, D. (2011). *Thinking, fast and slow.* New York: Farrar, Straus and Giroux.

Kalyuga, S. (2012). Instructional benefits of spoken words: A review of cognitive load factors. *Educational Research Review, 7,* 145–159. doi:10.1016/j.edurev.2011.12.002.

Kane, T.J., Gehlbach, H., Greenberg, M., Quinn, D., & Thal, D. (2015). *The Best Foot Forward project: Substituting teacher-collected video for in-person classroom observations. First year implementation report.* Cambridge, MA: Center for Education Policy Research, Harvard University.

Karabenick, S. (Ed.). (1998). *Strategic help seeking. Implications for learning and teaching.* Mahwah, NJ: Lawrence Erlbaum.

Kasworm, C. (2001). *A case study of adult learner experiences of an accelerated degree program. Paper presented at the Annual Meeting of the American Educational Research Association, Seattle 2001 (ED ED479317).*

Kearney, S. (2014). Understanding beginning teacher induction: A contextualized examination of best practice. *Cogent Education, 1*(1), 2–15. doi:10.1080/2331186X.2014.967477.

Kehle, T.J., & Gonzales, F. (1991). Self-modeling for children's emotional and social concerns. In P.W. Dowrick (Ed.), *Practical guide to using video in the behavioural sciences* (pp. 244–256). New York: John Wiley & Sons.

Kelchtermans, G. (2009). Who I am in how I teach is the message: Self-understanding, vulnerability and reflection. *Teachers and Teaching: Theory and Practice, 15*(2), 257–272. doi:10.1080/13540600902875332.

Kelman, H.C. (1974). Attitudes are alive and well and gainfully employed in the sphere of action. *American Psychologist, 29*(5), 310–324.

Kennedy, M. (1998). *Form and substance in inservice teacher education.* Arlington, VA: National Science Foundation (ED 472719).

Kennedy, M. (2016). How does professional development improve teaching? *Review of Educational Research, 86*(4), 945–980. doi:10.3102/0034654315626800.

Kersting, N.B. (2008). Using video clips of mathematics classroom instruction as item prompts to measure teachers' knowledge of teaching mathematics. *Educational and Psychological Measurement, 68*(5), 845–861.

Kersting, N.B., Givvin, K.B., Sotelo, F.L., & Stigler, J.W. (2010). Teachers' analyses of classroom video predict student learning of mathematics: Further explorations of a novel measure of teacher knowledge. *Journal of Teacher Education, 61*(1–2), 172–181. doi:10.1177/0013164407313369.

Kersting, N.B., Givvin, K.B., Thompson, B.J., Santagata, R., & Stigler, J.W. (2012). Measuring usable knowledge: Teachers' analyses of mathematics classroom videos predict teaching quality and student learning. *American Educational Research Journal, 49*(3), 568–589. doi:10.3102/0002831212437853.

Kersting, N.B., Sherin, B.L., & Stigler, J.W. (2014). Automated scoring of teachers' open-ended responses to video prompts: Bringing the classroom-video-analysis assessment to scale. *Educational and Psychological Measurement, 74*(6), 950–974. doi:10.1177/0013164414521634.

Kersting, N.B., Smith, J.E., & Vezino, B. (2021). Using authentic video clips of classroom instruction to capture teachers' moment-to-moment perceiving as knowledge-filtered noticing. *ZDM Mathematics Education, 53*, 109–118. doi:10.1007/s11858-020-01201-6.

Kiemer, K., Gröschner, A., Pehmer, A.-K., & Seidel, T. (2014). Teacher learning and student outcomes in the context of classroom discourse. Findings from a video-based teacher professional development programme. *Form@re, 14*(2), 51–62. doi:10.13128/formare-15124.

Kiemer, K., Gröschner, A., Pehmer, A.-K., & Seidel, T. (2015). Effects of a classroom discourse intervention on teachers' practice and students' motivation to learn mathematics and science. *Learning and Instruction, 35*, 94–103. doi:10.1016/j.learninstruc.2014.10.003.

King, A. (1993). From sage on the stage to guide on the side. *College Teaching, 41*(1), 30–35.

Kleinknecht, M., & Gröschner, A. (2016). Fostering preservice teachers' noticing with structured video feedback: Results of an online-and video-based intervention study. *Teaching and Teacher Education, 59*, 45–56. doi:10.1016/j.tate.2016.05.020.

Kleinknecht, M., & Schneider, J. (2013). What do teachers think and feel when analyzing videos of themselves and other teachers teaching? *Teaching and Teacher Education, 33*, 13–23. doi:10.1016/j.tate.2013.02.002.

Klinzing, H.G. (2002). Wie effektiv ist Microteaching? [How effective is microteaching?] *Zeitschrift für Pädagogik, 48*(2), 194–214.

Ko, R., & Rossen. S. (2010). *Teaching online. A practical guide.* New York: Routledge.

Kobarg, M. (2009). *Unterstützung unterrichtlicher Lernprozesse aus zwei Perspektiven. Eine Gegenüberstellung* [Teachers' instructional support of learning in the classroom contrasted from two perspectives]. Münster: Waxmann.

Koellner, K., & Jacobs, J. (2015). Distinguishing models of professional development: The case of an adaptive model's impact on teachers' knowledge, instruction, and student achievement. *Journal of Teacher Education*, *66*(1), 51–67. doi:10.1177/0022487114549599.

Kohen, Z., & Borko, H. (2019). Classroom discourse in mathematics lessons: The effect of a hybrid practice-based professional development program. *Professional Development in Education*. doi:10.1080/19415257.2019.1706186.

Korthagen, F.A.J., Kessels, J., Koster, B., Lagerwerf, B., & Wubbels, T. (2001). *Linking practice and theory. The pedagogy of realistic teacher education*. Mahwah, NJ: Lawrence Erlbaum Associates.

Korthagen, F.A.J., & Lagerwerf, B. (2001). Teachers' professional learning: How does it work? In F.A.J. Korthagen, J. Kessels, B. Koster, B. Lagerwerf, & T. Wubbels *Linking practice and theory. The pedagogy of realistic teacher education* (pp. 175–207). Mahwah, NJ: Lawrence Erlbaum Associates.

Korthagen, F.A.J., & Wubbels, T. (2001). Learning from practice. In F.A.J. Korthagen, J. Kessels, B. Koster, B. Lagerwerf, & T. Wubbels (Eds.), *Linking practice and theory. The pedagogy of realistic teacher education* (pp. 32–51). Mahwah, NJ: Lawrence Erlbaum Associates.

Kosko, K.W., Ferdig, R.E., & Zolfaghari, M. (2021). Preservice teachers' professional noticing when viewing standard and 360 video. *Journal of Teacher Education*, *72*(3), 284–297. doi:10.1177/0022487120939544.

Koster, B., Dengerink, J., Korthagen, F.A.J., & Lunenberg, M. (2008). Teacher educators working on their own professional development: Goals, activities and outcomes of a project for the professional development of teacher educators. *Teachers and Teaching: Theory and Practice*, *14*(5–6), 567–587. doi:10.1080/13540600802571411.

Koster, M., Bouwer, R., & Van den Bergh, H. (2017). Professional development of teachers in the implementation of a strategy-focused writing intervention program for elementary students. *Contemporary Educational Psychology*, *49*, 1–20. doi:10.1016/j.cedpsych.2016.10.002.

Koster, M., Tribushinina, E., De Jong, P.F., & Van den Bergh, B. (2015). Teaching children to write: A meta-analysis of writing intervention research. *Journal of Writing Research*, *7*(2), 249–274. doi:10.17239/jowr-2015.07.02.02.

Koumi, J. (2006). *Designing video and multimedia for open and flexible learning*. New York, NY: Routledge.

Koumi, J. (2015). Learning outcomes afforded by self-assessed, segmented video-print combinations. *Cogent Education*, *2*, 1–27.

Kounin, J.S. (1970). *Discipline and group management in classrooms*. New York: Holt, Rinehart, & Winston.

Kozulin, A., Gindis, B., Ageyev, V.S., & Miller, S.M. (Eds.). (2003). *Vygotsky's educational theory in cultural context*. Cambridge, UK: Cambridge University Press.

Kraft, M.A., Blazar, D., & Hogan, D. (2018). The effect of teacher coaching on instruction and achievement: A meta-analysis of the causal evidence. *Review of Educational Research*, *88*(4), 547–588. doi:10.3102/0034654318759268.

Kraft, M.A., & Hill, H.C. (2020). Developing ambitious mathematics instruction through web-based coaching: A randomized field trial. *American Educational Research Journal*, *57*(6), 2378–2414. doi:10.3102/0002831220916840.

Krammer, K. (2014). Fallbasiertes Lernen mit Unterrichtsvideos in der Lehrerinnen- und Lehrerbildung [Casebased learnng with classroom video in teacher education]. *Beiträge zur Lehrerinnen- und Lehrerbildung*, *32*(2), 164–176.

Krantz, P.J., MacDuff, G.S., Wadstrom, O., & McClannahan, L.E. (1991). Using video with developmentally disabled learners. In P.W. Dowrick (Ed.), *Practical guide to using video in the behavioural sciences* (pp. 256–267). New York: John Wiley & Sons.

Kuhn, T.S. (1970). *The structure of scientific revolutions. Second edition, Enlarged*. Chicago, IL: The University of Chicago Press.

Kunter, M., & Baumert, J. (2006). Who is the expert? Construct and criteria validity of student and teacher ratings of instruction. *Learning Environments Research*, *9*(3), 231–251. doi:10.1007/s10984-006-9015-7.

Kuntze, K., & Reiss, K. (2006). Evaluational research on a video-based in-service mathematics teacher training project – reported instructional practice and judgments on instructional quality. In J. Novotná, H. Moraová, M. Krátká, & N. Stehlíková (Eds.), *Proceedings 30th Conference of the International Group for the Psychology of Mathematics Education* (Vol. 4, pp. 1–8). Prague: Charles University.

Kyriakides, L., Creemers, B., Antoniou, P., & Demetriou, D. (2010). A synthesis of studies searching for school factors: Implications for theory and research. *British Educational Research Journal*, *36*(5), 807–830. doi:10.1080/01411920903165603.

Kyriakides, L., Creemers, B.P.M., & Antoniou, P. (2009). Teacher behaviour and student outcomes: Suggestions for research on teacher training and professional development. *Teaching and Teacher Education*, *25*(1), 12–23. doi:10.1016/j.tate.2008.06.001.

La Paro, K.M., Maynard, C., Thomason, A., & Scott-Little, C. (2011). Developing teachers' classroom interactions: A description of a video review process for early childhood education students. *Journal of Early Childhood Teacher Education*, *33*(3), 224–238. doi:10.1080/1 0901027.2012.705809.

Lacey, C. (1977). *The socialization of teachers*. London: Methuen.

Laurillard, D. (1993). *Rethinking university teaching. A framework for the effective use of educational technology*. London/New York: Routledge.

Lawrence Brown, D. (2004). Differentiated instruction: Inclusive strategies for standards-based learning that benefits the whole class. *American Secondary Education*, *32*(3), 34–62.

Leblanc, S. (2018). Analysis of video-based training approaches and professional development. *Contemporary Issues in Technology and Teacher Education*, *18*(1), 125–148.

Leblanc, S., & Ria, L. (2011). Designing the Néopass@ction platform based on modeling of beginning teachers' activity. *Design and Technology Education: An International Journal*, *19*(2), 40–51.

Lee, J.S., Ginsburg, H.P., & Preston, M.D. (2007). Analyzing videos to learn to think like an expert teacher … Early Childhood Mathematics Education Graduate Courses. *Beyond the Journal. Young Children on the Web*, *72*(3), 1–8.

Lee, Y., Kinzie, M.B., & Whittaker, J.V. (2012). Impact of online support for teachers' open-ended questioning in pre-k science activities. *Teaching and Teacher Education*, *28*(4), 568–577. doi:10.1016/j.tate.2012.01.002.

Leisink, J., & Kienstra, N. (2002). Videofragmenten. Kijken naar jezelf [Self-viewing with video fragments]. In C.N. Brouwer, T. Brouwers, N. Kienstra, J. Leisink, R. Liebrand, S. van Maanen et al. *Voor de klas. Voorbereidingen op de praktijk* [Learn and let learn. A handbook of teacher education methods] (pp. 101–109).

Lewin, K. (1951). *Field Theory in Social Science. Selected Theoretical Papers*. New York: Harper & Row.

Lewis, R., & Lovegrove, M. (1984). Teachers' classroom control procedures: Are students' preferences being met? *Journal of Education for Teaching*, *10*(2), 97–105.

Little, J.W. (1990). The persistence of privacy: Autonomy and initiative in teachers' professional relations. *Teachers College Record*, *91*(4), 509–536.

Littlejohn, A., & Pegler, C. (2007). *Preparing for blended e-learning*. New York: Routledge.

Liu, T.C. (2005). Web-based cognitive apprenticeship model for improving pre-service teachers' performances and attitudes towards instructional planning: Design and field experiment. *Educational Technology and Society*, *8*(2), 136–149.

Lo, C.K., & Hew, K.F. (2017). A critical review of flipped classroom challenges in K-12 education: Possible solutions and recommendations for future research. *Research and Practice in Technology Enhanced Learning*, *12*(4), 1–22.

Lockwood, F. (1998). *The design and production of self-instructional materials*. London: Kogan Page.

Loera-Varela, A., Flores, A.M., & Del Campo, A.F.M. (2018). *Using video-lessons to improve the quality of teaching*. Belmopan, Belize: Ministry of Education, Youth, Sports and Culture.

Lok, L. (2019). *Using video in teacher education and professional development activities to stimulate teaching for active learning in Cambodia*. Eindhoven: Eindhoven University of Technology.

Lortie, D.C. (1975). *School teacher*. Chicago, IL: The University of Chicago Press.

Lotan, M., & Gold, C. (2009). Meta-analysis of the effectiveness of individual intervention in the controlled multisensory environment (Snoezelen®) for individuals with intellectual disability. *Journal of Intellectual & Developmental Disability*, *34*(3), 207–215. doi:10.1080/13668250903080106.

Lovegrove, M.N., Lewis, R., Fall, C., & Lovegrove, H. (1985). Students' preferences for discipline practices in schools. *Teaching and Teacher Education*, *1*(4), 325–333.

Ludlow, B.L., & Duff, M.C. (2007). Copyright law and content protection mechanisms: Digital rights management for teacher educators. *Teacher Education and Special Education*, *30*(2), 93–102.

Lukeš, D. (2000). What do we know about educational videos: Research and practice. *Media and learning news*, webinar 4 March 2010.

Lundgren, U.P. (1973). *Pedagogical Frames and the Teaching Process. A Report from an Empirical Curriculum Project*. Gothenburg: Institute of Education, Gothenburg University.

Lunenberg, M., Dengerink, J., & Korthagen, F.A.J. (2013). *Het beroep van lerarenopleider. Professionele rollen, professioneel handelen en professionele ontwikkeling van lerarenopleiders. Reviewstudie in opdracht van NWO/PROO* [The profession of teacher educator. Professional roles, professional action and professional development of teacher educators. Review study commissioned by the Program for educational research of the Netherlands Organisation for Scientific Research]. Amsterdam: Vrije Universiteit.

Lussi Borer, V., & Flandin, S. (2016). *Designing in-school Collaborative Video Learning Lab: A video-enhanced imementation of an educational policy in France*. Presentation for the CIDREE event "Video-enhanced teacher development: From research to innovative practice" (13–14 October, Helsinki, Finland). Genève: Université de Genève.

Lussi Borer, V., Gaudin, C., Roche, L., & Flandin, S. (2015). *Teaching Transformations From Video-Based Induction Programs: Does It Make a Difference Whether The learning Objects Are Prescribed Or Not?* Presentation symposium "How much instruction and support do novice and expert teachers need to learn from classroom videos? Effects of video-based approaches in different stages of teacher education and teachers' professional development" of the Special Interest Group 11 Research in Teaching and Teacher Education at the the 16th biennial conference of the European Association for Research on Learning and Instruction (Limassol, Cyprus). Genève: Université de Genève.

Lussi Borer, V., & Muller, A. (2016). Designing collaborative video learning lab to transform teachers's work practices. In P.G. Rossi, & L. Fedeli (Eds.), *Integrating video into pre-service and in-service teacher training* (pp. 68–89). Hershey, PA: IGI Global.

Lussi Borer, V., & Ria, L. (2014). *Collaborative Video Learning Lab in Schools*. Presentation at the Special Interest Group 11 Research in Teaching and Teacher Education conference of the European Association for Research on Learning and Instruction (Chiemsee, Germany). Genève: Université de Genève.

Lussi Borer, V., Ria, L., Durand, M., & Muller, M. (2014). How do teachers appropriate learning objects through critical experiences? A study of a pilot in-school collaborative video learning lab. *Form@re*, *14*(2), 63–74. doi:10.13128/formare-15137.

Lussi-Borer, V., Muller, M., Perrin, N., Plazaola, I., & Durand, M. (2015). *Collaborative inquiry on teachers' activity in pilot collaborative video learning labs (CVLL)*. Presentation for the

CIDREE-IFÉ seminar "Professional vision and video-enhanced teacher development" (17 March, 2015, Lyon). Genève: Université de Genève.

Lyman, F. (1981). The responsive classroom discussion. In A.S. Anderson (Ed.), *Main-streaming digest* (pp. 109–113). College Park, MD: University of Maryland College of Education.

Lyver, D. (2005). *Basics of video sound.* Oxford: Focal Press.

MacDonald, E. (2011). When nice won't suffice. *Journal of Staff Development, 32*(3), 45–47.

MacLeod, G. (1995). Microteaching in teacher education. In L.W. Anderson, *International encyclopedia of teaching and teacher education. Second edition* (pp. 573–578). Oxford, UK/New York/Tokyo: Pergamon/Elsevier.

Madariaga, L., Nussbaum, M., Gutiérrez, I., Barahona, C., & Meneses, A. (2021). Assessment of user experience in video-based learning environments: From design guidelines to final product. *Computers & Education, 167,* 104176. doi:10.1016/j.compedu.2021.104176.

Major, L., & Watson, S. (2018). Using video to support in-service teacher professional development: The state of the field, limitations and possibilities. *Technology, Pedagogy and Education, 27*(1), 49–68. doi:10.1080/1475939X.2017.1361469.

Marsh, B., & Mitchell, N. (2014). The role of video in teacher professional development. *Teacher Development, 18*(3), 403–417. doi:10.1080/13664530.2014.938106.

Martin, S.N., & Siry, C. (2008). *Choosing the right tool for the job: An analysis of the utilization of video/multi-media resources in teacher education. Paper presented at the annual meeting of the American Educational Research Association.* Philadelphia, PA: Drexel University.

Martin-Kniep, G.O. (2004). *Developing learning communities through teacher expertise.* Thousand Oaks, CA: Corwin Press.

Mashburn, A.J., Downer, J.T., Hamre, B.K., Justice, L.M., & Pianta, R.C. (2010). Consultation for teachers and children's language and literacy development during pre-kindergarten. *Applied Developmental Science, 14*(4), 179–196. doi:10.1080/10888691.2010.516187.

Matsumura, L.C., Correnti, R., Walsh, M., Bickel, D.D., & Zook-Howell, D. (2019). Online content-focused coaching to improve classroom discussion quality. *Technology, Pedagogy and Education, 28*(2), 191–215. doi:10.1080/1475939X.2019.1577748.

Matsumura, L.C., Garnier, H.E., & Resnick, L.B. (2010). Implementing literacy coaching: The role of school resources. *Educational Evaluation and Policy Analysis, 32*(2), 249–272. doi:10.3102/0162373710363743.

Matsumura, L.C., Garnier, H.E., Slater, S.C., & Boston, M.B. (2008). Measuring instructional interactions 'at-scale'. *Educational Assessment, 13*(4), 267–300. doi:10.1080/10627190802602541.

Matsumura, L.C., Garnier, H.E., & Spybrook, J. (2013). Literacy coaching, reading comprehension instruction and student achievement: A multi-level mediation model. *Learning and Instruction, 25,* 35–48. doi:10.1016/j.learninstruc.2012.11.001.

Mayer, R.E. (2001). *Multimedia learning.* Cambridge, MA: Cambridge University Press.

Mayer, R.E. (2005). Introduction to multimedia learning. In R.E. Mayer (Ed.), *The Cambridge handbook of multimedia learning* (pp. 1–19). New York: Cambridge University Press.

Mayer, R.E. (2008). *Learning and instruction.* Upper Saddle River, NJ: Pearson.

Mayer, R.E., Fiorella, L., & Stull, A. (2020). Five ways to increase the effectiveness of instructional video. *Educational Technology Research and Development, 68*(3), 837–852. doi:10.1007/s11423-020-09749-6.

McCabe, M. (2004). *The divergent paths of alternative teaching routes. evidence of wide-ranging variation in state alternative-route teacher education programs. Paper prepared for the annual meeting of the American Educational Research Association.* Bethesda, MD: Education Week.

McKnight, P.C. (1980) Microteaching: Development from 1968 to 1978. *British Journal of Teacher Education, 6*(3), 214–227. doi:10.1080/0260747800060305.

Meelissen, M.R.M., Netten, A., Drent, M., Punter, R.A., Droop, M., & Verhoeven, L. (2012). *PIRLS- en TIMSS-2011. Trends in leerprestaties in lezen, rekenen en natuuronderwijs* [PIRLS and TIMSS 2011. Achievement trends in reading, mathematics and science education]. Nijmegen/Enschede: Radboud University Nijmegen/University of Twente.

Mehan, H. (1979). *Learning lessons. Social organization in the classroom.* Cambridge, MA: Harvard University Press.

Meloth, M., Good, A., & Sugar, W. (2008). Review of research on the use of video cases to improve preservice and inservice teachers' knowledge and skills. In K. McFerrin, R. Weber, R. Carlsen, & D.A. Willis (Eds.), *SITE 2008--Society for Information Technology & Teacher Education International Conference* (pp. 940–942). Waynesville, NC: Association for the Advancement of Computing in Education (AACE).

Mercer, N., & Dawes, L. (2014). The study of talk between teachers and students. *Oxford Review of Education, 40*(4), 430–445. doi:10.1080/03054985.2014.934087.

Merseth, K.K. (1996). Cases and case methods in teacher education. In A.J. Sikula, T.J. Buttery, & E. Guyton. *Handbook of research on teacher education* (pp. 722–744). New York: Simon & Shuster Macmillan.

Merseth, K.K., & Lacey, A.C. (1993). Weaving stronger fabric: The pedagogical promise of hypermedia and case methods in teacher education. *Teaching and Teacher Education, 9*(3), 283–299.

Michaels, S., O'Connor, C., & Resnick, L. (2008). Deliberative discourse idealized and realized: Accountable talk in the classroom and in civic life. *Studies in Philosophy and Education, 27*(4), 283–297. doi:10.1007/s11217-007-9071-1.

Mikami, A.Y., Gregory, A., Allen, J.P., Pianta, R.C., & Lun, J. (2011). Effects of a teacher professional development intervention on peer relationships in secondary classrooms. *School Psychology Review, 40*(3), 367–385.

Miles, M.B., & Huberman, A.M. (1994). *Qualitative data analysis. An expanded sourcebook.* Thousand Oaks, CA: Sage.

Miller, K.F. (2011). Situation awareness in teaching: What educators can learn from video-based research in other fields. In M.G. Sherin, V. Jacobs, & R. Philipp (Eds.), *Mathematics teacher noticing. Seeing through teachers' eyes* (pp. 51–66). New York: Routledge.

Miller, K.F., & Correa, C. (2009). *What are you looking at? Matters of perspective in watching classroom video. Paper presented at the 13th biennial conference of the European Association for Research on Learning and Instruction (Amsterdam).* Ann Arbor, MI: University of Michigan.

Miller, K.F., & Zhou, X. (2007). Learning from classroom video: What makes it compelling and what makes it hard. In R. Goldman, R. Pea, B. Barron, & S.J. Derry (Eds.), *Video research in the learning sciences* (pp. 321–334). Mahwah, NJ: Lawrence Erlbaum Associates.

Mills, G.E. (2013). *Action research. A guide for the teacher researcher.* Upper Saddle River, NJ: Merrill Prentice Hall.

Mischel, W., Shoda, Y., & Rodriguez, M.I. (1989). Delay of gratification in children. *Science, 244* (4907), 933–938.

Mohr, S., & Santagata, R. (2015). Changes in pre-service teachers' beliefs about mathematics teaching and learning during teacher preparation and effects of video-enhanced analysis of practice. *Orbis Scholae, 9*(2), 103–117.

Mol, S.E., & Bus, A.G. (2011). To read or not to read: A meta-analysis of print exposure from infancy to early adulthood. *Psychological Bulletin, 137*(2), 267–296. doi:10.1037/a0021890.

Mollo, V., & Falzon, P. (2004). Auto- and allo-confrontation as tools for reflective activities. *Applied Ergonomics, 35*(6), 531–540. doi:10.1016/j.apergo.2004.06.003.

Moretti, F.A., & Ginsburg, H.P. (2009). *Video interactions for teaching and learning (VITAL): A learning environment for courses in early childhood mathematics education. NSF final report.* New

York: Columbia Center for New Media Teaching and Learning (CCNMTL), Columbia University.

Morris, A.K., & Hiebert, J. (2009). Building a knowledge base for teacher education: An experience in K–8 mathematics teacher preparation. *The Elementary School Journal, 109*(5), 475–490. doi:10.1086/596994.

Müller-Fohrbrodt, G., Cloetta, B., & Dann, H.-D. (1978). *Der Praxisschock bei jungen Lehrern. Formen-Ursachen-Folgerungen. Eine zusammenfassende Bewertung der theoretischen und empirischen Erkenntnisse* [Practice shock in young teachers: Forms, causes, and consequences. An evaluative summary of theoretical insights and empirical evidence]. Stuttgart: Klett-Cotta.

Mumme, J., & Seago, N. (2003). *Examining teachers' development in representing and conceptualizing linear relationships within teaching practice. Paper presented at the annual meeting of the American Educational Research Association.* San Francisco: WestEd.

Musburger, R.B., & Ogden, M.R. (2014). *Single-camera video production.* Abingdon, UK: Routledge.

Nagro, S.A., & Cornelius, K.E. (2013). Evaluating the evidence base of video analysis: A special education teacher development tool. *Teacher Education and Special Education, 36*(4), 312–329. doi:10.1177/0888406413501090.

Neuman, S.B., & Cunningham, L. (2009). The impact of professional development and coaching on early language and literacy instructional practices. *American Educational Research Journal, 46*(2), 532–566. doi:10.3102/0002831208328088.

Noetel, M., Griffith, S., Delaney, O., Sanders, T., Parker, P., del Pozo Cruz, B., & Lonsdale, C. (2021). Video improves learning in higher education: A systematic review. *Review of Educational Research.* doi:10.3102/0034654321990713.

Nolan, J.F., & Hoover, L.A. (2011). *Teacher supervision and evaluation. Theory into practice.* Hoboken, NJ: John Wiley & Sons.

O'Dell, S.L. (1991). Producing video modeling tapes. In P.W. Dowrick (Ed.), *Practical guide to using video in the behavioural sciences* (pp. 186–203). New York: John Wiley & Sons.

O'Donnell, A.M., & King, A. (Eds.). (1999). *Cognitive perspectives on peer learning.* Mahwah, NJ: Lawrence Erlbaum.

OECD (2005). *Teachers matter. Attracting, developing and retaining effective teachers.* Paris: OECD. Accessed 3 June 2021 at http://www.oecd.org/education/school/attractingdevelopingandretainingeffectiveteachers-homepage.htm

OECD (2017). *Education at a glance 2017. OECD Indicators.* Paris: OECD Publishing. doi:10.187/eag-2017-en.

Oliveira, A.W. (2010). Improving teacher questioning in science inquiry discussions through professional development. *Journal of Research in Science Teaching: The Official Journal of the National Association for Research in Science Teaching, 47*(4), 422–453. doi 10.1002/tea.20345.

Oonk, W. (2009). *Theory-enriched practical knowledge in mathematics teacher education.* Leiden: ICLON, Universiteit Leiden.

Oosterheert, I.E., & Vermunt, J.D. (2003). Knowledge construction in learning to teach: The role of dynamic sources. *Teachers and Teaching, 9*(2), 157–173.

Open Science Collaboration (2015). Estimating the reproducibility of psychological science. *Science, 349*(6251), 1–8. doi:10.1126/Science.aac4716.

Opfer, V.D., & Pedder, D. (2011). Conceptualizing teacher professional learning. *Review of Educational Research, 81*(3), 376–407. doi:10.3102/0034654311413609.

Ortlieb, E., McVie, M.B., & Shanahan, L.E. (2015). *Video reflection in literacy teacher education and development. Lessons from research and practice.* Bingley, UK: Emerald.

Osborne, J.F., Borko, H., Fishman, E., Gomez Zaccarelli, F., Berson, E., Busch, K.C. et al. (2019). Impacts of a practice-based professional development program on elementary teachers' facilitation of and student engagement with scientific argumentation. *American Educational Research Journal, 56*(4), 1067–1112. doi:10.3102/0002831218812059.

Palincsar, A.S., & Brown, A.L. (1984). Reciprocal teaching of comprehension-fostering and comprehension-monitoring activities. *Cognition and Instruction, 1*(2), 117–175.

Pehmer, A.-K., Gröschner, A., & Seidel, T. (2015a). How teacher professional development regarding classroom dialogue affects students' higher-order learning. *Teaching and Teacher Education, 47*, 108–119. doi:10.1016/j.tate.2014.12.007.

Pehmer, A.-K., Gröschner, A., & Seidel, T. (2015b). Fostering and scaffolding student engagement in productive classroom discourse: Teachers' practice changes and reflections in light of teacher professional development. *Learning, Culture and Social Interaction, 7*, 12–27. doi:10.1016/j.lcsi.2015.05.001.

Perini, M., Cattaneo, A.A., & Tacconi, G. (2019). Using Hypervideo to support undergraduate students' reflection on work practices: A qualitative study. *International Journal of Educational Technology in Higher Education, 16*(1), 1–16. doi:10.1186/s41239-019-0156-z.

Petko, D., Prasse, D., & Reusser, K. (2014). Online-Plattformen für die Arbeit mit Unterrichtsvideos: Eine Übersicht [Online platforms for working with classroom videos. An overview]. *Beiträge zur Lehrerinnen-und Lehrerbildung, 32*(2), 247–261.

Pianta, R.C., & Hamre, B.K. (2009). Conceptualization, measurement, and improvement of classroom processes: Standardized observation can leverage capacity. *Educational Researcher, 38*(2), 109–119. doi:10.3102/0013189X09332374.

Pianta, R.C., Hamre, B.K., & Allen, J.P. (2012). Teacher-student relationships and engagement: Conceptualizing, measuring, and improving the capacity of classroom interactions. In S.L. Christenson, A.L. Reschly, & C. Wylie (Eds.), *Handbook of research on student engagement* (pp. 365–386). Boston, MA: Springer.

Pianta, R.C., La Paro, K., & Hamre, B.K. (2008). *Classroom assessment scoring system (CLASS).* Baltimore, MD: Paul H. Brookes.

Pianta, R.C., Mashburn, A.J., Downer, J.T., Hamre, B.K., & Justice, L. (2008). Effects of web-mediated professional development resources on teacher–child interactions in pre-kindergarten classrooms. *Early Childhood Research Quarterly, 23*(4), 431–451. doi:10.10116/j.ecresq.2008.02.001.

Picard, P., & Ria, L. (2011). Néopass@ction: A training tool for beginning teachers. In P. Picard, & L. Ria (Eds.), *Beginning teachers: A challenge for educational systems* (pp. 119–130) (hal-00804088). Lyon: École Normale Supérieur de Lyon.

Pieters, J., Voogt, J., & Pareja Roblin, N. (2019). *Collaborative curriculum design for sustainable innovation and teacher learning* (p. 424). Cham: Springer Nature. doi:10.1007/978-3-030-20062-6.

Piwowar, V., Barth, V.L., Ophardt, D., & Thiel, F. (2018). Evidence-based scripted videos on handling student misbehavior: The development and evaluation of video cases for teacher education, *Professional Development in Education, 44*(3), 369–384. doi:10.1080/19415257.2017.1316299.

Piwowar, V., Ophardt, D., & Thiel, F. (2013). *Videoclubs in teacher training programs for classroom management. Paper presented at the annual meeting of the American Educational Research Association.* Berlin: Freie Universität Berlin.

Piwowar, V., Thiel, F., & Ophardt, D. (2013). Training inservice teachers' competencies in classroom management. A quasi-experimental study with teachers of secondary schools. *Teaching and Teacher Education, 30*, 1–12. doi:10.1016/j.tate.2012.09.007.

Ploetzner, R., Massler, U., & Huppertz, P. (2005). Learning by collaborative analysis of digital video in distributed groups. In T. Okamoto, D. Albert, T. Honda, & F.W. Hesse (Eds.), *Proceedings of the second joint workshop on cognition and learning through media-communication for advanced e-learning* (pp. 140–145). Tokyo: Japanese Society for Information and Systems in Education.

Preston, C. (2013). *Phase One. Innovation in teaching and learning. Using web enabled video technology to build professional capital through reflective practice, coaching and collaboration.* Luton, UK: MirandaNet/University of Bedfordshire.

Preston, M.D. (2010). *Using Guided Experienes with Video to Help Teachers Interpret Children's Thinking with Appropriate Intellectual Modesty. Paper presented at the annual meeting of the American Educational Research Association.* New York: Teachers College/Columbia Center for New Media Teaching and Learning (CCNMTL), Columbia University.

Quinn, D.M., Kane, T.J., Greenberg, M., & Thal, D. (2018). Effects of a video-based teacher observation program on the de-privatization of instruction: Evidence from a randomized experiment. *Educational Administration Quarterly, 54*(4), 529–558.

Reisman, A., & Enumah, L. (2020). Using video to highlight curriculum-embedded opportunities for student discourse. *Journal of Teacher Education 71*(5), 551–567. doi:10.1177/0022487119895503.

Resnick, L.B., Asterhan, C.S.C., & Clarke, S.N. (Eds.). (2015a). *Socializing intelligence through academic talk and dialogue.* Washington, DC: American Educational Research Association.

Resnick, L.B., Asterhan, C.S.C., & Clarke, S.N. (2015b). Introduction. In L.B. Resnick, C.S.C. Asterhan, & S.N. Clarke (Eds.), *Socialzing intelligence through academic talk and dialogue* (pp. 1–13). Washington, DC: AERA.

Reusser, K. (2019). Unterricht als Kulturwerkstatt in bildungswissenschaftlich-psychologischer Sicht [Education as cultural work, considered from a pedagogical and psychological perspective]. In U. Steffens & R. Messner (Eds.), *Unterrichtsqualität. Konzepte und Bilanzen gelingenden Lehrens und Lernens* [*Quality of education. Concepts and assessments of successful teaching and learning*] (pp. 129–167). Münster: Waxmann.

Ria, L., Sève, C., Saury, J., Theureau, J., & Durand, M. (2003). Beginning teachers' situated emotions: A study of first classroom experiences. *Journal of Education for Teaching, 29*(3), 219–234. doi:10.1080/0260747032000120114.

Rich, P.J. (2015). Examining the role of others in video self-analysis. In B. Calandra, & P.J. Rich (Eds.), *Digital video for teacher education. Research and practice* (pp. 71–89). London/New York: Routledge.

Rich, P.J., & Hannafin, M. (2009a). Video annotation tools: Technologies to scaffold, structure, and transform teacher reflection. *Journal of Teacher Education, 60*(1), 52–67. doi:10.1177/0022487108328486.

Rich, P.J., & Hannafin, M. (2009b). Scaffolded video self-analysis: Discrepancies between preservice teachers' perceived and actual instructional decisions. *Journal of Computing in Higher Education, 21*(2), 128–145. doi:10.1007/s12528-009-9018-3.

Richards, J., Altshuler, M., Sherin, B.L., Sherin, M.G., & Leatherwood, C.J. (2021). Complexities and opportunities in teachers' generation of videos from their own classrooms. *Learning, Culture and Social Interaction, 28*, 100490. doi:10.1016/j.lcsi.2021.100490.

Riegel, U., & Macha, K. (Eds.). (2013). *Videobasierte Kompetenzforschung in den Fachdidaktiken* [Video-based competence research in the subject-specific pedagogies]. Münster: Waxmann.

Rijlaarsdam, G., Van den Bergh, H., Couzijn, M., Janssen, T., Braaksma, M., Tillema, T. et al. (2011). Writing. In S. Graham, A. Bus, S. Major, & L. Swanson (Eds.), *Application of educational psychology to learning and teaching* (Vol. 3, pp. 189–228). Washington, DC: American Psychological Association (APA Handbook).

Rimm-Kaufman, S.E., Voorhees, M.D., Snell, M.E., & La Paro, K.M. (2003). Improving the sensitivity and responsivity of preservice teachers toward young children with disabilities. *Topics in Early Childhood Special Education, 23*(3), 151–163.

Robinson, S.E. (2011). Teaching paraprofessionals of students with autism to implement pivotal response treatment in inclusive school settings using a brief video feedback training package. *Focus on Autism and Other Developmental Disabilities*, *26*(2), 105–118. doi:10.1177/1088357611407063.

Roche, L., & Gal-Petitfaux, N. (2017, March). Using 360° video in physical education teacher education. In P. Resta, & S. Smith (Eds.), *Society for information technology & teacher education international conference* (pp. 3420–3425). Waynesville, NC: Association for the Advancement of Computing in Education (AACE).

Roelofs, E. (2007). *Protocol bewijsvoering videodossiers: een stappenplan* [A stepwise protocol for assessing video portfolios]. Arnhem: CITO International.

Ronfeldt, M., Farmer, S.O., McQueen, K., & Grissom, J.A. (2015). Teacher collaboration in instructional teams and student achievement. *American Educational Research Journal*, *52*(3), 475–514. doi:10.3102/0002831215585562.

Rook, M.M., & McDonald, S.P. (2012, March). Digital records of practice: A Literature review of video analysis in teacher practice. In P. Resta (Ed.), *SITE 2012--Society for Information Technology & Teacher Education International Conference* (pp. 1441–1446). Association for the Advancement of Computing in Education (AACE).

Roschelle, J.M., Pea, R.D., Hoadley, C.M., Gordin, D.N., & Means, B.M. (2000). Changing how and what children learn in school with computer-based technologies. *Children and Computer Technology*, *10*(2), 76–101.

Rosenshine, B. (2010). *Principles of instruction*. Brussels: International Academy of Education.

Ross, L., & Nisbett, R.E. (2011). *The person and the situation: Perspectives of social psychology*. London: Pinter & Martin Publishers.

Roth, K.J. (2009). Using video studies to transform science teaching and learning: Results from the STeLLA professional development program. In T. Janík, & T. Seidel (Eds.), *The power of video studies* (pp. 225–243). Münster: Waxmann.

Roth, K.J., Bintz, J., Wickler, N.I., Hvidsten, C., Taylor, J., Beardsley, P.M. et al. (2017). Design principles for effective video-based professional development. *International Journal of STEM Education*, *4*(1), 4–31. doi:10.1186/s40594-017-0091-2.

Roth, K.J., Garnier, H.E., Chen, C., Lemmens, M., Schwille, K., & Wickler, N.I. (2011). Videobased lesson analysis: Effective science PD for teacher and student learning. *Journal of Research in Science Teaching*, *48*(2), 117–148. doi:10.1002/tea.20408.

Roth, K.J., Wilson, C.D., Taylor, J.A., Stuhlsatz, M.A., & Hvidsten, C. (2019). Comparing the effects of analysis-of-practice and content-based professional development on teacher and student outcomes in science. *American Educational Research Journal*, *56*(4), 1217–1253. doi: 10.1080/19345747.2016.1147628.

Rudduck, J., McIntyre, D. (2007). *Improving learning through Consulting Pupils*. London: Routledge.

Ryan, R., & Deci, E.L. (2000). Self-determination theory and the facilitation of intrinsic motivation, social development, and well-being. *American Psychologist*, *55*(1), 68–78.

Sabers, D.S., Cushing, K.S., & Berliner, D.C. (1991). Differences among teachers in a task characterized by simultaneity, multidimensional, and immediacy. *American Educational Research Journal*, *28*(1), 63–88.

Sacher, J. (2008). *Videographie in der Lehrerbildung – ein Literaturbericht* [Videography in teacher education – a literature study]. *TriOs, Forum für schulnahe Forschung, Schulentwicklung und Evaluation 3*(2).

Salmon, G. (2011). *E-moder@ting. The key to teaching and learning online. Third edition*. New York/London: Routledge.

Santagata, R., & Angelici, G. (2010). Studying the impact of the lesson analysis framework on preservice teachers' abilities to reflect on videos of classroom teaching. *Journal of Teacher Education*, *61*(4), 339–349. doi:10.1177/0022487110369555.

Santagata, R., & Bray, W. (2016). Professional development processes that promote teacher change: The case of a video-based program focused on leveraging students' mathematical errors, *Professional Development in Education, 42*(4). 547–568. doi:10.1080/19415257.2015.1082076.

Santagata, R., & Guarino, J. (2011). Using video to teach future teachers to learn from teaching. *ZDM, 43*(1), 133–145. doi:10.1007/s11858-010-0292-3.

Santagata, R., & Yeh, C. (2014). Learning to teach mathematics and to analyze teaching effectiveness: Evidence from a video-and practice-based approach. *Journal of Mathematics Teacher Education, 17*(6), 491–514. doi:10.1007/s10857-013-9263-2.

Santagata, R., & Yeh, C. (2016). The role of perception, interpretation, and decision making in the development of beginning teachers' competence. *ZDM, 48*(1–2), 153–165. doi:10.1007/s11858-015-0737-9.

Santagata, R., Zannoni, C., & Stigler, J.W. (2007). The role of lesson analysis in pre-service teacher education: An empirical investigation of teacher learning from a virtual video-based field experience. *Journal of Mathematics Teacher Education, 10*(2), 123–140. doi:10.1007/s10857-007-9029-9.

Santos Espino, J.M., Afonso Suárez, M.D., & González-Henríquez, J.J. (2020). Video for teaching: Classroom use, instructor self-production and teachers' preferences in presentation format. *Technology, Pedagogy and Education, 29*(2), 147–162. doi:10.1080/1475939X.2020.1726805.

Santos-Espino, J.M., Afonso-Suárez, M.D., & Guerra-Artal, C. (2016). Speakers and boards: A survey of instructional video styles in MOOCs. *Technical Communication, 63*(2), 101–115.

Sarason, S.B. (1996). *Revisiting "The culture of the school and the problem of change".* New York: Teachers College Press.

Sauli, F., Cattaneo, A.A., & Van der Meij, H. (2018). Hypervideo for educational purposes: A literature review on a multifaceted technological tool. *Technology, Pedagogy and Education, 27*(1), 115–134. doi:10.1080/1475939X.2017.1407357.

Scheepens, R. (2004). *Rapportage mentor meeloopdagen (MML)* [Report of mentor classroom visits]. Nijmegen: Urban Gymnasium Nijmegen.

Scheiner, T. (2016). Teacher noticing: Enlightening or blinding? *ZDM, 48*(1–2), 227–238. doi:10.1007/s11858-016-0771-2.

Schick, N. (2020). *Deep fakes and the infocalypse. What you urgently need to know.* London: Monoray.

Schildwacht, M.M.C. (2012). *Learning to notice. Teachers coaching teachers with video feedback.* Enschede: University of Twente.

Schindler, A.K., Gröschner, A., & Seidel, T. (2015). Teaching science effectively: A case study on student verbal engagement in classroom dialogue. *Orbis Scholae, 9*(2), 9–35.

Schön, D.A. (1983). *The reflective practitioner. How professionals think in action.* New York: Basic Books.

Schwindt, K. (2008). *Lehrpersonen betrachten Unterricht. Kriterien für die kompetente Unterrichtswahrnehmung* [Teachers viewing teaching. Criteria for competent viewing of teaching]. Münster: Waxmann.

Seago, N.M., Jacobs, J.K., Heck, D.J., Nelson, C.L., & Malzahn, K.A. (2014). Impacting teachers' understanding of geometric similarity: Results from field testing of the Learning and Teaching Geometry professional development materials. *Professional Development in Education, 40*(4), 627–653. doi:10.1080/19415257.2013.830144.

Šed'ová, K. (2017a). A case study of a transition to dialogic teaching as a process of gradual change. *Teaching and Teacher Education, 67*, 278–290. doi:10.1016/j.tate.2017.06.018.

Šed'ová, K. (2017b). Transforming teacher behaviour to increase student participation in classroom discourse. *Teacher Development, 21*(2), 225–242. doi:10.1080/13664530.2016. 1224775.

Šed'ová, K., Sedláček, M., & Švaříček, R. (2016). Teacher professional development as a means of transforming student classroom talk. *Teaching and Teacher Education, 57,* 14–25. doi:10.1016/j.tate.2016.03.005.

Šed'ová, K., Švaříček, R., Sedláček, M., & Šalamounová, Z. (2014). On the way to dialogic teaching: Action research as a means to change classroom discourse. *Studia paedagogica, 19*(4), 9–43.

Seidel, T., Stürmer, K., Blomberg, G., Kobarg, M., & Schwindt, K. (2011). Teacher learning from analysis of videotaped classroom situations: Does it make a difference whether teachers observe their own teaching or that of others? *Teaching and Teacher Education, 27*(2), 259–267. doi:10.1016/j.tate.2010.08.009.

Shanklin, N.L. (2007). *What supports do literacy coaches need from administration in order to succeed?* Denver, CO: Literacy Coaching Clearing House (ERIC document 530330).

Shen, J., & Bierlein Palmer, L. (2005). Attrition patterns of inadequately prepared teachers. In J.R. Dangel, & E.M. Guyton (Eds.), *Research on alternative and non-traditional education. Teacher education yearbook XIII* (pp. 143–159). Lanham, MD: The Association of Teacher Educators/Scarecrow Education.

Shepard, L.A. (2000). The role of assessment in a learning culture. *Educational Researcher, 29*(7), 4–14.

Sherin, M.G. (2001). Developing a professional vision of classroom events. In T. Wood, B.S. Nelson, & J. Warfield (Eds.), *Beyond classical pedagogy: Teaching elementary school mathematics* (pp. 75–93). Hillsdale, NJ: Erlbaum.

Sherin, M.G. (2003). Using video clubs to support conversations among teachers and researchers. *Action in Teacher Education, 24*(4), 33–45.

Sherin, M.G., & Han, S.Y. (2004). Teacher learning in the context of a video club. *Teaching and Teacher Education, 20*(2), 163–183. doi:10.1016/j.tate.2003.08.001.

Sherin, M.G., Jacobs, V., & Philipp, R. (Eds.). (2011). *Mathematics teacher noticing. Seeing through teachers' eyes.* New York: Routledge.

Sherin, M.G., Russ, R.S., Sherin, B.L., & Colestock, A. (2008). Professional vision in action: An exploratory study. *Issues in Teacher Education, 17*(2), 27–46.

Sherin, M.G., & Van Es, E.A. (2005). Using video to support teachers' ability to notice classroom interactions. *Journal of Technology and Teacher Education, 13*(3), 475–491.

Sherin, M.G., & Van Es, E.A. (2009). Effects of video club participation on teachers' professional vision. *Journal of Teacher Education, 60*(1), 20–37. doi:10.1177/0022487108328155.

Sherin, M.G. & Van Es, E.A. (2010). The influence of video clubs on teachers' thinking and practice. *Journal of Mathematics Teacher Education, 13*(2), 155–176. doi:10.1007/s10857-009-9130-3.

Shernoff, E.S., & Kratochwill, T.R. (2007). Transporting an evidence-based classroom management program for preschoolers with disruptive behavior problems to a school: An analysis of implementation, outcomes, and contextual variables. *School Psychology Quarterly, 22*(3), 449. doi:10.1037/1045-3830.22.3.449.

Shinkfield, A.J., & Stufflebeam, D.J. (Eds.). (1995). *Teacher evaluation. Guide to effective practice.* Dordrecht: Kluwer.

Shute, V.J. (2008). Focus on formative feedback. *Review of Educational Research, 78*(1), 153–189. doi:10.3102/0034654307313795.

Silver, R.E., Kogut, G., & Huynh, T.C.D. (2019). Learning "new" instructional strategies: Pedagogical innovation, teacher professional development, understanding and concerns. *Journal of Teacher Education, 70*(5), 552–566. doi:10.1177/0022487119844712.

Simons, N. (2017). *Newton Fund. Maths Teacher Training. South Africa 2016. Evaluation Report.* Penarth, UK: Peter Trevitt Consulting.

Simons, R.-J., Van der Linden, J., & Duffy, T. (2000). *New Learning.* Dordrecht/Boston/London: Kluwer Academic Publishers.

Sinclair, J., & Coulthard, M. (1975). *Towards an analysis of discourse: The English used by teachers and pupils.* London: Oxford University Press.

Sleeter, C. (2014). Toward teacher education research that informs policy. *Educational Researcher, 43*(3), 146–153. doi:10.3102/0013189X14528752.

Smith, P.J. (2003). Workplace learning and flexible delivery. *Review of Educational Research, 73*(1), 53–89.

Smith, T.M., & Ingersoll, R.M. (2004). What are the effects of induction and mentoring on beginning teacher turnover? *American Educational Research Journal, 41*(3), 681–715.

Snoeyink, R. (2010). Using video self-analysis to improve "withitness" of student teachers. *Journal of Digital Learning in Teacher Education, 26*(3), 101–110.

Sonnleitner, M., Manthey, B., & Prock, S. (2020). Der Einsatz von Videos in der Lehrkräftebildung aus Sicht von Datenschutz und Forschungsethik [Video use in teacher education from a data protection and research ethics perspective]. In K. Hauenschild, B. Schmidt-Thieme, D. Wolff, & S. Zourelidis (Eds.), *Videografie in der Lehrer*innenbildung. Aktuelle Zugänge, Herausforderungen und Potenziale* [Videography in teacher education. Recent perspectives, challenges and potential] (pp. 232–241). Hildesheim: Universitätsverlag Hildesheim. doi:10.18442/100.

Stahnke, R., Schueler, S., Roesken-Winter, B. (2016). Teachers' perception, interpretation, and decision-making: A systematic review of empirical mathematics education research. *ZDM, 48,* 1–27. doi:10.1007/s11858-016-0775-y.

Stanford, G. (1977). *Developing effective classroom groups.* New York: Hart Publishing.

Staub, F. (2003). *Content-Focused Coaching: Transforming mathematics lessons.* Portsmouth, NH: Heinemann.

Stephenson, J., Carter, M., & Arthur-Kelly, M. (2011). Professional learning for teachers without special education qualifications working with students with severe disabilities. *Teacher Education and Special Education, 34*(1), 7–20. doi:10.1177/0888406410384407.

Stigler, J.W., & Hiebert, J. (1999). *The teaching gap. What educators can learn from the world's best teachers.* New York: The Free Press.

Stigler, J.W., & Rankin, S. (1998). *TIMMS-R Video Study. Data collection manual.* Santa Monica, CA: Lessonlab.

Stigler, J.W., & Thompson, B.J. (2009). Thoughts on creating, accumulating, and utilizing shareable knowledge to improve teaching. *The Elementary School Journal, 109*(5), 442–457.

Stoll, L., Bolam, R., McMahon, A., Wallace, M., & Thomas, S. (2006). Professional learning communities: A review of the literature. *Journal of Educational Change, 7*(4), 221–258. doi:10.1007/s10833-006-0001-8.

Stones, E. (1994). *Quality teaching. A sample of cases.* London: Routledge.

Stronge, J.H. (2002). *Qualities of effective teachers.* Alexandria, VA: Association for Supervision and Curriculum Development (ISBN 0-87120-663-3).

Stuhlman, M.W., Hamre, B.K., Downer, J.T., & Pianta, R.C. (2007). *What should classroom observation measure. A practitioner's guide to conducting classroom observations.* Part 2. Charlottesville, VA: Center for Advanced Study of Teaching and Learning (CASTL)/University of Virginia.

Sun, J., & Van Es, E.A. (2015). An exploratory study of the influence that analyzing teaching has on preservice teachers' classroom practice. *Journal of Teacher Education*, *66*(3), 201–214. doi:10.1177/0022487115574103.

Supovitz, J.A. (2002). Developing communities of instructional practice. *Teachers College Record*, *104*(8), 1591–1626.

Sweller, J. (2005). Implications of cognitive load theory for multimedia learning. In R.E. Mayer (Ed.), *The Cambridge handbook of multimedia learning* (pp. 19–31). New York: Cambridge University Press.

Taylor, J.A., Roth, K., Wilson, C.D., Stuhlsatz, M.A., & Tipton, E. (2017). The effect of an analysis-of-practice, videocase-based, teacher professional development program on elementary students' science achievement. *Journal of Research on Educational Effectiveness*, *10*(2), 241–271. doi:10.1080/19345747.2016.1147628.

Tekkumru Kisa, M., & Stein, M.K. (2015). Learning to see teaching in new ways: A foundation for maintaining cognitive demand. *American Educational Research Journal*, *52*(1), 105–136. doi:10.3102/0002831214549452.

Tekkumru-Kisa, M., & Stein, M.K. (2017). A framework for planning and facilitating video-based professional development. *International Journal of STEM Education*, *4*(1), 28. doi:10.1186/s40594-017-0086-z.

Tharp, R.G., & Gallimore, R. (1988). *Rousing minds to life. Teaching, learning, and schooling in social context*. Cambridge, MA: Cambridge University Press.

The Economist (2020), *Virtual realities, technology quarterly*, October 3rd, 2020. London: The Economist.

Theureau, J. (2002). *Self confrontation interview as a component of an empirical and technological research programme*. Accessed 3 June 2021 at http://www.coursdaction.fr/06-English/2002-JT-C93ENG.pdf

Theureau, J. (2003). Course-of-action analysis and course-of-action centered design. In E. Hollnagel (Ed.), *Handbook of cognitive task design* (pp. 55–81). Boca Raton, FL: CRC Press.

Thomas, J. (2001). *Audio for distance education and open learning: A practical guide for planners and producers*. Vancouver: The Commonwealth of Learning and the International Extension College. Accessed 3 June 2021 at http://oasis.col.org/handle/11599/35

Tigchelaar, A.E., Brouwer, C.N., & Korthagen, F.A.J. (2008). Crossing horizons. Continuity and change in the learning of second-career teachers. *Teaching and Teacher Education*, *24*(6), 1530–1550. doi:10.1016/j.tate.2008.03.001.

Timperley, H., Wilson, A., Barrar, H., & Fung, I. (2007). *Teacher professional learning and development. Best evidence synthesis iteration*. Wellington: Ministry of Education. Accessed 3 June 2021 at https://www.educationcounts.govt.nz/publications/series/2515/15341

Tochon, F.V. (1999). *Video study groups for education, professional development, and change*. Madison, WI: Atwood Publishing.

Tochon, F.V. (2007). From video cases to video pedagogy: A framework for video feedback and reflection in pedagogical research praxis. In R. Goldman, R. Pea, B. Barron, & S.J. Derry (Eds.), *Video research in the learning sciences* (p. 53–67). Mahwah, NJ: Lawrence Erlbaum Associates.

Tochon, F.V. (2013). *Signs and symbols in education. Educational semiotics*. Blue Mounds, WI: Deep University Press.

Tomlinson, C.A. (2014). *Differentiated classroom. Responding to the needs of all learners*. Alexandria, VA: ASCD.

Topping, K., & Ehly, S. (Eds.). (1998). *Peer-assisted learning*. Mahwah, NJ: Lawrence Erlbaum Associates.

Tripp, T., & Rich, P.J. (2012). Using video to analyze one's own teaching. *British Journal of Educational Technology*, *43*(4), 678–704. doi:10.1111/j.1467–8535.2011.01234.x.

Tynjälä, P., & Heikkinen, H.L. (2011). Beginning teachers' transition from pre-service education to working life. *Zeitschrift für Erziehungswissenschaft, 14*(1), 11–33. doi:10.1007/s11618-011-0175-6.

Ulewicz, M., & Beatty, A. (Eds.). (2001). *The power of video technology in international comparative research in education.* Washington, DC: National Academies Press.

Van de Pol, J.E. (2012). *Scaffolding in teacher-student interaction: Exploring, measuring, promoting and evaluating scaffolding.* Amsterdam: University of Amsterdam. Accessed 3 June 2021 at http://dare.uva.nl/record/426432.

Van de Pol, J.E., Volman, M., & Beishuizen, J. (2010). Scaffolding in teacher–student interaction: A decade of research. *Educational Psychology Review, 22*(3), 271–296. doi:1.0.1007/s10648-010-9127-6.

Van de Pol, J.E., Volman, M., & Beishuizen, J. (2011). Patterns of contingent teaching in teacher–student interaction. *Learning and Instruction, 21*(1), 46–57. doi:10.1016/j.learninstruc.2009.10.004.

Van de Pol, J.E., Volman, M., & Beishuizen, J. (2012). Promoting teacher scaffolding in small-group work: A contingency perspective. *Teaching and Teacher Education, 28*(2), 193–205. doi:10.1016/j.tate.2011.09.009.

Van de Pol, J.E., Volman, M., Oort, F., & Beishuizen, J. (2014). Teacher scaffolding in small-group work: An intervention study. *Journal of the Learning Sciences, 23*(4), 600–650. doi:10.1080/10508406.2013.805300.

Van de Pol, J.E., Volman, M., Oort, F., & Beishuizen, J. (2015). The effects of scaffolding in the classroom: Support contingency and student independent working time in relation to student achievement, task effort and appreciation of support. *Instructional Science, 43*(5), 615–641. doi:10.1007/s11251-015-9351-z.

Van den Bogert, N. (2016). *On teachers' visual perception and interpretation of classroom events using eye tracking and collaborative tagging methodologies.* Eindhoven: Eindhoven School of Education, Eindhoven University of Technology.

Van Es, E.A. (2009). Participants' roles in the context of a video club. *The Journal of the Learning Sciences, 18*(1), 100–137. doi:10.1080/10508400802581668.

Van Es, E.A. (2012a). Examining the development of a teacher learning community: The case of a video club. *Teaching and Teacher Education, 28*(2), 182–192. doi:10.1016/j.tate.2011.09.005.

Van Es, E.A. (2012b). Using video to collaborate around problems of practice. *Teacher Education Quarterly, 39*(2), 103–116.

Van Es, E.A., Cashen, M., Barnhart, T., & Auger, A. (2017). Learning to notice mathematics instruction: Using video to develop preservice teachers' vision of ambitious pedagogy. *Cognition and Instruction, 35*(3), 165–187. doi:10.1080/07370008.2017.1317125.

Van Es, E.A., & Sherin, M.G. (2002). Learning to notice: Scaffolding new teachers' interpretations of classroom interactions. *Journal of Technology and Teacher Education, 10*(4), 571–596.

Van Es, E.A., & Sherin, M.G. (2006). How different video club designs support teachers in "learning to notice". *Journal of Computing in Teacher Education, 22*(4), 125–135.

Van Es, E.A., & Sherin, M.G. (2008). Mathematics teachers' "learning to notice" in the context of a video club. *Teaching and Teacher Education, 24*(2), 244–276. doi:10.1016/j.tate.2006.11.005.

Van Es, E.A., & Sherin, M.G. (2010). The influence of video clubs on teachers' thinking and practice. *Journal of Mathematics Teacher Education, 13*(2), 155–176. doi:10.1007/s10857-009-9130-3.

Van Es, E.A., Stockero, S.L., Sherin, M.G., Van Zoest, L.R., & Dyer, E. (2015). Making the most of teacher self-captured video. *Mathematics Teacher Educator, 4*(1), 6–19.

Van Es, E.A., Tunney, J., Goldsmith, L.T., & Seago, N. (2014). A framework for the facilitation of teachers' analysis of video. *Journal of Teacher Education*, 65(4), 340–356. doi:10.1177/0022487114534266.

Van Kesteren, B. (1993). Applications of De Groot's "learner report": A tool to identify educational objectives and learning experiences. *Studies in Educational Evaluation*, 19(1), 65–86.

Van Parreren, C.F. (1988). *Ontwikkelend onderwijs* [Formative teaching]. Leuven/Amersfoort: Acco.

Van Parreren, C.F. (1990). *Leren op school* [Learning in school]. Groningen: Wolters-Noordhoff.

Van Veen, K., Zwart, R., & Meirink, J. (2012). What makes teacher professional development effective? A literature review. In M. Kooy, & K. Van Veen. *Teacher learning that matters: International perspectives* (pp. 3–21). London: Routledge.

Veenman, S. (1984). Perceived problems of beginning teachers. *Review of Educational Research*, 54(2), 143–178.

Verhoeven, L., & Leeuwe, J. van (2008). Prediction of the development of reading comprehension: A longitudinal study. *Applied Cognitive Psychology*, 22, 407–423. doi:10.1002/acp.1414.

Vernooy, K. (2006). *Elk kind een lezer! Elk kind een lezer?* [Every child a reader! Every child a reader?]. Enschede: SPOE.

Vernooy, K. (2012). *Elk kind een lezer. Preventie van leesmoeilijkheden door effectief onderwijs* [Every child a reader. Prevention of reading difficulties through effective education]. Apeldoorn: Garant.

Vervoort, M. (2013). *Kijk op de praktijk. Rich media-cases in de lerarenopleiding* [A view on practice. Rich media cases in teacher education]. Enschede: Universiteit Twente.

Vescio, V., Ross, D., & Adams, A. (2008). A review of research on the impact of professional learning communities on teaching practice and student learning. *Teaching and Teacher Education*, 24(1), 80–91. doi:10.1016/j.tate.2007.01.004.

Voerman, L., Meijer, P.C., Korthagen, F.A.J., & Simons, R.J. (2015). Promoting effective teacher-feedback: From theory to practice through a multiple component trajectory for professional development. *Teachers and Teaching*, 21(8), 990–1009. doi:10.1080/13540602.2015.1005868.

Vygotsky, L.S. (1977). *Denken und Sprechen* [Thinking and speaking]. Frankfurt am Main: Fischer.

Walker, V.L., Douglas, K.H., & Brewer, C. (2019). Teacher-delivered training to promote paraprofessional implementation of systematic instruction. *Teacher Education and Special Education*, 43(3), 257–274. doi:10.1177/0888406419869029.

Wallace, M.R. (2009). Making sense of the links: Professional development, teaching practices, and student achievement. *Teachers College Record*, 111(2), 573–596.

Waller, W. (1932). *The sociology of teaching*. New York: Russel & Russsel, Inc./John Wiley & Sons.

Walshe, N., & Driver, P. (2019). Developing reflective trainee teacher practice with 360-degree video. *Teaching and Teacher Education*, 78, 97–105. doi:10.1016/j.tate.2018.11.009.

Wang, J., & Hartley, K. (2003). Video technology as a support for teacher education reform. *Journal of Technology and Teacher Education*, 11(1), 105–138.

Webb, N.M., Franke, M.L., Turrou, A.C., & Ing, M. (2015). An exploration of teacher practices in relation to profiles of small-group dialogue. In L.B. Resnick, C.S.C. Asterhan, & S.N. Clarke (Eds.), *Socializing intelligence through academic talk and dialogue* (pp. 87–99). Washington, DC: American Educational Research Association.

Weber, K.E., Gold, B., Prilop, C.N., & Kleinknecht, M. (2018). Promoting pre-service teachers' professional vision of classroom management during practical school training: Effects of a structured online-and video-based self-reflection and feedback intervention. *Teaching and Teacher Education*, *76*, 39–49. doi:10.1016/j.tate.2018.08.008.

Werner, C.D., Vermeer, H.J., Linting, M., & Van IJzendoorn, M.H. (2018). Video-feedback intervention in center-based child care: A randomized controlled trial. *Early Childhood Research Quarterly*, *42*, 93–104. doi:10.1016/j.ecresq.2017.07.005.

West, L., & Staub, F.C. (2003). *Content-focused coaching. Transforming mathematics lessons.* Portsmouth, NH: Heinemann.

Wideen, M., Mayer-Smith, J., & Moon, B. (1998). A critical analysis of the research on learning to teach: Making the case for an ecological perspective on inquiry. *Review of Educational Research*, *68*(2), 130–178.

Williams, M.A. (2004). *Exploring the Effects of Multimedia Case-based Learning Environment in Pre-service Science Teacher Education in Jamaica.* Enschede: University of Twente.

Wilson, S.F., & Berne, J. (1991). Teacher learning and the acquisition of professional knowledge: An examination of research on contemporary professional development. *Review of Research in Education*, *24*(1), 173–209.

Wright, M.R., Ellis, D.N., & Baxter, A. (2012). The effect of immediate or delayed video-based teacher self-evaluation on Head Start teachers' use of praise. *Journal of Research in Childhood Education*, *26*(2), 187–198. doi:10.1080/02568543.2012.657745.

Yasnitsky, A., Van der Veer, R., & Ferrari, M. (Eds.). (2014). *The Cambridge handbook of cultural-historical psychology.* Cambridge, UK: Cambridge University Press.

Yeh, C., & Santagata, R. (2015). Preservice teachers' learning to generate evidence-based hypotheses about the impact of mathematics teaching on learning. *Journal of Teacher Education*, *66*(1), 21–34. doi:10.1177/0022487114549470.

Yinger, R. (1979). Routines in teacher planning. *Theory Into Practice*, *18*(3), 163–169. doi:10.1080/00405847909542827.

Yousef, A.M.F., Chatti, M.A., & Schroeder, U. (2014). The state of video-based learning: A review and future perspectives. *International Journal on Advances in Life Sciences*, *6*(3/4), 122–135.

Yung, B.H.W., Yip, V.W.Y., Lai, C., & Lo, F.Y. (2010). *Towards a model of effective use of video for teacher professional development. Paper presented at the International Seminar, Professional Reflections, National Science Learning Centre, York, February, 2010.* Hong Kong: University of Hong Kong.

Zeichner, K.M., & Schulte, A.K. (2001). What we know and don't know from peer-reviewed research about alternative teacher certification programs. *Journal of Teacher Education*, *52*(4), 266–282.

Zhang, D., Zhou, L., Briggs, R.O., & Nunamaker, J.F. (2006). Instructional video in e-learning: Assessing the impact of interactive video on learning effectiveness. *Information & Management*, *43*, 15–27. doi:10.1016/j.im.2005.01.004.

Zwart, R.C., Wubbels, T., Bergen, T., & Bolhuis, S. (2009). Which characteristics of a reciprocal peer coaching context affect teacher learning as perceived by teachers and their students? *Journal of Teacher Education*, *60*, 243–257. doi:10.1177/0022487109336968.

ABBREVIATIONS

ACP	alternative certification programme
AERA	American Educational Research Association
ALACT	Action – Looking back on the action – Awareness of essential aspects – Creating alternative methods of action – Trial
AR	augmented reality
ATP	advanced traditional programme
BBC	British Broadcasting Corporation
BFF	Best Foot Forward
CAP	Content Acquisition Podcast
CASTL	Center for Advanced Study of Teaching and Learning
CD	compact disc
CDPM	Cognitive Development Process Model
CERP	Center for Education Policy Research
CFS	Child-Friendly School
CG	control group
CGI	Cognitively Guided Instruction
CHAT	cultural-historical activity theory
CIP	Caregiver Interaction Profile
CLASS	Classroom Assessment Scoring System
CPD	continued professional development
CSCL	computer-supported collaborative learning
CTD	constant time delay
CTML	Cognitive Theory of Multimedia Learning
CV	criterion variable
CVA	Classroom Video Analysis
CVLL	Collaborative Video Learning Lab
DV	digital video
DVC	Dialogic Video Cycle

DVD	digital video disc
Earli	European Association for Research on Learning and Instruction
ECE	early childhood education
ECEC	early childhood education and care
ES	effect size
FeTiP	Feedback-Theory into Practice
FFF	frequent, fast and focussed
HLM	hierarchical linear modelling
HV	hypervideo
ICT	information and communication technology
IG	intervention group
INTASC	Interstate New Teacher Assessment and Support Consortium
IPASS	Instructional Planning Assisting SyStem
IRE	Initiation-Response-Evaluation
IRF	Initiation-Response-Follow-up
IT	information technology
IV	instructional video
JAE	Joint Attention Engagement
KODEK	Kompetenzen des Klassenmanagements [Classroom Management Competencies]
LAF	Lesson Analysis Framework
LLT	Learning to Learn from Teaching
LTN	Learning to notice
M	mean
MAI	Munich Observation of Attention Inventory
MILE	Multimedia Interactive Learning Environment
MOOC	massive open online course
MT	Microteaching
MTP	MyTeachingPartner
NBPTS	National Board of Professional Teaching Standards
NCTM	National Council of Teachers of Mathematics
NHL	Noordelijke Hogeschool Leeuwarden
NGO	non-governmental organisation
NQT	newly qualified teacher
OECD	Organisation for Economic Cooperation and Development
PACT	Performance Assessment of California Teachers
PCK	pedagogical content knowledge
PD	professional development
PIRLS	Progress in International Reading Literacy Study
PLC	professional learning community
PTE	preservice teacher education
R&D	research and development
SCM	student-centred teaching methods
SD	standard deviation

SSW	segmenting, signalling and weeding
STeLLA	Science Teachers Learning from Lesson Analysis
STEM	science, technology, engineering and mathematics
SVG	structured viewing guide
TIMSS	Third International Mathematics and Science Study
TTI	Teaching Through Interactions
TUM	Technical University of Munich
UCI	University of California at Irvine
UNICEF	United Nations Children's Emergency Fund
UK	United Kingdom
US	United States
VAST	Video Analysis Support Tool
VET	vocational education and training
VHS	video home system
VIG	Video Interaction Guidance
VILMS	Video for Interactive Lesson preparation by Mentor and Student
VIPP-SD	Video-feedback Intervention to promote Positive Parenting and Sensitive Discipline
VITAL	Video Interactions for Teaching And Learning
VR	virtual reality
VRT	video-recorded teacher
VTL	Visual Teacher Learning
VSO	Voluntary Services Overseas

CREDITS

Permissions for quotations in this book were obtained from the respective copyright holders, when quotations from journals exceeded 50 words and quotations from books exceeded 300 words.

Chapter 1

Parts of the section *Quality standards for teacher learning* were derived from: Brouwer, C.N. (2007). Evaluating Alternative Teacher Education in the Netherlands. A Standards-based Synthesis. *European Journal of Teacher Education, 30*(1), 21–40.

Chapter 2

This chapter is based on a literature review begun in 2006, originally published in Dutch in: Brouwer, C.N. (2007). *Verbeelden van onderwijsbekwaamheid, een literatuurstudie naar het gebruik van digitale video ten behoeve van opleiding en professionele ontwikkeling van leraren* [Imaging teacher learning. A literature review on the use of digital video for preservice teacher education and professional development]. Heerlen: Open University of the Netherlands (reprinted 2010).

A summary of this review was presented at the annual meeting of the American Educational Research Association in New Orleans on 11 April 2011 and published in: Brouwer, C.N. (2011). *Imaging teacher learning. A literature review on the use of digital video for preservice teacher education and professional development.*

An updated version of this review was published in German in: Brouwer, C.N. (2014). Was lernen Lehrpersonen durch die Arbeit mit Videos? Ergebnisse eines Dezenniums empirischer Forschung [Visual Teacher Learning: Review of a decade of research]. *Beiträge zur Lehrerinnen- und Lehrerbildung 32*(2), 176–196.

Figure 2.1 is reproduced with permission from: Sauli, F., Cattaneo, A., & Van der Meij, H. (2018). Hypervideo for educational purposes: a literature review on a multifaceted technological tool. *Technology, Pedagogy and Education, 27*(1), p. 122.

Chapter 4

This chapter is reproduced with permission from Elsevier Publishers from: Brouwer, C.N., Besselink, E., Oosterheert, I. (2017). The power of video feedback with structured viewing guides. *Teaching and Teacher Education, 66*, 60–73.

Contributions to data collection and analysis were made by Coby Bos, Gert Muller and Marit Peters.

Chapter 5

This chapter is reproduced with permission from Taylor and Francis from: Brouwer, C.N., Robijns, F. (2015). In search of effective guidance for preservice teachers' viewing of classroom video. In Calandra, B., Rich, P. (Eds.), *Digital video for teacher education: Research and practice*. London/New York: Routledge (pp. 54–69).

Contributions to data collection and analysis were made by Coby Bos, Henk Hofman and Bart Joosten.

Chapter 6

Part of this chapter is based on findings presented at the annual meeting of the American Educational Research Association in San Diego on 14 April 2009 and published in Brouwer, C.N. (2009). *Teacher peer coaching with digital video. Evaluation of a four-year professional development program.*

We thank Barry Fishman and four anonymous reviewers of the *American Educational Research Journal* for their comments on an earlier version of this chapter.

Chapter 7

Figures 7.1 and 7.2 were adapted with permission from: Stigler, J., & Rankin, S. (1998). *TIMMS-R Video Study. Data collection manual*, (p. 9). Santa Monica, CA: Lessonlab.

Figure 7.3 is a photo taken during one of Niels Brouwer's lectures.

Figure 7.4 is a photo taken by co-author Eric Besselink, edited with his permission.

Figure 7.5 is a photo taken by Niels Brouwer.

Chapter 9

Figure 9.1 is a translation of the original Dutch version published in: Brouwer, C.N. (2002). Intervisie. Leraren leren van elkaar [Collegial consultation. Teachers learning from each other]. In Brouwer, C.N., Brouwers, T., Kienstra, N., Leisink, J., Liebrand, R., Van Maanen, S. et al. *Voor de klas. Voorbereidingen op de praktijk* [Learn and let learn. A handbook of teacher education methods] (pp. 109–131). Bussum: Coutinho.

Box 9.5 is an adapted translation from the same source.

AUTHOR INDEX

SUBJECT INDEX

Printed in the United States
by Baker & Taylor Publisher Services